£5.95

Accounting values and inflation

Accounting values and inflation

William T. Baxter

Professor of Accounting,
London School of Economics

*Sponsored by the Research Committee of the Institute
of Chartered Accountants in England and Wales*

London · New York · St Louis · San Francisco · Düsseldorf · Johannesburg · Kuala Lumpur · Mexico · Montreal · New Delhi · Panama · Paris · São Paulo · Singapore · Sydney · Toronto.

Published by
McGRAW-HILL Book Company (UK) Limited
MAIDENHEAD . BERKSHIRE . ENGLAND

Library of Congress Cataloging in Publication Data

Baxter, William Threipland, date
    Accounting values and inflation.

    Bibliography: p.
    Inflation (Finance) and accounting. I. Title.
HF5657.B34   332.4'1   74-20521
ISBN 0-07-084050-4

© William Baxter 1975

MADE AND PRINTED IN GREAT BRITAIN BY J. W. ARROWSMITH LTD., BRISTOL

Preface

Accounting grew up as a day-by-day record of business dealings. Its figures are a series of snapshots, each a glimpse of some event as it happened. They are faithful history. But usually they are left as historical records; the accountant does not touch them up when conditions change at later times. For instance, he continues to measure assets and inputs at their original cost, no matter how far their current values have moved. Particularly during inflation, the values are apt to move a long way. So now the question is whether the accountant should not try to update his figures.

One can imagine a science-fiction society in which money's purchasing power and the relative worth of assets never vary. In such a sleepy setting, historical accounts would be admirable. In the world as we know it, they invite criticism. With inflation, the criticism has grown loud. When prices are rising briskly, traditional accounts are beset by several ailments: their asset values become anachronisms; they ignore important forms of appreciation and loss; and an invisible error creeps into income measurement, so that income is overstated in profit and loss accounts—and then in tax assessments.

If, as seems likely, accounting now seeks to modify itself in response to the criticism, it will enter a new and exciting phase. In Britain, a first step has already been taken: the published accounts of quoted companies are to include a supplement showing figures adjusted for price-change. The next few years may in retrospect seem a major turning point.

The quest for improvement will not be plain sailing. We shall have to choose between different brands of reform; and a wrong choice may land us in many troubles. And we must accept that success will at best be partial. Here as elsewhere inflation is a powerful agent of evil, and our efforts will not offset it entirely. Still, a partial cure is better than none; we shall have cause to congratulate ourselves if we at least get out of the fire and back into the frying pan. If the accountant believes that his figures can be useful, then surely he must welcome any device that promises some improvement in them. Much of the argument against inflation accounting is, at bottom, argument for the outright rejection of accounts at any time.

This book amplifies the case against historical accounts, and discusses the pros and cons of reform. It sets out the various proposals for improvement—asset revaluation, measurement of loss on holding money, adjustment of input costs with price-indices, and so on. It describes the revaluation techniques that have proved workable in practice; and it tries to explain the new accounts with arithmetical examples.

However, when one starts to write about inflation accounting, one soon sees that the argument cannot be confined to a narrow area, but must range into unexpected places. The choice of technique must depend on views on principle. Often one cannot decide how to deal with inflation accounts without first making up one's mind on how certain difficult problems should be treated in times of general price stability. For instance, one must decide whether income is a matter of economic or physical growth; how depreciation should be measured; whether intangibles should be accorded the status of assets; and whether 'realization' is a pre-requisite of income recognition (i.e. upon the point at which the chicken is deemed to leave the egg). Unhappily, accounting literature is weak in its treatment of fundamentals; so a writer on inflation accounting must try to plug the gap, and (however modest his nature) is forced willy-nilly to attempt a most ambitious task. Several chapters of this book explore first principles. If these chapters do not get very far with the solutions, they at least suggest some of the problems.

The research committee of the Institute of Chartered Accountants in England and Wales has sponsored my book, and I am grateful for its aid. Needless to say, the committee is in no way responsible for my views.

I have to thank the editors of *The Accountant's Magazine* and *Economica* for permission to reproduce work from those journals. I am also grateful to the Institute of Chartered Accountants in England and Wales for permitting the full reproduction of SSAP7 which appears on pages 195–213.

Several classes of graduate students have helped me by discussing the final draft of this book, and it has benefited greatly from their forthright comments. I have been helped, too, by Professors Harold Barger and James Bonbright of Columbia University; and by many colleagues and secretaries at the London School of Economics, notably Michael Bromwich, Martin Churchill, Susan Dev, Harold Edey, John Flower, Edward French, Pamela Hodges, David Pendrill, and Peter Watson. I am most grateful to them all.

Contents

1. General and special price-change

This book uses the term 'price-change' in two senses. The first is *general* change—that is, such widespread change in the prices of goods and services that one can say the purchasing power of the money unit has altered, as during inflation. The other is change in the price of an individual good or service (with or without general change); this may be called specific or *special* change. Both are of great importance for accounting, but it is general change that has sparked off recent attacks on accepted practice, and this chapter starts with it.

The instability of money

Physical units and value units

We all started measuring things while we were still children; and, without knowing it, we acquired firm views on the units of measurement. We measured our heights with an inch-tape, our weights on a scale marked with pounds, and the price of eggs with money. If the number of inches rose, we believed ourselves to be growing tall; if the number of pounds rose, we were praised for eating manfully; if the number of pennies rose, eggs were dearer. Very naturally, we took the measuring units for granted. We did not wonder whether the inch-tape might somehow have shrunk, or part of the weights might have rubbed off; and neither did our small minds conceive of pennies losing their worth. 'Things are getting dear', we heard our elders say— not 'money is getting cheap'. Our fairy tales warned us of the moral risks of too much treasure; they gave no hint that precious metal, if created to the lavish standards of Aladdin's djinn, would cease

to be precious.[1] And so we learned a lesson that is uncommonly hard to unlearn, even though its error has since been shown to us over and over again, and sometimes in a most painful way.

Price as a ratio

A child who gained his early impressions in a crude barter economy might be more aware of the contrast between physical measures and value measures. On Monday, he sees twelve eggs exchange for twelve dried fish. On Tuesday, twelve eggs exchange for thirteen dried fish. Would he say 'eggs are dearer' or 'fish are cheaper'? The two statements seem equally likely and equally true. Neither eggs nor fish have special claims to be treated as a stable yardstick with which to value the other; $\frac{12}{12}$ has become $\frac{12}{13}$, and we have no grounds for regarding either the top or the bottom of the fraction as an absolute standard. All we know is that the relative esteem in which marketers hold eggs and fish has changed, and therefore the barter ratio has changed, too.

Next, suppose that dried fish is a staple and popular commodity in our crude market, so that people look on fish not only as food, but also as a convenient means of 'financing' other transactions and of storing wealth. Then fish will feature in many exchanges. So it can usefully be cited as the 'price' in each exchange, and as a standard for comparing the values of different goods. Our child, hearing fish mentioned more often than its virtues as food can merit, and finding it much sought after as a handy means for buying all other wares, will come to think of it as something apart from, and better than, these wares. Now he may

1

easily start treating fish as a unit of value that remains fixed when other values go up and down. If he does, he is wrong; a rise in the price of eggs may still be due, for instance, either to a dearth of eggs or a glut of fish.

We all know that, as markets grew, certain goods came to be used more and more as money. Silver, in particular, acquired a status that exceeded its due as the raw material of silversmiths. This status was enhanced further when it was cut into discs of standard size and stamped with the impressive symbols of the State. Anyone who often used the discs would in the end be apt to view them in a special light—as akin to physical measures rather than as exchangeable goods the value of which lies solely in the fickle tastes of the marketers (like the value of silver made instead into spoons). The seeming contrast between money and goods went even further when coins were replaced by paper notes and by credit in a bank's books.

Governments have done much to surround money with prestige, for example, by inflicting savage punishments on those who clipped coins, or who raised prices when the State was trying to peg them. Usually the State made itself the sole minter of coins, and exercised at least some control over notes and banking. However, our rulers were for long as puzzled as the rest of us by the contrasts between money and other measures (for instance, by the stubborn way in which prices went up when the mint increased the stock of money by putting less previous metal into each coin).

The behaviour of money was first explained by the French philosopher Bodin in the sixteenth century, but his words had little impact. Gradually, however, the truth spread: knowledgeable people came to see that market forces, rather than official pronouncements and threats, controlled the value of money—which altered whenever, for example, the changes in the quantity of money, or its speed of circulation, made people more (or less) eager to hold it.

To sum up. Perhaps because of early impressions, most of us stand in awe of money. We may see that price is an exchange ratio between a quantity of money and a quantity of goods, but we attach muddled notions of absolute value to the money. Yet a change in price merely reflects a change in the market's attitude to the two things concerned *relative to one another*; and there is scant reason to suppose that the market's esteem for money is constant and for goods variable.

Things-in-general as a stable measure of value

Let us hark back for a moment to our crude barter economy. We saw that a change in the egg:fish ratio from 12:12 to 12:13 might equally well be described by saying 'eggs are dearer' or 'fish is cheaper'. Would it make any difference if this change had been matched by changes in the ratios in which eggs were on the same day swapped for beans, and knives, and coffins—and for all other goods in the market? Certainly, this general shift in ratios would suggest that, if we wanted to find the *cause* of the egg:fish change, we should look not to fish but eggs; the latter seemed to be in more eager demand than before, perhaps because the tribe's fertility rites were imminent or the hens were not laying so well. Further, it is easier to sum up the position by saying 'eggs are dearer' instead of 'things-in-general are cheaper compared with eggs'. Yet the latter phrase is, perhaps, just as sound in logic when we are trying to understand what a price is.

When, however, we are trying to understand other problems, we may be justified in regarding a large sample of things-in-general as almost having a stable value, e.g., in terms of a given consumer's satisfactions. In this book, we shall have to think about 'keeping capital intact'. Money capital is not too hard to measure; accountants deem a man's money capital—of, say, £1000— to be intact so long as he still has assets whose book value (by various conventional rules mainly based on original cost) adds up to £1000. Nevertheless, he may well want to apply a more useful test (particularly if prices are restless) to find out whether he is still as well off in terms of purchasing power. For lack of a better test, we must assume that his real capital is intact so long as it enables him to buy the same bundle of 'things-in-general'.

This concept is admittedly not perfect. To measure 'things-in-general', we must rely on an index of many prices; and no price index that the statisticians can devise is free from flaws. Despite the flaws, however, a well-devised index can give at least a useful general impression.

Our troubles in this area are not merely matters of statistical technique (choice of goods and weights for the bundle of goods, etc.—see chapter 2). We also face more fundamental difficulties. In the last analysis, ideas such as 'capital' and 'wealth' must imply ability to yield satisfaction to human beings. But the philosophical concepts behind 'satisfaction' are exceedingly elusive; and there is no way in which we can gauge it. So, when we try to increase our skill at measuring wealth, we must not pitch our hopes too high. Our task becomes even harder when we try to compare wealth at different points in time.

Price-changes in history

If we hold money in undue respect, the reason is certainly not that money has behaved well in the past, but rather that our memories are short.

The temptation to degrade money is nearly as old as money itself. Under the strains of the Peloponnesian War, Athens took to inflation, by both debasement and devaluation (i.e., reducing the fineness and the amount of metal in coins); plated coins were also issued, and provided a currency whose metallic content had a value far below the legal value. The Romans in their turn took up the game, notably towards the end of the Empire; they 'attended more to the exploitation than the perfection of coining, with the result that their technique was poor, and they gave the world the inestimable curse of practical knowledge of all possible forms of inflation apart from the issue of paper money'.[2] The proposition that inflation was the cause of Rome's downfall may not be convincing, but is at least worth discussion.

Many examples of debased and ill-regulated currencies can be cited from later history. Macaulay paints the position in England about 1695, before Newton's reform at the Mint led to a fairly adequate supply of sound coins:[3]

Nothing could be purchased without a dispute. Over every counter there was wrangling from morning to night. The workman and his employer had a quarrel as regularly as the Saturday came round. On a fair day or a market day the clamours, the reproaches, the taunts, the curses, were incessant; and it was well if no booth

was overturned and no head broken. No merchant would contract to deliver goods without making some stipulation about the quality of the coin in which he was to be paid. Even men of business were often bewildered by the confusion into which all pecuniary transactions were thrown.

However, metal offered less scope for dilution than paper; fresh records were achieved when notes came into use. The American colonists of the eighteenth century showed ingenuity in experiments with paper issues (and quickly found out how prices responded).[4] The *assignats* of the French Revolution are notorious. The First and Second World Wars drove many countries to inflate in varying degrees; Germany's fantastic issues in the early 'twenties caused a social tragedy of the first order, and, indeed, go far to explain the rise of Nazism and the outbreak of the Second World War. Extreme inflation must have contributed powerfully to the collapse of Russia and Nationalist China.

Governments should not, of course, be blamed for all inflation. The relative attractions of money and things-in-general can change for many reasons. Prices rose when gold and silver poured into Europe after the discoveries of the late fifteenth century, and when gold was found in California in the mid-nineteenth century; they rose, too, when the Black Death reduced the population.

However, the lesson of history is not so much that money loses value as that its value changes. The increases in price have indeed outweighed the falls, but this should not make us forget how often falls took place, and how steep they were. Figure 1.1 shows price movements in England during some seven centuries. A study of these movements for 700 of the years suggests that prices fell in 328 years, were steady in 13, and rose in 359; further, if during this period 'we took a bet each year that the price level would be higher ten years from the date in question, we would be wrong more times than we would be right'[5] in all past centuries except the sixteenth and eighteenth. There was a markedly downward trend in the latter part of the nineteenth century; British prices fell by nearly one-third in the fifteen years after 1880,[6] and US prices were nearly halved between 1864 and 1894.[7] This half-century was the very time when accounting was

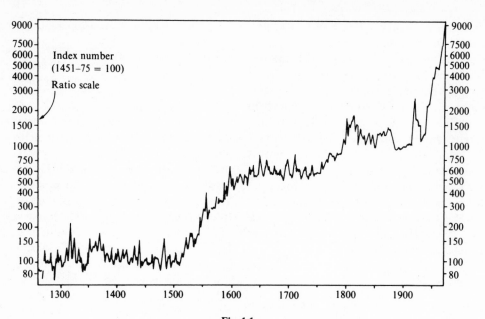

Fig. 1.1
Price of a composite unit of consumables in Southern England,
1264–1973

Source: E. H. Phelps Brown and Sheila V. Hopkins, 'Seven centuries of the prices of consumables, compared with builders' wage rates', *Economica*, November 1956, 229.

evolving fast to meet the needs of companies and tax officials—which may perhaps help to explain why accounting principles ignore the dangers of rising prices.

Deflation is unlikely to reach the speeds and proportions that have been achieved by some inflations. But, though less dramatic, it, too, has had profound social consequences. Thus, the deflation between the two world wars went hand in hand with unemployment on a dangerous and shameful scale. We may well believe that our civilization could not survive another slump of the same severity.

So we have had long and ample experience of changing prices; and their evil results are clearly established. To quote Macaulay again: 'It may well be doubted whether all the misery which had been inflicted on the English nation in a quarter of a century by bad kings, bad ministers, bad parliaments, and bad judges was equal to the misery caused in a single year by bad crowns and bad shillings.[8] Since Macaulay's day, we have had further lessons. Even a gentle inflation brings hard

times and a souring sense of injustice to those people—often the weakest and least vocal—who are not on the wage escalator. The astonishing thing is that we are so sluggish in our efforts to check steep price changes, and so ready to forget them. A stiff course in economic history should be compulsory for every schoolboy; it would certainly yield rich benefits to every investor.

Prospects of stability

After the Second World War, it was reasonable (remembering what happened after the First World War) to expect a slump. It did not come. For reasons that are not altogether clear (but probably include the impact of Keynes's doctrines, and the increased part that government expenditure now plays in total expenditure), prices have not fallen. Most of the former belligerents continued their wartime inflation: in America, the trend was mild; in Britain, somewhat steeper. Table 1.1 and Fig. 1.2 show the figures for the £ and $. If countries are arranged in order of monetary

4

TABLE 1.1
INDEX OF CONSUMER PRICES, 1948–70

	(1) UK	(2) USA
1948	100	100
1949	102	99
1950	105	100
1951	115	108
1952	122	110
1953	124	111
1954	126	111
1955	130	111
1956	136	113
1957	140	117
1958	144	120
1959	145	121
1960	147	123
1961	151	124
1962	157	126
1963	159	128
1964	165	129
1965	172	131
1966	179	135
1967	183	139
1968	192	144
1969	203	152
1970	217	161
1971	237	169
1972	254	174
1973	277	185

Sources: (1) *Central Statistical Office Bulletin.*
(2) I.M.F., *International Financial Statistics.*

stability during 1959–69, the list[9] includes:

	Average annual rate of inflation, 1959–69 %
Greece	1·9
USA	2·3
Germany	2·5
UK	3·5
Italy	3·6
France	3·9
Japan	5·3

These rates were tending to accelerate at the end of the decade. Some other lands have for many years abandoned themselves to inflation which, if not quite of the 'galloping' type, has at least been trotting briskly; for instance, the annual rates for Argentine and Brazil have averaged 30 per cent and 33 per cent.[10]

Thus, the £ and the US $ have now (1974) been losing value for over thirty years. However, in-flation has mostly gone hand-in-hand with brisk internal trade. A fortunate generation of young people has grown up with little experience of un-employment; unlike their parents, they take security for granted, and so can marry and rear families at an early age. Investors and statesmen have had a 30-year respite from the threat of catastrophic slump.

It is sometimes tempting to argue that govern-ments may at last be mastering powerful new ways of regulating economic affairs; that they are imbued with distaste for ever-mounting prices; and that accordingly they will soon be able to stop inflation—with enough skill to avoid over-shooting the mark and landing us in a slump. This would be a high achievement. Is it likely?

Reasons for more inflation

There are many reasons for thinking that inflation will persist. The strongest is the full-employment policy to which we are committed. Most of us believe that unemployment (beyond some small margin to cover movement from less useful to more useful jobs) is evil and dangerous—something that threatens alike our incomes as individuals and the welfare of our society. We will not tolerate a government that is lukewarm in fighting depres-sion. But measures that lessen unemployment often tend towards inflation; and likewise measures that check inflation tend to create unemployment.[11] Unless and until the two ailments can be disen-tangled, and we can find ways of treating them separately, humane governments will put up with some inflation as the lesser evil.

Our full-employment policy is reinforced by other factors. One of them may be the desire of governments for a brisk rate of economic growth. Another may be the influence of trade unions. Perhaps this influence may on occasion have been over-painted (sometimes wages of workers outside the unions, such as charwomen, rise more than the wages of members). But clearly the unions are not a negligible force, and tend to keep costs rising. Wage arbitration procedures are apt to push in the same direction.

So our chances of achieving price stability do not seem high. This being the case, we should face

Index ratio scale

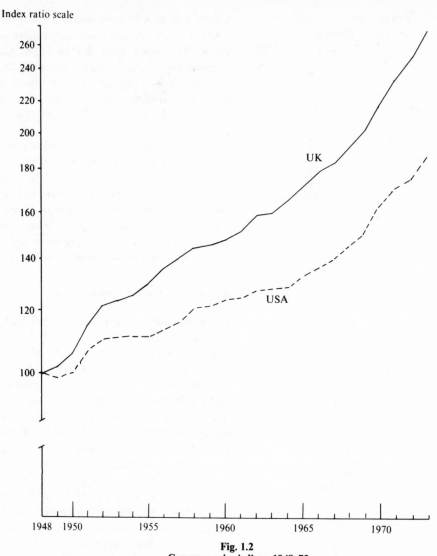

Fig. 1.2
Consumer price indices, 1948–73
Source: UK—*Central Statistical Office Bulletin*; USA—*IMF International Financial Statistics*.

up squarely to instability. One of the ways in which to do so is to admit that accounts based on the assumption of constant money values may be faulty and capable of improvement.

Prices, booms, and slumps

This book takes price-change for granted, without trying to explain its cause, nor does it try to explain trade activity. But it is worth while to have a brief look at both.

Prior to 1939, the up-and-down pattern of the business cycle was fairly clear. It tended to show in various ways—employment, output, incomes, and so on. History does not repeat itself exactly; but statisticians, trying to measure these cycles, have suggested that they lasted for roughly four years; perhaps longer beats were superimposed, so that every second or third cycle was more violent.[12] Whether such cycles survived the Second World War is not clear; we seem to have been going uphill most of the time, with only minor checks every four or five years. Conceivably, therefore, we are on a long-term upward surge which the old cyclical forces—plus any new ones—can sometimes slow down but not reverse.

Prices and trade activity usually move up and down together. So this book can reasonably assume that a change in prices goes along with a change in activity. But there are, of course, exceptions to this rule; and, indeed, the late 'sixties gave sombre hints that the modern economy may yet contrive to blend inflation with unemployment. Further, various prices and types of activity can move in different degree. There may be severe local unemployment (say, in steelmaking towns) when most prices are rising. Though the wholesale price index tends to keep closely in step with activity, the consumers' price index is less faithful. We usually can put off purchases of durable manufactures (productive machines, or consumers' goods such as radios), whereas our demand for non-durables (e.g., food and services) stays fairly steady; therefore, firms making durables are apt to feel slumps and booms more than firms making non-durables. A firm's production costs (e.g., wages and interest) may lag behind prices of goods; then manufacturing profits tend to fluctuate in a violent manner—and, as we shall see, accounts make these real changes look still more dramatic.

Special change

Special change calls for only a short introduction. We are all familiar enough with it. As children we learned that fruit becomes cheap when it is in season, and then gets dearer again as the months pass. Later, we saw how the price of a raw material or stock exchange security can undulate in dramatic style, and how the price of a newly-invented piece of equipment is apt to be high at first, and then to sink as other suppliers enter the market. And so on.

Special change is important for every firm that owns assets (unless the firm is exceptionally sheltered from market forces, or is odd in some other respect). It is particularly important where the assets take the form of inputs (raw materials, depreciating plant, etc.) that lead to sales after a timelag. During this turnover period, the assets are

at risk: thus a fall in the sale price of the finished goods on hand will cut down profit, and a fall in the replacement price of raw material stocks suggests that the sale prices may soon follow suit (and that the buyer has mistimed his purchases). On the other hand, a rise in those prices will often make for higher profits. In some firms, these market forces may be insignificant, i.e., may affect profit far less than, say, efficiency in manufacturing techniques, etc.; here the accounts will probably tend to concentrate on measuring efficiency. In others, the market forces are very important; here the accounts would be helpful if they gave some idea of the manager's flair for buying cheap and selling dear; but, rather surprisingly, the normal income statement throws little direct light on this point.

Special change in the prices of inputs and products can help or harm the firm in ways that are quick and, perhaps, obvious. But even fixed assets may 'turn over' in the long run; and so their special prices may sooner or later affect the firm's welfare. There is accordingly some case for arguing that the accounts should reflect the current special values of all the assets. In particular, they might draw attention to opportunities of selling under-utilized assets, etc., that is, to the opportunity cost of retaining them.

Interplay of special and general change

If the conditions for a laboratory experiment could be imposed on a human community, the experimenters could perhaps manipulate market forces in such a way that the price of every good and service would rise by precisely the same percentage. In real life, a general price rise of, say, 10 per cent must be some kind of 'average' rise: forces other than the money supply (e.g., gluts and shortages) will cause the prices of individual goods and services to move to varying extents above and below the 10 per cent average. General and special changes differ and intertwine.

A rise in the price of a certain good from £1000 to £1300 is a 30 per cent special change—regardless of what is happening to general prices. However, whether or not the owner of this asset feels much pleasure over his £300 of appreciation will in great degree depend on how general prices have behaved during the period. Naturally, he will prefer his special rise to outstrip the general rise.

Money gain *versus* real gain

Thus, he should use two different sums to test his progress:

		£
1.	Current price	1300
	Original price	1000
	Money gain	300

and (if general prices have risen by say 20 per cent):

		£
2.	Current price	1300
	Original price restated in current money, £1000 $\times \frac{120}{100}$	1200
	Real gain	100

The usual crude calculation, 1, shows *money* change, and the more testing, 2, shows *real* change —the surplus or shortfall between the special value and what this would have been if it had behaved like prices in general. In the example, the owner has beaten the general index to make a real gain of £100.

References

1. A notable exception is 'The Snake with the Golden Teeth'—J. B. S. Haldane, *My Friend Mr. Leakey*. London: Penguin Books, 1971, p. 128: 'The only other man I ever knew who had as much gold in his mouth was a pilot in the Yukon river in Canada, which goes past Klondyke, where there is a lot of gold. So gold is very cheap there. You can get a lot of gold for any ordinary sort of thing, like a loaf of bread or a book, so that means that everything else except gold is very dear.'

2. A. R. Burns, *Money and Monetary Policy in Early Times*. London: Kegan Paul, 1927, pp. 464–5.

3. T. B. Macaulay, *History of England*. London: Longmans, 1898. chapter 21, p. 94.

4. In 1705, £100 sterling exchanged for £135 of Massachusetts currency; in 1749, for £1000: J. M. Davis, *Currency and Banking in the Province of Massachusetts Bay*. New York: 1901, p. 367.

5. R. G. Lipsey, 'Does Money Always Depreciate?' *Lloyds Bank Review*, October 1960, p. 7. The rise in the eighteenth century may have been due to the development of banks (and

Summary

Our irrational faith in money

Mankind has been astonishingly reluctant to recognize that money is not stable. We have been slow to profit from experience, and quick to forget; men of high intelligence have often been no wiser than the fools. Except when some painful lesson is fresh in our minds, we have been apt to plan our affairs on the assumption that money has a fixed value—and to resent any contrary suggestion.

Accounting has shared the common attitude. For the most part, it has recorded values at historical cost, and ignored all subsequent changes in price.

Some accountants have been upset to a surprising extent by proposals for reforming this system. Such resentment may spring in part from loyalty to professional doctrines that for long were seldom criticised, and in part from dislike of scrapping hard-won mental equipment; perhaps it also reflects the general—and utterly misplaced—faith in the money unit.

Most accountants still seem to view their craft as something that is sound in fundamentals, but which has of late been exposed to shortsighted attack because of fleeting economic upsets. The aim of this chapter has been to suggest that, as both logic and experience stress the fickleness of money values, measurements based on historical cost are suspect right from the start.

so, as credit transfers in a banker's records would be almost impossible without debits and credits, in a sense of accounting).

6. Statist/Sauerbeck index of wholesale prices.

7. Snyder's index of the general price level.

8. Macaulay, *op. cit.*, p. 93.

9. O.E.C.D., *Inflation*, 1970.

10. I.M.F., *International Financial Statistics*. Figures for 1963–73.

11. 'which horn of the dilemma should public policy embrace: unemployment or inflation? If the choice has to be made, I do not think it can be made on grounds of principle. On the one hand it can be claimed that for Uncle Sam to debase the dollar is the height of immorality, especially since he is net debtor for a large amount. On the other hand it can equally well be urged that nothing is more immoral than the deliberate adoption of a policy that must create unemployment, cause businesses to fail, and lead to the loss of billions of dollars' worth of output. Hence, as with so many other choices in this unhappy world, the rate of substitution is critical. Obviously the wrecking of the currency through inflation would be too

high a price to pay for the avoidance of a small amount of unemployment. Nor would a 10–15 per cent unemployment rate be a price worth paying simply to avoid a trivial rise in the price level. Unfortunately it is extremely difficult to gauge the rate of substitution available to us, now or in the future. The terms of the trade-off are highly uncertain' (Harold Barger, *The Management of Money*, Chicago: Rand McNally, 1964, p. 302).

The book then quotes suggestions that about 5 per cent unemployment would be needed in the USA to maintain price stability, while a 4–5 per cent p.a. price rise would keep unemployment down to 3 per cent. British figures may be slightly different, but give the same general picture—see, e.g., A. W. Phillips, 'Employment, Inflation and Growth', *Economica*, February 1962, p. 1.

12. A. F. Burns and W. C. Mitchell, *Measuring Business Cycles*. New York: National Bureau of Economic Research, 1946.

2. Measuring price change

It is easy to talk about such and such a size of change in general or special prices. But the actual measurement is often beset by many troubles, of both principle and technique.

General price change is measured with a general price index. The statisticians try to provide us with suitable indices, but with incomplete success. The nature and limitations of their indices will be touched on in the next section.

Special change can be measured most accurately by direct study of the particular asset. Thus, an adequate current value for a stock exchange security may be found from its quotation in the stock exchange list; and a building can be valued by an appraiser. But, as a shortcut to approximate new values, a special index may be used for each class of asset (e.g., an index that shows the average movement in the prices of factory buildings). Such an index tries to reflect the price movements of a class of assets, with varying degrees of success.

General and special price indices

For those not familiar with price indices, the following discussion of their uses and limitations may be helpful. It will avoid technicalities, which can be found in textbooks on statistics.

General indices

A general index tries to measure how many £s or $s must be paid for a given quantity of goods and services at different times. Thus, a general index of consumption prices tries to measure the changing retail prices of a wide range of goods and services, and so may be said to show how the 'cost of living' is behaving. The statisticians who compile such an index must deal with—or skate over—many exceedingly awkward problems. What sort of goods and services are to serve as the standard? Today's housewife fills her basket with goods that differ from those chosen by her grandmother. The goods may have changed in quality. The modern housewife's loaf is branded, wrapped, and sliced. Her peas may be podded, packed, and frozen—and possibly tasteless. Her shoes may fit, look, and wear better (or worse) than her grandmother's. Technical changes may, indeed, have gone much farther than these examples suggest, and have brought entirely new commodities and services into use. Thus, electricity has ousted candles.

Moreover, tastes vary with circumstances and people. The statistician cannot, in fact, find a 'representative consumer'; there is no such thing as a 'typical' housewife. A given housewife's real income is apt to change; as it does so, she will vary the proportions of it that she spends on bread, beer, clothes, theatres, and other things. In addition, different housewives have different tastes and needs. Even if their incomes are equal, an elderly widow does not buy things in the same proportions as the adolescent, and a rise in the price of bread hurts the mother of six more than the bachelor-girl. Disparities of income heighten the contrasts: the rich stockbroker spends freely in directions that the poor student only dreams about.

So an index often does not match one's own experience; it records a two-point drop in the cost of living (due to a glut of vegetables), just when I become worried by the rise in bus-fares and you by the higher charges at Jamaican hotels. Even if a consumer has a special index for his own outlays, it may not suit him for long, since his consumption pattern will change along with his income, his family, his aesthetic development, and his state of health.

Price control and rationing widen the gap between a cost of living index and one's own experience. Thus, rent control checks the rise in the index, but tenants of uncontrolled houses may fare worse than the index suggests. During a war, the index may be fairly stable; however, if goods are sold in limited shares (or kept under the counter), the consumer feels worse off—and he probably switches to other kinds of goods.

Subsidies and indirect taxes also distort the index. If each citizen has to pay an extra £1 of income tax, the index is not directly affected. If, instead, he pays the same amount as a tax on beer, the index goes up.

For these and other reasons, it is not hard to find plenty of faults in a general index series; the skill and ingenuity of statisticians can lessen them, but cannot overcome them.

However, despite the defects of the general index, it is the best tool that we possess for tracing the value of our money over time. Normally, it does give a useful impression. To reject it in accounting is in effect to assume money's value to be stable; and this may lead to far worse error than use of the index does. When a series is based on prices of a remote year, we may not be sure whether the best figure for the present year is 390 or 410; we can be quite certain that it is not still 100.

Most suitable type of general index

How general should be the chosen general index of accounting reform (e.g., should it include capital goods)?

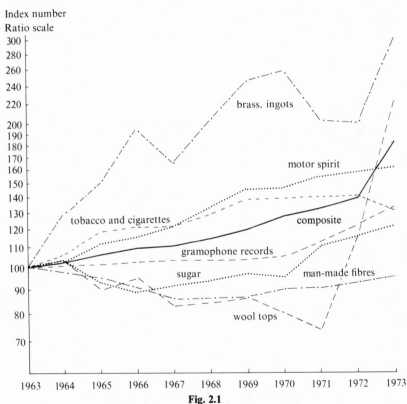

Fig. 2.1
Composite price index of manufactured products, and indices of various commodities included in it. Annual averages, 1963–73

Source: *Trade and Industry*.

11

Here one is dealing with a problem of *interpretation*—of giving as good an impression as possible of what certain figures meant at some past date. The most vivid and significant measuring-rod for most people must surely be one related to their own everyday experience, i.e., to their consumption. Further, an important (perhaps the most important) use of income figures is to give owners some picture of their material welfare, e.g., as a guide to their level of consumption;[1] this, too, points to a consumption index. So, probably, the best general index for our purpose is one geared to consumption—ideally, to the cost of living of the kind of man who owns a private business or shares in a company. Accountants should now be asking the statisticians to construct an index that tries to reflect the consumption of a 'typical shareholder'.

Special indices

Because they are much less ambitious in aim and simpler in structure, special indices may be less open to criticism than general indices. But they too are imperfect, e.g., an index of machinery prices may be far from typical of a given firm's machines, or at least of some of the machines.

There are, of course, many special indices: governments, journals, and research institutes compile and publish them liberally, for types of commodity, for wholesale prices, for capital goods and for sub-divisions of capital goods, for securities, and so on. If this wealth of numbers does not provide an index to meet your particular needs, you can often (given modest skill in statistics) construct a private one without much trouble.

A general index is compiled from many special prices, and so there may be some tendency for a movement in a general index to be matched by roughly similar movements in the underlying special prices. However, as was pointed out on p. 8, this association is often far from close.[2] Figure 2.1 shows the movements in a comprehensive index for manufactured goods and in the special indices of some of its components.

Thus it can happen that, when most prices are rising, the price of (say) sugar will fall. A firm dealing in sugar will then be doubly embarrassed: its stocks[3] lose part of their money value and still more of their real value.

References

1. In the UK, the Accounting Standards Steering Committee has recommended the use of the retail prices index—see *Accountancy*, February 1974, p. 9.

2. For a fuller account, see F. C. Mills, *The Behaviour of Prices*. New York: National Bureau of Economic Research, 1927.

3. Following the terser usage, I shall write 'stocks' rather than 'inventories'.

3. Price change makes accounting figures unlike

The critics of orthodox accounting point to several faults that appear when prices change. Historical figures of different dates then tend to be expressed in unlike units (e.g., £100 five years ago meant something different from £100 today); and the combination of such unlike units fosters various types of misinformation. Two of the more obvious are:

(1) Figures of different dates, even if each was correct at its own date, are not comparable. To arrange them side by side is to invite false impressions.

(2) If a year's accounts contain figures found by adding or subtracting unlike units (e.g., a profit found by subtracting an old cost from a current revenue), then these figures are in a significant sense incorrect even at the date of the accounts.

Trends

The first of these faults (non-comparability of figures of different dates) is important to anyone who tries to discern trends in a time series of accounting figures. For instance, company reports often include tables showing the main figures (e.g., sales, profits, and fixed assets) over the last ten years or so. This is excellent. But, as such a period has since 1939 invariably been one of inflation, the figures are almost sure to display an upward trend —whatever the physical turnover, the efficiency of management, and so on. The same holds for almost all other kinds of long-term accounting series.

To give better information to users, such figures ought to be made comparable. This can be done with an index; the arithmetic is simple and familiar enough. The main problem is what kind of index to choose.

Physical trends and the special index

Trends of physical activity can sometimes be detected by adjusting the money figures with a suitable special index. For example, suppose the manager of a shop wishes to find out the trend in the physical volume of sales over the years. He may (subject to provisos about the stability of the physical units and mix) sometimes obtain an adequate impression by deflating the money sales figures with a special index for the type of goods handled, so getting the figures shown below in italics.

Year	1	2	3
Sales	£4000	£7000	£10 000
Special index for these goods	100	200	300
Sales adjusted by index	*£4000*	*£3500*	*£3333*

The adjusted figures here suggest that the physical volume of sales has fallen—though the money figures suggest a steep rise. Similarly, trends in physical volume of stocks held, or of any type of fixed asset, can on occasion be best studied with the help of a special index for the particular asset.

Where one accounting figure covers several types of asset (for instance, stock usually comprises more than one commodity), the sub-total for each type should be separately adjusted with its own index. Or an adequate answer may be obtained by making up an index that is weighted to allow for the approximate volumes of each type.

The general index and trends

Where physical quantities do not matter, the general index may be more helpful than special indices. Thus, it usually affords the best means of comparing personal cash flows of different dates. Suppose a man's consumption outlays are:

Year	1	2	3
General index (average for year)	100	120	140
	£1000	£1320	£1680

The real trend in his style of living can be seen more clearly if he measures his outlays with a common footrule, by converting each year's £s into equivalent numbers of the £s of some convenient base date, say, year 1, i.e., into 'stabilized' figures (in italics):

Year	1	2	3
Outlays—average £s of year 1	*1000*	*1100*	*1200*

This series shows the trend plainly enough; the values are now comparable. His standard of living has been rising, though not so much as the raw figures suggest.

Choice of base date

In both this example and the earlier one on stocks, the revised figures for years 2 and 3 are statistical abstractions based on the average prices of year 1 (perhaps the actual prices of June of that year), and therefore divorced from those of year 3, when the man makes the study. He may feel that the figures will be a trifle less abstract if they are instead linked with the £s now current—that is, if they are adjusted with an index of year 3 instead of year 1. The year 3 average of 140 may serve; but the figure at 31 December, year 3, may be still better. Suppose it has by then risen to 150. The cash flows become:

Year	1	2	3
Outlays—£s of 31 December, year 3	*1500*	*1650*	*1800*

For that matter, the man could take as his base a £ of year 2, or of any other suitable date in history; or he could take the average £ of several successive years. His own convenience and understanding are the main tests.

Where fresh figures must be added each year to a long series, there is an obvious clerical economy in basing the adjustments on the £ of an early year. In this way, one avoids the annual readjustment of all the past figures to the new end-£. But such readjustment, though it entails more work, gives a contemporary and more meaningful picture, and so is often worth the trouble.

'Mixed' figures within an account

A series of unlike figures may be found within a single account. A good example is the account for retained earnings. Every year sees the addition of a new figure; an account for an old firm will hold a long range of additions, each expressed in a money unit peculiar to the given year. The successive figures can best be interpreted in terms of general purchasing power—the base-date equivalents of what the owners gave up when they ploughed back each year's bit of profit.

Example of mixed figures within an account

Suppose the owner has ploughed back profits of £1000 (year 1), £1089 (year 2), and £1176 (year 3). For a clear picture, this mixed series might be restated ('stabilized') in £s of (say) year 3, the factors being found from the general index series. If this has been 100, 110, and 120, the result is:

	(1) Historical figure £	(2) Factor	(3) Stabilized equivalent Year 3, £
Year 1	1000	$\frac{120}{100}$	*1200*
2	1089	$\frac{120}{110}$	*1188*
3	1176	$\frac{120}{120}$	*1176*
	3265		*3564*

In real terms, the sums retained each year have been sinking slightly.

The ledger account of column (1) adds up to £3265. But this total comes from the addition of unlike £s, and so has little meaning. The adjusted total of £3564 is better. It is the current equivalent, in terms of the purchasing power of year 3 £s, of all the past savings. For instance, if the owner wants to see whether his investments in the firm have maintained their value, the £3564 plus the year 3 equivalent of his original capital can sensibly be compared with a revalued total of the net assets.

Comparison of cost: revenue structure

To be most helpful, the comparison of accounts for different years should point clearly to any interesting developments. General price change tends to make such comparison hard. Once again, the user's task may be lightened by adjustment with the general index.

Examples of cost: revenue variation over time

Suppose that a firm's profits are £400 a year in a stable period before inflation starts (its costs being £1000 and its sales £1400). Then inflation sets in: next year, the general index rises smoothly from 100 (1 January) to 120 (31 December), and is at 110 'on average' during the year, say, at 30 June.

All sorts of things could happen to this firm's costs and revenues. Table 3.1 shows three of the many possibilities. The pre-inflation income account is given in column (1) on the left. To the right, under A, B and C, are some possible variants for the first year of inflation, namely:

A. *Ordinary figures vary exactly with the general price level.* Here sales go up in strict proportion to the general rise in prices—by one-tenth on the average, so the £1400 of revenue now becomes £1540 in the ordinary accounts (i.e., in accounts drawn up in the normal, familiar way), as in column (2). Similarly, costs move in step with the inflation, from £1000 to £1100. (It does not matter much whether we envisage a steady flow of small transactions over the whole year at prices increasing from, say, week to week, or a single outlay and revenue at 30 June.) Thus, profit rises from £400 to £440.

To help comparison with the pre-inflation accounts of (1), an extra column (3) restates our ordinary figures in opening £s. The stabilized figures, obtained by multiplying the ordinary figures by the factor $\frac{100}{110}$, show that sales are unchanged in real terms (and perhaps in physical volume), as are inputs; a profit of £440 earned on average at mid-year is worth only as much as 400 of the £s circulating before the inflation began. This firm has neither been helped nor harmed by the inflation, as its owners can buy the same quantity of goods and services as hitherto. Such consistent movements are not likely to occur in practice. A rise in general prices may for instance,

TABLE 3.1

COMPARISON OF INCOME ACCOUNTS DURING INFLATION

	Before inflation	*During first year of inflation*						
		A *Ordinary figures vary exactly with price level*		B *Ordinary figures are fixed*		C *Mixed case—say, sales vary, costs are fixed*		
	(1)	(2) Ordinary accounts	(3) Stabilized accounts	(4) Ordinary accounts	(5) Stabilized accounts	(6) Ordinary accounts	(7) Stabilized accounts	
	£	£	$£_0$	£	$£_0$	£	$£_0$	
Costs	1000	1100 $\times$ 10/11 =	1000	1000 $\times$ 10/11 =	909	1000 $\times$ 10/11 =	909	
Sales	1400	1540 $\times$ 10/11 =	1400	1400 $\times$ 10/11 =	1273	1540 $\times$ 10/11 =	1400	
Profit	400	440 $\times$ 10/11 =	400	400 $\times$ 10/11 =	364	540 $\times$ 10/11 =	491	

under the champagne-like effects of boom, be reinforced by a growth in the number of units sold; or the special prices of this particular firm may go up faster than the general index. Money profit will then rise by more than 10 per cent, and the firm's real income will rise, too, though by a lesser percentage than the money figures suggest.

B. *Ordinary figures are fixed.* Some firms' figures are not responsive to price changes. Thus, the rents earned by a property company may be subject to government control or long leases; interest from government stocks, etc., also remains constant.

Input prices may likewise be regulated by controls, long-term contracts, or trade union agreements.

Under B in Table 3.1, the ordinary figures for revenue and cost do not alter as prices rise—see (4). But the £s are now less desirable than in earlier days. The stabilized column (5), in consequence, shows that each item has sunk, and the unchanged profit of £400 in the ordinary accounts is worth only 364 pre-inflation £s.

In private life (as distinct from business), type B firms have their parallel in the *rentier*—the man who depends on a fixed income such as interest on government stocks. He is in clover if the price level falls (as in the early 'thirties); but in an inflation his real capital and income dwindle—despite static money figures—and so his lot may become tragic.

C. *Mixed case.* In practice, probably most items will change more or less in step with the inflation, but a few will be wildly eccentric. A vast range of possibilities exists. Example C deals with rising revenue (like example A) but fixed expense (like example B). The ordinary accounts (6) now show a much increased profit, and the stabilized accounts (7) confirm that this increase is both real and substantial. But they also show that it comes, not from the apparent rise in sales (steady in real terms), but from the decline in the real burden of expense—the unchanged payment of £1000 in the ordinary accounts now represents a sacrifice equal to only 909 starting £s.

However, mixed change is not kind to every type of enterprise. The landlord of houses subject to rent restriction has a fixed gross income, but his maintenance costs show a delicate awareness of upward pressures. He may, therefore, not earn enough even to keep his houses in repair; an appreciable number of homes in the UK each year sink into slumdom.

4. Concepts of wealth and income

A proposal for accounting reform should presumably be judged by both intellectual and pragmatic tests. Is it right in principle? Will it work? This chapter will attempt to suggest the tests of principle —that is, to describe an intellectual framework within which the proposals of later pages can be set and judged.

One of the accountant's main tasks is to keep track of wealth: he has to measure both wealth at a given time (e.g., in the balance sheet), and changes in wealth between given times (e.g., in the income statement). The first problem is thus how to do the measuring—what to include, and how to value; and the second is how to compare figures of different dates.

Alternative concepts for measuring wealth

There are many ways of tackling the first problem (and probably we all use all of them sometime or other, at least in our hazier thoughts). One group of concepts envisages wealth as the expectation of a stream of future benefits. Another looks to the existing assets; and, within this group, different concepts view the assets at various current or historical values.

Forward-looking concepts

An obvious example from the first group—the 'forward-looking' or *ex-ante* concepts—can be illustrated as follows. If the owner of a firm is asked at what price he would sell it, he may reason to himself 'By keeping the firm as a going-concern, I shall probably be able to take home various sums of money each year. I guess these will be about £x during the next twelve months, £y in the year after, then £z, and so on. So my price must be at least the total present value of £x, £y, £z, etc.' Let us say that the discounted value of these expected cash flows works out at £20 000.

Here, then, is one way of measuring the owner's wealth in the firm—and a profoundly important one, since it will guide him in deciding (among other things) whether or not to accept the buyer's offer. Such a concept is near kin to the discounted cash flow approach to internal capital budgets. It is highly personal and subjective. It looks at the expected future cash flows from the firm as a whole, and pays scant attention to the separate assets. These are relevant only so far as they will contribute directly to the flow (e.g., where they include cash in excess of working needs), or they can make the flow seem more secure and predictable (e.g., a shop in a prosperous street reassures investors more than a mine-shaft in a desert). Therefore, they tend to be of secondary importance when a firm is flourishing. However, when a firm is doing badly, the best plan may be to sell off the assets piecemeal, and then their separate values as scrap, etc. become relevant since these will constitute the future cash flow.

The owner in the above example, like the rest of us, probably does not normally carry in his mind any precise figure (such as the £20 000) of the value of his wealth. Unless he budgets in great detail, he will have only a vague impression; even if he does budget, he will admit that some of the estimates are likely to prove wildly wrong. Moreover, his value figure will vary over time with changes in his expectations, due, for instance, to new information and whether his mood is cheerful or not. Other people (such as potential buyers) may also form opinions about the future cash flows from the firm, and their valuations are likely to differ a good deal from the owner's £20 000.

Thus, we face a paradox. Forward-looking concepts are clear and attractive in principle, and do in fact guide us in our fundamental decisions; yet they can yield only shadowy figures that depend on personal opinion. Clearly, for routine accounting, they must give place to a concept of lowlier intellectual status, where the figures are, however, more precise, objective, and verifiable.

Under such an unanticipatory concept, the firm's wealth does not depend on what is expected to flow in hereafter but on what is known already. It can best be measured by listing the assets and liabilities one by one, valuing each on some objective basis, and finding their net total. But, alas, this is not as simple as it sounds, for there are many ways of measuring an asset's value. Two sets of concepts call for particular attention.

The accounting (historical-cost) concept

Accounting has evolved a concept the features of which are fairly well defined (though admittedly the edges are fuzzy and there are lots of exceptions and variants). Normally, it ignores all upward movements in an asset's value until they are vouched for by a clear-cut 'realization'; it aims to show the firm's actual achievement to date in winning solid wealth, rather than its prospects of future gain.[1] Thus, fixed assets may be kept indefinitely at their historical cost (or, to allow for depreciation, at some fraction of that cost); and current assets have traditionally (under the 'lower of cost or market' rule) been valued at historical cost or a lower figure. Therefore, accounting can be said to depend on a historical-cost concept— though the deference to history is probably a by-product of the realization test (so that 'realization concept' might be more apt).

The test has played, and still plays, a major role in accounting. Nevertheless, its standing should not be exaggerated. Sometimes it is not applied to certain assets, because, for instance, of a wish for still more caution (as where it is modified by the 'lower of cost or market' rule), or for convenience (as where 'work-in-process' is transferred at market prices through a long chain of subsidiary manufacturing companies, until in the end the original cost to the group of the raw materials can be found only with vast effort). Certain kinds of firm may abandon the realization test when valuing their stocks—e.g., some farms, producers of precious metals, and exotic plantations. (One suggested generalization is that the test is used where realization is difficult and the sale price is doubtful, and not used where realization is easy and the price is sure;[2] but the difficulties of finding cost may be the determining factor.) One way and another, the test is already observed with less than complete strictness, and I propose to treat it more as an aid to taxonomy and as a reminder of the need for caution than as a principle that bars future reform.

Doubts on realization date. Even where the test is loyally applied, there may be doubt about its interpretation. One set of criticisms concerns the nature and date of 'realization'. To some writers, the word implies merely physical usage (e.g., a factory's raw materials or depreciating plant may be said to be realized when they are consumed as input); far more often it implies an external transaction, such as a sale, that gives objective evidence of value growth. Even where an external sign is used, the choice of date can seldom be justified by anything more profound that a convention. Where the contract is for the sale of goods, etc., their realization date is normally deemed to be that at which the goods are sent off.[3] Where the contract is not for such sales (but is, e.g., for work by a building contractor or solicitor), the selected date may be that at which a claim for payment arises—a difficult matter, probably governed by the terms of the contract or by statute law, etc. But, to be on the safe side, accountants sometimes treat realization as occurring only at the later date of the cash receipt (e.g., where credit sales are beset by bad debts and lengthy delays of payment). Such caution may seem to put the figures beyond peril, but even cash receipts can afterwards be offset by, say, refunds for poor quality. Moreover, there are other circumstances that can make the realization date hard to define: for instance, when cash at a foreign branch appreciates because of favourable exchange movements, is the gain realized instantly or only on remittance?

Doubts on whether an asset exists. When cash is paid out, there may be doubt about whether any asset comes into being, i.e., whether the historical cost to be carried forward is zero or positive. Expenditures on research and advertising are examples.

This problem is not peculiar to the historical-cost concept, but is inherent in most asset-by-asset concepts.

Doubts on the size of historical cost. Where bits of historical cost can be charged to different periods or physical units, etc., the question 'How much is the historical cost?' often permits of more than one answer. Unfortunately, the accounting concept lacks a built-in logic for deciding which is right. So the accountant must willy-nilly rely on conventions, which may or may not happen to yield figures that make economic sense. He faces this choice between conventions when he must decide, for instance, on:

(1) ***The scope of historical cost.*** There may be doubt about the range of expenditures that should be included in an asset's historical cost. Thus, a manufacturer must decide whether to charge overhead—and, if so, how much—to his finished stocks and work-in-progress.

(2) ***Depreciation.*** The conventional methods of splitting up a depreciating asset's cost over the years of its life yield very different answers.

(3) ***Sequence.*** The size of some costs may hinge on order of physical movement, e.g., of materials issued from store—the first-in-first-out (Fifo) *versus* the last-in-first-out (Lifo) type of difficulty.

The use of current values would remove or at least lessen these problems. In particular, problem 3 impinges a good deal on reform proposals. And its existence is very damning to the accounting concept. One can hardly argue that economic magnitudes depend on such piffling trivialities as physical sequence (real or assumed). A concept that stumbles here must tend to be discredited *in toto*.

The current-value concept

Another approach measures each asset at its 'current value'. This phrase can mean several different things, which a later chapter will look at more carefully. One is current *sale price* (or more accurately the asset's net realizable value). Another is current *buying price* (replacement cost). Yet another is the type of cost employed by perceptive managers in their decision budgets (e.g., in measuring the sacrifice that would result from using up existing stores on a job). As we shall see later, this is found by considering the whole set of relevant values and then selecting the one that seems most informative in the given situation (so the procedure for finding it bears some resemblance to the familiar 'lower of cost or market' procedure, though the range of choice in the latter is less free). For reasons that will appear later, I call this figure 'deprival value'.

If an asset is revalued at a current figure, the accounts must perforce recognize gain or loss *before* realization. But caution at least suggests that such gain or loss should be kept apart from ordinary profit. So the accounts here should use some term such as 'unrealized gain' or 'unrealized holding gain' or 'unrealized appreciation'.

Should the term 'current value' be stretched to cover a historical cost that is updated with the general index? The resulting figure is still backward-looking, and therefore differs in principle from current market values; so it should probably be classed as a variant of the historical group.

Alternative concepts for measuring income

If wealth is compared at two different points of time, the growth is income.

This definition is not widely used. Accountants normally prefer one that compares revenues with costs—the approach of the profit and loss account. But the balance sheet approach seems to fit the facts and clarifies the problems of price change: this book will therefore make much use of it.

There are, however, a number of provisos to the bald definition above. Two of the more obvious ones are that allowance must be made (when the accounts are those of a firm) for wealth paid in by or out to the owners during the period (e.g., dividends) and that, as like must be compared with like, the same value concept must be applied at both points of time.

Needless to say, 'growth' and 'income' are sometimes negative. For convenience, this book will normally assume that such words include negative forms (and similarly that 'assets' covers 'negative assets', i.e., liabilities). It will also assume 'income' to be a general word that covers 'profit'; the latter is useful only in that it suggests an origin in trade, etc.

The simple diagram in Fig. 4.1 may help to introduce later steps in the argument. Time is shown on the horizontal OX axis, and value on the vertical OY axis. Total wealth at 1 January (by the given concept) is AB, and at 31 December it is CD; the growth ED is the income.

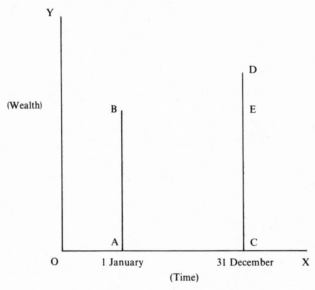

Fig. 4.1
Simple comparison of wealth over time

Value concepts lead to corresponding income concepts

The choice of value concept governs the sizes of AB and CD—and therefore of ED. Thus, income, like wealth itself, is the creature of value concepts; it must be defined by reference to the chosen concept.

If, then, there are x value concepts, there are x corresponding income concepts—possibly leading to x different income figures. A firm can legitimately have several different 'profits' for a year. To avoid imprecision, one would on some occasions need to say that profit is such and such a figure by such and such a concept.

Comparison units at different dates

A further difficulty now arises. CD's growth may or may not be due in some part to price change. If price change has taken place, one must—whatever the chosen concept—give thought to the kind of units in the vertical measures AB and CD; there is now a danger of the opening and closing wealth being no longer measured in like units.

Three possible types of unit for measuring both AB and CD (i.e., for calibrating OY) suggest themselves:

(1) *Money units.* Here one takes the money unit as the yardstick throughout, ignoring changes in both its purchasing power and special prices.

This is, of course, the ordinary accounting procedure.

(2) Real wealth units (i.e., units of constant purchasing power). Here one corrects for changes in the general price level, with the help of a general index. In effect, one calibrates OY with baskets of goods-in-general; AB and CD then reflect the number of baskets that seem equivalent to the total book values at 1 January and 31 December.

(3) Physical units. Here one corrects for change in the special prices of the various assets. If the firm has only one kind of asset (e.g., tons of a given stock), one could calibrate OY with physical units; AB and CD would then reflect the number of tons, etc., at 1 January and 31 December. Where there are several kinds of stock (i.e., in almost all real-life firms), one cannot calibrate OY with a physical unit. But one can achieve the same effect with money units by valuing both opening and closing stocks with a single set of prices; thus,

both AB and CD might be valued at the prices of date A, or (as under Lifo rules) of some remote base date.

Comparison between AB and CD would be absurd if the former were measured in, say, francs and the latter in lire. It likewise smacks of absurdity if the value of the money unit in the given country changes during the year: then, too, the opening and closing units can be deemed unlike. This is why orthodox accounting methods, based on money units, are now under fire; when prices change markedly, real wealth (or, perhaps, physical) units may be preferable.

Example of comparison units

Suppose a firm starts, at 1 January, with a capital of £100 in cash, and uses this to buy 100 tons of stock at £1 per ton. It turns over its stock several times during the year, and uses all the resulting revenue to buy fresh stock; the last such replacement takes place at 31 December. Prices are rising; the general index goes from 100 to 110, but the price of stock per ton goes from £1 to

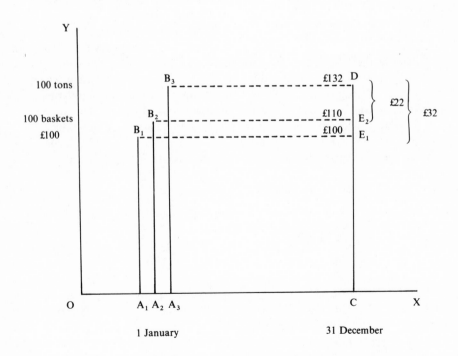

Fig. 4.2
Comparison of wealth using alternative units

21

£1·32. At 31 December, the only asset is still 100 tons of stock (i.e., all the sales receipts have been needed to maintain a constant physical volume), valued at £132.

Has the firm's wealth grown? One way of tackling the comparison is to accept the £132 figure for closing wealth, and to state the opening wealth in the three alternative units. In Fig. 4.2, opening wealth is shown by three different columns:

A_1B_1—100 money units.

Comparison of A_1B_1 with CD puts growth at E_1D. £100 has become £132; *money profit* is £32 (as in ordinary accounting).

A_2B_2—100 real-wealth units (baskets of goods-in-general).

At the end, 100 baskets cost £110; so opening wealth is restated at the equivalent of 110 end-£s, A_2B_2. This notional £110 grows to £132; *real profit* $(= CD - A_2B_2 = E_2D)$ is £22.

A_3B_3—100 physical units.

At the end, 100 tons cost £132, so opening wealth is restated at the equivalent of 132 end-£s, A_3B_3. By the physical maintenance test, there is no growth—a capital of £132 has merely been maintained; $A_3B_3 = CD$, and profit here happens to be zero.

Another way of making the comparisons is to leave alone the opening wealth and to apply the alternative measures to the closing wealth, making the latter reflect baskets and tons as well as money; to show this procedure in a diagram, one would compare a single column AB (100) with three versions of CD. Thus, the closing wealth of £132 can be stated as:

(1) (using the *money unit*) £132; profit is again £32. Or

(2) (using the *real-wealth unit*) an equivalent in opening £s, found with the general index:

$$132 \times \tfrac{100}{110} = \underline{\underline{120}}$$

reducing profit to 20 opening £s. Or

(3) (using the *physical unit*) an equivalent in another type of opening £ found with the special index:

$$132 \times \tfrac{100}{132} = \underline{\underline{100}}$$

and profit is again zero.

However, for the reasons set out on p. 14, the reader is likely to prefer the earlier kind of calculations, because these state the current profits in recent rather than remote £s.

Sub-concepts of income

It was pointed out on p. 20 that there are as many 'incomes' as there are value concepts, and succeeding pages added the further complexity of the alternative units of comparison. The accountant may thus seem to face a confusing welter of income figures.

However, it is not too hard at least to marshal these income figures in a comprehensible pattern. The first step is to make the fundamental choice of value method—whether to measure AB and CD by, for instance, the historical-cost or current-value concepts. Once the concept has been chosen, the next step is to decide on the comparison unit: the three possibilities may be regarded as giving rise to three sub-divisions within the chosen concept. Thus, the accountant who uses Fifo and ignores price change has in effect opted first for the historical-cost concept and then for its money-capital sub-concept.

In other words, if there are x feasible value concepts, and three ways of comparison for each, there are altogether $3x$ feasible sub-concepts of income. It follows that there are $3x$ possible ways of setting out the income statement, and that up to $3x$ different income figures are likely to emerge. They could be arranged in a table:

Comparison unit:	Money	Real wealth	Physical
Concept: Historical-cost			
Current:			
buying price			
selling price			
deprival value			
Etc., etc.			

Ordinary accounting profit fits into the box at the left-hand side of the top row.

The 'truth' of an income figure

Some readers may find it hard to swallow the notion that there are many rival 'incomes'. They may feel that only one can be 'true' and the rest must in some sense be impostors. Or they may liken the figures to those obtained during an experiment in a laboratory, where different readings presumably cluster round the result that would be given by extremely accurate measurement.

Such views are mistaken. There are some respectable arguments in favour of almost every one of the rivals (arguments of principle or ease of calculation); conversely, there are sensible objections to each one. Probably, indeed, it is a mistake to suppose that there is a 'true' income. What can be said is that some of the rivals are preferable to others because they are more useful. And 'useful' means not only honest, but also informative. Thus, the different figures should be thought of, not so much as nearer to or further from truth, but rather as more or less able to give information that is helpful to the reader. This ability may vary with the type of problem being studied—each version of profit may light up some aspect of a firm's progress better than other versions, or suit one kind of firm better than other kinds.[4]

For some legal purposes, admittedly it is convenient to enjoin the use of a particular concept. The ordinary accounting concept has obvious merits: it is familiar and (inflation apart) cautious, and most of its figures are based on objective data; its widespread use has therefore been sensible where the decisions are about cash payments (e.g., tax and dividends), since it reduces the scope for bickering and the danger of paying out cash before the revenue has been realized. But judicial blessings on this score do not make it more 'true' than any other version. Nor should they stop us from trying to improve it; for judges must in time give weight to reform that becomes accepted business practice.

If this view of income is right, the main test of proposals for reforming accounts during price change is whether the revised figures give a more useful picture of the firm and its progress than do orthodox figures. If the reformer can show this, he has made his point.

The uses of income figures

The last paragraph in the section above raises further questions: who are the users of the accounts, and when and why do they want information?

Clearly, there are many types of users, both inside a firm (e.g., directors and managers) and outside (e.g., actual and potential shareholders). And they will seek information on many problems, notably:

(1) *Consumption.* The individual investor wants information about each of his investments, in order to form some idea about whether he is growing richer or poorer—in particular, so that he can over the years regulate his consumption to whatever kind of pattern he deems most suitable. This is the view behind Professor Hicks's famous definition of income: 'The purpose of income calculations in practical affairs is to give people an indication of the amount which they can consume without impoverishing themselves. Following out this idea, it would seem that we ought to define a man's income as the maximum value which he can consume during a week, and still expect to be as well off at the end of the week as he was at the beginning.'[5] This consumption-power criterion is perhaps a corollary of the commonsense view that the main reason why we work is to earn our living—that the end of production is consumption.

(2) *Investment.* Present owners presumably want guidance on whether to keep or sell their shares, and so would welcome information that helps with comparisons between a particular company and other outlets for investment. Potential investors also want help with such comparisons. True, past performance is an unsure guide to future prospects; but the size and trend of the income figures, interpreted in the light of economic and other circumstances, can be useful aids.

(3) *Efficiency.* Both 'outsiders' and 'insiders' want to know about the efficiency of management; they may be helped if, for instance, they are enabled to work out the rate of return on

capital employed. Insiders may have a further need for detailed study of the efficiency of new methods, etc.; an income calculation should give guidance here, especially by providing costs that are meaningful.

(4) *Legal arrangements dependent on profit.* Often more than one person has a legal interest in profit—i.e., partners, different classes of share-holders, the tax-gatherer, and employees paid by commission on profit. Again, trustees may be required to pay income to one person during his life, and then capital to another. Some forms of government control are linked with profit; thus, public utilities may be enjoined to keep their profits under a stated ceiling, and one way of controlling prices is to limit profit margins.

And there may still be other users. Profits are sometimes cited during wage negotiations with trade unions; they may be relevant, too, in debates on social problems, a government's economic and fiscal policies, etc.

The different groups of users will seek somewhat different types of information. Investors are concerned with all types, but particularly types 1 and 2; and, as investors are an important (arguably the most important) group of users, surely the published income figure should be one that caters as well as possible for them. However, this view does not always dispose of all difficulty. The interests of different groups of investors may conflict: thus, over-caution probably tends to be bad for ordinary shareholders, whereas preference shareholders and long-term creditors may think that they benefit from it (if it holds down the ordinary dividend and so increases retained wealth).

If insiders want other sorts of accounts for use 3, there is nothing to stop them drafting extra accounts for their special purpose. Use 4 has played a big part in the historical development of accounting concepts. But it has perhaps been accorded more weight than its deserts warrant. Legal income should presumably be the figure that is in some sense most acceptable to people in general, i.e., it should follow tamely from uses 1 and 2. But, as the size of the legal income may well govern the size of cash payments for dividends, commission, tax, etc.,

the men who determine such income must be influenced by a wish to curtail disputes, delays, and excessive cash drains; their resulting rules may differ from those most helpful for the other uses.

It is, of course, one thing to want helpful information and another to get it. Like other human devices, income figures are imperfect.[6] Indeed, some critics say they are so bad that accountants should cease to publish them,[7] and should provide users instead with condensed cash accounts—thereby enabling each user somehow or other to form his own conception of the progress of the firm. Even if we reject this dark view, we must freely concede that any given figure, reformed or unreformed, is likely to have limitations in plenty, and will not tell readers everything they want to know.

The case for using multiple figures of income

Perhaps, therefore, accounting should aim at giving several income figures rather than one—at setting out different pictures of the firm side by side.

This would put users of reports on their guard, and might also remind them of the nature of accounting measurements. The new accounts need not be so cumbersome as they sound. A skilful draughtsman should be able to compress several alternatives into a simple table. For instance, Professors E. O. Edwards and P. W. Bell propose that the income statement should contain two alternative accounts in parallel.[8] The twin columns envisaged by this ingenious plan use the historical and the current-value (replacement-cost) concepts —and so end with ordinary accounting profit alongside a profit that includes the year's unrealized appreciation. For good measure, the accounting column is rearranged in a way that gives more information than is usual, by splitting accounting profit into its two elements of realized appreciation on stock, etc., and operating profit. (An example is appended to this chapter.)

Though orthodox accounts do not show alternative incomes in parallel, they often arrange the year's gain in successive slices that start with normal trade profit and then go on to less and less normal gains. Thus, a well-drafted income statement tends to separate ordinary from extraordinary items; and presumably it omits gains on the revaluation of fixed assets (and shows them in the balance sheet).

Income *versus* capital gain, etc.

The order and wording of the balance sheet can show abnormal gains in very different lights. Accountants are adept at arranging the figures in alternative ways that may or may not suggest income. Suppose a firm's capital is £1000, its profit from ordinary trade is £400, and it has realized a gain of £100 from sale of a fixed asset. Somewhat extreme alternative forms of the balance sheet might be:

(1)	£	(2)	£
Capital	1000	Capital	
Profit on:		Share capital	1000
trading 400		Reserve from	
sale of		sale of	
fixed asset 100		fixed asset	100
	500		
			1100
	1500	Profit	400
			1500

Forms 1 and 2 give quite different impressions of whether the £100 has the quality of income.

Where gains fall squarely within the historical-cost concept, attempts (by, e.g., tax experts) to treat some as income and others as non-income must tend to sound thin in logic; the attempted distinction will often hinge on 'usualness', and then must be arbitrary. However, where gains fall into different concepts, some distinction can be justified. Thus, reformed accounts might reasonably (in the interests of caution) separate realized from unrealized gains—even though the size of the figures on each side of the line may admittedly depend on rule-of-thumb, as when material costs rely on sequence (see p. 19) and machinery costs are 'realized' via depreciation charges of questionable size.

Various other solutions to this problem have been suggested, notably by lawyers. Thus, growth in 'fixed' assets has been distinguished from growth in 'circulating' assets; and the analogy of the tree and its fruit has been seized on eagerly.[9] Such solutions are too superficial to be of much service.

It does not get us out of the wood to call some gains 'capital'. The word seldom means more than 'unusual' or 'unforeseen'; and, though there may be some advantage in pointing to unusual or unexpected items (e.g., because windfalls do not affect our expectations, and thus our behaviour), these items may nonetheless seem in other respects to be income. There are, however, two exceptions:

(1) Suppose a testamentary trust starts with a capital £100 000, and invests this in irredeemable fixed-interest securities to earn £6000 a year, the market rate of interest then being 6 per cent. Later, the rate drops to 5 per cent, i.e., the value of the securities rises to £120 000. In one sense, there is here a gain of £20 000. If, however, the trustees now sold £20 000 of the securities and paid out the proceeds, future revenue would drop to only £5000 a year; the recipients of income might be delighted this year but very disappointed next year. So, where gain is due to change in the market rate of interest, at least part[10] of it may usefully be excluded from some definitions of income.

(2) Where there is gain in money terms but not real terms, it may sensibly be treated as a restatement in current £s of an unchanged real capital rather than an increase. But such treatment implies acceptance of the real-wealth sub-concept.

The discussion of capital gains, etc. in this section might have been broached in a rather different way—by questioning the earlier statement (p. 20) that all growth should be called *income*. Should not some forms of growth be excluded? Again, if an accountant decides that asset values should be written up to higher levels, does he thereby commit himself to a new income concept and a higher income figure?

The best answers to such questions probably hinge on the notion of multiple incomes. By the narrow test of a single concept (e.g., that employed by ordinary accounts), many forms of growth no doubt can be excluded. Once we admit the existence of the other concepts, we must concede that every gain has a place in some part of the framework (on p. 22), and so can be called income; our best plan, then, may be to set out several income figures to reflect the different concepts.

Price-change reforms and wealth concepts

Ill-results of ignoring price change

Accounts that ignore price change give poor information in several ways:

(a) They distort trends, etc. (as chapter 3 tried to show);
(b) they may, by what seem important tests, mis-state cost; and in consequence
(c) may likewise mis-state realized profit;
(d) they show assets at out-of-date values; and in consequence
(e) they ignore unrealized gain and loss.

These faults can be important for all the uses and users mentioned on pp. 23–24.

Reform means movement over the conceptual framework

There are many different proposals for curing the faults. Most of them involve some degree of switching within the conceptual framework already described. Thus, the reform of cost and profit figures must mean a switch at least from the money sub-concept to a real-value or physical sub-concept; and reform of asset values forces a switch from the historical to a current-value concept.

Because the orthodox accounting concept, despite its defects, confers certain safeguards (p. 23), plainly we should not abandon it without awareness of what we are about. We should appreciate the size of the conceptual change in a given reform proposal, the better to assess its risks as well as its benefits. And probably a change from the historical to the current concept is not justified during the stress of inflation if it would not seem defensible in more serene times. Therefore, a reformer strengthens his case by showing how his proposals fit into the full framework. He is less than honest if, bent on reform of concept, he slips this in as part of a seemingly modest programme for dealing with inflation.

Degrees of reform

It would be wrong to think that 'reform' must necessarily mean upheavals throughout a firm's accounting system. The proposals are many and varied, and contrast greatly in their scope. A short sketch of their range may now be helpful.

Proposals for reform can differ sharply from one another in matters of principle. Thus, one school of thought rejects the realization concept and treats unrealized appreciation as income, while a more timid school retains the realization test. There is argument, too, between the 'general-index man' (who backs the real-change sub-concept) and the 'special-index man' (who backs the physical-change sub-concept). The general-index man, in effect, adheres to the historical concept, and merely brings its figures up to date, and so (he tells us) offers the least radical kind of reform—something to be looked on more as a friend than an enemy of accepted practice, in that it makes the historical-cost system respectable. The merits of this debating-point are dubious; but the general-index man is on firm ground when he adds that his method is relatively simple. Probably this merit will (to judge from the trend in Britain) give it the edge over the special-index method, at least in the early stages of reform. But the controversy over the two methods will probably remain lively, and is of great importance for the accountant of the future.

Even when differences over concept and sub-concept have been resolved, there still may remain differences over the extent to which the agreed reforms should be adopted in a given situation. Various compromises and shortcuts are feasible and defensible. In other words, a reform programme should seldom be thought of as a seamless robe, to be accepted or rejected as a whole. On the contrary, its various parts should be considered one by one; and a firm may reasonably decide to adopt some parts in its internal accounts, and to reject or postpone others.

Appendix: Example of parallel income statements

It was suggested on p. 24 that a multiple income statement would be useful. Table 4.1 shows what such a statement might look like. This example follows the Edwards and Bell model. Its arithmetic assumes that three units of goods were bought in year 1, at the wholesale price of £10 apiece. They remain in stock till June of year 3, when two units are sold at the current retail price of £21. There are no other transactions. Accounting profit for year 3 is thus £22:

Income account, year 3

		£
Sales	2 units at 21	42
Cost of goods sold	2 units at 10	20
		—
	Profit	22
		=

Special prices (i.e., the wholesale buying prices per unit) during the three years are:

		£
		£
Year 1	Purchase date	10
Year 3	1 January	12
	30 June (sale date)	16
	31 December	17

(General prices here are ignored, but could readily be introduced into this form of calculation.)

With the aid of the special prices, the income account can be redrafted as in Table 4.1. This starts with (a), a preliminary calculation. Then, in (b), the account is split into two columns—the left-hand column leading to ordinary accounting profit, and the right-hand column to a current value profit.

TABLE 4.1

ACCOUNTS SHOWING TWO VERSIONS OF PROFIT

Income Account £

(a) *Current trading section*

		£
Sales		42
Cost of goods sold (as at 30 June, year 3) 2 × 16		32
Current operating profit		10

(b) *Alternatives treatment of profit*

	(1) Only realized gains shown	£	(2) Both realized and unrealized gains shown	£
(i) Current operating profit, b/d		10		10
(ii) Appreciation	Realized appreciation, during years 1–3, on assets sold 2 × (16–10)	12	All appreciation during year 3 only, on assets: sold 2 × (16–12) still held 1 × (17–12)	8 / 5
				13
Total	Accounting (= realized) profit:	—	'Business profit'	
For year		22		23
Brought forward		—		6
		22		29

Balance Sheets, year 3

	1 Jan. £	31 Dec £	1 Jan. £	31 Dec £
Cash	—	42	—	42
Stock	30	10	36	17
	30	52	36	59
Capital	30	30	30	30
Profit: realized		22		22
unrealized			6	7
				29
	30	52	36	59

'Current operating profit' *versus* 'holding gain'

It was noted on p. 8 that the normal income statement throws little light on the manager's skill at buying cheap and selling dear, i.e., at making 'holding gains' while the assets lie in stock. The twin parts of section (b) in Table 4.1 both try to repair this deficiency, by showing profit in its two parts:[11]

(i) Profit that would arise even if all relevant special prices were stable (the firm's reward for the narrow task of retailing, manufacturing, etc., as distinct from holding). This part may be called *current operating profit*; it is calculated in (a) above.

(ii) Special appreciation on the assets' values, i.e., *holding gain*.

Analysis of accounting profit

Column (1) in Table 4.1 is an elaboration of the ordinary profit calculation. It shows that the accounting profit here consists of £10 of current operating profit and £12 of realized holding gain (the £6 appreciation on each of the two units sold, from their purchase in year 1 to their sale in year 3). The total is £22, as in ordinary accounts. The balance sheet contains the ordinary figures.

This procedure reminds one of a familiar device of cost accounting. Where full records are kept of raw materials, and these are charged to jobs at current prices, then changes in their value while in stock must be measured and passed through the accounts. This costing variance resembles the realized holding gain of £12 in the example.

'Business profit'

Column (2) in Table 4.1, for the current-value concept, also starts with current operating profit. Its novelty centres round its treatment of holding gain.

There is a double objection to ignoring holding gain until it is realized (the ordinary procedure, shown clearly in column (1)). The gain in the given year's accounts then includes too much (since it may contain the appreciation of prior years, not just the year with which the accounts are supposed to deal), but also too little (since it fails to show unrealized appreciation of the current year). To overcome this double defect, Edwards and Bell use an alternative profit figure (which they have christened 'business profit'); it is made up of current operating profit plus appreciation on all stock (whether sold or retained) during the current year alone. In the example, two units appreciated by £8 between January and their sale date, and the unit still in stock by £5 between January and December. Total 'business profit' is £23.

As the balance sheets show, the link between the twin income accounts is change in unrealized holding gain:

	£
Accounting profit	22
Increase in unrealized gain, from £6 at start of year to £7 at end	1
'Business profit'	23

From deference to the cautious view that realized gain may be the safer guide for tax and dividend payments, column (2) throughout distinguishes realized and unrealized items.

References

1. 'The main purpose of accounting is to exhibit, for the proprietors of the business, the actual results in terms as nearly comparable as can be to the expected results; in terms, in other words, which make it possible for the proprietors to judge whether the business is a 'success' and fulfils those expectations in the light of which they invested their capital, and which they alone are ultimately capable of deciding' (Nicholas Kaldor, *An Expenditure Tax*, London, Allen and Unwin, 1955, pp. 67–8).

2. This idea is suggested in F. K. Wright's, 'A Theory of Financial Accounting', *Journal of Business Finance*, Autumn 1970.

3. 'Shipment is taken as the occasion for the credit to revenue. . . . In many cases, title doubtless actually passes at this point; but this is certainly not always the case' (W. A. Paton, *Accounting Theory*. New York: Ronald Press, 1922, p. 450).

4. 'If, indeed, one believed that annual profit was in some sense an objective phenomenon, one might well take the view that careful search was bound to disclose the appropriate formula, in the same way that a scientist by looking deeply into the nature of the real world is able sometimes to produce a formula describing, within very close approximations, a natural phenomenon, such as the propagation of light. But this is not the case. The terms "profit" and "income" are in fact used in our language to indicate a whole range of ideas. It is true that all these ideas have something in common. They all imply in

some sense the receipt of a benefit during a given period of time. But there the common element ends. In fact, the systematic use of any one of the many concepts of income arises only because thereby a convenient social purpose is fulfilled; and for different social purposes it is convenient to use different concepts' (H. C. Edey, 'Income and the Valuation of Stock-in-Trade', *The British Tax Review*, May–June 1962, p. 164).

5. J. R. Hicks, *Value and Capital*. Oxford: Oxford U.P., p. 174.

6. Professor Hicks ends his discussion of income with: 'We have come to see how very complex it is, how unattractive it looks when subjected to detailed analysis. We may now allow a doubt to escape us whether it does, in the last resort, stand up to analysis at all, whether we have not been chasing a will-o'-the-wisp' (*op. cit.*, p. 176).

7. 'We are led to the conclusion that periodic income is not an effective tool of financial planning or control. This conclusion seems to accord ill with the fact that income measurement has long been a central theme of accounting and the main preoccupation of the accounting profession. Yet this fact need not impress us. The practice of medicine once consisted largely of blood-letting . . . just as in the first half of this century we saw the income statement displace the balance-sheet in importance, so we may now be de-emphasizing the income statement in favour of a statement of fund flows or cash flows. Each of us sees the future differently, no doubt. But my own guess is that, so far as the history of accounting is concerned, the next twenty-five years may subsequently be seen to have been the twilight of income measurement' (D. Solomons, 'Economic and Accounting Concepts of Income', *Accounting Review*, July 1961, pp. 118–19).

8. E. O. Edwards and P. W. Bell, *The Theory and Measurement of Business Income*, Berkeley: University of California Press, 1960, p. 218. This important book approaches the problem of price change by pleading persuasively for special revaluation; the general index is introduced as a concluding refinement.

9. 'For a long time the relationship of income to capital was likened to the relation of the fruit to the tree. Just as there was no difficulty in separating the crop from the tree, so there need be no difficulty in distinguishing income from the capital which produced it. It was in line with this thinking that, for the first thirty-six years after Peel had re-introduced the income tax in Britain in 1842, no relief was given by the British tax code for the using up of fixed assets in the course of carrying on a business. The introduction of income tax depreciation allowances in Britain in 1878, and their growth in importance there and here since then, constitute a movement away from the idea that you can evaluate the fruit without giving thought to the value of the tree—that realized profits can be measured in disregard of what have sometimes been called "mere value changes" in the assets' (Solomons, *op. cit.*).

10. Professor Frank Paish explains the theoretical distinction between the 'income' and the 'non-income' parts in his 'Capital and Income', *Economica*, July 1940.

11. For a discussion of the pros and cons of this analysis, see David F. Drake and Nicholas Dopuch, 'On the Case for Dichotomizing Income', *Journal of Accounting Research*, Autumn 1965. Some accountants may object to putting appreciation into the limelight, and would prefer accounts to stress the technicalities of production and gloss over price fluctuations. They would argue that to (say) a manufacturer, the change in value of his raw materials is a factor of secondary weight; he should be judged by his skill on the workshop floor, not in the market. But change in the market value of assets is a reality of economic life, and the manager's prowess in this part of his work deserves to be shown as clearly as his prowess elsewhere.

5. Revaluation and stabilization

As earlier chapters have hinted, the essence of most proposals for the reform of accounts during inflation is the restatement of accounting figures of different dates in terms of the prices at a common base date. One example is the revaluation of assets at current prices.

When accountants talk about 'revaluation', they normally mean a limited degree of modernization—probably confined to the corner of the balance sheet that encloses the fixed assets. However, it is possible to restate every figure in both income account and balance sheet with the help of price-index factors, and so to create a consistent whole in terms of the price level of some chosen base date. We shall call this full treatment 'stabilization', by way of compliment to the accountant who first explained the matter in English and used the word in this sense.[1] Other words, such as 'revaluation', can then serve as names for some of the incomplete programmes.

Stabilized accounts

As chapter 3 explained, the real trends in a series of accounting figures can be made clearer by adjusting the raw figures with index factors. But stabilization has also a far more valuable function: it can cut out most of the flaws and inconsistencies that mar a given year's accounts after price change, and make such accounts almost as useful as they would have been in the absence of change.

Probably, no one can really appreciate the impact of price change on accounts unless he can stabilize them. We may decide in the end that stabilized accounts are too elaborate for this or that kind of report; but they are essential for an understanding of our subject, and so a serious student must drill himself in their use.

Analogy with foreign branch accounts

Stabilization will remind accountants of a more familiar subject—their treatment of figures for foreign branches, etc. When exchange rates are varying, the conversion of foreign money figures into home equivalents involves problems very like those of dealing with home price change. Suppose a businessman in Utopia (the 'head office') runs a branch in Britain. At the end of each year, the head-office accountant probably converts the British results from £s sterling into Utopian dollars (in order, for instance, to find the firm's total income). Let us say that the business year ends on 31 December; that the only branch asset is land; that branch profit is £400 p.a. (net rents received smoothly over the year, i.e., on average at 30 June); and that the branch balance sheets run:

	1 Jan. £ sterling	31 Dec. £ sterling
Fixed assets (land), at cost:		
At start of year	10 000	10 000
Bought with the year's profits, on average at 30 June		400
		10 400
Capital	10 000	10 000
Profit—net rents, earned on average at 30 June		400
		10 400

The head office accountant can translate these sterling figures into Utopian $s easily enough if the exchange rate is £100 = $100 throughout the year; then the closing sterling values are also the Utopian values.

But suppose, instead, that British prices start to rise on 1 January (when the general index in Britain stands at 100) and go up steadily—to 110 at mid-year and 120 at the end; that profits rise in harmony, and thus (being earned on average at mid-year) are £400 × $\frac{110}{100}$ = £440; that these profits are promptly invested in more land; and that the exchange rate exactly mirrors the depreciation of the £, so that:

At 1 January, £100 sterling exchanges for $100; at 30 June, £100 sterling exchanges for $\frac{100}{110}$ of $100, i.e., for $90·9; and
at 31 December, £100 sterling exchanges for $\frac{100}{120}$ of $100, i.e., for $83·3.

The usual procedure—which links well with the accounting conventions for valuing assets—is to convert the branch's opening assets and capital at their original exchange rate; additional fixed assets at the rate when bought; profit at the average rate for the year; and current assets at closing rate.[2] So the closing balance sheets are now:

	31 December		
	Sterling	Rate	$
	(1)	(2)	(3)
Fixed assets, at cost:			
Original	10 000	100	*10 000*
Bought with the year's profits, on average at 30 June	440	90·9	*400*
	10 440		*10 400*
Capital	10 000	100	*10 000*
Profit	440	90·9	*400*
	10 440		*10 400*

The converted results of column (3) show that the British income, up from 400 of the old £s to 440 of the new ones of mid-year, remains unchanged in the units that mean more to the Utopian owner (e.g., as a guide to his consumption or further investment in Britain). They also measure the different British assets in consistent terms, i.e., the total of $10 400 is no longer 'mixed' (see p. 14).

With stabilized accounts, in effect we pretend that the ordinary accounts are those of a foreign branch, and we convert them into the units of a conceptual head office in a far-off, happy land with stable money. Index factors (based on the price level of any convenient time) take the place of exchange rates. In simple examples, the mechanics are much the same as for the Utopian firm.

Example revaluation *versus* stabilization

The $ figures in the account in the lefthand column on this page are the same thing as British figures stabilized with 1 January as the base date, i.e., in *opening* £s. But stabilization in the money units of the close of the period—i.e., in *end-£s*—is, in fact, often preferable (see p. 14). If these closing units are used, the figures must be raised to match the rise in the closing index to 120. Table 5.1 shows what happens then; it also contrasts stabilization with the half-hearted reform of revaluation. It has three columns: (1) is for the ordinary figures, and (2) and (3) for their revalued and stabilized counterparts. Column (2) assumes that all the land has appreciated in step with general prices, i.e., that the special index for such land has behaved just like the general index:

(1) The *ordinary* form is, of course, the one in everyday use. Its figures are historical, and therefore out of harmony with current values; as they date back to times with different price levels, they are mutually inconsistent.
(2) The *revalued* form is being adopted by a growing minority of firms. It brings some or all of the assets up to date—but it leaves capital and profit alone, and therefore needs a balancing figure—the 'gain on revaluation of assets'.
(3) The *stabilized* form is seldom met with, even in textbooks. It completes the process of revaluation by extending it from the assets to the other balances, here capital and profit. These are raised by factors that match the time between their 'arrival' and the end of the year—

TABLE 5.1

SIMPLE BALANCE SHEET, IN ALTERNATIVE FORMS SHOWING
REVALUATION, AND STABILIZATION IN END–£s

	(1) Ordinary figures £	(2) Revaluation		(3) Stabilized figures end–£	
		Factor	£	*Factor*	
Fixed assets					
Original, bought at index 100	10 000	$\frac{120}{100}$	12 000	$\frac{120}{100}$	12 000
Bought with the year's profits, at index 110	440	$\frac{120}{110}$	480	$\frac{120}{110}$	480
	10 440		12 480		12 480
Capital, raised at index 100	10 000		10 000	$\frac{120}{100}$	12 000
Profit, earned at index 110	440		440	$\frac{120}{110}$	480
Gain on revaluation of assets			2 040		
	10 440		12 480		12 480

capital by $\frac{20}{100}$ and profit by $\frac{10}{110}$. Because the same factors are here applied to both assets and owner's balances (i.e., no real gain intrudes in this example), a balancing figure is not needed.

Most balance sheet figures are the sum of many entries at different dates with different price levels. Thus, more than one factor is in practice needed to revalue or stabilize each of these 'mixed' accounts. If, for instance, fixed assets or undistributed profits have grown from year to year, the totals must be analysed so that each increase can be separately multiplied by the factor appropriate to its date.

Nature of gain on revaluation

Revaluated accounts (column (2) in Table 5.1) need a balancing figure of £2040. This 'gain on revaluation' cannot but give an impression of growth. Such an impression is here misleading, since it reflects merely the cheapening of money. Most accountants distinguish such an unrealized gain on fixed assets from ordinary trade profits, and would regard the payment of dividends from it as dangerous. Orthodox theory can justify the distinction on the dual grounds that the asset is fixed and that it is unrealized. If, however, one abandons the money sub-concept, gain due to inflation becomes non-existent (whether or not it is realized). And this is exactly what the stabilized accounts show, so here stabilization and caution are allies.

It is important to make up one's mind firmly on the principle at stake in this example. In less clear examples, as later chapters will show, the illusory gain from inflation can seep undetected into realized trade profit; and orthodox accounting usually leaves it there.

Some problems of stabilization

Stabilization becomes less easy when the values in the accounts change at differing rates.

General *versus* special indices

Our simple example assumes that the general and the special indices rise equally. So it evades the problem of choosing between them when they differ.

The special index (like direct revaluation) gives more information about the size of assets. Thus, it seems the better tool for updating asset values.

But the owner's balances—capital, profits, etc.—are not linked with particular assets. They reflect a series of investments by the owner (cash paid in or dividends forgone) at various dates. The problem is how to interpret such historical moneys in the most meaningful way. The general index is probably the best device for enabling us to look at yesterday's cash flows through today's spectacles: if we want to see how the owner's wealth has fared in a period, there are strong grounds for using units that measure it in terms of his general purchasing power. And even if we are tempted to use a special index, we should have a hard time deciding which one is appropriate where the other side of the balance sheet covers a realistic range of assets with diverging indices.

We shall next adapt the example so as to introduce problems that arise when the values of the asset and of the owner's balances fail to march in step, i.e., when there is real change. We can conveniently distinguish two kinds of movement:

(1) Real-value change in non-money assets.
(2) Real-value change in money assets.

Each of these will also be discussed more fully in later chapters.

Real change in the values of non-money assets

Suppose in the example that, while the general index moves from 100 to 120, the special index moves from 100 to 130. Then the original land appreciates during the year from £10 000 to £13 000, instead of £12 000 as in Table 5.1. For simplicity, let us suppose too that the only asset is this original bit of land (i.e., that trade profit is zero, and so no land is bought at mid-year).

One school of reformers holds that such special change should be ignored: stabilized accounts should still value the assets at the revised historical cost of £12 000. A second school holds that the £13 000 figure should now be used, since it gives better information to the reader.

If the £13 000 is used, the surplus on revaluation is £3000; but £2000 of this is mere paper gain, due to inflation, and only £1000 is real gain. Stabilized accounts ignore the £2000, but will, if they are drafted on the lines favoured by the second school, show the £1000 as in Table 5.2.

This form of stabilization accordingly recognizes real but unrealized appreciation. It thus makes a radical move in the conceptual framework set out on p. 22. So an important problem of principle is here at stake.

A useful mental approach to this problem is to start by thinking about comparable special change in a time of general stability. If the value of an asset goes up by £1000 while the general index stays at 100, should the assets be revalued? Recognition of the £1000 then gives a more informative picture of the firm's wealth and progress, and accordingly may seem desirable. If so, it is desirable also when special change is superimposed on general change.

Stabilization and real change in the value of money assets

This discussion of real change has so far been simplified by leaving out money assets (cash, debtors, etc.). The next step is to bring them in.

Let us go back for a moment to the foreign-branch example in the account on p. 31. Suppose that the £440 of rents received at mid-year are held as cash (instead of being invested at once in more land). The closing balance sheet of the branch (see column (1) below) thus contains £440 of cash. For simplicity, the special index for land is assumed to coincide with the general index.

The closing exchange rate applicable to current assets 83·3 must be used to convert the £440 of cash, though the £440 of profit is still converted at the 90·9 mid-year rate; this reduces the Utopian figures for assets to less than those for capital plus profit, and so a balance is needed. In the context of

TABLE 5.2

SIMPLE BALANCE SHEET IN ALTERNATIVE FORMS, WITH REAL
APPRECIATION ON ASSETS

		(1) Ordinary £	(2) Revalued Factor	(2) Revalued £	(3) Stabilized Factor	(3) Stabilized end-£
Fixed assets	Cost	10 000	$\frac{130}{100}$	13 000	$\frac{130}{100}$	13 000
Owners' balances						
Capital	Historical	10 000		10 000	$\frac{120}{100}$	12 000
Appreciation (unrealized) on revaluation of assets						
Money		$10\,000 \times \frac{30}{100}$		3 000		
Real					$10\,000 \times \frac{130-120}{100}$	1 000
				13 000		13 000

foreign branches, it is rather misleadingly called 'loss on exchange'; in fact, it measures loss (or gain) from not making the exchange, i.e., from keeping cash at the branch instead of remitting it to the head office before the exchange rate fell. Because of the branch's inactivity, the head office lost 33 potential dollars.

	(1) Sterling	(2) Rate	(3) $
Fixed assets, at cost:			
Original	10 000	100	10 000
Cash	440	83·3	367
	10 440		10 367
Capital	10 000	100	10 000
Profit	440	90·9	400
'Loss on exchange'		balance	−33
	10 440		10 367

In a stabilized version of these accounts, the figures are the same as those in column (3) above if the opening £ is used as base. A loss (£33 opening £s) is shown; it measures the decline because of inflation in the value of cash held from July to December—i.e., the loss from holding money instead of land, etc. If the end-£ is used instead, the results are as shown in Table 5.3. Here the profit of 440 June-£s is equivalent to 480 end-£s. But the same cash figure (440) serves for both columns (1) and (2), since face value is the correct measure of money assets stabilized in the ene-£. A balance of

−40 end-£s is needed—to show how the value of the cash slipped down in comparison with things-in-general.

Gain and loss on money seems to fit under the heading of 'real change', just like the £1000 appreciation on land in Table 5.2. One could say that money has a very special index of its own; no matter how far the general index moves, this special index stays doggedly at 100, and every fluctuation in the general index alters the gap between the two indices, and so signals real gain or loss on money. Whether or not such gain or loss is *realized* is a nice point, which will be discussed in chapter 6.

Gain and loss on money can have immense importance for individuals, firms, and society. Yet ordinary accounts make not the least attempt to measure it. Here is one of the strongest arguments for stabilization.

Stabilization in £ of dates other than the end of year

When accounts are stabilized, the end-£ normally seems to be the most convenient unit to choose. But the raw figures can as easily be stabilized in £s of any other date (e.g., some of our examples have used opening £s, and a table comparing the results of many years might possibly use the £ of a remote date). Moreover, one of the virtues of stabilization is that any set of stabilized figures can be converted directly to another base with the help of a single factor. We can, for instance, turn the figures of column (3) on the balance sheet on p. 31 into those of column (3) in Table 5.1 by multiplying by $\frac{120}{100}$ throughout, and the reverse change can be made with the factor $\frac{100}{120}$.

TABLE 5.3

BALANCE SHEET SHOWING LOSS ON HOLDING MONEY

		(1) Ordinary £	Factor	(2) Stabilized end-£
Fixed assets	Cost	10 000	$\frac{120}{100}$	12 000
Cash		440		440
		10 440		12 440
Capital	Historical	10 000	$\frac{120}{100}$	12 000
Trade profit	Historical	440	$\frac{120}{110}$	480
Loss on holding money				−40
		10 440		12 440

34

The stabilized income statement

The income account also can be stabilized—that is, the costs and revenues of, say, each month can be restated in the £s of some base date. The results may be less dramatic than when the balance sheet is stabilized. But the new figures can be helpful if one wants to compare different years (and one accordingly gears all the statements to the same base date). And they are specially helpful where a statement is 'mixed', in the sense that costs are incurred at dates other than those of the corresponding revenues (e.g., where materials are bought in the summer for peak sales at Christmas); the twisted results of such timelags in ordinary statements will fill several later chapters.

The stabilized figures are, however, in one respect hard to digest. There are clearly strong grounds for stabilizing the income statement at the same base date as the balance sheet. For the latter, the end-£ usually seems the obvious unit. But an income statement that is stabilized in end-£s must disagree with the ordinary figures of earlier months, and thus its figures will seem unfamiliar and odd to managers, etc. They may during inflation, for instance, seem too big. (A partial remedy—when cost studies, etc., are being made—is to stabilize the relevant figures at some 'average' date, e.g., mid-year.) As an illustration, suppose one of a firm's ventures costs £1000 and brings in £1540; that both the outlay and the sale take place at mid-year, when the index stands at 110; and that the accounts are stabilized at the year-end, when the index is at 120. The ordinary and stabilized versions of the income statement will run:

	Ordinary	Stabilized	
	£	Factor	Closing £
Cost	1000	$\frac{120}{110}$	1091
Sale	1540	$\frac{120}{110}$	1680
Profit	540		589

The enlargement of the stabilized figures is at first disconcerting.

References

1. Professor Henry Whitcomb Sweeney, of the Graduate School of Business, Columbia University. His *Stabilized Accounting* (New York: Harper, 1936. Republished by Holt, Rhinehart and Winston, 1964) was based on German experience during the inflation of the 'twenties, and is still an excellent work on the mechanics of stabilization.

2. The rules are examined more fully in W. T. Baxter and B. S. Yamey, 'Theory of Foreign Branch Accounts', *Accounting Research*, April 1951.

6. Gain and loss on money

The proposal that accounts should show change in the value of money, as in the example in chapter 5, is more alien to ordinary practice than any other of the suggestions in this book. So, perhaps, we should treat such change as a grand climax, and postpone it until the end. But it is fundamental to our topic, and obtrudes on milder reforms; so it can conveniently be dealt with now.

Money assets and non-money assets

Stabilized accounts show the gain automatically because they give different treatment to:

(a) *Non-money assets* (such as land, buildings, etc.), whose values are free to float as the price level changes; and

(b) *Money assets* (such as cash and debtors), whose values are firmly fixed to the money unit. (It is unfortunate that *fixed* is the obvious adjective to use both in such phrases as 'fixed assets' and 'fixed money rights', which are at opposite ends of the inflation spectrum.)

The ordinary balance sheet splits its contents into current and non-current groups; the definitional distinction is none too clear, but usually hinges on the firm's ability and willingness to liquidate the asset within, say, twelve months. A stabilized balance sheet may marshal the figures into the same groups. But the process of stabilizing lays great stress on a different line of cleavage—between (a) and (b) above. Thus, for stabilization purposes all 'money assets', whether current or not, belong to the same family. The corresponding claims on the firm (e.g., creditors) also belong to it. If a balance sheet is stabilized in the end-£, all the members of this family are left at their face values (subject, perhaps, to discount for risk and delay). If it is stabilized in the £ of some other date, all members are multiplied by the same factor. Indeed, they might all be reduced to one net figure of money owned or owed (which would show the firm's structure in an interesting light, as in the example in Table 6.3), and then be stabilized *en bloc*.

Presumably firms do not obtain their asset structures by chance. The structure normally results from some sort of plan—an attempt to hold the assets best suited to economic and technical conditions. However, the plan may be marred by carelessness, shortsight, or bad luck. In particular, one may doubt whether most managers realize how much they stand to make or lose by regulating the volume of money assets.

Types of money assets and non-money assets

Many of the current assets (cash, debts due to the firm, etc.) are money assets, or near enough to be treated as such. Investments held as current assets may or may not be money assets: the value of some (e.g., government stocks) is closely linked to money, whereas the value of equities is free to fluctuate. Stocks, though current assets, are not tied to money; their values can change between acquisition dates and the end of the business year.

The heading 'investments in subsidiary companies' may cover dissimilar items. Loans to such companies are money assets, whereas holdings in the equities are non-money assets.

Fixed assets are almost invariably non-money assets. Deductions from their value (e.g., depreciation provisions) also must normally obey the same rules.

On the other side of the balance sheet, the equity of the ordinary shareholders (i.e., the balances for capital, retained profits, etc.) form a non-money group. Preference shares, however, carry rights that are defined mainly in rigid money terms, and thus may reasonably be subjected to much the same conversion rule as money assets; so may debentures and loans. Current liabilities to creditors fall into the money group, as do provisions for the payment of fixed sums of money.

Sometimes the item will have affinities with both groups, and then its classification must be arbitrary. Examples are participating preference shares and convertible loan stock.

Gearing

Inflation makes a money liability less burdensome, and so gives a 'gain on owing money' to those who are in debt. An important example is the company that is financed in substantial part by loans, preference shares, etc., rather than by equity capital. Such a company is said to have 'high gearing' (or 'leverage' in the USA). Inflation, in effect, transfers part of that company's wealth from the holders of the money claims to the holders of the equity; the latter obtain a gain on owing. Stabilization reveals this gain.

Gearing also affects annual cost. The borrowing costs of a company with gearing—interest and preference dividends[1]—do not rise during inflation (i.e., they fall in real terms), and its ordinary shareholders then reap an agreeable harvest.

Balance sheet example

By way of example, again consider (as in chapter 5) firms whose pre-inflation capital is £10 000; general prices again rise by 20 per cent as do the values of fixed assets, etc. But we now vary the patterns of assets and liabilities, and illustrate three of the possibilities:

[A] *Real values are constant.* Here the net money assets are assumed to be *nil* (throughout the year).

[B] *Money values are constant.* Here the wealth is assumed to consist entirely of money assets (throughout the year). So £10 000 is the net sum of cash, debtors, etc., less money liabilities.

[C] *Mixed structure.* A normal firm owns some money assets and some non-money assets. An interesting mixture is provided by high gearing.

To avoid complications, no trade profit appears; i.e., such profit is assumed to be zero, or to be paid out in dividends as fast as it is earned.

Table 6.1 sets out the differences between firms, A, B and C. The figures of each are shown (as in Table 5.1, p. 32) in three possible forms of balance sheet: (1) ordinary, (2) revalued, and (3) stabilized. As chapter 5 explained, the stabilized accounts are likely to use the £ of either the start or the end of the year as base unit. Both possibilities are shown here. Some rather dramatic contrasts emerge:

[A] *Constant real values.* Because it has no money, the assets of this firm can be shown in the stabilized accounts of column (3) at a figure that still represents their original value—stated as either 10 000 opening £s or 12 000 closing £s; there is no real gain or loss. The revalued accounts of column (2) show a £2000 'surplus on revaluation'. This suggests rightly that the managers have been clever to buy land and property; but a more apt title would be 'nominal gain from avoiding money assets'.

[B] *Constant money values.* Here the opening assets are again £10 000. Because the managers stick to a policy of holding money assets while money is losing value, the firm is clearly worse off at the end of the year. But the ordinary and the revalued accounts still put the assets at £10 000, i.e., show no loss. The $\frac{20}{120}$ fall in the value of money means that this sum is now worth only 8333 of the original £s; or, measuring in closing £s, it is worth 10 000 instead of the original 12 000.

We can expand the ownership side of the stabilized balance sheets to show what has happened. The full consequences of holding money then hit the eye: 1667 opening £s, or 2000 closing £s, have evaporated.

[C] *Mixed pattern.* Here our (somewhat extreme) example is a firm whose financial policy is superlative: it holds no money assets, and it is deeply in debt. Its debt is £20 000 borrowed on debenture, which, with the capital of £10 000, allows it to start the year with £30 000 invested in non-money assets.

TABLE 6.1
BALANCE SHEETS SHOWING EFFECTS OF OWNING MONEY

	(1) Ordinary £	(2) Revalued Factor	£	(3) Stabilized — In opening £ Factor	£	(3) Stabilized — In closing £ Factor	£
A. *Constant real values* (money zero)							
Land, property, etc.	Cost 10 000	$\frac{120}{100}$	12 000	$\frac{100}{100}$	10 000	$\frac{120}{100}$	12 000
Capital	Historical 10 000	Historical	10 000	$\frac{100}{100}$	10 000	$\frac{120}{100}$	12 000
Surplus on revaluation of fixed assets		Balance	2 000				
			12 000				
B. *Constant money values*							
Cash, etc.	Actual 10 000	Actual	10 000	$\frac{100}{120}$	8 333	Actual	10 000
Capital	Historical 10 000	Historical	10 000	$\frac{100}{100}$	10 000	$\frac{120}{100}$	12 000
Loss from holding money				$\frac{20}{120}(-10\,000)$	−1 667	$\frac{20}{100}(-10\,000)$	−2 000
					8 333		10 000
C. *Mixed pattern* with high gearing							
Fixed assets, etc.	Cost 30 000	$\frac{120}{100}$	36 000	$\frac{100}{100}$	30 000	$\frac{120}{100}$	36 000
Less Debentures	Actual 20 000	Actual	20 000	$\frac{100}{120}$	16 667	Actual	20 000
Net assets	10 000		16 000		13 333		16 000
Capital	Historical 10 000	Historical	10 000	$\frac{100}{100}$	10 000	$\frac{120}{100}$	12 000
Surplus on revaluation of fixed assets			6 000				
Gain from owing money				$\frac{20}{120} \times 20\,000$	3 333	$\frac{20}{100} \times 20\,000$	4 000
			16 000		13 333		16 000

At the end of the year, the assets have retained their real value. Debentures, however, have become a far lighter burden. Ordinary accounts give not the slightest hint of this important change; the totals are exactly the same for the firm in 3 as they are for accounts 1 and 2, which have fared so differently. Revalued accounts tell us that account 3 has done best, but overstate the gain and ascribe it to the fixed assets. Stabilized accounts correctly put the gain at 3333 original £s or 4000 current £s, and explain that it comes from borrowing: this part of the debentures has in real terms been cancelled. The gain should presumably not yet be deemed to be 'realized'; but it is an indication that the firm could now pay off its debentures more easily than at the start of the year (e.g., by selling fewer of its properties) and that in real terms the interest charge has shrunk. In fine, the firm gains much the same benefits as it would (in a time of stable prices) from a reconstruction scheme under which the debenture-holders are forced to scale down their claims to principal and interest by one-sixth.

Fixed interest and gearing

Table 3.1 (p. 15) illustrated real changes in cost and revenue structures. Fixed-interest receipts and payments are important examples of such changes.

A highly-geared company has a profit and loss account like example C on page 15; if the money cost of interest stays constant during inflation, real cost falls and the company gains. So, too, does the man who pays interest on (say) a mortgage over his home. Their snug position during inflation is the obverse of the *rentier's* discomfiture. Someone must get what the *rentier* loses; an interest-payer is one of the gainers. He might be called a negative *rentier*.

The dangers of gearing

If borrowing brings such easy gains, why are not all men of foresight deep in debt, and why are not all firms as highly geared as their credit status permits? One answer is, of course, that firms subject to marked ups and downs of trade may in the bad years be acutely embarrassed by high interest costs.

Another is that though high gearing is very pleasant if prices happen to rise, it can be disastrous if the cat jumps the other way. Then the real burden of paying the interest each year, and the capital at maturity, becomes heavier. (This possibility is illustrated in the appendix to this chapter). And a firm that has already borrowed heavily may in an emergency be unable to borrow more; in the USA, high gearing ('leverage') makes it impossible for a company to keep the coveted 'AA credit rating' in the reports of statistical services, upon which potential lenders presumably rely.

Businessmen have, therefore, mixed feelings about large liabilities. Those who are cautious by nature, or who were schooled in the tenets of the depression years, still dislike gearing.

Further, it becomes increasingly hard to sustain (or acquire) gearing as inflation continues. Each annual gain on owing must tend to reduce the real liabilities—and thus the potential future gains; in firm C, for instance, each gain reduces the real size of the debentures, and therefore the scope for further gain on them. To maintain the annual gains, the firm would have to borrow more each year. But lenders then become wary, and interest rates tend to rise with inflation.

Calculating the loss and gain on money

Where the ordinary trade profits are free from the errors (described in chapter 7) that beset less simple income accounts, one could find the loss (or gain) from holding money by merely putting a balancing figure into the stabilized balance sheet. But a separate computation always serves as a useful check. It may be drawn up like a calculation of day to day interest on a varying sum of money; index factors take the place of interest rates. (An example is given in the appendix to this chapter.)

Importance of failure to show results of holding money

How important is it that ordinary accounts give no inkling of the loss or gain from holding money? The next few pages will amplify the results of such movements—to the individual, to trust funds, to firms, and to the State—and so will try to establish the case for accounting reform in this matter.

Most managers and investors are appreciative when accounts show the size and source of various trading gains; we should all denounce accounts that failed to report large cash losses due, say, to theft; and we go to great pains to devise costing systems that pinpoint small wastes in a factory. So there is a presumption in favour of showing any sizeable profits or losses—including those on money.

The argument will, in any case, seem somewhat needless to anyone who remembers what has happened in major inflations. When prices go up steeply by the hour, people soon grasp the notion of loss from holding money. In 1923, German workmen would on payday race from job to shops in order to change their wages into goods before prices rose again.[2] In such extreme circumstances, figures for this loss or gain might well be the most significant part of accounts. They could still be helpful in less extreme circumstances.

Personal investment

Godliness and cleanliness may rank as the top virtues in the traditional code, but financial prudence cannot be far below. And financial prudence had fairly simple rules until 1914. The money unit seemed supremely trustworthy. A prudent youth started to build up his fortune by putting his savings into the bank; later he bought government stocks and life insurance; and finally—if he had ample money assets and strong nerves—he might 'speculate' in equities. A horror of debt was salutary; parents read out Mr Micawber's homily on overspending, and children grew up with an ingrained distaste for borrowing.

Unhappily, the money unit is no longer trustworthy. In the years following 1914, and again after 1939, the investor who put his faith in money lost disastrously. Balance sheet B (stabilized form) in Table 6.1 explains what happened to him. So the easy maxims of Victorian days now need qualification. Our early training in prudence—iterated by parents, teachers, and savings propaganda—is apt to distort our judgement of what is sound and cautious investment; we should now teach our own children to study price trends, and on occasion to prefer blue-chips to gilt-edges. It pays to run head-over-heels into debt when inflation is coming, and to go on borrowing as long as prices go on rising. Balance sheet C might record the fortunes of a successful private investor instead of a firm—of, say, the man who some years ago raised a loan to buy his home, and has thus since been subsidized by the lender. And his capital gains from owing money have also (as is explained on p. 38) their income counterpart in benefits from the falling real burden of fixed-interest charges.

The downfall of government stocks

In fact, the investor who put his savings into fixed-interest securities has in many instances done worse than balance sheet B suggests. Their capital values have fallen even in money terms, especially where redemption date is remote (see Fig. 6.1). The full story would be shown by stabilized accounts that allowed for the special index, i.e., the quotation of the particular security. An extreme case is provided by irredeemable securities with a low rate of interest, such as Britain's $2\frac{1}{2}$ per cent consols—'Daltons', in tribute to the Chancellor who issued them. If £100 of Daltons were bought at par when they were issued in 1947, the 1973 balance sheet ran somewhat as follows:

	Ordinary accounts £	Factor	Stabilized in 1947-£
Investment, £100			
$2\frac{1}{2}$ per cent consols			
Cost	100		
Current market value	17	$\frac{100}{300}$	6
Capital	100		100
Loss on holding government loan[3]			−94
			6

The stabilized column shows that this investor had lost over nine-tenths of his wealth through trusting in government securities. The wide use of such stabilized accounts might well have led to strong, and probably beneficial, political pressures against inflation.

To own is to speculate

We should probably all increase our understanding of economic affairs if we thought about our positions in terms of 'loss on holding money' rather than 'rising prices'.

For one thing, we should then see that we are all speculators. (The only exceptions are those who adopt literally the Christian rule of complete poverty.) When we own *any* asset, we are willy-nilly taking a chance—that the chosen asset will in time prove less (or more) desirable than some other asset. Ownership thus involves us in risk of doing worse (or better) than we expected; and surely this is the essence of speculation. Even when we avoid ways of investment that are normally labelled 'speculation', by holding our wealth in cash or the savings bank, we are still gambling on the behaviour of money: if it depreciates, then so does our wealth; if it appreciates, we gain just as surely as the dabbler in shares who makes a lucky deal.

It follows that no one can evade risk by following a passive investment policy—by leaving money on deposit with staid institutions or in government stocks. Inactivity may save the investor much bother, but the cost can be high.

The switch to equities

Because investment in gilt-edged securities had such sorry results, equities became popular even with small savers who would formerly never have considered holding anything except gilts.

The change has perhaps been well-advised on balance (see Fig. 6.1). However, investment in equities is far from a complete and comfortable panacea. Their appreciation is erratic at best. Sometimes the whole equity market slumps (perhaps just when a given investor must sell to meet an obligation), and then equity values go down much faster than the value of money is ever likely to do. Looking back over the post-war years with the wisdom of hindsight, it is easy to deride those who held money securities. But one could never at the time feel sure that inflation would continue, or that equities would not be hit by economic misfortune or government action such as dividend control.

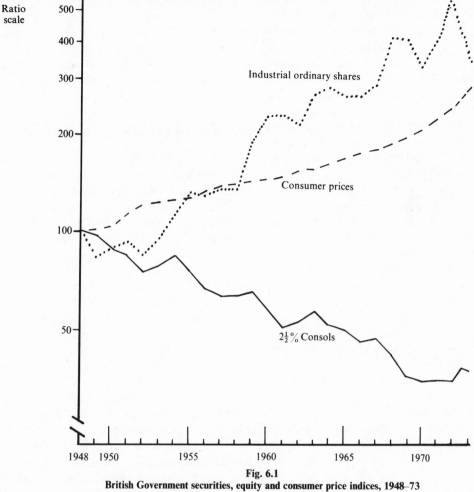

Fig. 6.1
British Government securities, equity and consumer price indices, 1948–73

Source: Central Statistical Office, *Annual Abstract of Statistics*.

Moreover, though an equity may free its owner from the risks of the money unit, it involves him in the risks of the individual company. Here he needs both judgement and luck. Some solid-looking companies—whose ordinary shares were at one stage strongly commended by experts—have managed to do badly even in prosperous times. Thus, the cautious investor in equities should spread his holdings over many companies, taking pains to choose varied industries and countries. If his means are too modest for direct investment in many companies, he should buy the equities of an investment trust or unit trust, which will spread his capital for him; no doubt this reasoning explains in part the popularity (and low yields) of such securities. However, though the trusts probably give long-term safety, in the short-run the prices of their shares can fluctuate in a disturbing way.

In short, wealth and worry go hand in hand. To maintain one's real capital, one must be vigilant, skilful, bold, and lucky.

Interest rates and inflation

Traditionally, the interest yield on gilt-edged securities has been below the earnings yield on equities (e.g., in 1938 the two British rates were about 3·4 per cent and 6·2 per cent); because of the greater commercial risk attaching to equities, the investor would not buy them unless they seemed to offer an extra return. However, as was noted on p. 39, inflation changed the market's preferences. Prices in the gilt-edged market fell—which is, of course, just another way of saying that interest yields rose. Thus, the gap between the two types of yield dwindled. In the UK, the gilt-edged interest yield rose above the earnings yield on equities in 1960. Many investors are now content with a low immediate yield on equities if there are reasonable prospects that dividends and capital value will rise with inflation. The growth-rate has become a weighty factor in investment decisions.

Some investment pundits from time to time tell us that the fixed-interest yield has become big enough to make money securities attractive despite the inflation risk. Whether or not this is true depends on one's expectations regarding the rates of inflation and one's own income tax. Suppose, for simplicity, that a debenture now yields $10\frac{1}{2}$ per cent, and an equity 3 per cent; and that a given investor expects the inflation to run at 5 per cent per annum (equity dividends keeping pace). Then he must, to maintain the real value of money securities that are worth £100 at the start of any year, invest a further £5 by the end of the year to make good the loss on holding money; whereas his equity dividends and prices will (hopefully) look after themselves. Accordingly, he should budget somewhat as in Table 6.2, substituting his own marginal rate of tax for the specimen rates shown—namely *nil*, $33\frac{1}{3}$ per cent, and $66\frac{2}{3}$ per cent: So the money investment is, on the given assumptions, worth while only to investors blessed with low tax rates (such as charities); to be as attractive

as equities to tax-payers with higher rates, the fixed-money security needs a gross yield of $10\frac{1}{2}$ per cent where tax is $33\frac{1}{3}$ per cent, and of no less than 18 per cent where the tax is $66\frac{2}{3}$ per cent. (But *redeemable* securities, if bought well below the sum repayable on redemption, may be more attractive to those with high tax rates.)

Securities that guarantee real income

Not unnaturally, investors have sought for securities that avoid both the commercial and the money risk. Convertible loans may sometimes answer their demands: so long however as companies can raise fixed-interest loans cheaply in real terms, the conditions attached to convertibles will remain niggardly. One occasionally hears of money concontracts with a 'gold clause' linking the debt with the price of gold.[4] Or the link may be with a price index;[5] thus in some countries (such as Israel), one can buy debentures whose 'fixed-money' rights are modified by movements in a named index. Though their fixed-money loans have proved grossly unfair, few governments have issued loans that are linked to an index— perhaps because increases in the sums paid as interest or at redemption would be a public admission of failure to check inflation. Yet many of us would accept a very modest yield in return for the State's guarantee to maintain the real value of our wealth; and index-linked loans would foster saving, and thus help to check inflation. A few states (notably Brazil) have included their loans in a comprehensive system of 'indexization' that covers also private obligations, wages, rents, tax rates, etc.

TABLE 6.2

COMPARISON OF HYPOTHETICAL REAL INCOME (AFTER TAX)
FROM MONEY INVESTMENTS AND EQUITIES

Type of investment	(1) Fixed money			(2) Equities		
Tax rate—(say)	Nil	$33\frac{1}{3}\%$	$66\frac{2}{3}\%$	Nil	$33\frac{1}{3}\%$	$66\frac{2}{3}\%$
Gross money income	$10\frac{1}{2}$	$10\frac{1}{2}$	$10\frac{1}{2}$	3	3	3
Less Tax	—	$3\frac{1}{2}$	7	—	1	2
Money income after tax	$10\frac{1}{2}$	7	$3\frac{1}{2}$	3	2	1
Loss on holding money during inflation	5	5	5	—	—	—
Net sum for spending	$5\frac{1}{2}$	2	$-1\frac{1}{2}$	3	2	1

Government equities

An unusually thoughtful investor may hanker after a different form of capital 'maintenance'. He may feel that, in years when the country's real national product per head is growing, even if his money income rises enough to let him buy a constant quantity of goods, etc., he is nevertheless falling behind other people. To feel satisfied, he would need to expand his consumption as much as his neighbours; what he wants to maintain is his *share* of the national product. There seems no reason why this wish should not be humoured (in return for a suitably low starting yield). The State could issue 'equity' loans, with interest linked to wages or the net national product (in money terms) per person. This scheme would have the advantage of saving the Treasury's face, since the money figure for net national product varies both with inflation and productivity, and so a rise in the interest rate might conceivably be due to praiseworthy reasons rather than inflation.

Investment by trustees, etc.

We rightly expect a high standard of care and prudence from men holding wealth in trust—for instance, those in charge of the investments of charities, local government, and educational and private trusts. Therefore, such men have traditionally been compelled to invest only in gilt-edged securities (though there are of course loopholes, e.g., a will can extend the range of investments). In Britain trustee securities were defined, by the Trustee Act, 1925, as a narrow range of fixed-interest investments whose safety was beyond question—so long as money itself was safe.

The end of the traditional safety rules

When money ceased to be safe, the real capital of the more prudent trusts began to fall. The account on page 40 illustrates what could happen then; in that example, some 94 per cent of the original real capital was lost—an odd result for a safety rule. This percentage of loss was probably higher, because Daltons were issued at an unusually low rate of interest, than that on the average trustee investment; yet there must have been plenty of

instances when persons in positions of trust (e.g., local government councillors) felt impelled to subscribe to securities paying a low rate of interest, out of patriotism or a wish to support cheap-money policies. If their accounts had included a column for stabilized figures, trustees would have seen just how disastrous the safety code was proving, and might then have forced the government to change the code.

There is a further objection to carrying investments at historical cost. When loss is not recognized unless and until investments are sold, trustees and managers are tempted to keep securities with a bad record even when the best policy for the future is to get rid of them.

In the UK, the Trustee Investment Act, 1961, widened the powers of trustees: up to one-half of a trust's capital (at the date when the trustees decide to adopt the provisions of the Act) may now be put into a 'wider-range fund', to be invested in equities (subject to certain conditions, e.g., the company's paid-up capital must be £1 000 000 or more, and the trustees must obtain 'proper advice' from an expert).

Such relaxations of the old rules are welcome, but make it hard for trustees to fulfil their duty of maintaining fairness between conflicting interests. The choice between low-yielding equities and high-yielding government securities may be hard. So may the choice of the particular equities. And, however well a trustee chooses the latter, beneficiaries will almost certainly be able later to point to others that would have proved even better; and, of course, the chosen shares may in fact do badly. On the other hand, to refrain from buying equities is likely in retrospect to be looked on as a sign of timidity and misjudgement, if not gross neglect.

The need for new rules on capital and revenue

Where different persons are entitled to a trust's income and capital, inflation makes it hard for the trustees to keep a fair balance between them. Presumably, the aim should be to maintain (at least) both income and capital in real terms. Investment in equities perhaps offers the best chance of doing so. But there must be some high rate of interest at which fixed-money securities become, at the given rate of tax, etc., more attractive than equities (see Table 6.2, p. 42); and then the trustees should be able to buy the fixed-money securities, and yet not harm the ultimate recipients of capital. If they had power to retain some of the annual interest and transfer it to capital (as loss on holding money assets during inflation—see column (1) in Table 6.2), real capital could be preserved; money income would at first be penalized, but would grow over the years as the retentions were invested and bore interest (i.e., real income too would be preserved). On the other hand, growth stocks may sometimes seem the best investment in all respects, save that dividend yield is below the average for sound equities; here the trustees should have power to transfer the annual shortfall from capital to revenue.

The ordinary rules of trust accounting have become inadequate because of inflation. Plainly,

new rules would need much careful thought, and might add another dimension to an already-complicated system. In essence, they would call for a move down the conceptual income framework (on p. 22) from the historical (and money) concept to the current-value (and real wealth) concept.

Investment by firms

By real-life standards, the gearing of firm C on p. 37 is somewhat exaggerated. Nevertheless, a majority of the big firms probably began the period of inflation with plenty of non-money assets and some long-term liabilities, and so have more resemblance to firm C than firms A or B. A summary of the balance sheets of some 700 large British companies in 1949 (see Table 6.3) shows that in total their money liabilities far exceeded their

TABLE 6.3

CONSOLIDATED BALANCE SHEETS OF 719 BRITISH COMPANIES
(PUBLISHED OCTOBER–DECEMBER 1949)[7]

	£m	£m	£m
Non-money assets			
Stocks			358
Trade investments			53
Fixed assets—cost		813	
Less Depreciation		183	
		==	630
Intangibles			51
			1092
Money liabilities			
Current liabilities		518	
Long-term liabilities:			
Debentures	158		
Preference capital	189		
	==	347	
		865	
Less Money assets			
Cash	177		
Debtors	235		
Securities	149		
	==	561	
		==	304
			788
Provided by the equity shareholders, thus:			
Ordinary capital		289	
Capital reserves, etc.		150	
Revenue reserves and profit		301	
Minority interest		48	
		==	788

money assets;[6] many of the companies must therefore have been highly geared, and must have made substantial gains from owing. Much has been written about the harm done by inflation to business, and (as will appear in later chapters) inflation does indeed inflict a harsh extra tax on many firms. We must, however, in fairness recognize that some firms obtain substantial benefit from the lightening of their money liabilities.

Investment and gearing

A shrewd investor will have an eye for gearing when he chooses his companies, etc. He will wish to see the make-up of both the liabilities and the assets. The next few paragraphs describe some of the outlets available to the small investor, and how far the published reports enable him to study gearing.

Investment trusts

Most investment trusts are rather like firm C (see p. 37). Their balance sheets typically show a high ratio of long-term loans to ordinary capital, and nowadays the assets consist largely of equities (possibly in companies that themselves have gearing). By buying ordinary shares in such a trust, therefore, one is in effect eking out one's own funds with borrowed money to acquire non-money assets; one gets the benefits of gearing as well as spread.

Split-level trusts[8] seem likely to carry the gearing process even farther. If they prove successful, they will enable investors to obtain either geared income or geared capital. Presumably the former will appeal to investors whose tax rate is low, and the latter to those whose rate is high.

Unit trusts

Unit trusts do not issue debentures, etc., and thus lack the means for capital gearing. Their published reports do not, in general, throw much direct light on to the composition and value movements of the underlying assets; but the list of investments may indirectly give guidance.

Life assurance

The chief liabilities of the life offices are to the policy-holders. Some of these liabilities (to holders of no-profit policies) resemble money claims; but others (to holders of with-profit policies) are nearer to equities, thanks to the variable bonuses that serve to distribute an office's fluctuating profits. The assets of the offices have traditionally been 'safe' money investments, such as government stocks and well-secured mortgages. This unenlightened investment structure was continued for a good many years after inflation became obvious. By the mid-'fifties, however, most British offices were forced by the competition of a few leaders to increase their holdings of non-money investments, and now ordinary shares and properties tend to form some 20 per cent to 45 per cent of the book-value of the assets. Because of this shift, and the higher yield now obtainable when new funds are invested in gilt-edged securities, bonus rates have risen considerably; if tax reliefs and the value of life-cover are allowed for, maturing with-profit policies perhaps give their holder a positive yield in real terms on the premiums that he has invested (though this yield may be less than he might have got from investment trusts, etc.). The real yield on no-profit policies must be slender or negative (though such policies may still be a sensible investment in the short-term for persons whose family responsibilities demand cheap cover).

A would-be policy-holder, if he is to choose rationally between the life offices that compete for his custom, should know how much and how well the office is investing in equities (asset gearing), and what proportions of the policy-holders' claims are in the with-profits and the no-profit funds (much the same thing as capital gearing). The published balance sheets have tended to be defective at both points. British practice was long for insurance offices to show assets by book-values only—i.e., cost, less such realized gains as the office chooses to subtract from cost—while the make-up of the insurance fund is not disclosed in the balance sheet (though it can be found by hunting through the valuation returns filed with the Department of Trade). This is a serious blemish in insurance accounts.

Many unit trusts took advantage of the life offices' lethargy by issuing life policies that are linked with equity units. Many of the offices in time followed suit. Thus, the distinction between the two forms of investment has lessened. The investor is now faced with a bewildering range of combinations (which include also property bonds, i.e., a mixture of insurance contract and investment in real estate). It is too soon to predict which combination is likely to do best.

The State's liabilities

If the government published its accounts in commercial form (an income statement and balance sheet), and these were stabilized, we should see that it is now the outstanding example of gearing.

The State's balance sheet

Most of the State's assets are non-money, e.g., mail vans, schools, and (one is tempted to add) past victories; on the other side of the balance sheet are vast money liabilities—the national debt. Thus, its position is reminiscent of that of firm C (on p. 37). The debt is incurred to finance wars, the nationalized industries, housing projects, etc. At the time when these investments are made, we automatically bear most of the real sacrifice at once, by consuming less (and so freeing resources for making munitions, building homes, etc.). A corresponding part of our money income is not spent by us but taken by the State to finance the investments. To lessen our grumbles, much of this money transfer is made as loan rather than tax. Afterwards, the loans are only an echo of the real sacrifice, yet their annual service may become an embarrassment. We flinch from paying enough tax to repay them quickly. So we cannot but look on inflation as an easy way out. By lowering the value of money, in effect we repudiate part of the loans, and so avoid having to pay obvious taxes. Or, to look at the matter in another way, we lessen the tax on our income, etc., by imposing an invisible capital levy on ourselves as holders of loan.[9] Unfortunately, this political manoeuvre has side-effects: much wealth is transferred from private creditors to private debtors.

The state's income statement

Stabilization would also show how gearing affects the State's income and expenditure. The account would have some likeness to firm C on p. 15. Much of the expenditure is fixed (interest on debt) or sluggish (pensions and professors' salaries); so in real terms these items are scaled down by inflation. By countenancing inflation, we can to some extent evade higher levels of tax, at the expense of the recipients of interest, etc. Collectively, we are negative *rentiers*. We are here behaving rather like our ancestors when they used the press-gang to man the navy, instead of sharing the burden fairly.

Inflation also cuts the real expenditure of nationalized industries, since these are mainly financed by fixed-interest securities. Presumably, the gain is passed on to us as consumers.

Some related accounting matters

Results of holding money should be segregated

Enough has been said to stress the vast importance, in times of changing prices, of a firm's skill in controlling its net money assets. Accounts showing a 'loss on holding money' or a 'gain on owing money' would provide one test of this skill.

In real life, policy on holding money is no doubt mixed up with other matters that are considered in chapter 7. One manager may deal with both money and these matters, and hardly notice the distinction. Yet they are so different in logic that we must—if we are to see clearly what is afoot—keep the two things severely apart in our analysis. This book will, therefore, always try to unravel the 'gain on money' from the other effects of inflation, even though they tend to be confused in practice.

Should gain on money be classed with ordinary profit?

One may concede that gain on money is a significant benefit, and yet hesitate over its treatment in accounts. Two problems present themselves. Can the gain be treated as a form of ordinary profit (often linked with realization—see p. 18), or is it more like unrealized appreciation on fixed assets? If it is to be accorded a place in ordinary accounts, what kind of entries are needed?

We shall be helped with the first problem if we follow the reasoning suggested on p. 33 and consider the treatment of comparable gain and loss in the time of stable prices. Appreciation on the stock exchange price of money investments (e.g., debentures) seems a comparable gain; depreciation on such investments and bad debts seem comparable losses. Unfortunately, the normal accounting rules do not here lend themselves to generalization. But the tendency is to treat the losses as ordinary expenses (particularly if the investments are classed as current), and the gains as income provided they are realized; no doubt both gain and loss are shown as 'extraordinary' where circumstances demand this. Another analogy is change in the value of liabilities. If a creditor is persuaded to cut down his claim (say, because supplies from him proved defective), the gain normally finds its way into the current trading results. If loan-holders agree to cut their claims as part of a reconstruction scheme, the gain is recognized, but probably (in the circumstances of a reconstruction) is set off against past loss or over-valued assets. If the stock exchange value of the company's loan or preference shares falls, the gain is ignored.

We might, perhaps, adapt these analogies to value change on money assets by making new rules that hinge on the quickness with which the good or bad results accrue. Value change on the *current* money assets and liabilities could then be bracketed with ordinary income (though it should be shown separately); and it might reasonably influence the size of dividends. Value change on *non-current* money items would not be classed as ordinary income. By this rule, value change on irredeemable loan would never be classed as ordinary income (though, of course, change in the real burden of the interest automatically affects income statements); value change on redeemable loan could reasonably be treated as income in the year of redemption. Admittedly, the distinction between current and non-current would here, as elsewhere, be arbitrary.

General price change makes realization harder than ever to define in cautious terms. Gain that is realized in the conventional sense can still be lost during inflation if it is left as a money asset. One might perhaps say that it is not certainly realized until cash is paid out as dividend[10] (or tax?). This is carrying caution far. I am tempted to put forward a slightly facetious alternative: if trade profit on non-money assets is not realized until it is turned into money assets, then gain on money assets is not realized until it is invested in non-money assets.

Correcting entries for money and loss

Money gain and loss is the product of stabilization, and can hardly seem at home in ordinary accounts. Assuming, however, for the sake of argument that a firm wants to make its ordinary accounts show the gain or loss, what sort of correcting entries are needed to force these figures into the historical framework?

Take, first, a loss on assets (such as the £2000 of firm B on p. 37). To tell the full story in ordinary accounts, we should make two closing adjustments:

(1) Show the year's potential nominal appreciation, by writing up cash and capital with a general-index factor.

(2) Then show that the potential has not been achieved, by writing down cash again and charging this loss against profit.

Adjustments (1) and (2) might be compressed into a single adjustment—a charge against profit and a credit to a new kind of capital account that in effect stabilizes the relevant part of capital, and might be called 'allowance for nominal capital appreciation due to inflation'. Thus, the ordinary balance sheet of firm B might become:

	£
Cash, etc.	10 000
Capital:	
Historical	10 000
Allowance for nominal appreciation due to inflation	2 000
	12 000
Loss on holding money	−2 000
	10 000

Firm C's £4000 'gain on owing' could be inserted into the accounts by showing it as a kind of profit ('unrealized real gain on owing money—£4000'), and writing up the asset to £34 000. But the latter figure is a somewhat indefensible mongrel; so (I consider) the asset should be raised instead to its full current value of £36 000. The ordinary balance sheet then becomes:

	£
Fixed assets, current value	36 000
Less Debentures	20 000
	16 000
Capital	
Historical	10 000
Inflation allowance	2 000
	12 000
Unrealized real gain	
On owing money	4 000
	16 000

Appendix: Further illustration of money-gains in stabilized accounts

It may be useful to illustrate stabilization a little further, by showing the arrival of extra money assets during the year. Assume that firm C (otherwise as described on p. 37) retains £540 of profit earned by a single set of transactions (including payment of a year's interest) at mid-year (index 110), or a series of transactions with the same average date; the ordinary and stabilized income figures are thus the ones explained in Table 5.1 (p. 37). If the net receipts of £540 are promptly reinvested in non-money assets (which appreciate with the general index), the figures for these assets and for their source (profit) remain equal, and stabilization is still a simple matter (much as it was in the example in Table 5.1). But let us now suppose that the new assets are kept as cash. The latter does not appreciate, and so stabilized cash and profits cannot remain equal. Columns (1) and (2) of Table 6.4 compare the ordinary and stabilized figures. Column (2) shows that the £4000 gain on the debentures is slightly offset by a £49 loss from holding the £540 of cash from mid-year.

It may be salutary to show also what happens to a highly-geared firm in a year when prices *drop*. In this second version of firm C's story, we suppose that the index falls from 100 to 80, being at 90 when profits are earned. As trade is likely to languish in such a recession, realism suggests that the profits should here be lower, say £260. Once again, the new assets are kept as cash. The ordinary and stabilized accounts appear in columns (3) and (4). The main interest of the column (4) balance sheet is that it shows clearly the disaster entailed by borrowing during deflation—a loss of £4000.

Before stabilized accounts can be drafted, special calculations of some of the figures are normally helpful. Here one should start by working out the gain on money assets.

Calculation of gain or loss on money assets

The gain during a period, in £s of the close of the period, is:

$$\text{Amount of money assets (net)} \times \frac{\text{Fall in index during period}}{\text{Index at start of period}}$$

Where the stabilization date is some date other than the close of the period, the answer must be multiplied by:

$$\frac{\text{Index at stabilization date}}{\text{Index at close of period}}$$

For complete accuracy, each period would have to be short—say 24 hours. In practice, one might well approximate by working in months, etc., and (in the absence of violent cash changes within a month) by using the opening balance (of net money assets) for each month. One could then, if the year runs from January, either:
(a) find the gain on the 1 January balance, from 1 January to 31 December; then find the gain on extra cash, etc., received by 1 February, from 1 February to 31 December; and so on. Or
(b) (more clumsily) find the gain on the 1 January balance, from 1 to 31 January; then find the gain on the 1 February balance, from 1 to 28 February, and, by adding the gain brought forward (adjusted with the February factor) find a cumulative total; and so on.
Table 6.5 applies both methods to the examples.

TABLE 6.4

SHOWING BALANCE SHEETS WITH NEW ASSETS IN THE FORM OF MONEY

	Index rises to 120			Index falls to 80		
	(1) Ordinary accounts £	Factor	(2) Stabilized accounts closing £	(3) Ordinary accounts £	Factor	(4) Stabilized accounts closing £
Income Account						
Gross profit—say	1 540	$\frac{120}{110}$	1 680	1 260	$\frac{80}{90}$	1 120
Interest on loan—say	1 000	$\frac{120}{110}$	1 091	1 000	$\frac{80}{90}$	889
Trade profit	540	$\frac{120}{110}$	589	260	$\frac{80}{90}$	231
Balance Sheet						
Fixed assets	30 000	$\frac{120}{100}$	36 000	30 000	$\frac{80}{100}$	24 000
Cash	540	Actual	540	260	Actual	260
	30 540		36 540	30 260		24 260
Less Debentures	20 000	Actual	20 000	20 000	Actual	20 000
Net assets	10 540		16 540	10 260		4 260
Capital	10 000	$\frac{120}{100}$	12 000	10 000	$\frac{80}{100}$	8 000
Trade profit	540	$\frac{120}{110}$	589	260	$\frac{80}{90}$	231
Gain on money:			£			£
Unrealized			4000		(Loss)	−4000
Realized			−49			29
			3 951			−3 971
	10 540		16 540	10 260		4 260

TABLE 6.5

CALCULATION OF GAIN AND LOSS ON MONEY

	Index rises from 100 to 120			Index falls from 100 to 80		
	Actual £	Factor	Gain in closing £	Actual £	Factor	Gain in closing £
Method (a)						
Debentures, 1 January	−20 000	$-\frac{20}{100}$	+4000	−20 000	$\frac{20}{100}$	−4000
Money received, 1 July	540	$-\frac{10}{110}$	− 49	260	$\frac{10}{90}$	+ 29
			3951			−3971
Method (b)						
1 January–30 June period						
Debentures, 1 January	−20 000	$-\frac{10}{100}$	+2000	−20 000	$\frac{10}{100}$	−2000
1 July–31 December period						
Adjustment of £2000 gain to June		$\frac{10}{110}$	+ 182		$-\frac{10}{90}$	+ 222
Money received	540			260		
Balance, 1 July	−19 460	$-\frac{10}{110}$	+1769	−19 740	$\frac{10}{90}$	−2193
Total gain or loss			+3951			−3971

References

1. Strictly, a preference dividend is of course not a legal 'cost'. But it is one in the economic sense (since it is the price paid for the use of resources); for our present purpose, loan interest and preference dividends are indistinguishable.

2. One tale of this time is specially poignant. An old couple, whose pension had become valueless, lived by selling off their furniture. Finally they sold their house, for an enormous number of marks. They went to collect this cash a week later. Prices had so risen during the week that the price was just enough to pay their tram-fares back again.

3. About two-thirds of the loss would have accrued if the loan still stood at par (i.e., is due to holding money rights), and one-third is due to change in market price.

4. In one British case, perhaps because of clumsy wording in the contract, a majority of the Court of Appeal declined to enforce a 'gold clause'—*Treseder-Griffin* v. *Co-operative Insurance Society Ltd.* [1956], 2 All E.R. 33. A yearly rental of £1900 was to be paid 'either in gold sterling or in Bank of England notes to the equivalent value in gold sterling'. The majority of judges plainly felt that, if they did not do battle against such contracts, sterling would become a 'discredited currency unable to look its enemy inflation in the face'. The economic arguments were perhaps not of the highest order, e.g., 'Sterling is the constant unit of value by which in the eye of the law everything else is measured. Prices of commodities may go up or down, other currencies may go up or down, but sterling remains the same'—Lord Denning. It was, however, conceded that rents may be tied to the value of minerals or corn. And similarly to a price index?

For legal interpretations of different forms of 'gold clause', see G. C. Cheshire, *Private International Law*. London: Butterworth, 1965, p. 226.

5. An example of the wording of such a clause is:

The landlord hereby demises unto the tenant all that [*parcels*] TO HOLD unto the tenant from the........day of........for the term of........years paying therefore

(a) the yearly rent of £........payable quarterly in advance on the usual quarter days without any deduction

(b) by way of additional rent a sum bearing the same proportion to the said sum of £........ as shall be borne by any increase in the Index of Retail Prices to the figure shown therein for the month of........19........ [*month of execution of lease*].

Provisos follow on, e.g., reference to arbitration if there is change in the reference base used to compile the index. See *Encyclopedia of Forms and Precedents*, 4th edn. London: Butterworth, 1965, Vol. 11, p. 302.

6. Another test of gearing is the percentage of loan and preference capital to equity (nominal values)—here over 40 per cent, a fairly high figure.

7. *The Economist*, 28 January 1950. Some of the 'securities' were probably equities, which, if reclassified as non-money assets, would increase the *net* borrowing of money.

8. Such companies issue two kinds of capital:
(1) *Income shares*. These are entitled to all the income during the trust's lifetime (which is normally set at some 20 years), and then a repayment of capital at par value only.
(2) *Capital shares*. These get no annual dividends, but all the residue at winding-up.
Thus, (1) in a sense have a highly-geared income (at the expense of (2)); and (2) have a highly-geared capital (at the expense of (1)).

9. During the fifties, this unauthorized levy on British holders of government securities ranged in annual size from £50 million to £780 million (respectively in 1959, when prices rose some 0·3 per cent, and in 1955, when prices rose some 4 per cent); only in 1959, did the levy yield less than death duties—Ralph Turvey, 'The Effect of Price-level Changes on Real Private Wealth in the United Kingdom, 1954–60', *Economica*, May 1962, pp. 174–5.

10. H. W. Sweeney, *Stabilized Accounting*. (New York: Harper, 1936. Republished by Holt, Rhinehart and Winston, 1964), p. 21, seems to adopt this strict view.

7. The timelag error in accounting profit. A. General price change

Chapter 6 accused the accountant of failing to report certain real gains. This chapter accuses him of reporting gains that do not exist.

'Mixed' money figures in the income statement

Subtracting cost of one date from revenue of another date

To understand this accusation, one must think again about 'mixed' sets of figures (chapter 3). In a time of general price change, a ledger account may contain entries that each deal with £s of different worth. For instance, in a year when prices are rising the transactions of January are expressed in more valuable £s than are those of the following December. Thus, unlike units are added and subtracted; the totals and balances become 'mixed' and perhaps meaningless; it is almost as if we subtracted 2 horses from 9 oranges.

The ledger account that is most vulnerable to this error is the profit and loss account. Typically, a firm must obtain and use inputs ahead of sales; and so the cost £s in that account are older than its revenue £s, and the balance (profit) is distorted. This book calls the distortion the 'timelag error'.

Unfortunately, the error cannot be analysed simply. Theory is here charged with controversy; and its application varies with the type of information needed and asset owned. Not surprisingly, this complexity has created much confusion in discussions on reform: almost anything said about the timelag can be either sensible or silly according to the context envisaged by the speaker. To avoid muddle, he should specify what context he has in mind.

Possible contexts

He should, in the first place, be clear on the familiar point of whether the price change is general or special. But a second point then obtrudes. Cost figures can be needed for different purposes. They may be used for income measurement, i.e., in the income statement. Or they may be used as guides to whether a particular job, etc., is worth while, i.e., as measures of sacrifice in budgets employed by managers when making decisions (and in any post-mortem cost accounts to check these budgets). And perhaps the two figures should not always be the same. So the first step in analysing any pronouncement on the timelag is to decide into which of the four boxes below it falls:

	Income statement	Decision budget
General change	(1)	(2)
Special change	(3)	(4)

We start with (1)—i.e., this chapter deals solely with the income statement in a period when general prices change but the relevant special indices move exactly in step with the general index, and so can be ignored.

Costs and revenues—simultaneous and separated

Costs and revenues can often be looked on as a series of linked pairs—inputs and corresponding sales. When there is no delay between input, sale, and the withdrawal of the resulting profit, the income statement is free from the timelag error even in a year of big price change. When there is delay, distortion follows.

Simultaneous costs and revenues. Suppose, for instance, that a man starts and ends a venture in January (general index 100) and another in July (general index 110), and that his income account for the year can be set out as shown in Table 7.1.

Each horizontal line here deals with the same kind of £s; taken separately, the January and July profits are sensible guides to, for instance, the sums available for drawings just after each venture. But the totals of each vertical column are mixed, and thus are of doubtful meaning—as in the total profit of £840.

Timelag between input and sale. However, production is often a lengthy matter, with inputs preceding outputs and sales. Here a timelag occurs between a cost and the corresponding output's realization; the debits and credits in the income account no longer form neat horizontal pairs, but are 'slanting', and so are recorded in £s of different dates and value. If the two ventures in the example each need a half-year turnover, the account in Table 7.1 changes into something like Table 7.2. This assumes that the general index goes up during each venture by

10 points, and that the sale prices also rise with the index. Thanks to the timelags, the profits on each venture—let alone their total—are now suspect.

Typically an income account contains some costs that synchronize with revenues, so forming horizontal pairs and doing little harm, and some slanting pairs. Then one may say that the cost column does not on average synchronize with the revenue column. When the average timelag between the two columns is big, the figure for profit is stretched in an odd fashion.

The balance sheet approach to profit measurement

Capital maintenance as the base line for income measurement

Earlier chapters have tended to define income more as growth in wealth than as a gap between revenues and costs. They have, in other words, treated capital maintenance as the base line for calculating income; the measurer's task is to see whether or not the initial capital has been maintained exactly. The same approach will serve to clarify reasoning on the timelag. Moreover, arithmetical illustrations to such problems are often more helpful if the figures

TABLE 7.1

INCOME ACCOUNT WITH NO TIMELAG BETWEEN INPUT AND SALE

Date	Index		Cost £	Sale £	Profit £
1 January	100	Venture 1	1000	1400	400
1 July	110	Venture 2	1100	1540	440
			2100?	2940?	840?

TABLE 7.2

INCOME ACCOUNT WITH SIX MONTHS' TIMELAG BETWEEN COST AND SALE

Date	Index		Cost £	Sale £	Profit £
1 January	100	Venture 1	1000		
30 June	110	Venture 1		1540	540?
1 July	110	Venture 2	1100		
31 December	120	Venture 2		1680	580?
			2100?	3220?	1120??

52

are put in successive balance sheets rather than a profit and loss account. Assets are mostly familiar and easy to envisage; costs and revenues are less clear—being mere measures of asset changes. So, probably, we see more of the truth when we compare the net assets at two dates than when we try to visualize the streams of arrivals and departures.[1]

Balance sheet illustration, with historical values

To illustrate the balance sheet approach, let us apply it to the first (January to June) venture in Table 7.2. The starting data and price changes are here much the same as those used in Table 3.1 (p. 15); we can treat this venture as an important extension to the range of sample firms (A, B, and C) shown there, and call it D.

We can trace firm D through all its stages by putting a series of balance sheets in successive columns. The approach of ordinary accounting needs columns for only three stages:

(1) Date of *opening figures*—1 January (index 100).
(2) Date when *stock bought*—later on 1 January (index 100).
(3) Date when *stock sold*—30 June (index 110).

TABLE 7.3

COMPARATIVE BALANCE SHEETS, USING HISTORICAL VALUES ONLY

Date	(1) Opening figures £	(2) Stock bought £	(3) Stock sold £
Cash	1000		1540
Stock		1000	
Initial capital:			
Historical figure	1000	1000	1000
Trade profit			540
			1540

Bearing in mind that profit ran at £400 per venture before the inflation began (see p. 15), we see that the owner of firm D has cause to feel delighted by the increase to £540. This promotes him to the level of C, the firm that is so successful because of its gearing; whereas he may well have thought that his business is in its nature more like firm A, whose profit merely keeps pace with inflation. He has often heard that a slow turnover is rather a bad thing; but, merely by having a slower turnover than firm A, he has far outpaced it in the race for profit.

Is there something spurious in this upward leap in the profit of firm D? The answer depends on our old problem of how to compare amounts of wealth at different dates. If we are content with pound notes as the unit, the increase is genuine: firm 4 began with 1000 bits of paper, and now has 1540 bits of paper; there is nothing wrong with our sum by the money sub-concept.

Consequences of using historical values

However, doubts about the usefulness of this paper measure begin to arise if the owner treats his accounts as a meaningful guide to action. We may reasonably suppose that his main problem is what to do next with his £1540—in particular, how much of it he needs to reinvest in the firm if his capital is not to be impaired, and how much is surplus. He now faces issues discussed in chapter 4, i.e., the nature of capital and income, and the wisdom of choosing the measures that give the most useful information. Here a good measure of income may be especially helpful in shaping his views on, e.g., how much to withdraw for consumption, and whether he has used the assets efficiently.

The historical measures suggest that he must put back £1000 as capital, and that his income is now running at £540 per centure. This is misleading on two different scores. First, it suggests that the rate of return has gone up from 40 per cent to

54 per cent per venture. But on the assumption that the firm's methods, etc., are unchanged, these profit rates depend solely on the behaviour of money; for instance, if the index now levelled off at 110, the rate would tend to revert to 40 per cent. Fifty-four per cent is thus a poor guide to the rate of future earnings. Secondly, and much more important, the future yield by a capital of only £1000 is likely to seem inadequate to the owner, notably because it will fail to maintain his real standard of life. We are assuming, it must be remembered, that the index measures the prices of consumers' goods (as well as business assets); henceforth, the profits on £1000 will tend to buy fewer of those goods, and so the owner will feel poorer than he did before the inflation.

This can be seen easily if we look into the next stage in the firm's story. The balance sheet of 30 June tempts the owner to withdraw £540; and, even if he himself has qualms about the wisdom of so doing, his tax collector will have none. Let us suppose that he does take out £540 for consumption and tax, and so leaves his money capital once again at exactly £1000. Then 1 July finds him about to undertake the next venture. But when he comes to buy more inputs—for a similar or any new type of venture—he realizes to his dismay that their prices have gone up by 10 per cent. His £1000 will now finance only about $\frac{10}{11}$ of his former trade, measured in real terms. He cannot automatically buy the whole July input envisaged in Table 7.2. He faces a painful choice between:

(1) Working henceforth at only $\frac{10}{11}$ of his former scale of real investment—earning perhaps the same money profit as before the inflation, but unable to buy as much with it as hitherto, i.e., with a reduced real capital by the consumption test. Indeed, even his money income will perhaps fall, since shortage of real capital may for example deprive him of quantity discounts, or force him to work with assets that are no longer in such good proportions to one another.[2] Or

(2) paying in, or borrowing, an extra £100. Then the firm can go on at the same real level; but the owner must pay interest, and the net level falls. His consumption is reduced as in (1).

In short, the owner's increase in drawings from £400 to £540 means that he takes out real capital.[3] Other things being unchanged, he must sooner or later see a consequent fall in his real income; to think otherwise is to regard the firm as a cornucopia. By the test of real consumption and investment, his accounts are untrustworthy guides.

Balance sheet illustration, with current values

The next step is to adapt the balance sheets to make them illustrate the 'real-capital maintenance' sub-concept. We must add a column to those in Table 7.3 to restate historical figures in current terms of the moment just before the sale. As the index has risen to 110 at this time, initial capital is now reset at £1100, and so also is the stock's cost:

TABLE 7.4

COMPARATIVE BALANCE SHEET, USING CURRENT VALUES

Date	(1) Opening figures £	(2) Stock bought £	(3) Just before sale £	(4) After sale £	(5) After sale, stabilized at 110 £
Cash	1000			1540	1540
Stock (current value)		1000	1100		
	══	══	══	══	══
Initial capital Historical figure	1000	1000	1000	1000	
Allowance for inflation			100	100	
Initial capital in current £s			1100	1100	1100
Trade profit				440	440
	1000	1000	1100	1540	1540
	══	══	══	══	══

By restating capital and stock in current £s, we reduce trade profit to £440, and so maintain capital at a level high enough to preserve the owner's standard of life.

This columnar analysis confirms our explanation of why and how distortion creeps into conventional balance sheets—wherein assets valued after the sale in new £s are placed alongside a capital still valued in old £s. If we attach weight to what money can buy, rather than to money *per se* (i.e., if we prefer the real-wealth sub-concept to the money sub-concept), then we should update initial capital as in column (3) in Table 7.4. The £100 nominal increase in initial capital may be called a capital reserve[4] or, better, an inflation allowance. Column (5) supports this interpretation by showing the figures of (4) in stabilized £s.

Cost, revenue, and the timelag

Distortion of the profit and loss account

It is easy to repeat the timelag argument in terms of cost and revenue, explaining how distortion arises when the price level changes between the dates of input and sale. It is also easy to explain the mechanics for correcting the profit and loss account. But the logic perhaps becomes less obvious than in the balance sheet approach, and must in the end fall back on capital maintenance.

The profit and loss account corresponding to the conventional balance sheet at firm D, at the stage of column (3) in Table 7.3, is set out below. To show what is really happening, a stabilized version is also given. Remember that, to obtain the stabilized counterparts, different factors must be applied to transactions of different dates. The

stabilized accounts show that real wealth is flowing in merely at the old rate, as in firm A (p. 15). The ordinary accounts, when compared with those of pre-inflation years, suggest instead that trade has been exceptionally good—that cost and profit are just like those of the fortunate firm C.

Thus, ordinary accounts give a rosy picture during inflation. They are likely to make the owner more cheerful than the facts warrant. So they may not only induce him to raise his real consumption, but also (as investment now seems to yield such easy winnings) to expand his business. If many other owners are also misled by their accounts, their combined actions may have social effects of some magnitude.

'Correction' of the cost error in the ordinary profit and loss account

The timelag error, as we have seen, arises when an account sets off cost of one price level against revenue of another. Table 7.5, for instance, subtracts January £s from June £s. It would be less apt to mislead if it subtracted like £s. The simplest way to make the £s uniform is to restate the costs at the June level, by inserting an 'inflation charge' among the ordinary figures to raise historical cost. (Note that we are here considering only something in the nature of first-aid to the ordinary profit and loss account. This restricted reform must be distinguished from full stabilization, which not only aligns cost and revenue £s, but also ensures that all the figures in both the profit and loss account and the balance sheet are expressed in some common unit.)

TABLE 7.5

PROFIT AND LOSS ACCOUNT WITH TIMELAG ERROR

		Index	(1) Ordinary accounts £	Factor	(2) Stabilized accounts £ of 30 June
1 January	Cost	100	1000	$\frac{110}{100}$	1100
30 June	Sale	110	1540	$\frac{110}{110}$	1540
	Profit		540		440

55

The size of the error equals the appreciation on historical cost between cost date and sale date. A convenient way to express it is as follows. Let C stand for the historical cost shown in the ordinary accounts, c for the general index at cost date, and s for that index at sale date. Then the error is $C(\frac{s}{c} - 1)$. To correct the figures in Table 7.5, raise the cost by £1000 $(\frac{110}{100} - 1)$, i.e., £100.

The correction can easily be put into the ordinary profit and loss account, e.g., in this way:

TABLE 7.6
PROFIT AND LOSS ACCOUNT WITH TIMELAG ERROR CORRECTED

	£
Cost:	
Historical	1000
Inflation charge to raise historical cost to current price level	100
Total current cost	1100
Sale	1540
Corrected profit	440

The inflation charge is, of course, the other end of the double entry that leads to the credit of £100 in Table 7.4, column 3.[5] Because 'inflation charges' are novel and controversial, it seems desirable that their presence in an account, and their size and method of calculation, should be made abundantly clear.

Nature and limitations of a 'corrected' income account

The 'corrected' ordinary account is, in this simple example, the same thing as an account stabilized at 30 June, as can be seen by comparing Table 7.6 with column (2) of Table 7.5.

So this form of correction appears here to do just what is needed to put right the cost and profit figures, within the ordinary framework and with far less labour than is demanded by the worksheets of full stabilization. And, indeed, it is an easy and effective trick for improving ordinary accounts (even where they are less simple than here), and has the great merit of calling for the bare minimum of change in familiar methods and figures. But it cannot claim to be more than a rough-and-ready cure. It suffers from two main faults. First, the correcting charge may not in practice be worked out with the same care and precision as fully stabilized figures (the case for approximation is touched on in an appendix to this chapter). Secondly, an income statement that is correct at some date *during* the year (average sale date) does not fit in with the balance sheet of the *end* of the year (ordinary or stabilized), and may not be a good basis for a dividend decision at a still later date. So the correction should be regarded as valuable first-aid rather than a complete solution.

Table 7.7 recapitulates these points, by comparing the rival forms of profit and loss account that are now at our disposal:

(1) *Ordinary accounts.* These make no attempt to correct the raw figures.

(2) *Ordinary accounts with timelag correction.* These try to stick as closely as possible to the form and figures of ordinary accounts, and yet to improve profit with a short-cut correction— the insertion of an inflation charge.

(3) *Stabilized accounts.* These adjust the crude costs and revenues with the help of a general index factor and so produce almost completely new sets of figures, all in homogeneous £s (of some chosen base date) and thus automatically free of the errors due to the time-lag and mixing.

The figures in Table 7.7 are set in accounts for the year to 31 December. The index is assumed to reach 120 at that date. Thus, the figures of column (3), being stabilized in end-£s, must differ from those of earlier months in (1) and (2). They must also show (if the profit has been retained in the form of cash) a loss on holding money from July to December.

TABLE 7.7

COMPARISON OF ORDINARY, CORRECTED, AND STABILIZED INCOME ACCOUNTS

	(1) Ordinary £	(2) Corrected £	Factor	(3) Stabilized end-£
Income statement				
Cost (index 100)	1000	1000	$\frac{120}{100}$	*1200*
Inflation charge		$1000 \times \frac{10}{100}$ 100		
		1100		
Sale (index 110)	1540	1540	$\frac{120}{110}$	*1680*
Trading profit	540	440	$\frac{120}{110}$	*480*
Balance sheet				
Cash	1540	1540		*1540*
Capital	1000	1000	$\frac{120}{100}$	*1200*
Inflation allowance		100		
Loss on holding money			$1540 \times \frac{-10}{110}$	*− 140*
Trading profit	540	440	$\frac{120}{110}$	*480*
	1540	1540		*1540*

Chief cost items subject to the timelag

In practice, the error is likely to be material for three kinds of cost:

(1) *Cost for capital gain calculations.* When fixed assets, investments, etc., are sold, their historical cost may have been carried forward for many years. If the gain is to be seen at its real size, the cost must be updated with an inflation charge.

(2) *Stocks.* There may be a timelag of at least some months between the purchase of stocks and their sale, engendering 'inventory profit'. (Stocks are so important that the whole of chapter 9 is devoted to them.)

(3) *Depreciation.* The life of a depreciating asset is normally long enough for the index to change greatly. So a considerable error is apt to arise when the later slices of historical cost are written off. (Chapter 10 deals with depreciation.)

As the error raises taxable income during inflation, one may regard it as imposing an extra tax, never authorized by Parliament, on the owners of stocks and depreciating assets.

Other items subject to the timelag

Any marked carrying-forward of historical figures can lead to the use of outdated values. Cost is the main but not the only culprit. 'Revenue received in advance' is also carried forward in the ledger, and not put into the profit and loss account until the date at which the revenue is deemed to be earned. This may lead to a different form of timelag error: when the historical revenue is credited in the profit and loss account, old-revenue £s are offset against new cost £s, and so (if prices are rising) profit is understated. Thus, magazine publishers (so far as they receive subscriptions in advance) and correspondence schools may habitually understate their profits.

Charges for tax, dividends, etc., may relate to dates many months away from average revenue date. For instance, the income statement may contain a closing adjustment for a final dividend to be paid some months after the end of the year. Here is another example of the subtraction of unlike £s. During inflation, such belated charges are in fact less expensive than the ordinary figures suggest. In cold logic, the charges should be reduced by 'inflation credits'.

Date of historical cost

The historical cost date (with index c in the formula on p. 56) is normally the date at which the firm invests in the input, and as at which the books record its acquisition. The date of c does not depend on whether the input is bought for cash or on credit: both forms of transaction at once change part of the firm's wealth from net money assets to non-money assets—which is what matters here. But credit, loans, etc., give rise to an interesting point that will be discussed on p. 59.

Consider, for instance, a contract whereby a year's tenancy of buildings is obtained for £1200. If the £1200 is due at the start of a year of inflation, these cost £s—whether the cash is paid forthwith or later—do not in value match the revenue £s of later months; to make them match, they must be corrected with an inflation charge (c being here the index at the start of year). If instead £100 is due monthly, probably each instalment will almost coincide in time with the month's revenue, and little or no cost correction is needed. This accords with commonsense. Inflation gives the former arrangement a higher real cost than the second, and so the owner (if he wants to maintain real capital) should take out less money, e.g., as monthly drawings.

Visible and concealed timelag errors

Where inputs are bought in one business year for the benefit of another, they will show up as assets in intervening balance sheets, and the scope for timelag error will be fairly obvious. But some inputs are bought for use within the same year, and then the annual accounts can give no hint of the error. To correct costs, therefore, one must look at both (1) inputs carried forward at a year-end, and (2) inputs acquired and consumed within the accounting year:

(1) *Inputs carried forward at a year-end.* Typically, a balance sheet may show machinery, stocks, rent paid in advance, and so forth. Such assets point to the likelihood of timelag error (though they give little indication of its size).

(2) *Inputs acquired and consumed within the same accounting year.* This source of error is most likely to be important where firms have peaks of activity within each year, for seasonal or other reasons. For instance, a maker of skis may buy heavily in the spring in order to meet the winter rush; and the maker of fireworks may incur costs throughout the year to build up stocks for sale near Guy Fawkes' Night or Fourth of July. If, as is not unusual, the accounting year ends after the peak (when stocks are at their lowest), the stock figure in the year-end accounts can give no hint of the timelags. Nevertheless, these lead to 'inventory profit' just as surely as if the stocks were recorded in inventory sheets at the year-end.

This type of distortion must usually be small compared with that under (1).

Sluggish sale prices

In most of the earlier examples, sales price has been made to respond freely and promptly to inflation. These buoyant figures seem not unrealistic; they are also a good means of stressing the upsurge in general prices between buying and selling dates. But they may leave some impression that increased sale prices are what cause the overstatement of profit. Such is not the case. The error comes from mixing £s of different worth: sale price is irrelevant.

So the error still occurs if sale prices are kept low, e.g., by the firm's own policy (notably selling at cost-plus), or by government controls. Then the profits in ordinary accounts are smaller than those envisaged in our examples; and real profits (after correction with an inflation charge) are smaller still, or perhaps negative.

The timelag and partnership rights[6]

Chapter 6 explained how the money-effect can transfer wealth between the various groups who finance a company (e.g., from loanholders to ordinary shareholders). In a partnership, a corresponding transfer can take place if the firm obtains fixed money loans (from outsiders or some of its own partners). But the timelag can induce a second and subtler transfer, in the following way.

The timelag error makes money capital appear as profit. This might not matter much if all the false profit could be retained and returned to capital, in the proportions needed to restore each partner's balance to its original real size. Such a cycle may exist where the partners share profits in the ratio of their capitals; but not where they share profits in another ratio. If partner X's fraction of the total capital exceeds his fraction of annual profit, the error diverts some of his real capital to his partners. If Y's fraction of profit exceeds his fraction of capital, then he gets some of his partners' real capital. We may guess that, where the capital fraction differs much from the profit-sharing fraction, X is likely to be the senior partner and Y the junior. If this is true, there must in recent years have been some levelling as between junior and senior partners—none the less real because neither side planned or detected it. Inflation here plays Robin Hood.

Example

As usual, one should use a rather extreme example to stress the facts. Suppose X and Y become partners in a venture that needs £100 000 of capital. X provides £80 000, and Y only £20 000; but X works only part-time, and Y full-time. They agree that these contributions of capital and work will be fairly compensated if all profits are split fifty-fifty. At its end, the venture brings in £150 000, so its uncorrected profit is £50 000; but, as the index rises from 100 to 150 during the period, the timelag error (50 per cent on the capital of £100 000) is also £50 000, and corrected profi is *nil*.

	Ordinary £	Corrected £
Cash, etc.	150 000	150 000
Partners' capitals		
X. Opening	80 000	80 000
Inflation allowance	$\frac{50}{100}$	40 000
Profit	25 000	—
	105 000	120 000
Y. Opening	20 000	20 000
Inflation allowance	$\frac{50}{100}$	10 000
Profit	25 000	—
	45 000	30 000
	150 000	150 000

Ordinary accounting here gives Y a handsome present, as one can see by comparing an ordinary balance sheet with the one that would have resulted if the timelag error had been corrected.

If (as is true of most professional firms) the partnership holds a substantial amount of work-in-progress, the timelag error may well be fairly high, and it may also be big where a capital gain arises. Any surplus when the partners' rights are restated at a retirement or admission is probably such a gain.

The time-lag and borrowed capital

Let us now go back to firm D (see p. 55). Thoughtful readers may have detected an unconvincing point in the treatment of its figures. Surely there is one circumstance, they may object, in which the owner of firm D *does* make a genuine profit of £540, not £440. What if he has borrowed the original £1000—does he not then end up £540 to the good after repaying his debt?

The answer is that he does. But now we have returned to the discussion of p. 46—the money-effect. His gain does not all come from trading; £100 of it comes because he was in debt.

Here the timelag is superimposed on gearing. Stabilized accounts would throw up two different facts, both obscure in ordinary accounts: (1) the ordinary profit is swollen by £100 of synthetic gain, which must be omitted in real calculations, reducing trade profit to £440; but (2) the firm's owner has made a gain of £100 from the scaling down (in real terms) of his debt. The ordinary closing balance sheet and its stabilized counterpart run as in Table 7.8.

Interplay of timelag and money-effect in practice

Both the timelag and the money-effect are sure to be present in most real firms. Even if there are no formal loans, the usual flow of credit purchases and sales will create money liabilities and assets, and so give rise to a money-effect.

Timelag and money-effect may well be interlinked on purpose. An alert firm will try to manipulate its current position so as to make the best of the market from the viewpoints alike of trade and finance. Thus, if the firm foresees higher prices, it may tighten up its credit terms to customers, and

TABLE 7.8
BALANCE SHEETS AFFECTED BY BOTH TIMELAG AND MONEY GAINS

	(1) *Ordinary balance sheet* £	(2) *(1) stabilized at 110* £
Cash	1540	1540
Less Loan	1000	1000
	540	540
Trade profit (after interest, etc.)	540	440
Gain on owing		100
		540

so lessen the vulnerable period on its debts. It may also buy supplies farther ahead. If it gets longer credit for such extra purchases, its suppliers suffer; if it borrows from the bank, its bank suffers; if it uses idle cash, it avoids losses on holding money. For instance, firm D in our example may well buy the repeat dose of input before 30 June, the sale date; it then seems to benefit by buying while prices are still low, but in real terms the benefit comes from the gain on owing, etc. (As was stressed on p. 38, however, a policy of heavy borrowing does not always end in success. Prices may start tumbling just after the purchase, and then the real gain is transmuted into real loss—as in the example on p. 49; and when further loans are wanted in a time of dire need they may prove unobtainable. In an uncertain world, borrowing is far from being the rather one-sided and unsporting manoeuvre that Table 7.8 suggests.)

When the purchases and sales are those of a busy firm, one must treat them not as discrete incidents but as streams of transactions. Plainly, the timelag errors and money-effects will here multiply and intertwine in a way that is hard to follow. But, no matter how complex their inter-relations, a clear-headed observer will try to keep them apart in his thinking, and to form at least an approximate idea of their separate sizes.

Falling prices

Nowadays, it comes natural to describe the timelag in terms of rising prices. But the argument holds equally well when prices are falling.

Example

The example in Table 7.7 can be adapted to deflation. Suppose again that profit has been £400 per venture while the index was stable. This year's venture begins at index 100, but the index falls to 90 at sale date and 80 at the year-end. For realism, the sale proceeds should be reduced, say by 10 per cent to £1260. Then the ordinary accounts run as in column (1) of Table 7.9; ordinary profit (£400 in stable times) falls steeply to only £260.

Capital maintenance in deflation

If the owner treats the accounts of column (1) as a guide, he will now leave at least £1000 in the firm (i.e., he will increase his real stake in it) by restricting his withdrawals to a £260 ceiling. A fall of this size may bring much suffering to him and his family. The low profits will also make him wary about further investment in productive assets, so that his extra cash will tend to lie idle. As other owners will likewise at such a time be prompted by their accounts to spend less on consumption and investment, real demand by the whole community may fall, making the slump worse than it would have been in the absence of accounts.

Yet, judged by the test of a constant living standard, the owner does not now need to leave a capital of £1000 in the business; £900 in June, and only £800 in December, should thereafter (thanks to lower prices in the shops) yield a big

TABLE 7.9

ORDINARY, CORRECTED, AND STABILIZED ACCOUNTS WITH FALLING PRICES

	(1) Ordinary £	(2) Income Corrected £		Factor	(3) Stabilized end–£
Income statement					
Cost (index 100)	1000		1000	$\frac{80}{100}$	800
Less Deflation credit		$1000 \times \frac{10}{100}$	100		
			900		
Sale (index 90)	1260		1260	$\frac{80}{90}$	1120
Trading profit	260		360		320
Balance sheet					
Cash	1260		1260		1260
Capital	1000		1000	$\frac{80}{100}$	800
Less Deflation adjustment			100		
			900		
Gain on holding money				$1260 \times \frac{10}{90}$	140
Trading profit	260		360		320
	1260		1260		1260

enough flow of cash drawings to maintain his old standard. More helpful accounts for June would write down initial capital by £100 as in column (2), and thus raise surplus from £260 to £360, the correct profit by the real-wealth sub-concept. A profit of £360 is the exact equivalent, at June prices, of the £400 that was the profit for the same real activity when the index stood at £100.

Profit correction

The first-aid correction of the accounts is again simple. In column (1), the cost £s of January are too big relative to the sale £s of June. So total cost must be reduced to allow for the rise in the value of the £ during the turnover period. The error is £1000($\frac{90}{100}$ − 1) = −£100. In column (2), £100 is deducted from cost in the income statement, and also from capital in the balance sheet.

Where space permits, the deduction in the income statement might be explained as:

Less Reduction to allow for fall in general
  prices during the turnover period   £100

But a short name is convenient: 'deflation credit' will perhaps serve. The corresponding deduction

in the balance sheet should be made from a suitable figure in the owner's equity (e.g., reserves, but ideally from an inflation allowance created on the upswing of the price cycle);[7] presumably, company law would frown on any change in the capital figure itself, though in fact the original £1000 is now equivalent to a lesser number of current £s.

Correction and caution

At first blush, the raising of profit in column (2) may be disturbing. It seems at odds with the normally cautious tenets of accounting. So this side of reform may be much harder to swallow than its counterpart for inflation. One must concede, for instance, that it would tend (if tax were based on the reformed figure) to put up a firm's tax at an awkward moment. Again, many directors will yearn for a strong liquid position when bad times threaten, and will regard low profit figures as a welcome pretext for cutting dividends.

The analogy of the 'dividend equalization reserve' may be helpful here. Some companies subject to profit fluctuations used to transfer profits in good years to such a reserve, and then retransfer enough to cover the dividends of poor years. The most prudent of directors should not object—if the productive assets have been kept in good heart and there is enough cash for all likely calls—to drafts on such a reserve in bad times. An inflation allowance may be thought of in the same light. But, in fact, the case for the higher profit figures rests on still stronger ground: they measure real growth better than uncorrected ones. Moreover, as was pointed out on p. 60, if low figures appear also in the annual reports of most other companies, they may aggravate depression and become self-defeating.

Stabilized accounts and deflation

Stabilized accounts confirm the reasoning of column (2) in Table 7.9. If they are based on the £ of June, stabilized profit is £360. In column (3), they are based instead on the £ of December (to conform with the usual custom of covering a whole year in accounts); the equivalent profit, because of the rise in money's worth, is then £320. Capital is likewise restated at only £800.

If the sale proceeds are kept as money assets from July to December, they appreciate in purchasing power. Accordingly column (3) shows a £140 gain on holding money.

Accounting opinion on the timelag error

Early reactions

Accountants have been much divided on the timelag error. Its existence was hardly recognized until after the Second World War. The stiff dose of inflation of the late 'forties made it big and conspicuous, particularly as it prompted businessmen to say hard things about their accounts and to demand tax reforms. The complaints stirred up unwonted interest in income theory; many articles on price-level change began to appear in accounting journals, and there were warm—even heated—debates on whether accounts could contain error.[8] For long, general opinion among accountants tended to be incredulous of this charge, and hostile to any reform; but the continuance of inflation, and much lively discussion, have gradually won many converts. The argument has been tepid when the price curve seemed to be flattening, and warm when it was mounting. Thus inflation has at least given a welcome fillip to accounting theory.

The accountant had several reasons for disliking and misunderstanding the case for reform. The very ease with which historical costs can be gathered in a ledger gave him something of a vested interest in such figures, so that he might well find it hard to admit their limitations. Again, he probably was confused by the intermixing of general with special price change; this clouds the problem by raising questions of whether inflation charges are costs or appropriations.

Inflation charges as costs or appropriations?

In the days when company accounting practice was taking shape (say, 1850–1914), few accountants had cause to worry over general price change. The only kind of price change that entered into their theory was special change. They decided that such movement is often irrelevant to income measurement, i.e., they preferred the money to the physical sub-concept; less reasonably, they decided too against asset revaluation. They therefore concluded that, where the financial difficulties of replacing dearer assets led to the gesture of transfers to reserve, the charges in income account were not costs but appropriations, and so must be put 'below the line'.

In the strict context of special price change, this procedure may well (as chapter 8 argues) be logical. Unfortunately, when accountants at last came to face general price change, many of them applied the old logic to the new facts. The adapted argument therefore runs: inflation raises asset values; a firm that wants its accounts to allow for this increase in the money value of inputs is no doubt wise; but it must treat the whole charge as an appropriation to reserve and not a cost.

This adapted argument is, of course, a rephasing, in terms of book-keeping entries, of the view that money is the best base line for measuring capital growth. If we accept this view, then the conservative accountant was right: inflation charges swell money capital, and so are savings and should be put below the line in income statements. If we prefer the real-wealth sub-concept, then he was wrong: inflation charges are essential for keeping real capital intact, and thus are true costs.

The impact of the conservative view has been powerful. Even when firms recognize the existence of the error and try to allow for it in their (unstabilized) accounts, they seldom do so by adjusting costs. Often they merely plough back more 'profit' (e.g., as omnibus reserves) than they would do in the absence of inflation, making no attempt to specify how big the error is; possibly they have only vague notions of its size. A few put concealed special charges among their costs, by revaluing fixed assets and then gearing the yearly depreciation charge to the increased value. A few others allow openly for general or special charges, but as appropriations rather than costs.

Organizations and orthodoxy

Corporate groups of accountants, like individuals, have varied in their reactions to the timelag error. Some refrained from making pronouncements on principle—which seems wise when such difficult problems of intellectual right and wrong are at stake. In the UK, the Institute of Chartered Accountants of Scotland maintained a strict neutrality, and so did its Irish counterpart. The Association of Certified and Corporate Accountants did likewise, but commissioned a useful bit of research by a joint committee of its members and staff of the *Economist*. The report[9] analysed the issues well, and favoured a liberal attitude. The American Accounting Association (of teachers of accounting) sponsored some valuable studies of the theory of price-level changes[10] and their effects on given companies.[11]

But, in general, the reaction of accounting bodies was hostile to reform; and perhaps it is salutary to recall—particularly as accountants now pin such high hopes on official 'standards'—how near-sighted some of the collective pronouncements on inflation have proved.

The Institute of Chartered Accountants in England and Wales first dealt with the topic in Recommendation XII (1949). This statement by the Council summarizes the arguments of the reformers and the conservatives. For example, the latter 'claim that not only is the suggested change

wrong in principle, but also that it strikes at the root of sound and objective accounting because of the practical difficulties of assessing the amounts which would be treated as charges to revenue if the new conception were adopted'. Then follows the Council's own analysis of the problem: this can hardly be described as either full or profound. Its conclusion is: 'the Council sees no need to modify the advice which it has already given', in favour of historical cost.

This document was well received by the accounting press, but outside comment was less favourable. For instance:[12]

> The institute...told the profession to bring to the attention of management the fact that equipment now costs more (which reminds one of grandma and sucking eggs). It pointed out a lot of difficulties. What does 'replacement' mean and how are changes in prices to be measured? Accountants ought to be searching their hearts whether a certificate that endorses a set of accounts as showing a true and fair view is justifiable in circumstances that clearly involve a continuing dilution of the substance of industry. One might suggest a new form of qualified certificate in such cases: 'Subject to the capital market providing sufficient resources to make good the drain that has occurred through wrong price policy, through inflation and through the taxation of capital made to masquerade as income, in our opinion such balance sheet and profit and loss account give a true and fair view, etc.'.

Possibly the Council realized that Recommendation XII was tending to bring accountants into discredit, for in 1952 it published Recommendation XV on the same subject. This is more cautious. It starts by conceding that 'it would be a major development in the building up of a coherent and logical structure of accounting principles if the limitations of accounts based on historical cost could be eliminated or reduced by the adoption of new principles'. Then it examines various proposals for reform, and points out certain difficulties in each—some important, others involving mere technicalities of law and book-keeping, and the rest springing from misunderstandings of the proposals. It concludes that 'the alternatives to historical cost which have so far been suggested appear to have serious defects and their logical application would raise social and economic issues going far beyond the realm of accountancy. The Council is therefore unable to regard any of the suggestions so far made as being acceptable alternatives to the existing accounting principles based on historical cost'. Historical cost should continue to be the basis on which profits are computed; and fixed assets should not (save in special circumstances) be written up. Nevertheless, experiment is desirable.

The American Institute of Certified Public Accountants also stood stoutly by historical cost.[13] In some ways, its attitude had much more serious consequences than that of the English Institute. For though the latter's views carry much weight, they are no more than the recommendations of a non-governmental group; some accountants and companies on occasion reject its advice.[14] But the views of the American Institute tend to be accepted *en bloc* by the Securities and Exchange Commission, which has legal power to prescribe the accounting principles used by the larger American companies in their published reports. This link between the Institute and the SEC has no doubt been beneficial in imposing good minimum standards upon the laggards. However, in one instance at least (see p. 102), it has also stopped the leaders from experimenting with new methods for dealing with inflation.

The timelag error has also exercised judges (in tax cases) and government committees on tax reform—in the UK and many other lands. Judges and committees for the most part took the same side as the conservative accountant, and stood firm for historical cost.[15] Not unnaturally, tax authorities everywhere tended to adopt with gratitude the official view of accountants, and in their income computations to disallow departures from historical costs.

The swing to reform

In the late 'sixties, the conservative attitude started to crumble. Thus, in 1968 the research committee of the Institute of Chartered Accountants in England and Wales published a well-balanced study.[16] This recommends that accountants should use supplementary calculations, geared to the general index, as an aid to understanding; and that companies should 'set aside to an Inflation Reserve any amount by which the conventional profit exceeds the profit recalculated in terms of current pounds'.

A few years later, the Accounting Standards Steering Committee (representing the main British bodies) issued a proposed 'standard' on *Accounting for Changes in the Purchasing Power of Money*.[18] In 1974, this became the Provisional Statement of Standard Accounting Practice No. 7. SSAP 7 recognizes the gravity of the timelag error, and seeks to correct it with general index factors. It calls on quoted companies to include a 'current purchasing power statement' as a supplement in their published reports. Its statement consists of a stablized income statement and balance sheet, and a note reconciling the historical and stabilized profit figures, i.e., listing the various forms of timelag and other errors (see p.176).

In the USA, the swing of opinion has not been so emphatic. But there are now (1974) strong hints that some comparable change in practice is pending.

Conservatism and accounting theory

Two further points are perhaps worth making.

First, it has often been said in defence of accounting that it is an empirical subject. It is not based on airy theorizing, but evolves to meet practical business needs. This view has probably been true at most stages of accounting history; but it may prove wrong where inflation is concerned. The needs of business now call for change; accounting leaders have in many cases sought to resist it by invoking theory, usually of the most sterile and pedantic type.

Secondly, accounting is often described as 'conservative'. Now this can mean many different things—some good, some not. For instance, the accountant is conservative when he uses methods that paint a firm's results in cautious hues and discourage reckless dividends; but he is also conservative when he uses methods that no longer work well but save him trouble. In the past, both forms of caution have tended to point to the same methods, and one could not tell which form was the stronger. With inflation, they point in opposite ways; cautious conservatism asks for reformed methods to maintain business capital, while sleepy conservatism supports the old methods that erode it. The outcome of the argument will show which strain of conservatism is dominant.

Appendix: Arithmetical troubles of correction and stabilization

The simplicity of the examples in this chapter leads to tidy and precise results (e.g., the equality of the stabilized and corrected profits set out on pp. 55 and 56). But in real life, alas, the figures are seldom so amenable. The number of costs and revenues in a year will be great. These costs and revenues are apt to form unwieldy patterns (some spread evenly over the year, some bunched, and some carried forward from or to other years), and do not always centre on mid-year. The price level continues to change after the central date has passed. Further, inputs do not always link up surely with individual sales. Even if they do, many firms lack the detailed cost records that trace the flow of costs from input to sale. Thus, it is often hard, if not impossible, to correct profit or to stabilize exactly, and some rough-and-ready arithmetic may be inevitable.

Example. Profit correction and stabilization

In Table 7.10, the figures are less simple and regular than those of earlier examples. The second half-year's venture is much bigger than the first, so that the 'centre of gravity' is near to December. The index goes up at an accelerating pace, from 220 at the first input to 280 at the last sale and 285 at the year-end. Therefore, as correction of the timelag error must be linked with the 'average sales date', the corrected accounts are *not* the same thing as accounts stabilized at mid-year, and also differ considerably from those stabilized at the year-end.

Because inflation has been so brisk during the year, both correction and stabilization take a big bite out of accounting profit. The inflation charge is the difference between the totals of columns (4) and (1), £41. It cuts down the ordinary profit of £120, column (3), to a corrected profit of £79, column (5). Stabilized profit in the end-£ is £86, column (8).[19]

TABLE 7.10

LESS SIMPLE INCOME ACCOUNT—ORDINARY, CORRECTED, AND STABILIZED FIGURES

Date	General index		(1) Cost	(2) Sale	(3) Profit	(4) Cost raised to current index	(5) Corrected profit (2)–(4)	(6) Cost	(7) Sale	(8) Profit
			£	£	£	£	£	£ stabilized at 31 December (index 285)		
14 February	220	Input	110							
15 April	230	Sale		140	30	115	25	142·5	173·5	31
15 September	250	Input	300							
15 December	280	Sale		390	90	336	54	342	397	55
			410	530	120	451	79	484·5	570·5	86

Columns grouped as: (1)–(3) *Ordinary Accounts* (Cost, Sale, Profit); (4)–(5) *Accounts with Cost Correction* (Cost raised to current index, Corrected profit (2)–(4)); (6)–(8) *Stabilized Accounts* (Cost, Sale, Profit).

References

1. This is at adds with the view, nowadays popular with many leading accountants, that the income statement is significant, whereas the balance sheet is merely a cold-store for unripe costs and revenues (see B. S. Yamey, 'Some Topics in the History of Financial Accounting in England, 1500–1900', in W. T. Baxter and S. Davidson, *Studies in Accounting Theory*, 2nd ed., Sweet E. Maxwell, Irwin, 1962, p. 38). In fact, the two accounts depend on one another, and thus to belittle the values in the balance sheet is also to belittle the values in profit and loss account.

2. These points are developed by Professor F. W. Paish, *Business Finance*, Pitman, 1953, p. 66.

3. As revenues, like costs, have gone up 10 per cent, drawings can rise to £440 without impairing real capital. So £100 of the £540 is a withdrawal of real capital.

4. 'Capital reserve' may suggest an addition to capital in its narrow, legal sense. This is only part of the truth. Here 'initial capital' is the whole of the owner's investment at the start of this accounting period, and may consist of accumulated profit as well as legal capital (in a partnership, current accounts as well as capital accounts). Both of these become understated in ordinary accounts during inflation. Part of the inflation allowance is thus a corrective to accumulated profit, and can scarcely be dealt with as a capital reserve.

5. If the correction is made by a closing adjustment, the journal entry might be:

		£	£
Cost of goods sold, etc.	dr	100	
Inflation allowance	cr		100

Adjustment of historical cost to current level with factor $\frac{110}{100}$.

That is, an extra cost is charged, and an addition to capital is created. The wording of the journal entry avoids infringement of the useful book-keeping rule that links the word 'costs' with balance sheet 'provisions', and 'appropriations' with 'reserves'.

6. See my 'Inflation and Partnership Rights,' *The Account-ant's Magazine*, February 1962.

7. Thus, the full journal entry is:

Inflation allowance	dr	£100	
Cost-of-goods sold, etc.	cr		£100

8. This early ferment is reflected in the papers on 'Fluctuating Price Levels in Relation to Accounts', read at the Sixth International Congress of Accounting, 1952. K. Lacey's book, *Profit Measurement and Price Changes*, Pitman, 1952, was another stimulating contribution.

9. Association of Certified and Corporate Accountants, Taxation and Research Committee, *Accounting for Inflation*, Gee, 1952.

10. Ralph C. Jones, *Effects of Price Level Changes on Business Income, Capital and Taxes*, American Accounting Association, 1956; and Perry Mason, *Price Level Changes and Financial Statement: Basic Concepts and Methods*, American Accounting Association, 1956.

11. Thanks to this work, it is possible to compare the ordinary and the stabilized results of four companies from 1940 to 1952, and to see how far the ordinary figures misrepresent the real results—Ralph C. Jones. *Case Studies of Four Companies*, American Accounting Association, 1955; see also his 'Effect of inflation on Capital and Profits: The Record of Nine Steel Companies', *Journal of Accountancy*, January 1949. Comparable British figures may be found in W. T. Baxter, 'Inflation and the Accounts of Steel Companies', *Accountancy*, May and June 1959.

12. Roland Bird, deputy editor of *The Economist*, in a lecture at the Institute of Chartered Accountants in England and Wales, printed in *The Accountant*, 3 February 1951.

13. See, e.g., American Institute of Certified Public Accountants (formerly American Institute of Accountants), Accounting Research Bulletin No. 43, 1953. However, the Institute also sponsored some able publications (by individuals) with contrary views, e.g., S. S. Alexander, M. Bronfenbrenner, S. Fabricant, and C. Warburton, *Five Monographs on Business Income*, American Institute of Accountants, 1950. More recently, R. T. Sprouse and Maurice Moonitz have proposed somewhat radical changes in a work published under the auspices of the Institute's research organization—*A Tentative Set of Broad Accounting Principles for Business Enterprises*, American Institute of Certified Public Accountants, 1962 And this attitude is also found in the Institute's *Research Study No. 6*, 1963.

14. For example, Imperial Chemical Industries revalued its assets in 1950, just after Recommendation XII appeared.

15. See, e.g., the reports of the (Tucker) Committee on the Taxation of Trading Profits (Cmd. 8189), 1951 and of the Royal Commission on the Taxation of Profits and Income, HMSO, 1955.

16. Research Foundation of the ICA, 'Accounting for Stewardship in a Period of Inflation', 1968.

17. *Exposure Draft* 8, 1973; see also the two 'Working Guides' published by the English Institute.

18. *Exposure Draft* 8, 1973. See also the two 'working guides' published by the English Institute.

19. Had the stabilization date been mid-year (say, index 245), the stabilized profit would have been $245/285 \times £86$, i.e., £74. It would have been £79.8 at average sales date (index 264.8, found by dividing historical sales by their stabilized equivalent at index 100), somewhere in the autumn.

8. The timelag error. B. Special price change

Chapter 7 tried to show how general price change creates a timelag error in the income statement. Its subject was thus box (1) in the table on p. 51. This chapter deals with special change. So its subject is box (3).

The issues at stake here are just one part of the larger problem—whether the updating of historical costs is best done by applying a *general* index or by using *special* values (found either by direct reappraisal of assets or the adjustment of each historical cost with a special index). Views on this point are divided, and are likely to become more so. The reformer who pleads for special values will perhaps allow himself to be called 'the special-index man'.[1] His arguments concern the three familiar areas—the measurement of (1) asset values; (2) costs for decisions; and (3) income, and thus the timelag problem.

Measurement of assets, costs, and income

(1) *Asset values.* If asset values are to be stated in current terms, the case of the special-index man is completely convincing. The only alternative to special revaluation is the updating of historical cost with a general index: the resulting values are hybrids that cannot command much respect.

(2) *Costs for management decision.* The costs needed for internal decision budgets (the right-handed column of the table on p. 51) should show the sacrifice from devoting assets to the plan under consideration. Deprival value is designed for this purpose; usually it is replacement cost, and then reflects special prices. So here, too, the special-index man's case is normally overwhelming.

(3) *Income and the timelag error.* When the argument shifts to income, the case becomes less obvious. Whether or not special change brings a further dose of timelag error is a highly contentious question, on which we should not be too dogmatic. To a considerable extent, what here is right and wrong depends on the *objectives* of the men concerned: the objective defines cost. The special-index man assumes the main objective to be the maintenance by the firm of an effective team of assets. The general-index man assumes it to be successful investment by shareholders, etc.— success being defined in terms of increase in the owner's command of general goods. The accountant has no right to question the wisdom of other men's objectives. But, as the men who use his statements fall into different groups, he must ask who are his real masters, and what information this group needs to achieve its aim.

We have now returned to the question discussed on pp. 20–24, i.e., what is the best method when prices change, of comparing wealth *at different dates* in order to measure its growth. We may agree entirely that the owner's wealth at each date should be found by valuing his assets at their current special prices, and yet question whether a special index is the best tool for updating the figures so found at date 1 to make them comparable with the new figures so found at date 2. In the context of the income statement, date 1 is that at which an input is acquired, and date 2 is that at which the corresponding output is sold: our task is to find how best to 'translate' the date 1 value of the owner's investment in input to date 2 £s, so that he can compare cost and sale in like terms, and be sure that the profit is genuine growth after the bit of capital invested in the input has been maintained. For the 'translation', the special-index man relies on the sub-concept of physical capital maintenance; as we shall see, this raises issues that are difficult and, indeed, far transcend accounting.

The problem can be seen most clearly if one starts by considering special change when general prices are stable, i.e., when the change in the special asset's price, during an otherwise stable period, has no perceptible effect on the owner's index of general prices—say, because sales of the special asset are too small a part of the market's total transactions. So, until it reaches its final pages, this chapter will assume an unchanging general index.

Special price alters while general index remains stable

Maintaining the owner's capital or physical assets?

The argument of chapter 7 stressed the aim of capital maintenance, and defined the latter in terms of the owner's investment. The timelag error emerged as an unfortunate trick of reckoning that leads to the sapping of his wealth, measured in terms of his ability to buy another bundle of goods (perhaps for private consumption) comparable with the old bundle in desirability, but not necessarily in physical quantity or shape. There has been little need to talk of the replacement of particular assets.

In some ways, it would have seemed easier and more persuasive to frame that argument in terms of physical asset replacement. The firm whose accounts are given on p. 54 could be described as buying 1000 kg of a stated type of stock on 1 January, at £1 per kilogram. It sells this stock on 30 June at £1·54; it then pays out £540 as drawings and tax, and retains £1000 to buy a repeat dose of the same goods. But they now cost £1·1 per kilogram, so the firm can replace only 909 kg. Historical cost has failed to maintain the assets at their initial level. QED.

In fact, the argument on p. 54 tried to show that, with general price change, the historical-cost approach fails because it makes the firm less able to maintain the real value of the owner's investment, regardless of physical form. Its stress was on the assets' power to maintain the owner's standard of life, and not on their shape and number.

Numerical example

The problem can be illustrated by again using the earlier figures (see pp. 56–61). These dealt with a capital of £1000, invested in a single input. The new assumption is that the general index stays at 100, but the special index rises to 110. The physical nature of the input now impinges on the argument; it can, for instance, be envisaged as 1000 kg of stock, bought at a wholesale price of £1 and sold at retail when this price has risen to £1·1.

Balance sheet approach

The series of balance sheets in Table 7.4 can be repeated without changing the assets. But the wording of the capital section now needs to be revised. Table 8.1 opposite tries to give an analysis acceptable to the special-index man. Because capital maintenance is defined in physical terms, profit is only £440. The special-index man ignores the £100 *real holding gain*, i.e., real appreciation on inputs during the timelag between their acquisition and sale.

An equally full analysis, which rejects the ideal of physical capital maintenance, would restate the lower part of Table 8.1 in some such way as:

	(1) £	(2) £	(3) £	(4) £
Initial capital	1000	1000	1000	1000
Gains during year:				
From holding stock			100	100
Current operating profit				440
			100	540
	1000	1000	1000	1540

TABLE 8.1

COMPARATIVE BALANCE SHEETS, SHOWING SPECIAL APPRECIATION
IN TIME OF GENERAL PRICE STABILITY

Date	(1) Opening figures £	(2) Stock bought £	(3) After price change £	(4) After sale £
Cash	1000			1540
Stock (current value)		1000	1100	
Capital—defined as the cost of 1000 kg of input:				
Initial cost	1000	1000	1000	1000
Increase in cost			100	100
			1100	1100
Trade profit				440
	1000	1000	1100	1540

So, by the re-analysis, the total profit is £540: conventional accounting is right (providing always that the general index has not changed). This total is made up of £100 of holding gain during the timelag, and £440 of current operating profit (see Table 4.1).

Profit and loss approach

The special-index man corrects the timelag in the profit and loss account by charging input at current replacement cost. If his extra charge is shown separately, as in column (2) below, it may be called a 'provision for the increased replacement cost of the asset' (the credit in the balance sheet receiving some such name as 'allowance for increase in cost

of replacing assets'). Superficially, column (2) seems to do the same thing as the account in Table 7.6 (p. 56). But the two accounts deal with different situations, and in fact do different things. In Table 7.6, the £100 extra charge makes up for a fall in the value of the £, and restores the cost to its original real level—thus maintaining the owner's real capital. In Table 8.2, the extra charge registers a rise in the cost of the particular input while the £'s value is constant, and so increases the charge in real terms and expands real capital. By the general-index test, profit is the £540 of column (1), and, if the owner decides to plough back £100 of this profit, his decision does not turn the £100 into a cost of this year's operations.

TABLE 8.2

PROFIT AND LOSS ACCOUNT,
WITH COST CORRECTED BY SPECIAL INDEX

	(1) Ordinary accounting £	(2) Special-index accounting £
Cost		
Historical	1000	1000
Provision for increased replacement cost		100
Replacement cost		1100
Sale	1540	1540
Profit	540	440

The special-index man argues that, as the input appreciated by £100, the current sacrifice from using it up is indeed the £1100 of column (2). This is true, but then column (2) should show *both* the £100 appreciation and the £100 cost; you cannot logically record the exit of wealth whose entry you have ignored. So the net profit is still £540.

Normally, those who use the special index do not in fact show the nature of their costs so frankly as the above account. They get much the same results obscurely, e.g., by using Lifo or by writing up plant and then charging correspondingly more depreciation.

The special-index case put badly

Perhaps the most revealing way to canvass the pros and cons of the special-index case is to set this out in its weakest light, and then to see how its advocates would make it more persuasive.

At its crudest, then, the case runs like this. Suppose I make my living as a speculator in stock exchange securities. One of my purchases is 1000 shares in the XY Company for £1000. Later, I sell them for £700, i.e., the special index has fallen from 100 to 70 (the general index remaining constant). An ordinary trading account for my venture compares the £1000 cost with the £700 sale, and tells me I have lost £300. The special-index theory says that—despite the obvious worsening in my position—I have lost nothing (i.e., profit is zero): for my £700 will buy another 1000 shares in XY, i.e., covers replacement cost, and thus my physical assets are exactly maintained.

Now, why does my exposition sound so weak? A special-index man can make it sound far more convincing by using an example that differs from mine on several points.

Points favourable to the special-index case

(1) *Cash strain of asset replacement.* The special-index man would take, not a discrete venture, but a firm with a stream of transactions from a composite team of assets; failure to replace any asset physically here tends to upset the whole stream, perhaps disastrously. Further, he would suppose that the special price of the given input is not dropping but rising. Given these two conditions, a change in input price means the firm is faced with an imperative problem of finance. Its officials will long to conserve enough cash to replace the dearer inputs at the same physical level, and thereby keep activity at a pitch that they deem satisfactory. They will gratefully embrace any doctrine that may lead to lower dividends and perhaps tax.

(2) *Unchanged future receipts.* My example glossed over the question of whether or not the fall in the value of my shares heralded a fall in XY's future dividends, etc. The special-index man does not neglect this point. He concedes that higher input prices sometimes result in higher sale prices and margins. But his favourite example is the firm that cannot pass on higher costs to customers. For it, a rise in input prices spells lower future profits. Admittedly, it is glad to hold a store of inputs at their moment of appreciation, but thereafter the rise is an unrelieved misfortune. To count it as income would be absurd.

(3) *Distinction between firm and owner.* The special-index man keeps apart the firm and its owners. He is happy to let owners measure their personal incomes in whatever way seems good to them (e.g., with general-index adjustment if general prices change). But he accords to the firm the status of an independent body, important in its own right, remote from the tests of personal consumption, and entitled to its own measures of income. Indeed, the accountant's attitude to this matter 'depends on whether one tends to look on a firm from without or from within, and this depends on what one's environment has been'.[2] Logic is thus coloured by one's environment, and 'one's subconscious ideas on for whom or for what accounting systems are maintained', i.e., by whether one looks at the firm's wealth through the eyes of the outside equity-holder or through those of 'the entity itself'. Accountants in public practice are concerned to protect the interests of shareholders, and tend to favour the general index; accountants in business tend to favour the special index.

Consideration of points

Each of the above points is beset with difficulties. Point 3, in particular, raises philosophical issues that a book on accounting must approach with humility.

(1) The suggestion that income is changed by the *cash strain of asset replacement* cannot be brushed aside lightly, especially in a book advocating the view (see p. 23) that an income concept must be judged by its informativeness. Is not an income figure highly informative if it warns owners of the need to restrict dividends in order to finance new assets? One possible answer is that we should not judge it in isolation. A single figure may not be the best means of giving information on varied matters: two or more figures may be clearer. When real replacement costs are rising, the owners may be better served by an income figure that ignores the increase, plus a cash account or forecast, than by an income figure that tries to be maid-of-all-work.

Another answer runs thus. Suppose a factory has for some years made a steady profit of £x p.a. Suddenly, it is acutely short of cash. A conscientious accountant cannot announce without investigation that income has dropped. If the sole change in the situation is that the firm is now spending heavily on building a second factory, most of us (including the special-index man) would say that its income is still £x—no matter how crippling the cash strain: the income figure of £x, coupled with a clear explanation of cash needs, gives better information than a lower income figure. Plainly, then, the cash need is not the main test. What really matters is whether the cash shortage is deemed to be due to an *expansion* of the assets or merely to their *maintenance*, i.e., the problem hinges on how one defines 'expansion' and 'maintenance'. The definitions of the special-index man ignore real expansion that is unaccompanied by physical expansion, and so enable him in such cases to blend income measurement with cash conservation.

(2) The link between *asset values and future receipts* provides more solid grounds for thought.

A rise in the value of an equity investment may be due to a rise in either the given company's dividends, etc., or the general market yield on all equities. In the latter case, the investor who consumes the appreciation during the week (see p. 23) is as well off at the end as at the beginning in terms of capital, but not in terms of future receipts; such change in the market's capitalization rate thus produces a dubious form of income (perhaps justifying the phrase 'capital gain'—see p. 25)—which most of us would however deem to bring some degree of benefit. Where instead the company's rate of dividend rises, the owner can consume the appreciation and still be as well off at the end of the week in terms of both capital and future dividends. Or he can leave the gain invested, and so secure a higher standard of 'well-offness' in future weeks. In either case, the gain meets more of the tests of income.

A comparable analysis can be made of holding gain on inputs. Stock appreciation, for instance, may or may not herald higher future profits. Where the firm can pass on higher costs, and future profits and dividends are likely to rise, holding gain brings unmixed benefit. Where instead the firm cannot pass on higher tinuing benefits, i.e., it somewhat resembles the 'capital gain' due to change in market rates of costs, the appreciation does not herald concapitalization; here the special-index case becomes much stronger.

However, it must often in practice be hard to separate the two possibilities with any feeling of assurance. And, perhaps, the onlooker may without undue cynicism doubt whether many firms are inhibited from passing on costs, in the long run at least. Economic logic suggests that, in an industry where asset prices become high relative to profits, firms will tend at replacement date to switch to other industries, while potential competitors will stay out until reduced supply forces prices up to a level again yielding normal profit.

(3) To say that the firm is privileged as a *separate entity* is, I suspect, to stray on to very thin ice. The notion seems to imply that firms, by virtue of being separate entities, have a right to

continued existence and growth, regardless of their economic and social contributions. It thus has obvious appeal to the employees of a firm: and it strengthens the hand of those managers with a paternalist attitude to shareholders and other 'outsiders', enabling them to build up what are (by real-wealth standards) secret reserves.

When one appeals to the entity theory of accounts, presumably one does not mean that splitting up figures in accounts, as between a trader's business and his home, etc., somehow endows the business with special status. The analysis implies no more than that the separate figures are useful; the trader is helped by knowing, for instance, how much he spends on the shop and how much on his wife. In much the same way, the economist is helped in his reasoning when he unravels man-the-consumer from man-the-firm.

The law goes a long step further. There is plainly much convenience in, for example, the legal fiction that a corporation is a person.

But the status accorded to the entity by some accounting theorists presumably derives mainly from the view that a business is run by more than one man, and that a group of men—working together as, say, a church, gild, or firm—acquires a personality of its own, demanding our special respect. This line of argument leads us into the realm of political philosophy, and far beyond the competence of one who, like me, is trained only as an accountant. Apparently, some serious philosophers, as well as demagogues like Mussolini, have attributed 'the red blood of real corporate personality' to the group, asking whether it has a 'personality beyond the persons of its members, and a will beyond their wills'. An opposing view is stated by Ernest Barker. He sees in the group not an extra person, but merely an 'organizing idea' (presumably a set of common aims, standards, and loyalties). 'What has happened is that this idea has entered into a continuous succession of persons...a new personality has not arisen, but a new organizing idea has served as a scheme of composition for existing personalities.' Thus, he cuts down the group's status.

'When we talk of real persons, we attach to them an intrinsic value as such, because we feel that all personality has value. At that rate we should see value in the Mafia or Camorra. If one talks rather of ideas, one can keep something more of critical poise...one can deflate a bubble idea with a prick of logic.'[3]

Clearly, an entity theory of accounting should be spelled out with some caution.

The owners *versus* the entity

Earlier pages have tended to look at problems through the eyes of the entity's owners rather than those of the entity itself. This may have struck readers as naïve and a century or more behind the times—especially where the entity is a vast company with a legion of owners, or is far removed from human owners by virtue of being a sub-sub-subsidiary. Yet there is, perhaps, a sound reason for stressing human judgement.

The soulless corporation can trade in the market in the same way as a human being, and so there seems nothing irrational about using market values in (say) its balance sheets, etc. But some of its fundamental value figures must rely, at least by analogy, on external judgements by humans. When net assets must be compared at different dates, I have some difficulty in understanding how a non-human can feel whether the December pile is 'as good as' the January pile; the general-index man overcomes this difficulty, the special-index man does not.

Economic and physical quantities

There is a further reason for preferring the owner to the entity. If one fails to do so, one runs the risk of confusing physical with economic qualities. The latter do not depend on number, size, etc., but on scarcity and capacity to meet human wants. 'There is no quality in things taken out of their relation to men which can make them economic goods'; wealth (in the sense of a flow of economic goods) 'is not wealth because of its substantial qualities. It is wealth because it is scarce. We cannot define wealth in physical terms as we can define food in terms of vitamin content or calorific value

.... So, too, when we think of productive power in the economic sense, we do not mean something absolute—something capable of physical computation.'[4]

The special-index man seems perilously near to forgetting such ideas. Yet it is doubtful if he can without them even decide how to define the physical size that he seeks to maintain. Does physical size mean for instance the *number* of, e.g., items of stock, regardless of other attributes? Or their weight? Or (where these are important) qualities such as thermal content? With plant, does it mean the machines themselves or capacity to produce physical units of product? And what does total physical size mean (e.g., as one type of asset grows old and useless, how far do very different replacements fill up this physical gap)? What if the firm decides not to make any replacement? And how special should the special index be, i.e., should it mirror prices of the one asset, or all the firm's assets, or the industry's assets?[5] The answer must lie in some rather woolly concept of maintaining an activity level that is satisfactory to various human beings—perhaps the level that keeps workers in jobs, preserves management's morale, and provides customers with their usual purchases. If this be so, physical quantity is really a clumsy guide to certain human wants.

Such truths are easier to read than to believe. If, for instance, a firm starts a year with one ton of opening stock costing £1000, and after a fortunate series of sales and purchases ends with a closing stock of three tons costing £3000, accountants will readily register a gain of £2000; but if closing stock is one ton costing £3000, they are not so sure. Those who follow Lifo think the physical expansion is an essential condition for the gain's existence. In their trading accounts, they raise the figure for closing stock (and hence profit) by the £2000 cost of the physical increments, but ignore the value change where the physical size is constant. In terms of economic reality the two gains seem equally desirable. With both, the owner is richer by £2000, regardless of the number of tons. With both, he has ploughed back his profit as extra investment—again regardless of the number of tons: the increased value of one ton seems in this sense to be just the same 'expansion' of assets as the increase marked by physical growth. In less simple problems (e.g., where the units are depreciating assets, or the gain is unrealized), the issue is less clear. With them too, however, the accountant must decide whether holding gain on one physical unit is tantamount to profit and its reinvestment, or whether increase in the number of units is a necessary condition. This is the heart of the matter.

Conclusions on the special-index view

This chapter began by suggesting that right and wrong here depend largely on objectives. If the maintenance of a viable set of physical assets is really what lies closest to the owners' hearts (an implausible assumption where there are many shareholders), we must not challenge their value judgment. But where the hearts in question are those of managers, we may ask whether these men are not too authoritarian in measuring profit in a way that suits themselves rather than owners, and which, moreover, fosters automatic reinvestment, regardless of its fruitfulness, and so may lead to the inefficient use of resources. The democratic alternative is to show real profit, and then leave the owners to opt for expansion or distribution. This is what is done by the franker figures of the general-index method (i.e., by the method adopted in the British *Provisional Statement of Standard Accounting Practice No. 7*).

All in all, it seems to me that though the special-index man's treatment of asset values and decision costs is right, he has not yet proved his case where the timelag error is concerned; and that (in the absence of general price change) income should be found by subtracting historical rather than replacement cost from revenue. His income accounts are normally incomplete, in that they charge out gain whose prior arrival they have ignored. In addition, his method is particularly harmful if (as logical symmetry requires) it shows no loss when input prices fall calamitously; his neglect of price decline is a yawning gap in his exposition.

The only time when the special-index case appears valid is when input appreciation is not due to change in expected net receipts, but in their capitalization rate (p. 71). Then the gain is so different from other forms of income that it might well be excluded or at least carefully segregated. But such gains seem likely to be rare, hard to distinguish, and harder to quantify. So we may doubt whether they deserve much space in a reform programme.

Where the special-index approach may bring tax benefits, a new factor comes into the argument; and no doubt the special-index man does not exclude such benefits from his thoughts. Should tax law embrace the physical sub-concept, and exempt profit that is used to finance physical expansion? If so, the reason is not that the gain is unreal, but rather that the extra investment is thought by the nation to merit encouragement.

How to combine replacement cost with historical income

Even if replacement cost is rejected as a basis for measuring income, there may be some convenience in showing it in the income statement. Where the assets have been revalued, replacement-cost depreciation ties in with the balance sheet better than historical depreciation; and the use of current costs should be encouraged wherever they may influence decisions. Replacement cost can be substituted for historical cost, without changing real profit, if the difference (holding gain) is also recognized by the income statement, as an addition to revenues. This procedure has the merit of giving extra information about the profit by analysing it as current operating profit and holding gain (see also p. 28) and so showing how successful the firm's stock-holding policies have proved.

As an example, column (1) of Table 8.2 might be redrafted as in Table 8.3, thus:

TABLE 8.3

PROFIT AND LOSS ACCOUNT
COMBINING HISTORICAL COST
INCOME WITH INPUT AT REPLACEMENT
COST

	£
Input, at replacement cost	1100
Sale	1540
Current operating profit	440
Holding gain on input	100
Accounting profit	540

Special change in times of general change

The notion of special change in a time of otherwise stable prices is a help to analysis but hardly smacks of real life. In practice, reform must be able to deal with simultaneous and unequal changes in both indices. The arithmetic of such reform may be a trifle laborious, but the principle is simple.

General-index viewpoint on special change

If one accepts the general-index case, one ignores special change (in the narrow context of income measurement), and after general change still corrects income by converting costs with the general index, as in chapter 7.

Or, if one prefers to show costs at special replacement level and yet keep the same corrected income figure, one must also add the real holding gain (the difference between special and general costs) to revenue, thus neutralizing the extra cost.

To illustrate, let us once more use our main numerical example. Suppose that I again hold input (costing £1000) from January to mid-year, while the general index moves from 100 to 110; but now let the special index at the same time rise to 132, so that replacement cost is £1320. Sales prices are likely to rise in sympathy with costs, say, to £1848. Column (1) of Table 8.4 shows the new ordinary accounts.

The special-index view is that the timelag error on cost should be corrected by converting the input's historical cost to its current replacement level, as in column (2), i.e., by creating a replacement allowance of $\frac{32}{100} \times$ £1000 = £320.

The general-index view leads to an extra charge of only $\frac{10}{100} \times$ £1000 = £100, as in column (3). Or, if the full analysis is wanted, cost can be raised to the replacement level of £1320 by adding a further £220 of real appreciation, and then revenue should also be raised by this £220. Column (4) shows this variant of the general-index method.

Stabilization and special-index change

The earlier tables, it must be remembered, show merely the minimum adjustments needed in the ordinary accounts to correct the timelag error on costs. They do not try to give stabilized figures for, e.g., assets and capital.

Full stabilization also removes the timelag error. But the stabilized figures must vary with the brand of correction that is chosen as 'right' and used in preliminary workings. Thus, the stabilized income statement could here be built on the special-index approach of column (2) in Table 8.4, or the general-index approach of either columns (3) or (4). In fact, the example in column (5) builds on (4). It uses the end of the year as base date, and assumes the general index to be 120 then. So it must slightly change all the historical figures of column (4); the end-£ equivalent of the 748 mid-year £s of profit is $\frac{12}{11} \times £748 = £816$.

Example

Table 8.4 thus interprets the results in altogether five of the possible ways:
(1) as in ordinary accounts;
(2) as in accounts where the timelag error in the income statement is corrected by the special-index method;
(3) as in accounts where that error is corrected by the general-index method;
(4) as in (3), but with replacement cost and real holding gain shown;
(5) as in (4), with both income statement and balance sheet stabilized in £s at the end of the year.

TABLE 8.4

ACCOUNTS ILLUSTRATING SPECIAL CHANGE SUPERIMPOSED ON GENERAL CHANGE

	(1) Ordinary accounts £	(2) Special-index correction £	(3) General-index correction £	(4) Real holding gain and replacement cost shown £	(5) Stabilized end-£
Income statement					
Input					
Historical cost	1000				
Replacement cost		1320		1320	*1440*
General-index correction			1100		
Sale	1848	1848	1848	1848	*2016*
Profit					
Accounting	848				
Corrected with special index		528			
Corrected with general index			748		
Current operating				528	*576*
Holding gain (real)				220	*240*
				748	*816*
Balance sheet					
Cash	1848	1848	1848	1848	*1848*
Capital	1000	1000	1000	1000	*1200*
Replacement allowance		320			
Inflation allowance			100	100	
		1320	1100	1100	
Profit	848	528	748	748	*816*
Loss on holding money ($\frac{10}{110} \times 1848$)					*−168*
	1848	1848	1848	1848	*1848*

Tax on capital gain

It was pointed out on p. 57 that one of the important costs subject to the timelag is the cost in a capital gain calculation. For example, the man who sells the home that he bought thirty years ago probably makes a gain of several hundred per cent: to find whether he has made any real gain, he needs to raise the historical cost with a general-index factor.

The point is very relevant to capital gains tax. Such a tax can be harsh where money gain exceeds real gain.[6] Justice suggests that inflation charges (in my view, based on the general index) should be permissible deductions in computing the taxable gain. If, for instance, Table 8.4 dealt with a capital transaction subject to tax, the taxable amount should be £748 only, as in columns (3) and (4).

A consistent application of the special-index man's argument to such isolated transactions would appear often to reduce the gain to zero. If, for instance, I buy shares at £1 and next day sell them for £10, I have presumably by his test made no gain at all, since the replacement price of the shares is £10. This result would be naïve in the context of tax, and seems further to weaken the special-index case.

References

1. The phrase was coined by R. S. Gynther, *Accounting for Price Level Changes: Theory and Procedure*, Pergamon Press, 1966. I am in debt to his book (a spirited defence of the special index) for much of the detail in later pages.

2. This paragraph relies heavily on Gynther, *op. cit.*; the quotations are from pp. *x* and 44.

3. The quotations are all from Ernest Barker, *Church, State, and Study*, Methuen, 1930, pp. 160–3.

4. L. Robbins, *The Nature and Significance of Economic Science*, Macmillan, 1949, pp. 46–47

5. See E. S. Hendricksen, *Accounting Theory*, Irwin, 1965.

6. See A. J. Merrett, 'The Capital Gains Tax', *Lloyds Bank Review*, October, 1965.

9 The timelag error. C. Stocks

A discussion of stocks may not add much to what chapters 7 and 8 have already said about principles. But it is needed because the 'cost of goods sold' is a much less simple figure than the costs used so far. Moreover, some of the methods of valuing stocks (i.e., of finding the closing stock for the balance sheet, and the corresponding credit in the income statement) can change the cost-of-goods-sold and thus the timelag error, and so we must extend the argument to cover valuation too. For simplicity, our examples will deal with the stocks of a merchant; but the argument normally holds also for, e.g., a manufacturer's raw materials, work-in-progress, and finished goods.

Difficulties of defining the historical cost of stocks

Most of the usual methods of valuing stocks make extensive use of historical cost. This is consistent with the accountant's way of valuing other assets; and it sounds objective and easy. Yet, as was pointed out, on p. 19, there are great difficulties in finding the historical cost of stocks, as well as further difficulties in justifying it if it can be found. Particularly in manufacturing, these difficulties are often the result of 'jointness'—a given outlay helps to make a pool of stock units, some of which are sold during the year and some left at the end. So the cost figure for closing stock can vary with choice of *ingredients* (e.g., should overheads be included?) and of *sequence* (which unit goes out first?). The ingredients problem is not important for understanding the timelag; all that need be said is that a bigger overhead content leads to a bigger stock carry-forward, and thus (when prices change) may result in a bigger timelag error. But the sequence in which units are handed out decides which units are charged to the income statement and which are left in the closing stock, and different units may have different historical costs; so the sequence affects the cost-of-goods-sold and the error.

Valuation methods: the Ifo family

A firm may, for instance, price stock issues by the *first-in-first-out* or *last-in-first-out* systems (familiarly abridged to Fifo and Lifo). However, these are often a matter of *assumed* rather than actual sequence, i.e., the firm may merely value the units *as if* one or other of the two patterns is followed, regardless of the actual physical flow.[1] A less common member of the Ifo family is *highest-in-first-out* (Hifo); it cautiously assumes that the dearest units are issued first, leaving the cheapest units as closing stock. None of the family can be defended as more than a convenient makeshift; to link value with a past physical event is an affront to economic logic. The problem would vanish if issues and closing stock were valued at current prices; so long as they are valued by reference to past costs, the latter must be allocated between units by some mere rule-of-thumb.

There are many other methods of valuing stock (some of which are mentioned in chapter 12). All those using historical cost are likely to create time-lag errors. Fifo and Lifo will serve to illustrate the point, and so this chapter deals mainly with them.

Example of Fifo and Lifo

The simple example in chapters 7 and 8 (i.e., a pre-inflation cost of £1000 and sales of £1400) still meets our needs when the firm deals in stocks; but the £1000 now becomes the net total of several items—say, stock at beginning and purchases, less stock at end. Suitable figures are set out in Table 9.1. This supposes that 500 stock units, costing £1 apiece, are always held, and the turnover period is six months. For simplicity, it supposes too that transactions are concentrated into a few busy days: thus all the 500 units of stock at beginning are bought as a single lot on 30 September in the preceding year, and 500 units are simultaneously sold and replaced on 31 March and again on 30 September in the current year. If prices are steady throughout the period (index 100), a year's trading account will run (by both Fifo and Lifo).

TABLE 9.1

INCOME ACCOUNT WITH STOCKS—STABLE PRICES

		£
Stock at beginning	500 units	500
Purchases	1000 units	1000
	1500 units	1500
Less Stock at end	500 units	500
Cost of goods sold	1000 units	1000
Sales		1400
Profit		400

So the outcome is a profit of £400, as before.

How does inflation change this? As usual, we begin on the assumption that the general and special indices coincide. Let us again say the index moves up steadily from 100 to 120 between 1 January and 31 December. Our figures will, however, be easier to compare with the other examples if we suppose that the upswing in prices began *earlier* than the start of this year—say, that the index was only at 95 on the preceding 30 September, so that opening stock cost only £475. Another lot of 500 units was bought at 31 March (index 105) for £525, to set off a sale of 500 units then. A third lot was bought at 30 September

(index 115) for £575. Fifo treats this last lot as the end-stock, which is therefore valued at £575. The figures are set out in Table 9.2—first as stores records, and then as final accounts.

The table gives also the Lifo interpretation of the same data. Each 500-unit lot of purchases is supposed to arrive just before a sale of 500 units; Lifo deems the incoming lot to be issued for the sale, so the original stock nucleus is left undisturbed. The choice of base date for the balance sheet values depends on the firm's history. Here we assume it to be a date, such as 30 September of the preceding year, when the index stood at 95. But if Lifo was first applied to 500 units when the index stood at say 50, and if volume has not since dipped at a year-end to below the original amount, then both opening and closing stock would here be valued at £250. The essence of Lifo is that the stock nucleus is always valued at the same rate, i.e., appreciation is ignored.

The Fifo income account confirms what was perhaps to be expected. The timelag error persists unchanged when there are opening and closing stocks—at any event, if these are measured à-la-Fifo; we have without undue trouble arranged our figures so that the cost, accounting profit, and error are again the same as in the staple example on pp. 55–6.

Comparing the Fifo and Lifo income statements, one sees that Lifo during inflation lowers the closing stock (to a level that may be far less than values of the current year), and thereby raises the cost-of-goods-sold (to something more like current cost). As a result, profit is here less than by Fifo.

Timelag in the physical flow of stocks

To understand the timelag error on stocks, one should perhaps think of the two sides of the profit and loss account as if they showed physical movements of inputs and outputs strung out *by date*. Thus, the left-hand side might list the successive purchases of stock units (starting at the top with the earliest unit affecting the year), while the right-hand side might list the sales of the same units. Such accounts can be represented as diagrams. Figure 9.1 shows three possible patterns. The left-hand side (AB) of each oblong lists the

TABLE 9.2

COMPARISON OF FIFO AND LIFO

Stores account
Dr.   Cr.

			Fifo and Lifo					Fifo		Lifo	
		Units	Price	£		Units	Price	£	Price	£
1 January	Balance	500	0·95	475						
31 March	Purchase	500	1·05	525	Issue	500	0·95	475	1·05	525
30 September	Purchase	500	1·15	575	Issue	500	1·05	525	1·15	575
31 December					Balance	500	1·15	575	0·95	475
		1500		1575		1500		1575		1575

Income statement

	Fifo	Lifo
Stock at beginning	475	475
Purchases	1100	1100
	1575	1575
Less Stock at close	575	475
Cost of goods sold	1000	1100
Sales	1540	1540
Profit	540	440

Balance sheets include

	Fifo	Lifo
Stocks	575	475
Profit	540	440

successive inputs as dots, A being (say) at 1 January and B at 31 December; and the right-hand side (CD) lists the successive outputs. Thus, E may represent one input, and F the sale of that unit. The diagram tries to suggest the timing of movements, but not their physical or money sizes.

Where each unit is held for almost no time at all (i.e., purchase synchronizes with sale), inputs and sales form horizontal pairs, and can be shown as the horizontal lines of the left-hand oblong (1). Thus, E and F may represent a single transaction in July. There can be no opening or closing stocks in this oblong. The timelag error here is negligible.

Where stocks are built up for a seasonal sales peak, one possible pattern is that of oblong (2). This shows more frequent purchases in the top half of AB, and more frequent sales in the lower half of CD: stocks are bought in the spring for big sales in the autumn, and so the broken lines slope down from the left during the turnover months. If prices change, a timelag error here

occurs within the year (even though there are no opening or closing stocks). In short, any physical undulation of stock may give rise to the error.

Opening and closing stocks are shown in column (3). GA is the purchases, made towards the close of the preceding year, that become the opening stock of the current year on Fifo assumptions. AB is the purchases of the current year. HB is deemed by Fifo to become the current year's closing stock, to be sold early in the next year. This leaves GH as the cost-of-goods-sold, tied slantingly to the year's sales (CD); Fifo cuts away closing stock (HB) from the year's costs, and leaves an earlier set of cost £s (GH) to be matched against current sales £s.

Lifo's assumptions make the broken lines of column (3) more horizontal. With constant real stocks, it produces an account corresponding to oblong (1). With changing volumes, the pattern cannot be shown in a simple diagram; but the net effect of Lifo is still to link costs with revenues that are almost contemporary.

Fifo

The next step is to analyse Fifo accounts in more detail, and to see how their timelag error can be corrected.

Anatomy of Fifo

It may be as well to remind oneself of the effect on the income statement of the entries for opening and closing stocks. The accountant seeks to charge no more or less than the historical cost of the units sold, just as if all purchases are on arrival stored away in a warehouse and charged against revenue, still at original cost, only when they are issued to customers. But, unless he keeps stores accounts, he does not know this cost figure. His nearest substitute is purchases; so he takes the latter, and trims it by cutting off the units unsold at the end and sticking on those held at the start. Under Fifo (provided all units flow through the shop in regular order, and there are no mark-downs due to spoilage, etc.) his resultant cost-of-goods-sold is the purchases for roughly a twelve-month period starting before the start of the accounting year and ending before its end (GH in oblong (3) in Fig. 9.1). By subtracting the cost of the later purchases (closing stock) from the cost of the whole year's purchases, he deprives those later purchases of all influence on the year's trading cost and profit.

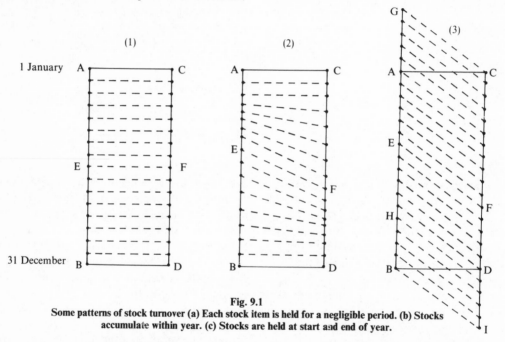

Fig. 9.1
Some patterns of stock turnover (a) Each stock item is held for a negligible period. (b) Stocks accumulate within year. (c) Stocks are held at start and end of year.

Thus, in the Fifo income statement of Table 9.2 the cost-of-goods-sold is made up of two lots of purchases—first, goods bought on 30 September in the preceding year, shown as stock-at-beginning and costing £475 and secondly, goods bought on 31 March in the current year for £525, and deemed to constitute the goods sold at 30 September. The table might be clearer if it showed only what happens to these two lots of purchases, i.e., left out the closing stock. Table 9.3 does this. It also demonstrates how profit can be corrected by the shortcut of an inflation charge. This arrangement shows more plainly that the timelag error arises because the 'cost year' precedes the 'revenue year'. Our minds should link the error with cost-of-goods-sold rather than closing stock; the error can be present even if closing stock is left out of the account.

More realistic flow patterns

In real life, the figures may run less smoothly than in our example. For instance, the purchases and

80

TABLE 9.3

INCOME ACCOUNT WITH PURCHASES ANALYSED ON FIFO ASSUMPTION

Date	Index		Cost £	Sales £
Previous				
30 Sept.	95	Lot 1. Stock at beginning	475	
Current				
31 Mar.	105	Lot 1. Sold		735
		Lot 2. Purchase of first half-year	525	
30 Sept.	115	Lot 2. Sold		805
		Lot 3. Purchase of second half-year (= end-stock) £575		
		Historical cost	1000	
		Inflation charge	100	
		Corrected historical cost	1100	
		Corrected profit	440	
			1540	1540

sales may consist of many items, each with a different date. But often they can be treated as a few large lots, without much loss of accuracy. Thus, the opening stock of £475 will normally consist of many small lots, purchased mainly between 1 July and 31 December of the previous year; but, if those purchases were made at a fairly steady rate, they may perhaps be looked on as a single lot bought on 30 September, i.e., at an index of 95 'on average'—strictly, a weighted average. During the year covered by the account, there were no seasonal peaks, and so purchases and sales may here be treated as occurring on average at 30 June when the index was 110. And the closing stock (i.e., the purchases of July to December) may be treated as a single lot bought on 30 September.

When the goods are not sold in strict order, some of the closing stock items will no doubt be purchased before some of the items in cost-of-goods-sold; the two physical groups overlap. But, though the exposition is now less neat, the sense is not changed: under Fifo, the cost of closing stock is excised, and the error is caused solely by time lags on the items that have been sold. Other things being equal, a rise in the volume of elderly items in closing stock must suggest a fall in this year's timelag, and a rise in next year's.

Another real-life complication is change in the physical size of the stock. Thus, closing stock may differ from opening stock in physical size, and seasonal or other causes may lead to ups-and-downs during the year (see column (2) in Fig. 9.1); such changes bring further error, and make correction more troublesome.

Calculation of the inflation charge

How is the inflation charge best calculated when there are stocks? In the example, one can readily convert historical cost (£1000) into £s of sale date: the costs are incurred on average at general index 100, and the sales take place at 110, so corrected cost is $\frac{110}{100} \times £1000$, i.e., £1100; the corresponding charge is £100. Or one can work out the appreciation on each lot:

	Historical cost £	Factor	Raised historical cost £	Inflation charge £
Lot 1	475	$\frac{105}{95}$	525	50
Lot 2	525	$\frac{115}{105}$	575	50
Total inflation charge				100

Note, again, that the charge has been found from the cost-of-goods-sold, and without reference to closing stock.

In less simple firms, there are innumerable lots. Moreover, one cannot suppose that a given lot of purchases will neatly constitute one lot of sales; there will be some overspill into other sales and end-stock. Unless full store records are kept, one cannot then find the exact charge; some less precise procedure may be inevitable. The most obvious procedure is to find an approximate charge with the aid of the opening and closing stocks. In some circumstances, such a figure may be fairly accurate. The exact charge is the sum of many smaller charges, each caused by inflation during the turnover of one of the stock items that together make up the cost-of-goods-sold. Suppose that a firm's stock always consists of a single unit, sold at the end of each month and replaced at once. Then twelve small inflation charges will emerge during the year, and their sum is the correction for cost-of-goods-sold. But the sum equals the charge on one unit for a whole year, i.e., the appreciation on one unit between the dates of the opening and the closing inventories. Similarly, where many units are held, the difference between opening and closing stock values is still the year's inflation charge—provided always that there has been no change in the real investment in stock (as shown, e.g., by stabilized values).

Such stability is assumed in our simple example. So the error can there be found more readily than earlier calculations suggest. It is the appreciation on the stocks between the two valuation dates: £575 − £475 = £100.

In practice, such stability is most improbable. The more real investment varies, the less likely is the difference between opening and closing stocks to reflect the whole error. (Appendix 1 of this chapter explains a rather lengthier method of approximation.)

Stocks other than merchandise

For a firm other than that of a merchant (e.g., a factory), the argument runs much the same as above. But purchases are here apt to be only a part of the factory's costs; the other costs, such as wages and depreciation, may or may not be treated as ingredients of manufactured stock values, and carried forward. The facts do not stand out so plainly as in the case of the trader, but the same reasoning holds. And here the firm is more likely to keep stores records, and so may find the cost-of-goods-sold direct from the 'issues' to customers, instead of indirectly by adjusting purchases, etc., with the opening and closing stocks.

Loose tools are often classed in the balance sheet alongside plant, i.e., in the fixed assets section. But their value is usually found by an annual stocktaking; and the figures may well be calculated in much the same way as when stocks of goods are valued at Fifo. Where this is so, the treatment for stocks should be applied also to loose tools: the annual charge for their 'using-up' tends during inflation to be understated in the income statement, and should be raised with an inflation charge.

'Inventory profit'

The extra accounting profit that springs from the error on cost-of-goods-sold (e.g., the £100 in the illustration above) is often called 'inventory profit' The preceding pages suggest that the phrase is not altogether a happy one. It is apt to evoke mental pictures of the inventory sheets that are drawn up at the end of a year, and so to encourage the idea that the error is confined to appreciation in stocks held at the start and end. As we have seen, error can arise too from stock fluctuations *during* the year—which are not reflected in the closing inventory.

'Inventory profit' is thus doubly misleading. The profit is spurious, and its size does not depend on closing inventories. 'Error on cost-of-goods-sold' seems preferable.

Special change—real holding gain

When the cost price of stock moves but general prices remain stable, the historical cost-of-goods-sold is the correct figure to set against revenue (if the conclusions of chapter 8 are sound); there is no need for special index charges. If the price movement is upward, and the firm wants to finance the real expansion from internal sources, it should treat any consequent charges against income as appropriations, not costs.

Similarly, when real change is superimposed on general price change, Fifo and an inflation charge do all that is needed by the sub-concept of real capital maintenance.

Nevertheless, as was suggested on p. 72, the cost figures in the income statement will be more informative if they are linked with special prices; but this in turn demands a second change: realized real appreciation must be brought in as a profit (thus offsetting the extra cost, and leaving the profit balance unaltered). The double change has the additional merit of enabling the accountant to distinguish between the 'current operating' and 'real holding gain' components of profit—see p. 28.

The special-index man will challenge these statements. He insists that the cost-of-goods-sold should be raised to special replacement level (with no credit of real holding gain). His adjustment may take the form of an unconcealed addition to the costs, but is more often masked as a method of stock valuation (e.g., Lifo), and then tends to be inaccurate even by his standards.

Special-index example

Suppose all the facts in Table 9.3 still obtain, save that the buying price of stocks rises in September by an extra 23 points—pushing up the special index to 138 on 30 September, and so raising the cost of the September purchases (unchanged in physical volume) from £575 to £690 (i.e., an extra £115) and giving a real holding gain of £115 on the goods in stock. Then the trading results are as shown in Table 9.4. Column (1) gives the new ordinary accounts; and column (2) shows the general-index correction—still £100, as calculated on p. 82.

Column (3) puts the replacement cost charge at £215, the figure needed to raise the £1000 historical cost to current level (i.e., to the cost of the purchases). It thus reduces profit to £325, the current operating profit. By the canons of the special-index man, this is the correct profit, and he would rule off the account here; but those who disagree with him can restore the profit to the general-index level of column (2) by adding the £115 real holding gain. This roundabout course gives some useful information. The trend of current operating profit

TABLE 9.4

INCOME ACCOUNT WITH REAL APPRECIATION ON STOCKS

Date	General index	Special index		(1) Ordinary account	(2) General-index correction	(3) Special-index correction
				£	£	£
Previous 30 Sept.	95	95	Stock at beginning—Lot 1	475		
Current year						
31 Mar.	105	105	Purchases: First half-year—Lot 2	525	as (1)	as (1)
30 Sept.	115	138	Second half-year—Lot 3	690		
				1215		
				1690		
			Less Closing stock—Lot 3	690		
			Cost-of-goods-sold (historical)	1000	1000	1000
			Inflation charge (general index)		100	
			Replacement charge (special index)			215
			Corrected cost		1100	
			Replacement cost			1215
31 Mar. and 30 Sept.			Sales	1540	1540	1540
			Profit—accounting	540		
			current operating			325
			real realized holding gain			115
			corrected accounting		440	440

over the years may draw attention to this year's rather poor results (compared with those of the base year—see Table 9.1; the drop in profit is perhaps due to not raising the autumn sale prices in step with buying prices. But the realized appreciation figure shows some compensating gain, due to the buyer's skill in ordering new stocks (lot 2) before their steep price rise.

Lifo

If the last unit is supposed to be sold first, then stock-at-beginning can be thought of as remaining untouched throughout the year (provided physical stock does not fall below its opening level), forming a kind of permanent nucleus. At the end of the year, still valued at its original historical cost, it becomes stock-at-end. Where there are physical increments or decrements during the year, various treatments are possible (and logic cannot help much with the choice): because of the obvious importance of the US Treasury's rules on the subject, these tend to be dominant, but some non-American firms may nevertheless use other interpretations.

General price change and Lifo

Once again, it is wise to start with simple assumptions—that general and special price movements are the same, and that physical stock is constant. The example in Table 9.2 shows what happens here. In it, Lifo profit is again £440, as when corrected profit was found by Fifo and an inflation charge (see Table 9.3). So here Lifo has taken us to the same answer—by a route that is agreeably short and free from arithmetical hardships. Lifo's

net effect is to knock off something from a credit (closing stock), whereas an inflation charge adds something to a debit (cost-of-goods-sold). So long as the two somethings are equal, the two methods give the same result.

Anatomy of Lifo

Lifo's working can be made clearer if the various transactions are shown separately. They are conceived to run thus:

TABLE 9.5

INCOME ACCOUNT WITH STOCKS
VALUED BY LIFO

	Cost £	Sales £
Beginning lot (carried forward as closing stock)	475	
March lot—purchased and sold	525 ⟶	735
September lot—purchased and sold	575 ⟶	805
Cost of goods sold	1100	
Profit	440	
Sales		1540

Comparison of this table with the corresponding analysis of Fifo (Table 9.3) shows how Lifo can in very simple circumstances circumvent the timelag.

Special prices and Lifo

In the example, Lifo transmutes the purchases into cost-of-goods-sold, i.e., charges the latter at replacement cost. This effect becomes more obvious when special price diverges from general price. The example in Table 9.4 dealt with such divergence; if column (1) of that table used Lifo, it would run:

TABLE 9.6

INCOME STATEMENT—LIFO AND REAL APPRECIATION

Date	Index		Cost £	Sales £	Lifo profit £
Previous 30 Sept.	95	Stock at beginning	475		
Current 31 Mar.	105	Purchase of first half-year	525 ⟶	735	210
30 Sept.	115	Purchase of second half-year	690 ⟶	805	115
			1690		
		Less Closing stock	475		
			1215	1540	325

These figures are reminiscent of column (3) (for the replacement-cost provision linked with the special index) in Table 9.4; the cost-of-goods-sold is again replacement cost (£1215) and profit again £325. Thus Lifo acts like a replacement-cost provision rather than an inflation charge. At least in the conditions assumed by this example, Lifo profit is 'current operating profit'—see p. 28—and so leaves out all holding gain (here the £115 of real stock appreciation), even though this gain is both real and realized. (Appendix 2 of this chapter shows that this result holds wherever physical stock stays constant, but elsewhere can be upset).

Changes in physical volume

There is some dispute among the votaries of Lifo over the proper treatment of physical changes (and the point can hardly be resolved by appeal to economic logic, since the latter must regard physical sequence as beside the point—see p. 73). But accretions in any year (i.e., expansions of the basic quantity) tend to be valued thereafter at a historical cost of that year; and this cost is excised if the volume falls again.[2]

When physical stock is constant, as in the examples, one can state that Lifo fits in with the sub-concept of physical capital maintenance. Where physical stock changes, this statement ceases to hold precisely, though the imprecision would seem slight enough to be forgiven. With such change, too, Lifo may not produce a cost-of-goods-sold that exactly equals replacement cost. But its tendency will still be to cut profit down to current operating profit (and so suppress holding gain). It still acts more like a replacement cost provision than an inflation charge.

Popularity of Lifo

The examples suggest rightly that in many normal situations (i.e., where physical stocks are fairly constant, and general and special prices do not diverge excessively), Lifo is superior to simple Fifo for dealing with inflation, and is a plausible rival to Fifo plus an inflation charge. The latter calls for the insertion of an awkward and alien figure; the former is hardly noticeable. The latter can be justified only by reference to fundamentals; the

former can be explained readily in the specious terms of physical or cost flow.

Thus, one need not be surprised at the enthusiasm with which Lifo is advocated by many reformers. Their propaganda has had fair success; Lifo seems to have won more general acceptance than most other devices for reform. True, its use for tax purposes has in the UK been rejected by the courts.[3] However, it has become common in America. In 1938, it achieved the distinction of being accepted by American tax law for income-tax assessment in a narrow range of industries; and Congress during the next ten years liberalized the rules until all taxpayers could opt for Lifo. A number of provisos were made—e.g., the taxpayer must use Lifo in his own book-keeping as well as in tax calculations, and his decision is irrevocable.[4] The tax benefits were sometimes great: 'during the period 1941–47, net income before taxes for the 18 stores submitting complete data was reduced by 8·7% by Lifo...the annual reduction in income ranged from 4·2% in 1945 to 17·1% in 1941, a year in which department store prices rose about 15%.'[5]

Defects of Lifo

When Lifo has such practical advantages and political allure, anyone who quarrels with its use may seem pedantic. However, it has in my view many faults, notably the following:
(1) Lifo is unlikely in practice to give exact correction (general or special). It will tend to be inaccurate when physical increments and decrements affect closing stock (see Appendix 2 of this chapter). And where there are fluctuations *within* a year, i.e., not reflected in the opening and closing stocks, a method of correction that relies exclusively on these two figures cannot be accurate. Perhaps the most vivid way to see the point at issue is to imagine an extreme case in which a trader each year lets his stocks sink to nothing by the end of December and starts to build them up again in January; plainly, Lifo here fails entirely. And, though few real firms reduce their stock to nothing, many (e.g., retail drapers) reduce it substantially, and tend to choose a business year ending at

the date when stock is at its nadir. A cure built on such a low figure will not offset the error of busier times. If, on the other hand, the stocks are unusually high at the start and end of the year, Lifo may overshoot the mark, acting in just the same way as too big an inflation charge. If the business year ends when stocks are at their 'normal' size, Lifo has its best chance to function well.

(2) Lifo sounds simple (compared, for instance, with Fifo plus an inflation charge), but it is often not so simple as it sounds. Many of its early users were firms handling raw materials (meat packers, non-ferrous metal mines, etc.);[6] their stocks consist of a relatively limited number of physical types whose nature does not vary much over time, and thus comparison of the opening and closing quantities of each type is not unreasonable. With most other firms, however, the nature and mix of types can vary fast; e.g., a grocer may decide to switch from one make or size of soap tablet to another, to hold less tea and more marmalade, or to add a very different line. This difficulty has forced the friends of Lifo to relax their primitive and literal rules (which could apply only to firms handling standard types of goods), and to substitute fairly elaborate calculations, often based on index numbers. (Someday, perhaps the historians of accounting will distinguish between 'paleolific' and 'neolific' ages.) The current cost of the 'pool' of varied goods that makes up closing stock is deflated with the help of an index approximately to base-date level (like stabilized figures).[7] A department store may have to use a different index for each department.

(3) Increases and decreases in physical volume must be valued by some arbitrary rule. And they can have odd and unwelcome effects on profit. If stock sinks during a year, the 'decrement' is removed from end-stock, and so in effect charged as cost-of-goods-sold—at perhaps the low acquisition rates of many years ago. Costs are therefore small compared with Fifo, and profit large. This is particularly true if stock sinks to below base volume, as happened in many American firms during the lean years of the Second World War; the resulting profits were so high that in 1942 the US Congress was cajoled into granting special tax relief to firms hit in this way.[8]

(4) It seems desirable, for the sake of clarity and comparability with other firms, that the income account should show the size of important price-level adjustments; but Lifo in effect deducts a hidden provision from stock-at-end. Further, the current assets section of the balance sheet is more helpful and realistic if stock is shown at current cost (which Fifo is near to), rather than as a more mixed figure whose core is valued in remote £s. (But this objection to Lifo could be overcome, e.g., by showing a Fifo value among the assets of the balance sheet, and transferring the difference between the Fifo and Lifo values from profit to some kind of stock allowance. No one seems to advocate a possible variant of Lifo by which both opening and closing stock of a year would be valued at the year's *closing* prices).

In general, Lifo leads to a conservative stock value in the balance sheet, because the base date is chosen when prices are expected to rise. But eventually the cat may jump the other way, and current prices may fall below those of base date. The rules for dealing with this situation are not clear; if (as under American tax regulations) they exclude a proviso on the lines of 'lower of cost or market', Lifo must then yield a falsely high balance sheet value, and a profit sometimes above Fifo profit (as in the example in Table 9.7 below).

(5) There is plausible evidence that Lifo's need for stable stock figures (if its tax benefits are to be maximized) may interfere with the buying policies of firms, and even upset markets:[9]

> If you have too little inventory compared with your Lifo base, you buy up stock; when six or seven companies are trying to do the same thing you run the market ragged. Should you be too high on certain goods in comparison with your Lifo base, you cut prices to move out goods. Thus operating decisions are colored by the operation of the accounting system.

So the Lifo tail may wag the business dog.

(6) The case was put (pp. 74–5) for permitting adjustment with the general index only, and treating extra change in the special price as profit. On this view, Lifo violates the fundamental premise that income depends on real capital maintenance. Lifo takes the maintenance of physical stock, not real capital, as its benchmark. It cannot be justified unless a very odd income concept can be justified.

Wrongly or rightly, then, Lifo income leaves out special appreciation on stocks. In countries whose tax code accepts Lifo, firms can (when the special index rises more than the general index) avoid tax on real appreciation, which our analysis suggests to be genuine profit and part of the fruits of ordinary trade. Conversely, when the general index rises more than the special index, such firms can pay tax that would be avoided if the law recognized Fifo plus an inflation charge.

Lifo *versus* inflation charges

We may conclude from these arguments that Lifo is on less sure ground than Fifo plus an inflation charge. Instead of adding a calculated and defensible charge to costs, Lifo-users put an unduly small stock-at-end on the other side of the income account, and hope this error will cancel the unexplored timelag error. Their income theory is implausible, their profit may be inaccurate even on their own premises, and their method covers up important figures.

Whether these objections will in fact prove strong enough to discredit Lifo is another matter. If we concede that any remedy must in real life be rather rough and ready, perhaps we should not condemn Lifo too harshly. It is already in wide use, is fairly well understood, and may be more acceptable politically than a direct and intelligent method. These are not inconsiderable merits.

It would be unfair to the more thoughtful advocates of special-index reform to accuse them of blind support for Lifo. They are sensitive to its crudities, and would no doubt prefer to use some more accurate and candid device (such as a special-index charge) to correct profit. To less perceptive reformers, however, Lifo and special correction may well seem synonymous.

Other aspects

Falling prices

It is, perhaps, worth while to compare Fifo and Lifo when prices are dropping, and also to look at the working of the 'lower of cost or market' rule.

Lower of cost of market. When current values of any stock items fall beneath historical costs, caution suggests that the lower figures should be substituted—the 'lower of cost or market' rule (here shortened to Coma). Thus, in bad times the Fifo cost of closing stocks may be changed into a market value of the year-end. The choice between types of market value plunges the accountant into further dilemmas, the main candidates being perhaps net realizable value and replacement cost. His most cautious plan would be to pick the lower of these, but practice seems currently to favour net realizable value. The rule is applied to each separate item; as the other items remain at cost, the result of this 'pick and choose' system is a mixed total of old and new values.

However, Coma is not used invariably. In particular, where the chosen method already uses a form of historical cost that is considered sufficiently cautious, the cost figure may be retained even if current value happens to be less; thus the Lifo regulations of the US Treasury forbid the substitution of current value.

Example of falling prices. Our usual example can help again. Table 9.7 shows the new twist. To make the figures harmonize with those in earlier tables, one must envisage a year set in a longer stretch of price fall. The opening stock is on Fifo assumptions bought for £525 before the year began, when both general and special indices stood at 105; the Lifo figure is, say, £500. Lot 1 of the purchases is bought at 31 March, when the indices are at 95. Lot 2 (the end-stock) is bought for £310 at 30 September, when the general index is at 85 and the special index has tumbled to 62.

TABLE 9.7

INCOME STATEMENTS—FALLING PRICES AND VARIOUS VALUATION METHODS

Date	Index General	Special		(1) Fifo £	(2) Fifo and Coma £	(3) Lifo £
Preceding						
30 Sept.	105	105	Stock at beginning	·525		500
					as (1)	
Current						
31 Mar.	95	95	Purchases: first half-year	475		475
30 Sept.	85	62	second half-year	310		310
				785		785
				1310	1310	1285
31 Dec.	80	57	*Less* Closing stock	310	285	500
			Cost-of-goods-sold	1000	1025	785
30 June	90	90	Sales	1260	1260	1260
			Ordinary profit	260	235	475
			Add Deflation credit	100	118	
			Corrected profit	360	353	

By the end of the year, the two indices stand at 80 and 57, and the Coma value of the end-stock is only £285.

The ordinary Fifo profit has dropped to £260 (column (1)). This is too low by the test of real capital maintenance—it should be corrected to £360 by the insertion of a deflation credit of £100 (best looked on as a reduction of the cost-of-goods-sold). If Coma is superimposed on Fifo, as in column (2) (i.e., if the accountant recognizes unrealized holding loss), ordinary profit falls to £235, i.e., by £25. But the October–December drop in the general index, from 85 to 80, means that part of this fall ($\frac{5}{85} \times £310 = £18$) is merely notional, and the real loss is only £7. So the total timelag error is £100 as in column (1) plus an extra £18, i.e., £118; Coma here cuts corrected profit by very little. Column (3) deals with Lifo (and assumes that Coma would not be superimposed). Because of Lifo's rigid way of valuing stock at both ends of the account, profit is not allowed to droop as under Fifo. In this example, indeed, it is much higher than the Fifo versions. The difference is the realized holding loss, £525 − £310 = £215. So Lifo is not always cautious.

Stabilized accounts and the error on cost-of-goods-sold

In its attempt to lay bare the error in the clearest way, this chapter has used ordinary accounts as its examples, and merely updated the cost £s to make them match the revenue £s. This limited correction is another example of the 'first-aid' mentioned on p. 55—as distinct from stabilization of all the items in both the income statement and balance sheet. Stabilization also will correct the error. But its curative action does not stand out plainly, and so it seems less suitable for a first exposition. In particular, the stabilized accounts may not show which of the possible corrective methods is in use: the accountant cannot stabilize without first choosing between, e.g., the maintenance of real and physical capital, and his choice should be obvious.

For an example, let us look again at Table 9.4, and stabilize its figures—in the £ of 31 December, when the general index (GI) has reached 120 and the special index (SI) 140. Several types of stabilized accounts, analysing profit by different criteria, suggest themselves. The one used below springs from column (3) Table 9.4 (cost corrected with SI,

TABLE 9.8

EXAMPLE OF STABILIZED ACCOUNTS WITH STOCKS

				(1) Ordinary accounts—costs correct with SI and income with GI £		(2) Stabilized version of (1) end–£
Income statement	GI	SI				
Previous						
30 Sept.	95	95	Lot 1. Opening stock	475		
Current			Purchases			
31 Mar.	105	105	Lot 2	525	$\times \frac{120}{105}$	*600*
30 Sept.	115	138	Lot 3	690	$\times \frac{120}{115}$	*720*
				1215		
				1690		
30 Sept.	115	138	*Less* Closing stock, Lot 3	690		
			Cost-of-goods-sold			
			Historical	1000		
			Replacement charge	215		
			Replacement	1215		*1320*
			Sales:			
31 Mar.	105		Lot 1	735	$\times \frac{120}{105}$	*840*
30 Sept.	115		Lot 2	805	$\times \frac{120}{115}$	*840*
				1540		1680
			Profit			
			Current operating	325		*360*
			Real realized holding	115	$\times \frac{120}{115}$	*120*
			Corrected accounting	440		*480*
Balance sheet			Cash	325		*325*
			Stock	690		*700*
				1015		1025
			Capital	475	$\times \frac{120}{95}$	*600*
			Inflation charge	100		
			Real profit—Realized	440		*480*
			Unrealized[10]			*−20*
			Loss on holding money[11]			*−35*
				1015		*1025*

income with GI). It assumes that opening capital (equal to the stock) was £475, and that real appreciation on closing stock (between its purchase date and 31 December) should be recognized.[10]

Appendix 1: Approximate inflation charges

It may be useful to illustrate a simple way of finding approximate general (or special) index charges when real stock-on-hand is not constant.

Table 9.9 shows the income statement for a calendar year of a firm with many purchases. The turnover period is some three months; the stock in a balance sheet is thus (on Fifo assumptions) bought at about 15 November, and the mid-point of the 'stock year' is about 15 May. The special index is assumed to rise faster than the general index, and physical stock to grow somewhat, so that the total investment in stocks grows considerably.

TABLE 9.9

INCOME STATEMENT WITH COMPLEX STOCK CHANGES

Date	Indices			£
	General	Special		
Preceding				
15 Nov.	95	95	Opening stock (Fifo)	950
Current year			Purchases	4350
				5300
15 Nov.	99	110	Less Closing stock (Fifo)	1320
			Cost of goods sold	3980

The approximation method assumes that the extra physical stock is bought as a single lot in the middle of the stock year, so that the error consists of: (1) appreciation on the opening stock for the first half of that year, plus (2) appreciation on the expanded stock for the second half. (1) can be found by calculating appreciation on the opening stock, and (2) by discounting the closing stock. Let us say that the general and special indices stand at 96·5 and 101 on 15 May. Then the calculation is:

Period	Known Stock	Appreciation		
		General	Special	
	£	£	£	
November–May	(Opening) 950	$\times \dfrac{96\cdot5 - 95}{95} = 15$	$\times \dfrac{101 - 95}{95} = 60$	
May–November	(Closing) 1320	$\times \dfrac{99 - 96\cdot5}{99} = 33$	$\times \dfrac{110 - 101}{110} = 108$	
	Approximate charges for year	48	168	

So uncorrected profit should be reduced by £48 (general-index test) or £168 (special-index test).

This method will become more inaccurate if the sales do not centre on the middle of the business year or the stock transactions on the middle of the stock year (although this fault may be lessened by choosing more representative dates). And, as it depends on opening and closing stocks, it cannot allow for peaks within the year.

Appendix 2: Arithmetic of stocks

Fifo

The formula used on p. 56 to show the timelag error, $C\left(\dfrac{s}{c} - 1\right)$, still holds where there are stocks, if C is understood to be the ordinary accounting figure for cost-of-goods-sold under Fifo rules, c the general index at the date of weighted average cost-of-goods-sold, and s that index at sales date.

For a more detailed scrutiny of stocks, however, we must split up C, and show it as:

B, i.e., stock at beginning, bought when index stands at b; plus

P, i.e., purchases of goods, when index stands at p; less

E, i.e., stock at end, bought when index stands at e.

Now, the typical trading account in effect runs:

$$\left. \begin{array}{c} \text{Beginning stock} \\ + \\ \text{Purchases} \\ + \\ \text{Gross profit} \end{array} \right\} = \left\{ \begin{array}{c} \text{Sales} \\ + \\ \text{End stock} \end{array} \right.$$

We may shorten this to:

$$B + P + G = S + E \qquad (1)$$

During price change, G is the uncorrected gross profit. Let the general indices be b, p, s, and e at the dates respectively of B, P, S, and E. Then, historical costs must be raised to find

corrected gross profit, i.e., $\quad S - \left(B\dfrac{s}{b} + P\dfrac{s}{p} - E\dfrac{s}{e}\right)$

From eqn (1),
uncorrected gross profit $\quad = S - (B + P - E)$

Subtraction gives the timelag error $\quad = B\left(\dfrac{s}{b} - 1\right) + P\left(\dfrac{s}{p} - 1\right) - E\left(\dfrac{s}{e} - 1\right)$ (2)

Thus, the error is the money appreciation on each cost item between its own date and sales date.

Where real investment in stocks is constant, as in Table 9.2, the error can be found more shortly. Because purchases here match sales, p becomes equal to s, so $P\left(\dfrac{s}{p} - 1\right)$ is zero; opening and closing stocks are the same in size, so $E = B\dfrac{e}{b}$. The error in equation (2) shrinks to:

$$B\left(\frac{s}{b} - 1\right) - B\frac{e}{b}\left(\frac{s}{e} - 1\right)$$

$$= B\left(\frac{e}{b} - 1\right) \tag{3}$$

i.e., the error is here the appreciation on the opening stock during the 'stock year'. So firms whose stock does not vary much can approximately offset the error by the use of simple tricks based on opening and closing stock figures.

By substituting the special index for the general, the above formula can be adapted to represent special appreciation.

Lifo

Normally, Lifo is linked with the special index. So the symbols below should be regarded as representing that index.

Lifo's exact result depends on what treatment is —rather arbitrarily—given to changes in the volume of real investment in stock.

(a) *Constant physical stock throughout year*. Let us start with the firm whose physical stock is constant throughout the stock year. (This is somewhat notional if the type of goods varies. It is meant to suggest absence of real investment change, apart from that needed to finance the difference between special and general inflation, i.e., real appreciation.)

When Lifo is first adopted, stock is given its base value, Bb. During a given subsequent year in a spell of inflation, stock at beginning is still Bb under Lifo (B under Fifo); the unchanged stock at end is also Bb $\left(B\dfrac{e}{b}\text{ under Fifo}\right)$.

Putting stocks in a trading account changes the profit figure from what it would be if stocks were ignored. The numerical extent of this change, given constant physical stocks, is:

under Fifo, an increase of $\qquad B\dfrac{e}{b} - B$

under Lifo, an increase of $\qquad$ —

net effect of change from Fifo to Lifo $= B\dfrac{e}{b} - B$

Thus, with constant physical stock the result of using Lifo instead of Fifo (i.e., Lifo's curative property) is a reduction in profit of $B\dfrac{e}{b} - B$ or $B\left(\dfrac{e}{b} - 1\right)$. Equation (3) above shows this to be the special appreciation (given constant physical stock); so the 'Lifo cure' here offsets exactly the special appreciation, i.e., adds both the inflation charge (by the general index) and real appreciation to Fifo cost.

(b) *Physical stock is the same at beginning and end, but varies during year*. Where physical volume at beginning equals that at end, but there is fluctuation *during* the year, the special appreciation (per equation (2)) is $B\left(\dfrac{s}{b} - 1\right) + P\left(\dfrac{s}{p} - 1\right) - E\left(\dfrac{s}{e} - 1\right)$.

The Lifo cure takes care of the first and last of these terms (see (a) above), but ignores $P\left(\dfrac{s}{p} - 1\right)$, and so profit is swollen by this amount (partly inflation profit, partly real holding gain).

(c) Increase in physical stocks carried forward. As the physical purchases at some point during the year exceed the physical sales, Lifo must at the following year-end add some value I to the base stock to allow for the increment—perhaps after it has been several times sold and replaced at higher prices. The effect of I varies according to which of the permissible values is allotted to it. If it is valued at its first acquisition price (as seems consistent with the rest of Lifo), then the reasoning in (a) applies: Lifo offsets all appreciation on I (as well as on the base stock). But if it is valued at an average rate for the year, or at Fifo, the cost-of-goods-sold is thereby lessened, and so profit for that one year includes some special appreciation; this is $I\left(\dfrac{x}{i} - 1\right)$, where x is the index used to revalue the increase, and i is the index at I's first acquisition;

to this extent, Lifo fails to measure income by the special-index canon.

(d) Decrease in real stock. Let us suppose that L, the total of a given year's stock at beginning by Lifo, includes D (a value still based on an acquisition-year index x) which is liquidated during the year. Then the Lifo profit is

$$S - (L + P - [L - D]) = S - P - D$$

Correct (special-index) profit is

$$S - P\frac{s}{p} - D\frac{s}{x}$$

Subtraction gives the Lifo error

$$P\frac{s}{p} - P + D\frac{s}{x} - D$$

$$= P\left(\frac{s}{p} - 1\right) + D\left(\frac{s}{x} - 1\right)$$

Even if $P\left(\dfrac{s}{p} - 1\right)$ happens to be *nil*, Lifo must here give a profit that includes special appreciation on D between the date of x and the average sale date.

References

1. Some accountants speak of the flow of costs rather than of physical units. Viscount Simonds described how this approach is used with Lifo:

It must in the first place be explained that Lifo does not mean that the metal last to be received into stock is in fact the first to be processed and sold. On the contrary the actual physical flow of the raw material is regarded as irrelevant: that which was purchased in previous years and was in stock at the opening of the relevant financial year or that which was purchased during that year may have been processed and the products sold during that year: this is of no account. It is to cost that Lifo looks, and in the simplest terms it means that the cost per pound of the metal most recently purchased and added to stock is the cost per pound of metal content to be charged against the next sale of processed metal products. It is the necessary corollary of this that to the stock which is in fact in hand at the end of the year there must be attributed the cost of metal which has not yet been exhausted by the cost attributed to metal consumed; this has been called the unabsorbed residue of cost.—*Minister of National Revenue* v. *Anaconda American Brass Ltd.* [1956] 2 W.L.R. at pp. 35, 36.

This has an agreeable air of sophistication, and makes the argument sound better. But it still has all the faults inherent in value theories based on cost; and it hardly seems to prove that any given sequence assumption is better than the rest.

2. C. D. Hellyar, 'The Lifo Method of Stock Valuation', *The Accountant*, 14 June 1952, gives full examples of different methods of dealing with increases and decreases. The methods laid down by the US tax regulations are: (1) in the year of adoption, all opening inventory units are valued at average cost; (2) any physical increase in a year is valued at its cost (earliest, average, or latest of the year), and this sum is carried forward in subsequent years; (3) any physical decrease ('liquidation') leads to the omission of the latest items in the preceding inventory, valued at whatever historical cost was chosen at stage (2) and then stage (1) (Tax Code, 1961, section 472).

3. *Minister of National Revenue* v. *Anaconda American Brass, Ltd.* [1956] 2 W.L.R. 31; [1956] 1 All E.R. 20. The base-stock method was likewise rejected in *Patrick* v. *Broadstone Mills, Ltd.* [1954] 1 W.L.R. 158; [1954] 1 All E.R. 163. Thus, the principle of 'lower of cost (Fifo) or market' now seems to reign in British tax practice. See H. C. Edey, 'Valuation of Stock in Trade for Income Tax Purposes', *British Tax Review*, June 1956.

4. A full description of Lifo (covering history, technique, statistical results and tax rules) is given by J. K. Butters and P. Niland, *Inventory Accounting and Policies*, Harvard University Press, 1949.

5. *Ibid.*, p. 37.

6. *Ibid.*, p. 55.

7. The phrase 'dollar-value method' is often used to describe Lifo when applied to a changing pool of varied goods.

8. Z. S. Zannetos, 'Involuntary Liquidations of Lifo inventories', *Accounting Research*, October 1954.

9. A comment quoted by Butters and Niland, *op. cit.*, p. 121.

10. Real holding loss on closing stock between 30 September and 31 December:

$$£690 \left(\tfrac{120}{115} - \tfrac{140}{138} \right) = £20$$

11. Loss on holding money:

31 March–31 December

$$£210 \times \frac{120 - 105}{105} = £30$$

30 September–31 December

$$115 \times \frac{120 - 115}{105} = 5$$

$$£325 \qquad\qquad £35$$

10. The timelag error. D. Depreciation[1]

Chapter 13 will discuss possible ways of improving the stereotyped 'depreciation methods' by which accountants write down the historical cost of depreciating assets. This chapter takes the methods as given, and asks how far their charges are subject to the timelag error.

The error, as we have seen, occurs when any input is charged in £s whose value does not match that of the corresponding revenue £s. The argument would seem to apply with equal force to stocks, depreciating plant, and any other asset that 'circulates' through the income or appropriation accounts (e.g., an intangible asset that is written down).

'Primary' and 'secondary' assets

In discussions of depreciation, it is useful to speak of the *primary asset* and *secondary assets*. The former is the depreciating asset that is being studied. The latter are the extra assets acquired as a result of providing for depreciation (i.e., the extra assets that the firm accumulates over the life of the primary asset to offset its fall in value, and so maintain total wealth). These phrases need not imply 'fixed assets' and 'current assets'. When sales are made, it is normally the liquid assets that grow. Thereafter, if such assets are retained to offset depreciation, they will in time be invested in whatever ways seem most rewarding, and thus become diffused throughout the asset structure, e.g., as stocks and even other depreciating assets.

Depreciation and change in secondary-asset values

It is worth while to pause at this stage to make up one's mind on a point that often creeps into discussions of depreciation and price change. Suppose that a factory has a machine costing £1000 in a period when the prices of things-in-general and the machine are stable. The firm sets about providing for depreciation by building up secondary assets that will in the end cost £1000. However, some of these secondary assets happen to lose or gain in value—because, e.g., of theft, deterioration, or special price movements. Can one argue that this secondary loss or gain changes the amount to be set aside as *depreciation*, i.e., that depreciation cost is no longer £1000? The answer must surely be no: the exhaustion of the primary asset still involves a sacrifice of £1000; the secondary change is due in the main to other forces, and should be classified separately and not added to or subtracted from the £1000.[2] If, say, the secondary assets are stolen, the owner may have to take drastic measures (perhaps cutting his dividend), but this does not mean that he has failed to measure depreciation.

Next, consider the same problem when price change is widespread. One must as usual distinguish between the following.

General change affecting all assets alike. Because such changes in money value affect all assets and equity claims to the same degree, they are nominal, and thus do not upset the argument. If, for instance, all prices rise by 10 per cent, one should deem depreciation provisions already in existence, and secondary-asset values, to go up in money terms by 10 per cent (a change that would be duly shown in accounts stabilized in end-£s); no surplus or loss occurs, and no new problem arises.

Real change. The secondary assets are, in fact, unlikely to appreciate exactly in step with the general index, say because they include money assets. The difference is real loss or gain. Applying the argument of earlier paragraphs, one should treat this in the obvious way, e.g., charging it as 'loss on holding money' (and trying to stop such loss in future); it does not give grounds for extra charges to 'top up' the accumulated depreciation provision for the primary asset.

General price change

We shall, as usual, start with general price change alone. We shall suppose that the price of a new depreciating asset moves in step with the general index; and that the prices of all the firm's other assets do the same—which implies its net money assets to be zero.

Book-keeping for general-index adjustments

Once again, the simplest way to correct the profit and loss account is to supplement the normal cost (i.e., historical depreciation) with an inflation charge. In the balance sheet, the supplements can again be credited to the inflation allowance (in the owners' group of balances); if, instead, they are subtracted from the original price of the asset, along with normal cumulative depreciation, the net balance may soon become incongruously small or even negative. At the end of the life of the machine, the accumulated credits in the inflation allowance should not be touched. They are a lasting re-expression of the owners' capital, etc., to be kept permanently unless a fall in the price level justifies transfers of 'deflation credits' back to the income statement.

Example

Let us adapt our staple example by turning its annual cost figure (£1000) into a charge for depreciation. Suppose that a capital of £4000 has just been

TABLE 10.1

ACCOUNTS SHOWING GENERAL INDEX CORRECTION OF
DEPRECIATION CHARGE

	£	Ordinary figures corrected £
Income statement		
Sales		1540
Depreciation:		
Historical	1000	
Inflation charge £1000 × ($\frac{110}{100}$ − 1)	100	
		1100
Corrected profit (= dividend)		440
Balance sheet		
Primary asset		
Historical cost		4000
Less Depreciation on historical cost		1000.
		3000
Secondary assets (1540 − 440)		1100
		4100
Capital		
Legal		4000
Inflation		100
		4100

95

invested at general index 100 in a machine with a four-year life, and that a historical charge of £1000 is each year being written off under the straight-line system of depreciation. Inflation sets in, and general prices rise by 20 points per year, i.e., by 10 per cent at average sales date of the first year. Corrected profit is paid out as dividend. If the ordinary accounts of the year are given 'first-aid' correction for the timelag error, they run as in Table 10.1.[13]

The error's pattern over the asset's whole life

The size of the timelag error on any given input depends on the size of $\frac{s}{c}$ (see p. 56), which in turn tends to grow with the length of the time between the cost and the resulting sale. Thus, one can expect the error to rise as the 'turnover period' of the input lengthens. Many depreciating assets have long lives; the inflation charge on such an asset may therefore in late life be high relative to the historical-cost charge.

Suppose, in our example, that the inflation continues throughout the four-year life of the machine, with the index mounting by 20 points a year. Table 10.2 shows the charges over the whole life. Column (3) gives the historical-cost charges. Column (4) gives the inflation factor, reflecting the increase in prices between the purchase date of the year's input and the assumed average sale date of the resulting output. Each successive historical charge is, in terms of buying power, more

inadequate than its predecessor; so the inflation charges rise as in column (5), until in the fourth year they reach 70 per cent of the historical charge. In most countries, the rate of inflation has been slower than the example suggests. On the other hand, many machines last far longer than four years, and so the deficiency of the final historical charges may reach or surpass this degree of short-fall.

In a given income account, the relative sizes of the errors on cost-of-goods and depreciation will largely depend on the particular firm's investments in stock and plant. A merchant probably has a large stock error and an insignificant depreciation error. In heavy industry, especially if firms are old-established, the depreciation error may be the bigger; the British steel industry, for instance, seems to have had a depreciation error some 50 per cent higher than the cost-of-goods error.[4] Perhaps the cost-of-goods error is apt to jump up and down from year to year (and so affect profits in a way that catches the eye), whereas the depreciation error tends over the years to follow a fairly sober course.

Need earlier provisions be adjusted?

Looking at the £100 inflation charge calculated with the June index of the first year, one may ask whether it is big enough, since by 31 December the index has risen past 110 to 120. Should not a further charge be made against income, to raise this £100 to £200 at the year-end? The answer seems to be that £100 is the right sum, i.e., it is

TABLE 10.2

DEPRECIATION OVER ASSET'S WHOLE LIFE

(1)	(2)	(3)	(4)	(5) Yearly correction	(6)	(7)	(8) Equivalents in end of year 4 prices	(9)	(10)
Year	General index	Historical-cost charge (i.e., year 0 prices) £	Factor	Inflation charge £	Total (i.e., current prices) (3) + (5) £	Factor	Historical-cost charge (3) × (7) £	Inflation charge (5) × (7) £	Total (8) + (9) £
0	100								
0·5	110	1000	$\frac{10}{100}$	100	1100	$\frac{180}{110}$	1636	164	1800
1·5	130	1000	$\frac{30}{100}$	300	1300	$\frac{180}{130}$	1385	415	1800
2·5	150	1000	$\frac{50}{100}$	500	1500	$\frac{180}{150}$	1200	600	1800
3·5	170	1000	$\frac{70}{100}$	700	1700	$\frac{180}{170}$	1059	741	1800
4	180								
		4000		1600	5600		5280	1920	7200

what is needed to maintain the purchasing power of the original capital. 1100 mid-year £s are the same thing (in purchasing power) as 1200 end-£s; so our charge of only £100 raises the depreciation provision sufficiently, and no subsequent topping-up charge against profit is needed. A revaluation of the secondary assets would support this view. Revenue normally flows in throughout the year, on average (say) at mid-year; the firm can thus invest surplus revenue in non-money secondary assets while their price index is still on average at 110. Because of the general rise in prices, secondary assets worth £1100 at June become worth £1200 at December; real wealth is intact.

Similar reasoning answers another question that is often put. The initial investment of £4000 (at index 100) has the same buying power as 7200 of the £s current at the end of year 4 (index 180). Even the augmented charges that column (6) in Table 10.2 envisages (£1100 in year 1, £1300 in year 2, and so on) will not provide anything like such a high figure; in fact, column (6) adds up to only £5600. Must we each year not merely augment the historical charge of £1000 with an inflation charge, but also look back and top-up still further all the accumulated provisions of earlier years?

Such compound increases are not needed. The question betrays the confusion spread by 'mixed' accounts, such as those for cumulative depreciation and the inflation charges. To see things clearly, one must turn from the mixed figures of columns (1)–(6) to their stabilized counterparts, (7)–(10). These retell the whole story of the cumulative provision in terms of the £s at the end of year 4. They explain how the earlier figures have in real terms grown in pace with inflation. Column (10) shows that the final values of the depreciation charges add up to 7200 end-£s at the close of the life of the asset, i.e., maintain capital exactly.[5] In effect, topping-up has already taken place automatically and invisibly. Or, looking at the question from the asset side of the balance sheet, one can suppose each year's depreciation provisions to be invested fairly soon in whatever secondary assets the firm thinks most suitable; if these are non-money (as our analysis has so far assumed), they should thenceforth tend to appreciate with the inflation, and so maintain their real value.

In fact, non-money assets may not be bought at once, nor are they likely to appreciate with such textbook precision. But as was suggested on p. 94, any variance should be ascribed to the faults or merits of the firm's financial and investment policies, and not to the reckoning of the depreciation charges. If these allow for inflation, then the managers have done that part of their job in full, and need not bother further with the old entries.

However, analysis is not action: management has merely exchanged one burden for another. It must still take pains to see that the real value of the secondary assets is maintained, and make good any shortfall, e.g., by restricting dividends. This is another reason why the careful measurement of asset values is important.

Special price change

Next, consider the situation in which general prices are fairly constant, but the replacement price of the primary asset changes.

Here the reasoning of chapter 8 suggests that historical-cost depreciation gives the best profit figure. Any extra sums provided for replacement are voluntary appropriations, not costs. If, instead, replacement-cost depreciation, found by revaluing the asset or applying the special index, is charged in the income statement for the sake of information, then the excess must be regarded as realized appreciation and added to revenue (much as in the examples in Table 8.3 and Table 9.4).

The special-index viewpoint

The special-index man would have us charge replacement cost, but would not permit the addition to revenue. He supports this view (see p. 70) by pointing to the troubles that will beset some firms if they do not save the full amount needed to replace an old machine with another of the same physical capacity. These troubles are real enough. The counter-argument does not deny the wisdom of putting aside the extra sums for replacement, but considers these not to be costs but voluntary appropriations to pay for what is really expansion.

This point can be made more vivid with the 'Rolls-Royce won in a raffle' approach. If you pay 5p for a raffle ticket and win a £10 000 car, should your friends congratulate you on your luck, or commiserate with you because your depreciation costs will now go up? The commiseraton view is sound enough so far as it goes: you will indeed suffer loss in future years as your car wears out, and will have to charge extra depreciation. Why then does commiseration strike you as nonsense? Because it recognizes your *loss* of wealth, but not your *prior gain* of that wealth: it calls for debits in your profit and loss account, but ignores a potential credit. To give a full picture, the account should show both the initial gain and the later losses; over the years, the gain and loss cancel, and you are back where you began, i.e. you have exactly maintained your original capital of 5p. If you decide to replace your Rolls at the end of its life with a second one, then you are bent on expanding your assets (compared with their original size), and must seek the extra finance as best you can. And this view would still seem to hold where there is real appreciation in the value of a machine bought in the ordinary way (though here the lesson is not rammed home by the advent of an extra physical asset, and so is less obvious). Real depreciation thereafter goes up, but only because the firm first makes a real gain from the appreciation of its asset; over the years, the two real movements cancel.

Replacement cost can be intolerably high

If the special index rises sharply, the replacement cost charge for the current year could be high. Moreover, if replacement-cost accounting is not to fail in its aim, presumably the provisions of former years must be topped up, i.e., the situation is no longer so comfortable as that described on p. 97, where general price change automatically raised the former provisions. Or, perhaps, this year's provisions should attempt to meet the estimated *future*, not the current, replacement cost. (Where input can be replaced at once—as with stocks—current cost is the same thing as replacement cost. Where it will not be replaced for a long time—as with most depreciating assets—current cost may prove a very poor guide to ultimate replacement cost, and can be defended

only as a shortcut that avoids guesswork about remote prices.) One way and another, the charge could reach an embarrassing size, and indeed might cut profit to a level at which no dividend could ever be paid. Only a very stern breed of owners would wish to save on this heroic scale: most men would instead make post-replacement plans for working on a lower physical level of activity, or for financing the same physical level by raising fresh capital from outside (as with any other kind of economic expansion).

'But', the special-index man may object, 'your argument holds good only on your implausible assumption that the real values of the secondary assets are stable. In practice, they may appreciate, too. Indeed, they are likely to do so if they take the form of more machines like the primary one; then they can provide the extra saving needed for replacement'.

Here we return to the discussion on p. 94. In my view, the secondary earnings (e.g., interest or appreciation) do not tell us anything about the size of the depreciation provision to be built up during the life of the primary asset—that depends entirely on the choice of capital-maintenance concept. If the secondary appreciation is big, plainly it may ease the financial strain of replacement; but it should be looked on as extra revenue, leaving the total depreciation charges unaffected.[6]

Other aspects of the special-index case

The special-index case has obvious allure for firms seeking an excuse to pass on increased replacement costs to others, e.g., for monopolists who must justify high prices for their products before a government commission. A monopolist should be allowed to raise his prices by enough to cover 'interest' on increase in asset values. If, however, he is allowed also to charge extra real depreciation, yet leave out the real appreciation, his customers will make him a present of the real expansion of his business.

However, special prices can fall as well as rise. Indeed, real fall is very likely with machines, because of improving technology. Then an owner who charges only replacement-cost depreciation will have good cause to doubt whether he is maintaining his capital in a satisfactory sense. And what happens when a firm decides not to replace the asset? Is depreciation here zero?

Revaluation and revised depreciation charges

In practice, the starting-point for any recognition of special price change is likely to be a revaluation of the primary asset. Then a revised depreciation charge follows as a byproduct. It covers both (a) the historical-cost charge, and (b) an extra replacement-cost charge. So it gives the special-index man just what he wants (at least until the revaluation becomes out of date). By the test of real capital maintenance, (b) is not a cost; and, as its size is concealed, it can be regarded as a transfer to a secret reserve. For instance, if the firm in our example believes in revaluation, and the replacement price of the machine rises 5 per cent just

after purchase, the gross book-value would be put up from £4000 to £4200, and then the depreciation charge would presumably be raised from £1000 to £1050. Normally, this is the end of the matter, i.e., income is cut down by £50 as in column (1) of Table 10.3. But this reduction offends the test of real capital maintenance, which is satisfied only if the £50 is brought back into income (see p. 74), as in column (2).

Columns (1) and (2) both raise the asset value by £200 to £4200, and thereafter write off this increased figure like ordinary depreciation. In column (1), the £200 credit is kept as a permanent addition to capital. Column (2) treats it as a form of (unrealized) income—which it is, if real capital is used as a benchmark. When slices of it are deemed to become realized, they are transferred from the balance sheet to revenue (e.g., the £50 in the table).

TABLE 10.3

ACCOUNTS SHOWING SPECIAL REVALUATION (GENERAL PRICES CONSTANT)

	(1) Physical capital maintained £	(2) Real capital maintained £
Income statement		
Sales	1540	1540
Cost (depreciation calculated on replacement price of £4200)	1050	1050
Current operating profit		490
Add Realized holding gain		50
Total profit (= dividend)	490	540
Balance sheet		
Primary asset		
Current value (new)	4200	4200
Less Depreciation	1050	1050
	3150	3150
Secondary assets: 1540 − 490	1050	
1540 − 540		1000
	4200	4150
Capital	4000	4000
Revaluation gain on primary asset:		
At revaluation date	200	
At balance sheet date		150
	4200	4150

Mid-year or end-year depreciation charge?

By using a one-step price rise, Table 10.3 skirts round a difficulty. In its income statement, cost is in effect measured in mid-year values, and yet ties in neatly with an asset value of balance sheet date. But suppose the index goes on rising after mid-year, so that mid-year and end-year £s differ in value. Should the year's depreciation charge then tie in with the mid- or end-year index? Suppose the input consisted of a single unit of stores, all converted into product and sold at mid-year, and not replaced. Here the logic of charging the input at the price of mid-year (rather than end-year) seems plain; the mind is not distracted by a figure in the end balance sheet. Why, then, should the logic change when similar assets are still held at balance sheet date? If this view is right, the year's depreciation charge should reflect the prices of input date (approximately mid-year in most cases). In the above example, it should still be £1150— even though such a charge cannot tie-in with the asset's value in the balance sheet.

In the example of Table 10.3, suppose the price of a new asset rises between July and December to £5000. Then, though the income statements are unchanged, i.e., depreciation remains at only £1050, the balance sheet value of the asset must be written down by £1250. The 'revaluation gain' takes care of the difference between the two depreciation figures:

	(2) £
Balance sheet	
Primary asset	
Current value (new)	5000
Less Depreciation	1250
	3750
Secondary assets	1000
	4750
Capital	4000
Revaluation gain (1000 − 250)	750
	4750

Real change combined with general change

The last stage in the argument must deal with the position where both general and special indices change, but to differing degrees. Here the mechanics become a trifle more intricate, but the principles stay the same.

Unravelling general and real changes

In this true-to-life situation, the total holding gain on a year's input (i.e., the excess of special-index depreciation over historical-cost depreciation) should for clear understanding be split into two parts:

(1) that part found with the general index—the inflation charge on pp. 95–6;
(2) the remainder, i.e., real holding gain (or real 'cost saving') on the asset during its 'turnover'.

If the argument of earlier pages is valid, the inflation charge is still the proper means for correcting income; the real gain merely adds extra information to both sides of an income account.

Example

To illustrate this matter with our main example, let us say that both general and special indices start the year at 100; that the general index again rises to 110 at mid-year (and so the income statement should by the test of real capital maintenance be like that in Table 10.1, with corrected income still at £440); but that the special index reaches 115 by mid-year. Thus, the year's input grows in money value by £150, and in real value by £50, while waiting to be consumed. If the accountant wants to spell out the whole story, he needs accounts somewhat along the lines of Table 10.4. The income statement must show the £50 as both a cost and a gain. A balance sheet based on historical cost would still be the same as that in Table 10.1; but if, as seems preferable, the asset is revalued with the special index (assumed to reach, say, 125 by the end of the year), the balance sheet will run as in Table 10.4. For the reasons given in the left-hand column, the depreciation charge in the income statement does not here tie in exactly with the balance sheet figure:

TABLE 10.4

DEPRECIATION CHARGE ADJUSTED FOR GENERAL AND REAL CHANGE

Income statement	£	£
Sales		1540
Depreciation:		
Historical cost	1000	
Inflation charge	100	
Real realized holding gain	50	
Current replacement cost		1150
Current operating profit		390
Real realized holding gain		50
Corrected profit (= dividend)		440
Balance sheet		
Primary asset—revalued at 125		5000
Less Depreciation $(1000 \times \frac{125}{100})$		1250
		3750
Secondary assets $(1540 - 440)$		1100
		4850
Capital		4000
Revaluation gain on primary asset $(1000 - 250)$		750
Inflation allowance		100
		4850

Possibly, full stabilization in end-£s is more sensible than this half-hearted adaptation of the ordinary figures. (The Appendix to this chapter gives an example.)

Other matters

Records of date

To calculate inflation charges, etc., one must know all the relevant dates. Therefore, adequate plant records are needed; and published reports could helpfully show both cost and depreciation figures for all disposals. A firm with many depreciating assets should, for easy calculation, group them according to purchase years; the same index factor can then be applied to the total historical cost of each group.

Finance of replacement

Much of the recent interest in 'accounting for inflation' springs from concern over the finance of plant replacement. This is important, and historical depreciation can indeed be crassly insufficient.

Even if such depreciation is eked out with inflation charges, replacement may still bring worries where the special index outstrips the general one, or the secondary assets fail to appreciate in step with the general index (say, because they are cash-heavy).

On the other hand, one must be careful not to exaggerate the case. A fair-minded person (even if he is still convinced of the need for reform) must concede that historical provisions are not so inadequate as they look: because the figures are 'mixed' (see p. 97), they give a false impression. In Table 10.2, for instance, the bare historical total of £4000 (column (3)) has at the end a current value of £5280 (column (8)); this falls short of needs, but not so badly as the mixed accounts suggest.[7]

Replacement when there are many depreciating assets

Again, though it seems right to take a single asset as the starting-point for a study of replacement, one should be wary about generalizing from such simple arithmetic.

In practice, the flow of depreciation funds can become an intricate pattern; often it can be comprehended only in terms of complex formulae. A firm may have many assets, with uneven lifespans; it can choose between several depreciation methods (and in particular can adopt 'accelerated' methods that make the heaviest charges in the early years of the life of an asset); it gets tax concessions on new assets; and its total plant is tending to grow. Only a rash person would dogmatize on the net effect of all these factors. But there are some grounds for thinking that a growing firm, using accelerated depreciation methods, can meet replacement burdens (even during inflation) with less strain than our one-asset example would suggest.[8]

Accelerated depreciation allowances

In general, accountants recognize the gravity of the timelag error, but dislike to abandon traditional methods. So they may try to meet the depreciation shortfall by speeding up the normal process of writing off historical cost. Thus, they may adopt a depreciation formula that makes heavy charges in the early part of the life of the asset (perhaps justifying this by pointing to abnormal physical activity in the early years); or they may write off an arbitrary initial allowance in the first year. 'Sometimes a gross amount is picked out of the air, and a formula found that will fit that figure.'[9] There may well have been a general tendency to switch from the straight-line to the 'fixed percentage of the declining balance' and (in the USA) the 'sum of the digits' methods.

All such tricks for speeding up depreciation are useful during inflation. Thanks to them, the firm can set aside receipts earlier than it would do otherwise, and so is more able to buy new assets before their price has risen much. However, so long as any part of the price of the asset is recovered in later years, via depreciation charges based on historical cost, the recoveries are bound to be inadequate. The only satisfactory course for those who regard historical cost as sacrosanct is to write off 100 per cent depreciation as soon as the asset is bought. From this angle, the unfashionable method of allowing for plant costs by charging renewals instead of depreciation may in some circumstances work well.

The US Steel experiment

The trend to accelerated depreciation is illustrated by the odd story of US Steel.

In 1947, the company already valued most of its inventories by Lifo. It then decided that principles accepted by the courts for 'short-term inventories' were 'just as applicable to costing the wear and exhaustion of long-term inventories... that it was prudent for it to give some recognition to these increased replacement costs rather than to sit idly by and witness the unwitting liquidation of its business'. Accordingly, it 'increased its provision for wear and exhaustion from $87·7 million based on original cost to $114·0 million, or by 30 per cent. This was a step towards stating wear and exhaustion in an amount which will recover in current dollars of diminished buying power the same purchasing power as the original expenditure'.[10]

The auditors pointed out in their report that depreciation was 'in excess of the amount determined in accordance with the generally accepted accounting principle heretofore followed'. The implication was that the auditors disapproved.

The Securities and Exchange Commission, following the official line of the American Institute of Accountants, in due course told the company that the new treatment could not be accepted in future accounts.

The company's 1948 Report adopted yet another treatment, to meet 'the stated position of the American Institute of Accountants, which is supported by the Securities and Exchange Commission'. Depreciation was put back onto historical cost, but with acceleration. An extra 10 per cent of an acquisition's cost was written off for each of the first two years of its life, on the grounds that the plant was in those years operating at well above the normal peace-time rate. The change, applied retroactively, raised the 1947 charges still further—and the SEC accepted the higher figures.

Tax concessions

Tax authorities in countries where inflation is mild tend to disallow inflation charges, etc., in computations of income for tax purposes. But they have been more generous about accepting the accelerated methods.

As a grudging concession to rising prices, British tax law in 1945 began to make various arbitrary arrangements that reduced tax in the first year of the life of the asset. These arrangements have been continued, on and off, according to each Chancellor's views about the need to soothe industry and stimulate investment.[11] It may be that they give business as a whole just about as much relief as if inflation charges were recognized in computing income for tax purposes.[12] But this does not mean that individual firms get the right amount of help. For instance, where the firm's tax bill is negligible because its profits are low, it may never receive the extra help. Concessions based on the general price index would probably match needs more closely and fairly.

Depreciation and borrowed money

Plant is likely to be financed in part with borrowed funds. And 'one of the most controversial questions in connection with price-level depreciation'—to quote from a memorandum by a large auditing firm—'is whether or not the amount computed for the price-level increase therein should be reduced for the effect of long-term debt so that only the portion relating to the stockholders' equity would be recorded. In other words, if the total capitalization consisted of 40% long-term debt and 60% stockholders' equity, should recognition be given to only 60% of the price-level increases?'[13]

This is another example of the matter discussed on p. 59. For the reasons set out there, an adequate analysis of profit must deal with, and show separately, both (a) the whole gain on owing, and (b) the whole inflation charge. To set any part of (a) against (b), and so reduce the extra depreciation charge to a small net figure, is to hide both the true cost of plant and the gain on owing.

The matter is often germane to public-utility accounts. Thus, the reports of the Port of London Authority have pointed out that, if depreciation had been charged at replacement instead of historical cost, the extra charge would have turned the surpluses of some years into deficits. However, as loan capital (less money investments) was about £30 000 000, readers of the report can guess that gain on owing could well cancel the deficits.

Lenders of capital are here subsidizing the users of the port.

Stabilization

To show the effects of the timelag error as simply as possible, this chapter has confined itself to the 'first-aid' correction of the ordinary accounts. Full stabilization (of all the figures in both income statement and balance sheet) would also cure the error. But it would, as a preliminary, require choice between the various theories explained in this chapter; and its detailed workings would be rather like the arithmetic of the tables above. (The Appendix below illustrates the matter.)

Appendix: Illustration to various types of price-level reform

A simple illustration may help to contrast some of the alternative reforms that have been suggested for depreciation accounting.

Data

A new firm's transactions are:

19x0	31 December	Receives £1000 capital and uses it to buy a machine. General and special indices = 100.
19x1	1 January	General index rises to 110, and special index to 115; thereafter they stay at these levels.
	30 June	£550 rents received for hire of machine for the year.

Possible treatments

Some alternative versions of the accounts are given in Table 10.5. They are:

(A) *Ordinary accounts.* (Column (1)).

(B) *Accounts with timelag error corrected (but without asset revaluation).* In column (2), cost is adjusted with the general index, i.e., income is found by the real-capital sub-concept.

Column (3) uses the same income sub-concept as (2), but cost is adjusted with the special index, and the resulting £5 real gain is credited.

In column (4), income is found by the physical sub-concept, i.e., cost is adjusted with the special index but the £5 is not credited.

(C) *Stabilized accounts, in end-£s.* After the timelag error on cost has been cured under account 2, the corrected accounts can be stabilized in various ways. All historical figures can be raised with the general index; column (2) then turns into column (5). Further, the depreciating asset can be raised with the special index; column (3) then turns into (6), and (4) into (7):

TABLE 10.5
VARIOUS FORMS OF PRICE-LEVEL ADJUSTMENT FOR A DEPRECIATING ASSET

Type of capital maintained	A. Ordinary accounts (1) £	B. Correction of timelag error			C. Full stabilization closing £		
		Real (2) £	Real (current cost shown) (3) £	Physical (4) £	(2) adjusted (5) end-£	(3) adjusted (6) end-£	(4) adjusted (7) end-£
Income statement							
Depreciation. Historical	100	100	100	100			
Adjusting charge		10	15	15			
Total charge	100	110	115	115	*as*	*as*	*as*
Rent	550	550	550	550	*(2)*	*(3)*	*(4)*
Current operating profit			435				
Realized real appreciation		115 − 110 5					
Profit	450	440	440	435	440	440	435
Balance sheet							
Asset—Cost (new)	1000	Details as in (1)			1100	1150	*as*
Less Depreciation	100				110	115	*(6)*
	900				990	1035	
Cash	550				550	550	
	1450				1540	1585	1585
Capital	1000	1000	1000	1000	1100	1100	1100
Allowance—inflation		10	10				
—replacement cost				15			5
Profit—realized	450	440	440	435	440	440	435
—unrealized						45	45
	1450	1450	1450	1450	1540	1585	1585

Workings

The most methodical and safe way in which to work out the adjusted figures is probably to use a ledger with an extra column for stabilized figures. Table 10.6 suggests how this could be done.

Accounts (3a), (3b), and (4a) are needed only if the machine's real change in value is recognized, i.e., the remaining accounts are adequate for correction and stabilization with the general index alone:

TABLE 10.6

WORKINGS FOR TABLE 10.5 IN LEDGER FORM

Dr.	Stabilized end–£	Ordinary £				Stabilized end–£	Ordinary £ Cr.
(1)			*Capital*				
			Opening balance	b/d		*1100*	1000
(2)			*Profit and Loss*				
Depreciation (4)	*110*	100	Rent			*550*	550
Depreciation addition			Real realized gain	(3b)		*5*	5
inflation (4a)		10					
real (4a)	*5*	5					
Profit c/d	*440*	440					
	555	555				*555*	555
			Profit	b/d		*440*	440
(3)			*Machine (historical cost)*				
Opening balance	*1100*	1000					
(3a)			*Machine (addition to value)*				
Gain on revaluation							
inflation		100					
real	*50*	50					
(3b)	*50*	150					
(3c)			*Gain on revaluation of machine*				
Inflation allowance (6)		10	Machine (addition)				
Profit and loss (gain *realized*) (2)	*5*	5	inflation				100
			real			*50*	50
Balance c/d	*45*	135					
	50	150	(3a)			*50*	150
			Balance	b/d		*45*	135
(4)			*Cumulative depreciation (historical)*				
			Profit and loss	(2)		*110*	100
(4a)			*Cumulative depreciation (addition, to write of the addition to asset)*				
			Profit and loss	(2)		*5*	15
(5)			*Cash*				
Closing balance c/d	*550*	550					
(6) (4)			*Inflation allowance*				
			Gain on revaluation	(3b)			10

References

1. Depreciation and price change is discussed at length in the essays by W. A. Paton, S. Davidson, D. Solomons, Carman C. Blough, Paul Grady, and George Terborgh, in *Studies in Accounting Theory*, (eds.) W. T. Baxter and S. Davidson, Sweet & Maxwell; Irvin, 1962.

2. This depreciation problem, like many others, can be fully understood only by using compound interest, as in the 'annuity method' of writing down assets. The 'interest' of such methods would seem to be the earnings of the secondary assets, i.e., the secondary (not primary) earnings rate gives the rate for

the depreciation formulae. Secondary earnings swollen by real appreciation are tantamount to a higher interest rate. A rise in the rate alters the *yearly incidence* of depreciation charges but not the *total* to be accumulated over the asset's life (i.e., makes DD' in Fig. 13.5 start lower and end higher, but does not change the total area DD'F). See W. T. Baxter and N. Carrier, 'Depreciation, Replacement Price, and Cost-of-Capital', *Journal of Accounting Research*, Spring 1971.

3. A comparable form has been adopted by several American companies. Thus, the Iowa–Illinois Gas and Electric Company began in 1958 to use similar entries (save that they are based on a special index, for public utility plant). The extra credit in the balance sheet (under the heading 'Shareholders' Equity' ran 'Capital maintained by recovery of fair value depreciation'; and the extra charge in the income statement is described as 'Fair value'. A note sets out the principles, citing the Iowa legal decision that authorizes the charge. The auditors' certificate contains the words: 'Although generally accepted accounting principles presently provide that depreciation shall be based upon cost, it is our opinion that these principles should be changed with respect to depreciation to recognize increased price levels. We approve of the practice adopted by the company, since it results, in our opinion, in a fairer statement of income than that resulting from the application of generally accepted accounting opinions.' A second income account gives the results on the historical-cost basis.

4. To judge from general-index adjustments for the period 1949–57. See W. T. Baxter, 'Inflation and the Accounts of Steel Companies', *Accountancy*, May and June 1959.

5. See also H. Norris, 'Depreciation Allocations in Relation to Financial Capital, Real Capital and Productive Capacity', *Accounting Research*, July 1949; A. R. Prest, 'National Income of the United Kingdom', *Economic Journal*, March 1948. W. J. Trumbull, 'Price Level Depreciation and Replacement Cost', *Accounting Review*, January 1958, has a neat demonstration of what happens if depreciation provisions are invested in other depreciating assets.

6. Meticulous accounting (an elaboration of the annuity method) could and would allow for real-value change in both the primary and secondary assets, e.g., by revaluing the primary asset each year, and redistributing the yearly depreciation charges (without changing their total). See Baxter and Carrier, *op. cit.*

7. An engaging bit of special pleading runs:
Have you heard about the $12,000 lathe which took more than a million dollars to replace? In 1942, Thompson Products Co., Inc., Cleveland, Ohio, bought a new lathe. The machine cost $12,000. Under Federal tax laws the cost could be depreciated over a 14-year period. So, last year when the lathe had to be replaced, Thompson had $12,000 set aside, plus an additional $1,000 which was the resale value of the old lathe. However, the same model lathe that had sold for $12,000 in 1942 was selling now for $35,000, and a new model with attachments to meet advanced needs of the industry cost $67,000. But there was only $13,000 available to buy the $67,000 machine. The additional $54,000 had to come from another source: profits. But in order to clear the $54,000 Thompson had to make a $114,000 profit before taxes; in order to make that much profit, the company had to sell more than $1,125,000 of its products. In short, it took sales of well over a million dollars before the company could replace one machine so three Thompson employees— one on each shift—would still have jobs.

8. E. D. Domar, 'The Case for Accelerated Depreciation', *Quarterly Journal of Economics*, February 1953; and 'Depreciation, Replacement and Growth', *Economic Journal*, March 1953. Page 11 of the latter suggests that the straight-line depreciation covers replacement if average life is 30 years and the growth rate is 3 per cent (the usual estimates for the American economy), provided the inflation rate does not go much above 4 per cent.

9. A comment quoted in E. Cary Brown, *Depreciation Adjustments for Price Changes*, Harvard School of Business Administration, 1952, p. 54—a book that discusses the whole subject very fully.

10. *Annual Report*, 1947. A somewhat similar increase in the depreciation charge was made by du Pont, with a similar outcome.

11. R. M. Bird, 'Depreciation Allowances and Counter-cyclical Policy', *Canadian Tax Journal*, May–June and July–August 1963.

12. For British figures, see *National Income Blue Book*, estimates for consumption of fixed capital by companies, and the tax depreciation allowances (in the notes).

13. Arthur Andersen & Co., *Memorandum on Price-Level Depreciation*, Chicago, 1959.

11. The timelag error. E. The accountant's contribution to the trade cycle

The timelag error not only upsets individual firms, but also may have broader social consequences, notably through its possible influence on the trade cycle.[1] When prices rise, it overstates the profits of innumerable firms; when prices fall, it understates them. Such mass alternations seem likely to have a feedback effect on the cycle, and to aggravate its ups and downs. If this is true, the accountant must bear some of the blame for the major social ills of boom and slump—a rhythm that was of great importance at least prior to 1939, and may well reassert itself at some future time.

Expectations and activity

The case against him assumes that economic activity is influenced by mental attitudes, and that the latter are influenced by reported profits. The cumulative effect of countless profit figures on attitudes (the argument runs) must be great: not only is each manager made to feel more bold or cautious by the swings in his own firm's results, but the general investor also reacts to the reports from his companies (particularly if profit swings are backed up by dividend changes). The direct stimulus of the company reports will be reinforced by echoes elsewhere, for instance, in stock-brokers' circulars and the financial columns of newspapers: people of all ranks may well decide to spend less or more after seeing headlines that shriek of dramatic loss or profit.

The main way in which such mental attitudes could affect activity is generally supposed to be via investment. Cheerful profits give a rosy tinge to expectations, and thus tempt businessmen to expand. Gloomy figures make them pessimistic and unventuresome. Their hopes and fears may be shared by bankers, etc., and so will tend to influence credit. The error may also affect activity by changing the pattern of saving. During booms, exaggerated profit figures make management less tough with unions and shareholders, and these more importunate towards management. Thus, potential savings of companies are distributed. The recipients are unlikely to save all this extra income, and so total saving sinks, and consumption demand rises. The accountant's error may at such times increase demand in a second way: because he underestimates the firm's costs, its sales prices may be too low (on the assumption that many prices are based on cost-plus, and thus lag behind input prices), and then will not ration demand adequately.

Counter-arguments on the error

There are, however, important counter-arguments. They have been marshalled forcefully by Professor Delmas D. Ray.[2] He is unimpressed by the view that the error affects investment. Relying largely on surveys of the reasons given by businessmen for their decisions, he suggests that technological needs for improved plant are a main cause of investment; and that, in cases where such needs are not predominant, the sales outlook rather than profit is what counts. He also reminds us that large firms may be less influenced by a wish to maximize profits than was formerly supposed; and that, even if businessmen want to invest more, their cash position puts a ceiling on their programmes. He adds that knowledge of the accounting error is now widespread and must tend to offset its impact, while high tax payments (based on the error) damp down the elation of the boom. Nor does he accept all the arguments about saving and consumption. Wages (he maintains) are raised mainly because of factors other than reported profits, e.g., cost of living; dividends are limited by the cash balance, and for the most part go to a wealthy few whose consumption will not be changed much; the influence of cost-plus is weakening, and anyway its 'cost' is increasingly current rather than historical.

Such criticisms are weighty. But they do not (in my view) carry full conviction. For instance, it is doubtless true that many accountants and businessmen know in a general way that the error exists, but probably few of them could say how big it is in their own firm and what are its results on the profit, etc. In addition, the accounts are written and authenticated, whereas one's reservations are mental and untested. The analysts who write for financial journals have so far failed signally to distinguish between uncorrected profits and corrected profits. Total income from private firms is roughly as big as that from incorporated firms, so presumably erroneous figures can have a considerable influence through unsophisticated owner-managers if not through directors and wealthy shareholders. Again, the size of a firm's cash balance admittedly has some restraining effect on investment and dividends; but inflated profits make it easy to raise more money by new issues and bank loans (and the small investor or local banker is most unlikely to question the accountant's golden figures). Tax may indeed diminish the error's effects. But tax is not assessed at 100 per cent; some part of a profit increase remains to cheer the appropriation account. Further, the date at which tax is paid may seem remote: under British tax law, a spurt in profit is unlikely to raise tax payments until a year or more has passed, and so there is a long period before the cash is drained off.

However, the essence of the matter is that so much depends on expectations, and no one (not even the decision-maker himself, in his most self-analytical mood) can measure the various influences that colour expectations. A defender of accounting may conceivably be right in saying that the error has scant effect. But the opposite view seems more plausible. Surely the businessman's outlook cannot but respond to marked changes in his profit figures—particularly when these synchronize with similar changes in the figures of most other firms (sometimes accentuated by high gearing), in dividend payments, and in quotations for company securities. It is hard to believe that such reiterated changes in so many quarters do not affect his views of the future and his willingness to shoulder risk.

Our understanding of this matter, and of the error's impact on a given firm as prices go up and down, will be helped if we now look at the *timing* of the error at various stages in the cycle.

Timing of the depreciation error

Let us take depreciation first. The error—see p. 56—is $C\left(\dfrac{s}{c} - 1\right)$, where C is the historical charge for input, and the general index is c at acquisition date and s at sale date. With depreciation, C is the slice of original cost that is written off each year. By the straight-line method, it is a constant quantity in all years of the asset's life; and even if other methods are used, the total (for a mature firm with many machines, etc.) tends to be fairly constant. c is also a constant throughout the asset's life. But s varies each year, since it represents the price level at which output is sold during that year, i.e., it is the average of the price indices at the dates of all sale transactions, weighted by their sizes. For the whole firm, $C\left(\dfrac{s}{c} - 1\right)$ thus tends strongly to move up and down with prices.

In Fig. 11.1a, we assume that plant is bought at the start of year 1, when prices have just reached the median level of an imaginary cycle, and the index stands at, say, 100. Their course is then assumed to follow the unbroken curve AB. The annual depreciation charge in accounts, being based on original cost, will follow the straight line CD. The vertical distance between AB and CD

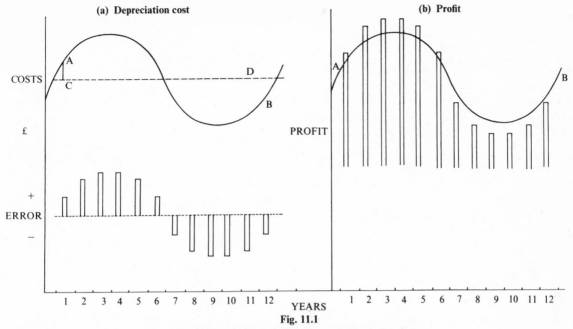

Fig. 11.1

Annual depreciation charge and error over the trade cycle

Source: *Economica*

suggests the error's size in each of the years. When s exceeds 100 (as in the years till the end of year 6), historical cost is less than its equivalent in terms of current £s—for instance, at the middle of year 1, by AC; accordingly the accounts now understate costs and overstate profit. The error's contribution to the profit figures for each year may perhaps be best suggested by the height of the pillars at the foot of the diagram. Those pillars which rise above zero indicate an increase in the accounting profits; such an increase is found during all years with prices above 100. In years 7 to 12, prices are below 100, and the error depresses low profits still further. The positive and negative errors will—in these improbably symmetrical conditions—cancel out exactly over the whole cycle.

We can speak of the error's effect on costs with some certainty. However, one must be much more cautious in describing its size relative to profits; this will depend on factors that vary greatly from firm to firm. Depreciation cost can be large or small compared with profit. Thus, the error will be negligible where a firm owns little plant, but substantial in for example an electric power undertaking. Again, the profits of the given firm may not move in proportion to price changes. But perhaps we

are not oversimplifying too grossly if we picture corrected profits (i.e., profits cured of the timelag error) as following some such cyclical pattern as the curve AB in Fig. 11.1b, while the uncorrected profits have an accentuated rhythm rather like that of the pillars. The error extends the pillars in good years, and cuts them short in bad years.

Had the plant not been bought at the mid-point of price movements, the error's pattern in Fig. 11.1a would not be symmetrical about CD, and the positive and negative errors would be less likely to cancel over the years. In Fig. 11.2, for instance, prices again follow the curve AB. Plant is bought at the peak price of year 3; and therefore c will never fall below s. In the other years of the cycle, cost will always be overstated, and accounting profit will in consequence always be less than corrected profit. Here the firm tends to set aside more secondary assets than will be needed for replacing the plant at anything less than peak prices (if the price of this asset moves in much the same way as the general index), and so expands its real capital unwittingly. At the other extreme, where plant is bought at the nadir, accounting profit will tend in all years to be swollen because of the skimpy depreciation policy, and the firm may

109

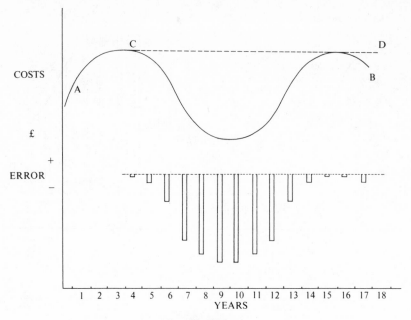

Fig. 11.2
Depreciation and error where plant is bought at price peak

Source: *Economica*

have to borrow extra funds at replacement day. In short, whatever the time of purchase, the error fluctuates in direct response to the price cycle and accentuates the rhythm of uncorrected profits.

If prices become stable (at any level other than that of purchase date), the error will persist but will no longer fluctuate. Suppose, for instance, that prices rise from year 0 (purchase date of an asset) to year 8, and then become steady, i.e., follow the curve AB in Fig. 11.3. As the pillars show, the error rises too, and then becomes stable in years 8 to 11. (It is odd that the agitation for tax concessions to offset the error dies down when a price rise is checked. A substantial depreciation error can persist thereafter, as the diagram indicates; firms with old plants have still as strong a case as ever for tax concessions.) But when the asset's life ends (year 11), the understated cost goes too. Probably the asset will now be replaced at increased prices, so that depreciation cost tends to rise abruptly (perhaps like ED). At any rate, the error disappears. The process of asset renewal must always limit the size of the error, and make its explanation less simple.

After allowing for all such qualifications, however, it seems probable that movements of the depreciation error will approximately coincide, in timing and pattern, with movements in prices and perhaps in corrected profits. Thus, the error is likely to serve the cycle as a prompt and often powerful ally by intensifying the prevailing mood.

Timing of the cost-of-goods-sold error

How does $C\left(\dfrac{s}{c} - 1\right)$ behave when we pass from

plant to goods? For merchants, etc., C (the historical cost-of-goods sold) tends to be a big part of the year's costs—far bigger than depreciation. s is again the cost index at the weighted average date of the year's sale transactions—say, mid-year. c is the cost index at the weighted average date of the year's purchases. Because goods have normally a quick turnover (compared with machines), c here tends to keep changing—i.e., it is far more volatile than when it relates to depreciation, and more likely to follow hard on the heels of s. The cost-of-

110

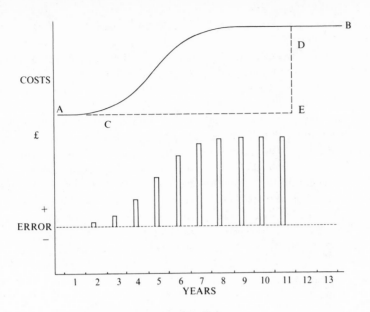

Fig. 11.3
The error on yearly depreciation cost after prices become stable

Source: *Economica*

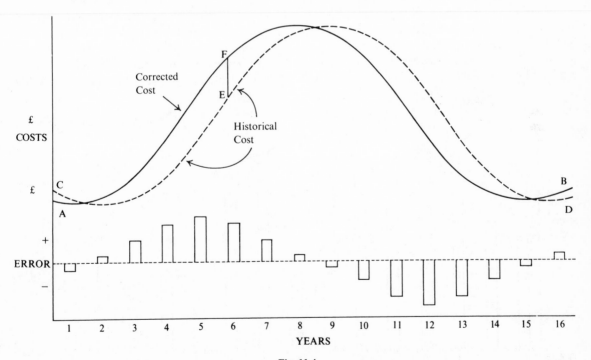

Fig. 11.4
Cost of goods sold and error over a cycle

Source: *Economica*

goods-sold error may thus have a pattern quite different from the depreciation error.

In Fig. 11.4, the broken curve CD represents the Fifo historical charges for cost-of-goods-sold, in a firm where the physical flow of goods is constant; its rise and fall is thus due solely to price change. General-index correction of the cost at any point E gives some new point, say F (above E when the index has risen during the turnover time). If general prices follow much the same rhythm as the special prices of goods, the curve for corrected cost will run somewhat like AFB, i.e., it can be got by shifting CD to the left by the space of the turnover time. The error is the vertical distance between the two curves (e.g., in year 6, EF). The total contribution by the error to each year's accounting profit may again be shown by the heights of the pillars at the foot of the diagram.

In years of rising prices, $C\left(\dfrac{s}{c} - 1\right)$ is positive, and

so the error restrains accounting cost and thereby lifts accounting profit. But, in contrast to the depreciation error, the cost-of-goods-sold error shrinks to *nil* soon after prices cease to rise (in half the turnover period), e.g., in the months about the end of year 8; and thereafter, on the downgrade, it becomes negative.

The error can move from its positive to its negative extremes either slowly or abruptly, according to the shape of the price curve. (With the depreciation error, this transition lasts from peak to trough.) The curve in Fig. 11.4 rises at its fastest in year 5, thereafter rises at a decelerating pace, and culminates in a gently rounded peak; corresponding movements take place on the downgrade. With such a 'sine-shaped' curve, the error's upward trend is reversed (in year 6) well before the peak is reached, at the point where AB and CD cease to run parallel and start to converge; and the new trend lasts till the curves are once more parallel (year 12).[3] When the price curve has a less rounded peak and trough than in our example, the trend of the error will change more steeply.

Thus, the cost-of-goods-sold error seems likely to have earlier and more dramatic tendencies than the depreciation error. But whether it in fact has noteworthy effects will depend on both the price curve and the kind of business (e.g., the impact on costs is more likely to be big if the turnover period is long, and material costs form a large part of total costs). Given suitable circumstances, accounting profit might be distorted as in Fig. 11.5. Here we assume the course of the price-index (shown as the unbroken curve AB) and the error to be the same as in Fig. 11.4; we assume also that

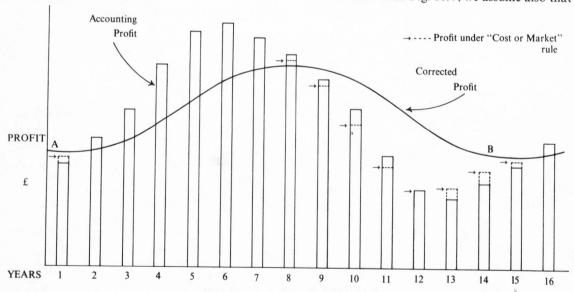

Fig. 11.5
Profit subject to cost-of-goods-sold error—complete cycle

corrected profit follows much the same pattern as the price index. The height of the pillar for, say, year 6 shows the corrected profit for 6 (from the base up to the line AB) and then the error (from AB upwards—corresponding to the distance EF in Fig. 11.4. The broken lines at the top of pillars 8 to 15 will be explained later. In this example, accounting profit starts to wane in year 7, although the peak in prices and profits is not reached until the middle of year 8. The circumstances needed to bring about this premature fall are:

(1) as the summit draws near, prices must rise at a decelerating pace; and
(2) the error must be large relative to profit, so that the decline in the error outweighs the rise in corrected profit (see years 7 and 8).

Condition 1, it seems reasonable to think, will obtain not infrequently. Condition 2 depends on factors such as the length of the turnover; however, even if these are too weak to make accounting profit fall, they may damp its upward trend.

On the down-grade of prices, our example reflects the same forces. In years 14 and 15, because prices are falling at a decelerating rate, the negative error moves so fast to zero that it raises accounting profit (though the nadir of prices and correct profits is not reached till the mid-point of year 15).

If our diagram correctly shows a tendency found in a fairly large number of firms, then surely the error should play a bigger part than it has done hitherto in discussions of the trade cycle. Just as the 'accelerator'[4] is said to alter the demand for capital goods before general activity reaches its turning-points—perhaps thereby causing the general crisis or the recovery—so accounting may alter mental attitudes prematurely, and thus contribute to changes in activity.

It is not hard to find flaws in the diagram in Fig. 11.5. In real life, the pattern of profits will doubtless not correspond closely to its curves. One reason is that firms are unlikely to carry constant physical stocks throughout the cycle. If stocks are reduced in the slump, the error will also dwindle at that stage,[5] i.e., will do less to encourage recovery than it did to bring about the fall. Another factor that may vary physically is sales. If, as seems likely, these grow in the boom and fall in the slump, they will probably give a bias to

corrected profit; but the error would not seem to be affected thereby (save by any consequential changes in physical stock). Again, sale prices may not be adjusted promptly when general prices change; in particular, they may lag because the firm fixes them at historical cost plus a constant mark-up—a policy likely to cause further changes in customers' demand, and so in physical volume of sales. Thus, one cannot (till many empirical studies have been made) treat any abstract diagram as an accurate photo of profit patterns. The case against conventional accounting is not so clear as Fig. 11.5 suggests.

However, though we cannot say that accounting profit always anticipates the general trend of the cycle, we can hardly avoid the conclusion that accounting cost may have a most unfortunate influence at crucial points in the cycle. Just when confidence begins to waver, delayed high charges for goods find their way into the accounts; the error has its least desirable effect at the worst possible moment.

Coma and the error

This chapter has so far supposed that closing stock is valued at historical cost (found on first-in-first-out assumptions), i.e., at the price level of a date preceding the end of the business year (on average, by half the turnover period). In fact, this may not be true on the down-grade of prices. For then the overriding rule of 'Cost or Market, whichever is the lower' is often applied. The precise interpretation of this cautious formula varies from firm to firm (see p. 88), but its general effect must on the downgrade be to depress stock values to below their historical cost.

The rule leaves our argument unchanged so far as the up-grade of prices goes. But in the year during which prices start to fall, market value is substituted in the income account for the (higher) cost value of closing stock, though opening stock is—somewhat inconsistently—still shown at cost. Thus, a smaller sum is deducted from the charges, and accounting cost is increased; in effect, the cost-of-goods-sold is loaded with both the usual error for the year, and a bit of next year's error. Under this double assault, profit may fall abruptly. In

Fig. 11.5, the decrease is suggested by the broken line cutting off the top of the profit column for year 8.

In subsequent years of the down-grade, both opening and closing stocks are valued at market. This pessimism at both ends of the income account puts a brake on the working of the rule. The net effect of the rule seems to be substantially as follows (assuming the physical quantity of stock does not change violently, and the price curve is free from kinks). Profit is reduced so long as the price curve is falling at an accelerating pace (years 8 to 11 in Fig. 11.5). If the pace becomes constant, for the space of an accounting year plus the preceding months during which opening stock is bought, profit is the same as if the rule did not exist (year 12). If prices fall at a decelerating pace (years 13 and 14), the rule actually makes accounting profit less conservative,[6] and so speeds up the illusion of recovery—and perhaps the actual recovery too. In the last year of the operation of the rule, closing stock reverts to cost, but opening stock stays at market, and so still keeps down the cost-of-goods-sold, and raises accounting profit.

There are strong arguments for valuing stocks at end-of-year prices, i.e., for recognizing unrealized loss (as with Coma) or gain, provided the timelag error is cured by some such method as that outlined in Table 9.7. Without such correction, Coma's effect is to reinforce the error on the down-grade and to make accounting profit respond more skittishly then to each change in price trends. No doubt, Coma does sometimes help a given firm (by making managers more cautious and watchful of liquid resources); but its social consequences may well have been bad.

Conclusions

To sum up. Because of the error, accounting profits overpaint the state of trade. The depreciation error tends to make the high-price years (both before and after the peak) look better, and the low-price years look worse. The stock error lifts profits in all years when prices are rising, and depresses profit throughout the down-grade; it seems likely to exaggerate the rate of change in the trend of correct profit, and may on occasion produce falling profit figures before the price rise has ended, and rising figures before recovery has begun.[7]

It is reasonable to conclude that an error so widespread and so emphatic in its rhythm must indeed influence business sentiment. It seems particularly likely to strengthen the factors that link the rate of price change with (after a timelag) investment and demand; it may well act in a way analogous to the accelerator. If this is so, the error must make the economy less stable.[8]

References

1. The trade-cycle effects have been explored, in particular, by K. Lacey: see, for example, his *Profit Measurement and Price Changes*, Pitman, 1952. They are discussed in G. Haberler, *Prosperity and Depression*, Columbia University Press, 1941, pp. 49–50; Erich Schiff, *Kapitalbildung und Kapitalaufzehrung im Konjunkturverlauf*, Wiener Institut für Wirtschafts und Konjunkturforschung, 1933, pp. 113–34; and Delmas D. Ray: *Accounting and Business Fluctuations*, University of Florida Press, 1960.

2. Ray, *op. cit.*

3. But probably a sine-shaped curve is more pleasing to the eye than true to the facts—Arthur F. Burns and Wesley C. Mitchell, *Measuring Business Cycles*, National Bureau of Economic Research, 1946, p. 251.

4. The accelerator principle is that a given percentage change in the output of consumer goods leads to a larger percentage change in the output of the capital equipment needed to make them.

5. In general, stocks appear to have a cycle very like the sales cycle, but with a narrower amplitude and a lag of some months (the number of months varying with different types of stock)—M. Abramovitz, *Inventories and Business Cycles*, National Bureau of Economic Research, 1950, pp. 93–6 and 144–5.

6. Let E and B be the physical quantities of stock-at-end and stock-at-beginning in an income account for year n (when prices are falling). Let c_n and c_{n-1} be the prices at which stock-at-end and stock-at-beginning are valued at cost, and m_n and m_{n-1} at market. Then the inclusion of stocks in an income account changes profit by:

If stocks are valued at cost $Ec_n - Bc_{n-1}$

If stocks are valued at market $Em_n - Bm_{n-1}$

So switching from cost to market changes profit by $E(c_n - m_n) - B(c_{n-1} - m_{n-1})$.

Suppose that physical stock is constant. Then E and B are equal: therefore the rule depresses profit if $(c_n - m_n)$ exceeds $(c_{n-1} - m_{n-1})$, i.e., if prices are falling at an accelerating pace; the rule raises profit if $(c_n - m_n)$ is less than $(c_{n-1} - m_{n-1})$; and it has no effect when $(c_n - m_n)$ equals $(c_{n-1} - m_{n-1})$.

If E and B are not equal, the pattern is modified. For example, if physical stocks sink during a depression and so E is less than B, the switch from cost to market depresses profit less than if stocks are constant; the broken lines in Fig. 11.5 become higher in all years. But the modification seems to be slight unless physical stock changes to a remarkable degree.

7. Where accounts include both depreciating assets and stocks, the composite pattern of the errors will probably look rather like the pillars in Fig. 11.4, but the depreciation error will push each pillar somewhat to the right (so that the highest error is nearer to, but still comes before, the price peak); the depreciation error will also give the accounting-cost curve a greater amplitude than the replacement-cost curve.

8. See A. W. Phillips, 'Stabilisation Policy in a Closed Economy', *Economic Journal*, June 1954, pp. 311–4 for a mathematical demonstration that, when one component of demand depends on the rate of change of prices, the system is made less stable. The accounting error is presumably one of the reasons for such dependence.

Diagrams are taken from W. T. Baxter, 'The Accountants' Contribution to the Trade Cycle', *Economica*, 1955, p. 99.

12. Asset revaluation

Price change is apt to prompt demands for up-to-date values in the balance sheet (and the mild reform of general index adjustment is not likely to still these demands). So we are now brought face to face with all the problems of whether and how to revalue the assets and liabilities. Such revaluation may be limited to certain items, or cover almost the whole balance sheet. It may be treated as a once-and-for-all step, or as a periodic routine. It may or may not be part of the more general reforms discussed earlier, e.g., full stabilization. It may or may not be part of the formal process of measuring income—though, where it is not, any gain or loss on revaluation must tend to give much the same impression as figures that are labelled income; and therefore the overtones of income measurement always seem relevant.

A discussion of revaluation must consider the aims of revaluation, not only to decide whether revaluation is worth while, but also because the aims influence the choice of methods.

The firm's value *versus* the sum of the net asset values

A preliminary point deserves attention. Sometimes one must value the firm as a whole (e.g., to find a suitable price for a takeover bid). Then one should normally use the *ex-ante* concept of p. 17, i.e., try to estimate the present value of the future cash flow (of dividends, etc.) that an owner can expect from the firm. The accounting statement that would help the valuer might here be the firm's cash budget rather than its balance sheet. Usually the figures of the latter play little direct part in the *ex-ante* calculation (particularly now that the 'super-profits' or 'goodwill' method of valuing has

fallen from grace). Certainly the value of the whole firm is unlikely to be the same as the net total of assets less liabilities on the balance sheet. Thus, the former must tend to fluctuate, like share prices, with every change in both the prospects of the firm and general market sentiment.

Where the prospects are reasonably good, one usually expects the price of the whole to exceed the sum of the net assets. For instance, one can imagine a valuer deciding that the expected flow of dividends and final capital proceeds is worth £100 000, when the net assets add up to only £80 000. Does the £20 000 gap between the two figures necessarily mean that the separate asset values have been estimated wrongly, or that some shadowy £20 000 asset has been omitted from the list, or that the separate values are useless? I think the answer to all three questions is no. If two values are calculated by different concepts, a gap is entirely proper. Even if methods of valuing each asset are reformed and refined out of all recognition, some gap should still persist.

What good are asset values?

A more pertinent question is whether, if the balance sheet contributes so little to the fundamental *ex-ante* calculation, revaluation of the assets is worthwhile—and perhaps even whether the balance sheet is worth publishing. A wise man will answer rather hesitantly. But it seems not unreasonable to hold that the balance sheet, with all its faults, provides a kind of information that the human mind still needs. The *ex-ante* calculation gives one kind of picture; a list of the existing resources gives another; both can be helpful. Experience tells us, for instance, that the firm normally must have physical resources to generate its future receipts; therefore, information about these resources is of interest. We have learned, too, that the firm needs liquid assets if it is to stay solvent; therefore, to assess the liquid position, we want to see the current sections of the balance sheet. Even when an *ex-ante* valuation is being made, the asset values are useful at least as background evidence of the size and certainty of the cash-flow figures— evidence that may, on occasion, make the valuer trim his estimate of these figures (e.g., if liquid assets exceed the firm's likely need, they may perhaps be used to raise dividends).

Imperfect information is often better than no information. Certainly we should recognize all the imperfections of the balance sheet: but to dismiss it as worthless seems too clever by half.

Pros and cons

The case for revaluation

People turn to the balance sheet for an impression of the firm's general nature, size, and ownership structure; they look to it also for help with more detailed problems of asset strength, liquidity, etc. Thus, the argument for updating the balance sheet is that managers, investors, etc., rely on it when making important judgements, and are misled if it fails to reflect the current facts.[1] So far as possible, a balance sheet ought to be a realistic model of the firm. But historical costs, even when the general index rests stable, must sooner or later cease to indicate current values. Over the years, the special prices of some assets are likely to rise, and those of others to fall. If, in addition, general prices move as far and fast as has been normal since 1914, the gap between historical cost and current value may become much bigger. Then a conventional balance sheet of all save the newest firms no longer is a realistic photograph.

The balance sheet may help with at least five areas of activity:

Investment in shares. Decisions on investment in a company's securities can be influenced by the values of its assets. To be sure, the overriding consideration is the estimate of future cash benefits (dividends and final proceeds); the stock exchange price of a share may be remote from the 'asset value per share'. But asset values are useful secondary evidence: normally they give at least some notion of the earnings potential, the nature and efficiency of the asset structure, and whether there will be any break-up receipts if things go wrong. As one company chairman has put it: 'True, net assets do not produce profits any more than mere possession of the tools automatically enables a man to exercise a craft. But a company which possesses enough good "tools" in the form of assets can recover more quickly from bad times and expand even further in good times than concerns with more limited resources.'[2] Further, money values are the only common denominator by which one can compare or appreciate diverse lists of 'tools'. It is easy to sneer at journalistic phrases like 'Fire at £10 million factory', but the words may convey a useful impression. Value totals will inevitably be used to compare the size of different companies, etc., and to find the 'asset cover' for loan or preference capital. Even the man who speaks slightingly of the importance of the separate assets would probably think several times before investing in a company with an attractive earnings yield but unusual asset values.

The balance sheet enables an analyst to use ratios (e.g., of current assets to current liabilities) and turnover rates (e.g., of stock). In particular, many investors and managers treat ratios of *earnings to capital employed* as useful guides. Again, a person studying the efficiency of a whole sector of the economy (industry X *versus* industry Y, big *versus* small firms, foreign subsidiaries *versus* home-controlled companies, and so on) often seeks help from these ratios. Possibly their usefulness is overrated.[3] But without asset revaluation, they must inevitably lose whatever virtue they may otherwise possess. They will then lead to false comparisons between companies whose assets vary in age and type. They will tend during inflation to show a company with old assets in too good a light (especially if the timelag error is large). Indeed, such a company's dividends and earnings may sink to a level that is absurdly low in relation to the current values of the assets, and yet is high in relation to book-values. Then shareholders and the financial press are lulled; and even the managers themselves may believe that they are doing a sound job, and can rest on their oars. The seemingly high return on capital may prompt trade unions to demand a larger share of such easy money.

Takeovers and proxy battles are relevant here, because they give such powerful evidence of the extent to which historical figures deceive. The big takeovers of the 'fifties could hardly have evoked such shocked headlines if investors had not been utterly ignorant of the values at stake. It is surely wrong that the high current value of assets should come as a surprise to their owners and managers; that, deceived perhaps by a seemingly adequate ratio of earnings to assets, managers should for years allow the performance of their firm to lag behind its full potential, to the detriment of both shareholders and consumers; and that shareholders who happen to sell just before the bid should get a price much lower than that obtaining afterwards. Doubtless some of the struggles have tinges of sharp practice, and are harsh to staff. In general, however, we can hardly object to the transfer of assets from less to more fruitful uses.

Nowadays, the opposite fault of overvaluation is not often met. But there have been times, notably during the depression of the 'thirties, when it was a source of complaint in the USA. New share issues (the allegation ran) could be floated on the strength of fixed assets valued at a cost price that was excessive compared with current value.[4]

Thus, a balance sheet based on historical cost fails to give important information to actual and potential shareholders, to the analysts[5] who advise them, and to managers. Their decisions will therefore tend to be less sound than if current values were used. This harms us collectively as well as individually; because we lack clearer pictures of the relative prowess of different firms, industries, and regions, the nation's flow of new capital may be misdirected.

Creditor protection. Creditors constitute another kind of 'investors'. A traditional aim of the balance sheet has been to tell them about the firm's ability to meet their claims, i.e., how far the claims are covered by the value of the assets. Plainly, up-to-date figures meet this aim better than old ones.

Or, looking at the matter from the firm's standpoint, one can say that sound current values will help to obtain longer credit and fresh loans.

In insurance accounts, policy-holders with pending claims deserve much the same treatment as creditors. The current value of the assets is again important, and state regulations should insist on it being shown.

Managers appraisal of progress and new projects. The task of managers is made harder by lack of current values. Without these, it is hard to size up the past profitability of ventures. Where, for instance, a firm owns several divisions, etc., its manager will have trouble in comparing their performances unless their assets are valued in a consistent and up-to-date way. Bad figures may impair the efficiency of many firms—and therefore of the whole economy.

Management accountants, like outside investors, make much use of the *ratio of earnings to capital employed*. This ratio is expected to help alike with internal studies of a given firm[6] and with inter-firm comparisons, with post-mortems and with decisions on future ventures. But old asset values can reduce the ratio to nonsense.

When managers are weighing up proposed new projects, valuation may be important for their decision budgets. Assets to be bought specially for the project will be costed at the price to be paid for them, i.e., their current value. If assets already owned (e.g., stores) are to be devoted to the project, they too should be costed at their current value; their historical cost may be a very poor measure of the sacrifice involved (as most managers quickly realize when prices begin to rise fast). A good manager must treat bygones as bygones, and cost all inputs in current terms; yet, where historical figures persist in the accounts, the bygones tend to creep into even sophisticated budgets.

Insurance. It is hard to believe that insurance cover is kept at the right level if managers have no idea of the current values of assets.

Laxness in the matter of fire insurance brings such obvious perils that one may perhaps be pardoned, where managers profess to have no up-to-date values at their disposal, for feeling some incredulity.

Income measurement. Out-of-date figures in one part of the ledger are apt to lead to out-of-date figures in another; thus low values for plant go hand-in-hand with low charges for depreciation, and so foster the timelag error. And the lack of figures for real appreciation (or loss) on assets robs 'income' of one of its dimensions.

Incidental benefits

The process of revaluing may yield certain incidental benefits. Thus, because it will in some cases require managers to think about the best future role of assets, it will draw attention to the need to replace those that are ageing and obsolete; to consequent problems of finance; and to the possibility of redeveloping assets, or (sometimes very important) of selling them when their market values have risen above the values of their services.

Up-to-date asset values may be particularly useful to firms whose costs are subject to public scrutiny. Where the State buys goods from monopolistic suppliers (e.g., munitions, drugs for the health service, etc.) at agreed prices, such values can help investigators to decide whether the profits are a normal return on capital employed. The same may hold where the state regulates public utilities.

There are sometimes legal, as well as economic, grounds for using current values. In the UK, shares qualify as trustee investments (under the Trustee Investments Act, 1961) if *inter alia* the company has an issued and paid-up capital of at least one million pounds. Some companies below this status-line could with propriety revalue and then issue enough bonus shares to qualify.

Opposition to revaluation

Though the case for revaluation is so strong, the vast majority of firms do not revalue. Thus, the counter-arguments must be strong too. The main ones are: (1) revaluation is troublesome and costly; (2) it opens the door to guesswork and deception; (3) it would displease shareholders when prices fall; and (4) it offends against principle.

Argument 1 cannot be lightly dismissed. Revaluation must bring extra work, some of it by senior staff or expensive consultants. Moreover, it is not likely to be a once-and-for-all affair; price change

is always with us, and so further work will be needed to keep the values up to date. Where the firm and the price change are small, this objection may well be conclusive. Where they are big, it is less so: once we grant that large-scale investment must necessarily lead to absentee ownership, then we must grant also that good communications between firm and owners will be troublesome and costly; the provision of useful statistics for the owners is part of the price to be paid for bigness and remote control. And careful planning can here, as in most other accounting work, point the way to many economies and shortcuts.

Argument 2, that revaluation involves too much guesswork, is also worthy of respect. But accounting is more and more finding that in some areas (notably management decision) figures cannot be both sure and informative. We must give up some sureness if we are to get more information.

Precision and sureness are good things, but they are less so in some contexts than others. Where, for instance, tax assessment depends on an income figure, they are important since they affect the size of cash payments; and therefore a strait-jacket of rigid rules may here be defensible. But does the same apply where the aim is to give readers of a balance sheet a general impression of the assets? Most readers will prefer figures that are helpful though mildly unsure to ones that are misleading but seem precise.

Revaluation admittedly brings a risk of window-dressing and even dishonest manipulation. But this risk can be kept low by the use of suitable checks and new audit methods. Some of these are described in a later chapter.

Argument 2 is not something to be disposed of in a couple of paragraphs. This whole book is in a sense a reply to it—a plea for cautious experiment, with plenty of checks, to see whether current values can be used safely.

Argument 3, that write-downs during slumps would displease shareholders, is less serious. Some companies, notably British investment trusts, already show current values; and under the 'lower-of-cost-or-market' rule, companies dealing in raw materials, etc., must sometimes report heavy falls in stock values. In such cases, the shareholders seem able to take the bad with the good. And probably most investors would agree that topical figures, even when gloomy, serve them better than historical costs.

Argument 4, that revaluation violates principle (of historical cost, conservatism, etc.), has featured in pronouncements by various important accounting bodies. Thanks to the educative power of inflation, it is nowadays being used more sparingly. To my mind, it is far less respectable than the other objections. Our historical cost 'principle' is really not much more than a belated rationalization, thought up by theorists anxious to justify a procedure that in fact just grew from the book-keeper's daily routine. This procedure became widespread because it was well suited to the needs of the times. There seems no good reason why we should not now adapt it to present needs.

The accountant has not in fact applied the historical-cost principle consistently. His 'lower-of-cost-or-market' rule for current assets is a clear breach. On occasion, he may even revalue fixed assets; thus, in a consolidated balance sheet he sometimes deems it sound practice to revalue individual assets of a newly-acquired subsidiary. Some American companies in the volatile 1919–34 era wrote assets up and down freely.[7] Since 1945, many countries that have suffered from severe inflation have for a time used tax rules permitting revaluation (e.g., France and Italy); and these breaches of principle seem to have been welcome and beneficent. If today we knew nothing about accounting, and had to think out a system *ab initio*, is it likely that we should prefer old to new values on grounds of principle? Surely the overriding principle in statistical matters is that the more informative is preferable to the less informative.

How do we revalue?

If we accept that we must revalue the assets and liabilities, we must next consider the best way of doing so. We may, of course, entrust the whole task to an outside appraiser, or change the old figures blindly with an index. But critical users of the accounts will then ask what (if anything) the results mean. If the job is to be done properly, the accountant must give thought to the nature of value, and also to the fundamental rules of accounting;

and then he will soon see how sketchy some of these rules are, even in times of relative price stability.

For most assets, there are several possible values, corresponding to the concept chosen (see p. 17). So a valuer should first explore the principles, and decide which concept to use. Even when he has chosen his concept, however, he can still have trouble in applying it, e.g., in finding the needed figures. Thus, revaluation may not be easy. With physical measurement, one can reasonably suppose that technical skill will sooner or later yield fairly precise figures, and that they will obey familiar principles. With values, this may not hold. Values stem from human wants, and so must be elusive. We should approach our task with limited expectations and some pessimism.

The next few pages explore the principles, and thus try to find a not inadequate concept for revaluing. The rest of the chapter shows how far this can be applied to various types of assets and liabilities. However, depreciating assets are such a big subject that they are left to chapter 13.

The principles

A valuer must choose between concepts

If a biologist were told to find the 'growth' of rats, he might reasonably start by asking whether the most revealing unit of measurement would be one of weight, or length, or something else. For valuation problems, likewise, one should choose the most revealing kind of value (historical, current, etc.) for the given task. So, when a professional appraiser is told to make a valuation, he must first ask what it is for. Unthinking clients are apt to be startled by the question, and even to suspect that it has shady overtones. It need have none. The appraiser is entirely right to use one concept for, say, business assets that are to be sold piece-meal, another if they are to be sold as a going team, a third if the valuation is for fire insurance, and so on. In accounting, the main reason for valuing is of course to find figures for annual reports.

Earlier chapters, in dealing with the different concepts of capital and income, suggested that the user of the figures should choose the concept that most adequately answers his questions—that there is no better test of the concept's 'truth' or 'rightness'. Much the same applies to the valuation of separate assets. An unprejudiced valuer will choose, from the long list of concepts (see chapter 4), the one that gives the best information to the particular user. For accounts, 'best information' is apt to mean the figures that are most helpful for economic decisions.

Difficulties of picking the best value concept

When the values are for use in a balance sheet, the trouble about choosing between the concepts is that the demands of the users of the balance sheet are varied and sometimes vague: it should give them a general picture of the assets' nature, should show the 'size of the tools', should tie in with income measurement, and so on. Moreover, the chosen value should so far as possible be objective, verifiable, and found readily from common transactions. And it should give maximum information not only when each asset is viewed separately but also when the separate figures are summed in a grand total. None of the obvious values stands out clearly as the fittest for such multiple requirements. Obviously the successful candidate in this competition will not be as good as we could wish, and will suit some assets less well than others (e.g., since work-in-progress is remote from market transactions, its link with market prices must be thin). We are here in a no-man's-land between accounting, economics, and appraisal, and cannot expect much help from any of them.

One suggested solution is to show *several* values for each asset, i.e., to issue multiple accounts. There is much to be said for this plan, costly and complicated though it might be. But it would still leave important problems of choice: someone would still have to decide that one set of figures was the best for a given purpose, e.g., the measurement of taxable income.

Individual asset values and their total

These matters can be put rather differently, by saying that the best candidate must meet two tests, the first concerned with any given asset viewed separately, and the second with the total of these separate values.

(a) *Separate assets.* If we accept that an asset should be valued at a current market price, we still have to choose between buying and sale price. The case for either of these candidates is greatly strengthened if the figure has proved its helpfulness for practical purposes within the firm, i.e., forms part of a manager's calculations on the best use of the asset. Some assets often feature in transactions, and so lend themself readily to this requirement. Others are less obliging; thus, most work-in-progress is from its nature unlikely to be bought or sold in any market.

(b) *Sum of the separate asset values.* The sum of the separate values (i.e., the total net assets) should if possible constitute a meaningful figure in its own right. As was pointed out on p. 116, this cannot usually equal the value of the firm as a going-concern; but it could for instance be the likely total proceeds from selling off the assets piecemeal, or the total capital that could justifiably be used to buy an equivalent set of assets piecemeal, e.g., if the firm were to set up another branch of the same size. Otherwise, we can hardly claim that the balance sheet shows the 'size of the tools' in any helpful sense, or treat its yearly increase as income.

Viewed in this light, some 'assets' (notably intangibles such as research) hardly seem to contribute to a meaningful total. As we shall see, this is one of the most awkward problems in accounting.

Sometimes the two tests may point in conflicting ways. Then one must perforce choose between them. On the whole, (b) is perhaps the more telling.

Market price *versus* personal assessments of worthwhileness

In thinking about these things, it is important to distinguish between market price and the figure at which a given person might deem a given transaction to be worth his while. This applies to decisions alike on consumption and production. Thus, when a householder is considering whether to buy an extra pound of sugar, or whether to sell his antique clock, he compares the price with his satisfaction from its ownership (marginal utility) to see whether the transaction would be worth while. When a manager is considering whether to buy a new machine, he compares its price with its likely future contribution (marginal revenue production) by way of higher revenue or lower costs, and so judges whether the purchase is worth while. Every buyer and seller has a private set of values that he contrasts with market value to decide to what extent (if any) he will buy or sell—a matter described at length by textbooks on economics. Where the good, etc., cannot be finely subdivided, a considerable gulf may separate market price and the personal assessment of even the marginal unit. This seems a likely situation with fixed assets. For instance, the village taxi-driver may pay £2000 for his one-and-only taxi because he gauges its contribution at £5000, but may decide not to buy an extra taxi because he gauges its extra contribution at only £1700. He might maximize his profit if he could buy one-and-a-fraction taxis, but their indivisibility makes this impossible; his best plan may be to hire an extra taxi for short periods.

A consumer's estimates of his marginal utility must plainly be highly subjective, and will often lack the crispness of money figures. A manager's estimate of contribution (e.g., in discounted cash-flow budgets for judging the worthwhileness of new equipment) employs money figures, and so may look coldly factual. But here, too, the figures must often be speculative, particularly where the asset will last a long time: though they take the form of money figures (sales of product, mainte-nance costs, etc.), they must depend on very personal and changeable views on dates, quanti-ties, probabilities, discount rates, etc., and so may well have much the same subjective and unsure quality as estimates of utility.

Finding market values

When an appraiser estimates the market value of an asset, he is trying to guess what its price would be if a sale really took place. He is greatly helped if he knows of actual dealings in similar assets. For then he can compare the given asset (which we may call the 'unknown') with a similar asset (the 'known'); and he can ask how far the actual price of the 'known' is a guide to the poten-tial price for the 'unknown'. Thus, to estimate the sale value of a house, he should know the sale prices of similar houses at recent dates.

Various difficulties can beset him. One is that there may be no exactly similar 'known'. When, for instance, a house is to be valued, it may differ somewhat from neighbouring houses in size, design, appeal, etc. Even here, however, the valuer should probably work from the known to the unknown; he must in effect combine several knowns, instead of relying on a single one. He presumably begins by finding the price at which a not-too-unlike house has been sold at a not-too-remote date. Treating this as his starting-point, he next tries to allow suitably for the variances between it and the unknown. If, for example, the unknown differs in area, he may argue that market prices work out at so much per square foot, and use this rate to allow for the variance. If he is valuing unquoted shares, he may find the price of shares in comparable quoted companies, and then adjust this suitably—subtracting something to allow for adverse variances such as the poorer market in the unquoted shares, and adding some-thing if there are favourable variances. But these 'somethings' may not be the subject of clear market dealings, and so may be debatable: thus, the price of a known share may have risen when it got a quotation, but how far was this due to getting the quotation and how far to other new forces? The variances must often be concerned with subtle matters. In particular, how does the market allow for different degrees of risk? And all the knowns will tend to fluctuate quickly and often, with the general tone of the market.

The idea of a known and unknown can often clarify difficult steps in accounting valuation. Suppose, for instance, that unquoted shares are the subject, and there is doubt over the suggested price because the company is highly geared. The sensible procedure must surely be to ask whether the known shares were in companies with comparable gearing, and, if not, how much the variance should be.

A good valuer has a wide knowledge and intui-tive judgement of market prices; even so, his synthetic figures must often be arbitrary and unreliable. When he lacks a clear known, he must peer into markets of his imagination to find a hypothetical price—the sum that might be paid if such an asset were in fact on offer; like the judge who had to value unquoted shares, he 'must enter a dim world peopled by the indeterminate spirits of fictitious or unborn sales'.[8]

Difficulties of defining market value [9]

Sub-divisions of the market. A good can well have more than one market value for a given person, since he may deal in what are, for practical purposes, different markets, and on different sides of the counter. Thus, he may buy cheap at wholesale and sell dear at retail. Or his markets may lie in different lands linked by slow and costly communications.

If he both buys and sells in the same market, his buying price may or may not be near his sale price. Sometimes the two are separated only by a small brokers' commission, etc.;[10] thus, a wheat merchant may have access to an almost perfect market, and then the sale and purchase prices of his stocks will indeed be almost the same. At the other end of the scale, the market can be small, the units unlike, and marketers ill-informed. Such defects are particularly likely where the asset is 'specific' to the given firm. For instance, a manufacturer who needs a highly specialized machine must usually have it made to order; if he sells it thereafter, nobody else may have much use for it, and it may fetch only a small fraction of its purchase price. Likewise, there is probably a big gap between the purchase and sale prices of my toothbrush, clothes, etc.; these, too, seem to be highly specific.

The gap can arise from another cause. Before the asset can fetch the best sale price, it may need an overhaul, etc. Or it may need to be adapted or changed in some more fundamental way. Under this head should probably be put the cost of uprooting and transporting it. Plant may be embedded in cement foundations. Crops or minerals may lie in a remote store. If an oil refinery stands in a desert, the costs of dismantling and taking away the parts may reduce their net sale prices to paltry sums.

Where there is a range of possible prices, the chosen standard must (to give serviceable information) be the one for which the firm would opt in actual transactions. Buying price must be the lowest available and similarly sale price must be the highest.

Sometimes, goods can be sold either in single units or by the gross, etc.; or indeed the whole stock can be sold *en bloc*. Likewise, a machine can be sold as a whole or split into separate components; or all the machines in a plant can be sold together, with or without spares and other stores. What is the unit for valuation?

This question shows up the crudeness of the asset-by-asset approach; the accounting rules on the point are vague. The least unsatisfactory answer is that the chosen physical unit must feature in the firm's common dealings and calculations, and must reflect the most advantageous scale of marketing. Thus, if buying price if taken as standard, and the firm has found that its best plan is to buy a gross of articles at a time, the buying price per gross seems the right choice (and, where a lesser number remain on hand, they should be valued as a fraction of a gross); if the best plan is to buy a machine rather than its parts or a whole team of machines, the price per machine seems the right choice.

Units in their present state or after transformation into product? When sale and purchase prices are contrasted, usually one assumes that both relate to the asset in its current physical state. Thus, 'the sale price of our factory's raw materials' suggests the resale of those materials, without physical change, in the market for raw materials. But the most rewarding course with such assets may well be to turn them into finished goods. Then their 'sale price' could mean something far from raw-material price, namely, the net realizable value of finished products less future costs of manufacture, etc. The same may hold for work-in-progress. Why stop here? Almost all the assets in a firm (e.g., depreciating machines) can be valued as contributions to output (either extra revenue or cost savings), and may in fact be most unlikely to be sold in any other form. Clearly 'sale price' may be highly ambiguous.

For various reasons, then, 'market value' demands a clear definition of the market, of whether the asset is being bought or sold, and of its size; and the definition of 'sale value' must further distinguish between the asset's sale in its present physical state and its contribution to future sales in whatever physical state pays best.

We must next look more closely at the different kinds of value, to decide which of them is most likely to be the best 'standard' for the balance sheet.

Sale price as standard

Sale price (net of selling costs, etc.) is in some ways an attractive candidate for the role of valuation standard. Thus, the total of potential receipts from the piecemeal sale of all assets is a statistic that creditors may well deem important (and 'creditors' also covers, e.g., the policy-holders of an insurance office and any government department that acts as their watchdog). Again the advocates of sale price argue that a manager wants to know how much money he could marshal for new projects, i.e., how much he could at a pinch raise by selling off assets piecemeal. Valuation at sale price gives him this figure, and may also give him a rough notion of how much he could raise from creditors, mortgagees, etc. Further, it can draw attention to assets that the firm would be wise to get rid of (because their sale price is high relative to their earnings in the firm). In the same way, the sum of the sale prices has meaning as the minimum potential proceeds from going out of business and selling all the assets piecemeal; it may thus be the benefit forgone by staying in business, and so an ingredient in the most momentous budget of all. And it can be useful for other decisions. For example, in budgets for showing whether or not a machine should be replaced by a new model, the old machine should usually be put in at sale price. In short, 'the single financial property which is uniformly relevant at a point of time for all future actions in markets is the market selling price or realizable price of any or all goods held'.[11]

This is all very true. On the other hand, the chances that a healthy firm will scrap the assets needed for everyday production are hardly big; and

so their sale prices are not likely to feature in everyday decisions. The latter are far more often concerned with normal production and investment, for which different values are needed. Admittedly, the ability to raise cash for new projects is to some degree linked with the sale prices of the assets; sale and lease-back is an excellent example. But, otherwise, one can scarcely imagine a manufacturer selling off chunks of his plant to finance its output: only a crisis or fundamental change of role would normally justify such dismemberment. An extra venture is usually financed from the more liquid assets only, or by borrowing; and potential lenders and investors tend to be impressed even more by the prospect of high and sustained earnings than by scrap values (though certainly these can be comforting background information). Moreover, 'sale price' can cover a range of urgency from a leisurely sale in the ordinary course of business to sale in a distress situation at almost any price. If the assets will not in fact be sold in any probable circumstances, a realistic valuer should presumably envisage some improbable circumstances. But what would be the least improbable circumstances that would cause a wholesale scrapping of fixed assets? The near-bankruptcy of the firm? And is this conceivable unless there is a general crisis and slump, with a consequent collapse of sale prices? Once a valuer is forced to work on artificially gloomy assumptions, there seems no end to the spiralling catastrophies that he must envisage. I might argue that the most plausible sale price of my piano is what it will fetch as firewood during the next ice-age; and yet that price hardly seems to add much information to my current balance sheet.

With highly specific assets, moreover, sale price may be far below purchase price; and then it is a bad measure of 'size', and leads to an excessive earnings: assets ratio. It may lead also to absurd results if it is linked with income measurement: where the firm must at once write off the difference between a new asset's cost and sale price, the accounts may show a loss if the firm buys useful but specific machines, and a profit if it buys unsuitable machines with a high resale value.

There is some case for using sale price for stocks in the rare situation where the excellence of the market guarantees that the firm can sell its whole ouput without trouble or uncertainty. This probably justifies some plantations and mines in valuing stocks at net realizable value (see p. 19). In general, however, sale price hardly seems to be a good standard, save when assets are on their last legs or the firm is on the brink of liquidation.

The *retail method* of valuing stocks, at sale price minus average gross profit margin, does not seem to fit into this section. It usually is better looked on as a shortcut to valuation at approximate historical cost.

Contribution to net revenue as standard

Another possible candidate is the asset's contribution to net revenue, either by raising receipts or lowering outlays (see p. 122).

This figure can be of great service in some kinds of calculation, e.g., in the 'capital budgets' (often using discounted cash flows—DCF) for showing whether the initial purchase of a given type of asset is worth while. But that does not make it a strong candidate for the balance sheet. One reason is that its size is so much a matter of personal expectations—with some assets, about complex possibilities in the remote future. Many other value standards involve at least some element of expectation (e.g., on the future life of a depreciating asset); but a large element would be a disadvantage in routine accounting, particularly if it entailed elaborate budgets for each of many assets. Another reason is that the contribution figure does not usually give the kind of information that it is the task of annual accounts to purvey. The relation of the contribution to the value of a single asset will be explained on p. 127. If the contribution is used for all the assets in turn, it often offends test (b) (p. 121) by making the sum of their separate values absurdly high. Consider a firm whose value as a going-concern does not by any useful method of assessment exceed £20 000. Suppose it has two assets, A and B, both essential to production and both hard to replace. If A is destroyed (say, by fire), the owner may in desperation decide that its contribution justifies payment of a very high price, perhaps approaching £20 000, for quick replacement. If B instead is destroyed, he feels the same about it.

But the total of these values, nearly £40 000, far exceeds the value of the whole. And the more links there are in the chain of assets, the more astronomic will the total become.

Because 'capital budgets' are now so trendy, there is a natural temptation to apply their methods (e.g., the DCF measurement of future contributions) to a wide range of tasks. But they do not seem suitable for finding balance sheet values; not only may the sum of their separate values be preposterously high, but the methods offend budget logic in a way that will be explained on p. 126.

Replacement cost as standard

As we shall see, replacement cost (i.e., current buying price) has strong arguments in its favour, and fewer defects than sale price or contribution.

But there are times when it too does not seem suitable. In particular, the owner may think the asset not worth replacing—because its contribution has declined (e.g., a machine becomes out of date, merchandise becomes unfashionable), or its replacement price has grown too high, etc. Sometimes replacement is 'impossible' (e.g., because a given model is no longer made); but here the argument will be simpler if it is couched in terms of a forbiddingly high price rather than physical shortage.

'Deprival value' as standard

If the reasoning of earlier pages is sound, what is needed as 'standard' is a concept that normally uses replacement cost, but on suitable occasions substitutes a lesser value. Such a standard is grounded in common sense. If, for instance, a works manager is drafting a budget to compare the costs and revenues of a proposed job that will use up material already in store, normally he can reason: 'When the stores are issued, I'll have to order more of them. So the sacrifice caused by their use is their replacement price.' But sometimes the stores will not be worth replacing (e.g., because they have become obsolete); and then he will rightly argue that the sacrifice must be less than replacement cost. Or one might make the issues more vivid by imagining some melodramatic situation. For instance, if a thief threatens to make off with one of your assets, but offers to refrain if you pay enough, what is the highest sum that he can prise from you? Usually your ceiling will be replacement cost—i.e., this is here deprival value. But sometimes you will stick at a lower figure, because you do not deem the asset worth replacing; here the lower figure takes over as deprival value. Or insurance compensation may serve as an analogy. If an insurance company offers you compensation for an asset that is lost, say, by fire, deprival value is the sum—replacement cost or less, according to your opinion of the asset—that will in your own eyes seem just as good as the asset, i.e., will 'make you whole'.

Finding deprival value

If, then, a valuer is to use the deprival concept, he must decide whether an asset would, if lost, be replaced; and, if it is not worth its replacement cost, what lesser sum its future services, etc., are worth. He may be helped if he keeps in mind a diagram showing the alternative figures—at its simplest:

Deprival value
= lower of

Replacement cost   Value of
                        future services, etc.

The 'value of future services, etc.' is clearly the more difficult branch; the figures that might be appropriate in various circumstances will be explained on pp. 129–30.

Usually, the easiest way to find deprival value is to draw up alternative budgets (in one's head or on paper) showing the future cash flows that are dependent on the possession or loss of the asset. The valuer thus adopts the economist's 'what difference does it make?' approach, and compares alternatives. Since the owner has already taken the step of acquiring the asset, the 'difference' does not here hinge on the advantages of its acquisition but *on the disadvantages of its loss*. His two alternative courses are:

(1) to continue in possession; or
(2) not to continue in possession, e.g., to deprive himself of the asset by using it up on a job.

Plainly, his future cash flow will normally be worse under alternative 2 (say, because he will have to pay for replacement) than under alternative 1. The gap between the alternatives is the benefit of ownership, i.e., the value of the asset by this concept.

Thus, the concept has a negative twist, and hinges on the loss from deprival rather than the gain from acquisition.[12] So perhaps a good name for us to give it is *deprival value*. It was probably first discussed in depth (as 'value to the owner') by Professor J. C. Bonbright of Columbia Business School.[13] It has the great advantage of being the right figure for many everyday management decisions: if the decision is on, say, whether or not to do a job (the stores example above), the manager should cost inputs already owned by asking what bad effects their using-up will have on the future cash book. If thoughtful managers already employ this approach in deciding how best to deploy their assets, perhaps it is a sound guide too for appraising each asset at revaluation time. At any rate, it is practical, increasingly familiar, and subject to a clear logic.

It was suggested on p. 121 that the best standard of value would meet two tests. The first, test (a), is that the figures must be helpful for decisions on the use of the separate asset; deprival value meets this test. The other, test (b), is that the standard must show the 'size' of the total assets in an informative way. Deprival value seems to meet (b) too: it yields figures the total of which shows how much the firm would (given adequate earnings prospects) feel justified in paying for an equally productive set of assets—if, for instance, it were (for some reason such as a fire) deprived of its existing set and had to start afresh, or if it wanted to start a duplicate business in another area. (But, of course, this does not mean that the net sum of the deprival values is the same thing as the *ex-ante* value of the whole firm. The latter, as was pointed out on p. 116, is likely to exceed the sum of the separate asset values, however found. Where the *ex-ante* value is less than the sum of the separate deprival values, this sum still serves a useful purpose in pointing to the skimpiness of the receipts relative to the 'tools', and perhaps to the desirability of going out of business—either at once or when some costly asset needs renewal.)

Deprival value and alternative cash budgets

When we set about finding deprival value, we are in effect drafting two cash budgets for the owner. The one assumes that he owns and uses the asset, the other that he loses it. The difference is the advantage of ownership, i.e., the suggested value.

Its size will vary greatly with the circumstances of the particular asset. If a deprived owner's best policy would be to replace the lost asset, replacement price must clearly loom large in the budgets. Indeed, one may then be able to say without more ado that replacement cost measures the value of the asset exactly, and that there is no need to draft the budgets; here the valuer's task is made simple. However, it is the reasoning of the budgets that gives logic to even a simple valuation, and budgets become essential when the facts are complex, e.g., when a half-worn asset would be replaced by a new and very different model. So we must look at the budgets with some care. I propose, for shortness, to call their two columns the *Have* and *Have Not* budgets. To begin with, we shall suppose that the replacement would be an exactly similar physical unit.

Illustration: alternative budgets and exact replacement

As a simple example, suppose that an item in a shopkeeper's stock is expected to sell for £8 (net of future selling and delivery costs), can be replaced for £4·8 and is so profitable compared with other lines that the shopkeeper would (if it were lost to the shop, say, because he took it for home consumption) replace it with an exact duplicate. A possible way of calculating its value is given in Table 12.1; this may seem unduly pompous for such straightforward facts, but sets out the essentials in what seems the clearest manner. Column (1) shows what the relevant cash flows will be if the asset stays at the owner's disposal and he sells it in the ordinary way. Column (2) shows what they will be if, instead, it is lost but then replaced and sold. This owner, if deprived of the asset, can and will 'make himself whole' by buying a duplicate for the replacement price of £4·8. This sum emerges as the difference between the two columns, and is the 'differential' or 'deprival' value of the asset. So we are here in the simple situation where replacement cost meets our need.

Why the contribution to future revenue is often irrelevant to deprival value

Because the asset or its replacement will both sell for £8, that figure appears in both columns (1) and (2) in the example above—and so does not affect the answer, and might just as well have been left out.

This amplifies what was said about asset values and contributions to future revenue or cost savings on p. 125. If a deprived owner would in

TABLE 12.1
ALTERNATIVE BUDGETS TO SHOW THE ROLE OF REPLACEMENT COST IN FINDING DEPRIVAL VALUE

	Future cash flow if the asset:	
	(1)	(2)
	stays at owner's disposal ('Have' budget)	*is lost and replaced* ('Have Not' budget)
	£	£
Outlay:		
Replacement cost of duplicate		−4·8
Revenue:		
Sale proceeds	8	8
Net receipts	8	3·2
Difference (= advantage of owning asset)	4·8	

fact replace an asset, and the contribution is common to both columns, the contribution is not part of his loss on deprival; replacement cost is enough to restore his position in full. A purist would maintain that economy of style and marginal logic demand the exclusion of the contribution from both columns.

In other words, so long as the contribution exceeds replacement cost, it is irrelevant, and *deprival value can then be found without reference to the asset's future earnings or cost savings.* This seems one of the hardest steps in the argument. Yet it accords with everyday behaviour. If your living depends on your having a car, and the car is stolen, you do not ask the insurance office for say £1 000 000—the present value of all your future earnings to age 65. You are content to ask for a more modest sum, the car's replacement cost: with this, you can replace promptly, and still earn your full income. The £1 000 000 does not depend on ownership of this car but of a car.

Thus, the figures in deprival budgets must often differ from those used in other sets of budgets in which the asset's contribution is an essential ingredient, e.g., in capital budgets. We must distinguish between stage (1) when the firm is deciding whether to install a new kind of machine for the first time, and stage (2) when it has owned the asset for some time and wants to value it.

(1) *Capital budgets.* These may show that, say, extra land costing £1000 will raise revenue (or cut costs) by equal annual sums whose present value is £1500.

(2) *Deprival budgets.* If on the strength of this finding the firm goes ahead and buys the land, the £1500 contribution becomes 'fixed', and can be omitted from both the Have and Have Not columns of later budgets that assume the continued use of this or an equally productive plot of land. So the £1500 is irrelevant to deprival budgets; for instance, £1000 will normally be enough compensation if the state expropriates the land to widen a road and the firm can for £1000 buy an equally productive plot.

In short, different figures are needed for studying different sets of alternatives—e.g., in capital budgets (for studying 'an asset *versus* no asset'), and in deprival budgets ('this asset *versus* its replacement').

But, on occasion, the contribution does affect deprival value. In the example above, suppose the best alternative plot that is available yields lesser annual sums whose present value is only £1100; to be fair, compensation must here be raised to £1000 + (£1500 − £1100) = £1400, i.e., the deprival value budgets must allow for the change in revenue prospects. Again, annual revenue from a depreciating asset sometimes changes because of the ageing of the asset. In such situations, the valuer faces all the troubles of the capital budgeter, and may have to probe into present values of dim anticipations. But these situations are perhaps less likely than the simple one. If a single tool in an assembly line wears out, or the office clock becomes unreliable, the firm's sales rarely dry up; given normal foresight and replacement facilities, the ill-result of the failure of the asset is limited to payment of replacement cost. (But I must warn readers that many distinguished theorists reject this view, notably in the context of depreciation; thus, some of them hold that a depreciating asset should always be valued by discounting its future revenues or cost savings.)[14]

The comparison lies between the best alternatives

For the two deprival budgets to be helpful, they must show what will happen on realistic assumptions, e.g., that the owner will make the best of his chances in each of the two sets of circumstances, by picking the course that offers the best cash flow prospects (after discounting for time and risk). Each column in Table 12.1 may thus be the best of a wide range of possible budgets. The Have column (1) may picture the most profitable of many ways of using the asset; the Have Not column (2) may picture the least costly of many ways in which a deprived owner could make the best of a bad job.

Sometimes one gets a clearer picture by including several of these extra budgets in the table. For instance, column (1) in Table 12.3 is split into budgets (a) and (b) to show the results of two alternative courses open to an undeprived owner; the deprival value emerges from a comparison of the more rewarding of (1a) and (1b) (in fact (1a)) with column (2). Similarly, column (2) may be subdivided into budgets (2a), (2b), etc., to show the results of the alternative courses open to the deprived owner; then the differential value will emerge from a comparison of (1) with the least damaging of (2a), (2b), etc.

Where the asset is not worth replacing

So far, we have considered assets whose replacement is worth while, e.g., whose revenue exceeds replacement cost. But sometimes the asset is not worth replacing. This may be because replacement price has risen (at the extreme, to the immense height at which one says the asset is 'unobtainable'). Or the contribution may have fallen, e.g., merchandise may have become unfashionable, or factory stores may have become less useful because of changes in methods or product. In such cases, deprival will not result in the owner buying an exact replacement. Indeed, where the contribution is low, he may already be planning to get rid of assets of this type as fast as possible. So here the cost of an exact replacement should not be put in the budgets. Deprival robs the firm not of this cost, but of whatever the asset can still contribute (in its best use) to the firm's cash flow. In other words, *when the contribution is less than replacement cost it becomes a relevant part of the deprival budgets.* Contribution sets a lower limit to deprival value.

As was said above, a low contribution can take one or other of two possible forms—(a) the net proceeds from selling off the asset, or (b) the cost savings from keeping and using it.

(a) *Net realizable value as deprival value.* Where the asset in question is stock intended for sale (e.g., an article in a shop), the highest contribution will usually still come from sale. Then deprival value is sale price less any future costs of completion, selling, etc.—i.e., is net realizable value.

Suppose, for instance, the asset of Table 12.1 does not sell when priced at £8, and the owner decides that his best course is to sell it off at a price of, say, only £4. After the sale, he will not pay the replacement cost of £4·8 for a duplicate that may also sell for £4 or less, i.e., he will not replace; and likewise if he is deprived now he will not replace. Thus, the replacement cost of £4·8 has ceased to be of interest, and should be left out of both the Have and Have Not columns. The new budgets are those of Table 12.2.

The sale price of an old or unsuccessful asset may be very low indeed. Thus, the best plan may be to get rid of it for any price that it will fetch: a fixed asset may be sold off in the secondhand market or as junk, and merchandise at a bargain sale; one can use 'scrap value' for the rock-bottom values provided by such disappointing sale prices. At scrapping, some assets may have no value. Worse still, an owner may need to pay to get rid of his white elephants (as when he must fence off a disused quarry). So one must sometimes put zero, or a negative sum, into column (1) of the table.

(b) *Cost saving as deprival value.* Sometimes deprival value lies in a zone between replacement cost and net realizable value. The asset is not worth replacing, but it is still worth keeping because of its contribution to future cost savings (i.e., this

TABLE 12.2

ALTERNATIVE BUDGETS TO SHOW ROLE OF NET REALIZABLE
VALUE WHEN THIS IS BELOW REPLACEMENT COST

| | Future cash flow if the asset: | |
	(1) stays at owner's disposal ('Have' budget) £	(2) is lost and not replaced ('Have Not' budget) £
Revenue—net proceeds	4	—
Difference (= advantage of owning asset)	4	

So here the asset's deprival value is its resale price as scrap, £4.

129

contribution is worth more than net realizable value). Here the discounted present value of the cost savings is the deprival value.

As an example, take a new machine that was expected to save £1600 of wages, but now seems likely, because of changes in methods, to save only £500; maintenance will cost £30. (These figures are discounted present values for the expected future life.) Its replacement cost is £900, so the owner will not replace it. He can get only £400 by selling it now (and nothing later on). The formal budgets for comparing his (1) 'Have' and (2) 'Have Not' positions run:

The cash flows shown in (1b) are better than those in (1a), i.e., the owner's best plan is to keep the asset in use. So budget (1a) can be ignored. Comparison of (1b) with (2) shows that the benefit of owning the asset, i.e., the desired value figure, is £470.

Sometimes the contribution of the asset from use is subject to a 'discount' that at first blush seems different from the ordinary time-discount that may be used to find present values of remote budget figures (but, like time-discount, is based on opportunity cost). This possibility arises where the asset acts as a constraint on new activities, e.g., where old factory equipment takes up floor space

TABLE 12.3

ALTERNATIVE BUDGETS TO ILLUSTRATE ZONE BETWEEN
REPLACEMENT COST AND SCRAP PRICE

	Future cash flow if the asset:		
	(1)		(2)
	stays at owner's disposal and is to be		is lost
	(a) Sold	(b) Used	
	£	£	£
Gains: Scrap proceeds	400	—	—
Wage saving	—	500	—
Outlays: Maintenance	—	−30	—
Net gain	400	470	—
Difference between (1b) and (2) (=advantage of owning asset)		470	

that must be cleared before an extra product can be made. Suppose, for instance, that the asset of Table 12.3 is blocking other plans in some such way, and these opportunities can contribute net benefits worth £20. Then the owner should be willing to give up the asset for only £470 − £20 = £450, to be

free to go ahead with the other plan and reap its £20; deprival value drops to £450. To spell out the story in full, one might put the £20 gain into the budgets that show the cash flows if the asset is no longer owned, i.e., into (1a) and (2). Then the budgets run:

TABLE 12.4

ALTERNATIVE BUDGETS WHERE THE ASSET BLOCKS OTHER GAINS

	Future cash flow if the asset:		
	(1)		(2)
	stays at owner's disposal and is to be		is lost
	(a) Sold	(b) Used	
	£	£	£
Gains: Scrap proceeds	400	—	—
New benefits made possible	20	—	20
Wage saving	—	500	—
Outlays: Maintenance	—	−30	—
	420	470	20
Difference between (1b) and (2) (= advantage of owning asset)		450	

130

Thanks to the new opportunity now open to the owner, he can be made whole by an immediate payment of only £450. This sum is, in an unexpected but accurate sense, the discounted value of the old asset's contribution, i.e., it is here deprival value.

So, when an asset is not worth its replacement cost, one must ask whether the owner will now sell it, or keep it for use. Here deprival value is the higher of net realizable value or value in use.

Summary

One might summarize the above section as follows. The owner of an asset will aim to reap whatever benefits it can contribute in its best role (as shown, perhaps, in a capital budget justifying the acquisition of an asset of this kind). If he is deprived of it, however, he does not necessarily lose these benefits. Where the benefits exceed replacement cost, he will limit his loss by buying or making a replacement, and thus replacement cost measures value to the owner. Where the benefits are less than replacement cost, the latter drops out of the picture. The benefits themselves here constitute value to the owner, i.e., he must estimate the future contribution of the asset to the cash receipts to be won or the cash payments to be obviated. So, to value an asset, one must play a game of make-believe, and imagine the various consequences of deprival. Valuation is a selective process, with (for stocks or similar assets) three possible answers: (1) replacement cost; (2) net realizable value; and (3) cost savings. We can now expand the diagram on p. 126 to:

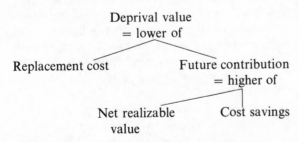

Deprival value
= lower of

Replacement cost   Future contribution
= higher of

Net realizable   Cost savings
value

But so far we have assumed the potential replacement to be an asset more-or-less identical with the present one. The reasoning must be modified where replacement would be very different.

Where the asset will be replaced by a different type of asset

An asset can differ from its potential replacement in many respects. Thus, the demands of customers or the methods of the firm may have changed in ways that call for a changed kind of asset, or (particularly where technology is improving fast) the model on sale today may bear little likeness to the model bought some years ago. This is apt to seem a major stumbling block to the calculation of value. But in fact it is not, though admittedly it may make the valuer envisage a more elaborate series of figures. Provided deprival would trigger off a series of consequential cash flows, one can still compare Have and Have Not budgets, and thus find a deprival value for the existing asset. The comparison of two sets of cash flows is what matters, even where the Have Not column envisages a very different 'replacement'.

Machines provide the obvious example. Their design may improve from year to year. Their optimum size and price may change (e.g., a rise in attendants' wages may justify more automation). The deprived owner of a 7-year-old machine might prefer to buy a brand-new machine rather than another that is 7 years old. And so on. Here 're-placement cost' can no longer be interpreted literally, and the Have Not budget may have to range over a long chain of altered flows; for instance, where the owner of a half-worn machine would (if he were deprived) buy a brand-new machine of better design, the ill-results of deprival must be partly offset by the longer life of the new machine and better performance, i.e., the budget must allow not only for the price of the new machine, but also the benefit of lower running costs, etc. The arithmetic will be illustrated in chapter 13, on depreciating assets.

Where the replacement would not be an exact duplicate, perhaps 'replacement cost' is not always the best phrase to indicate what the valuer should have in mind. Some other phrase, such as 'outlay obviation' or 'cost postponement' may on occasion be clearer. Bur 'replacement cost' is so apt for simple valuations that it seems worth retaining wherever possible, provided one can remember that its meaning must on occasion be stretched a long way.

Sometimes, however, the changes consequent on deprival would be so great that 'replacement cost' no longer seems applicable. In terms of the diagram on p. 131, the left arm for 'replacement cost' here gives way to one of the right arms, probably that for 'cost savings'. For instance, the cheapest 'replacement' for a little-used machine may be the occasional hire of another machine, or the use of more labour: then the potential payments for rent or wages measure the cost saving, i.e., the deprival value. Or the asset may have been demoted to uses for which it was not originally intended, so obviating the need to buy other assets which, even if they look entirely dissimilar to it, have thereby become its replacement. For instance, where a furniture factory has bought too much timber, and the highest contribution will come from burning it in the furnace and so saving coal, its deprival value is the replacement cost of an appropriate quantity of coal. A 'replacement cost' may thus still be the key figure, but it is now the measure of cost savings; the asset whose replacement outlay is obviated (e.g., the coal) may be remote and unexpected.

Circumstances envisaged by deprival budgets

Loss by deprival must vary with circumstances. For example, when the deprived owner is in desperate haste to replace, he may pay a price far higher than when he can buy in leisurely style. Therefore, if 'deprival value' is not to cover a whole spectrum of possible figures, we must try to decide on a suitable background of assumptions, i.e., to set out the circumstances envisaged at a general revaluation. If the figures are to help with normal investment decisions, etc., they must reflect normal circumstances. Earlier pages have tried to meet this point by envisaging a firm depriving itself of assets during its everyday activities, as when a manager prices stores, etc., for use in production. The 'willing buyer and willing seller' of the appraiser may also be helpful. Perhaps we can list the main points thus:

Assumptions should be reasonable and likely. The budgets should be drafted on reasonable and likely assumptions—about the particular owner, the particular asset, and the particular circumstances.

Owner will try to minimize loss. The Have Not budget must assume the owner to take all practicable steps to minimize his loss.

Plenty of time is available. As was pointed out above, if an owner has to replace an asset in haste, replacement cost may be higher than if he can approach the task with ample time. On dramatic assumptions, then, he can revalue his assets at high figures.[15] Such figures conflict with our aim of showing the 'size' of assets in a way that helps business judgement in ordinary circumstances— enabling us (for instance) to compare the resources of one firm with those of another, or to form some idea of how much money a new firm would today need to build up a collection of like assets at a realistically economical pace. Given this aim, we should assume that the asset can be replaced without any suggestion of haste or duress. We are seeking the prices that will obtain when the firm makes its typical investments in assets.

As an example, suppose that a blizzard isolates a factory at balance sheet date. The fuel stock is running low. So long as the snow lasts, the value of fuel should surely be exceedingly high for purposes of decisions on short-term usage. But the same high figure in the annual accounts would be unhelpful. The replacement price at times of easy delivery will give a better view of the assets, when the accounts are read by normal readers at normal dates.

Plenty of cash available. Difficulties could arise, similarly, in *financing* replacement where an owner really was deprived (e.g., fire loss not covered by insurance). He might not have enough ready cash, and therefore might need to borrow at high rates of interest or to pinch his other activities. Here, then, is another possible constraint that may push up the value of an existing asset and lead to dramatic figures that do not fit our picture of placid and efficient working. So we must assume the firm to have access to enough cash to replace the old asset in the most economical way (e.g., buying an expensive new machine where this will in the long run prove more economical than a worn one).

Time discount. A valuer who recognizes that value depends on comparisons will try to show that a £ due some years hence is less attractive than a £

already in the till. So, where the figures are high enough and the times are long enough to be material, he will discount future receipts and payments in his alternative budgets, at the firm's appropriate rate.

An asset's value can vary though its own prospects are unchanged

When an asset's value is defined as a gap between budgets, its size must vary not only with any change in the asset's own budget, but also with change in the budget of the potential replacement. If, for instance, the replacement's budget improves, then the value of the asset drops—even though its future contribution still looks as good as ever. Value is a matter of *comparison*.

Take machinery as an example. Though an owner's expectations of service from a machine may be quite unchanged, his relative opinion of it must fall if improvements in design raise the attractions of new models. Though the Have budget remains the same, the Have Not budget becomes less unfavourable; and so the difference (deprival value) is narrowed.

Assets hard to value

There are some assets that seem ill-fitted for valuation by the deprival or probably any other method. Their links with the market are too weak to provide the needed price data. Obvious examples are the work-in-progress and finished goods of some factories, long-term contracts, and intangibles. A wise man will admit that his chosen method for valuing such assets is merely a makeshift. But certain proxy figures suggest themselves.

A factory's work-in-progress and finished goods

Accounts use a wide range of stock-valuation methods. Indeed, this wealth of possibilities is itself evidence that any guiding logic is hard to find.

Methods used. The stocks of a factory may be valued at historical cost. But then, as was pointed out on p. 77, the firm must link cost with some physical *sequence*, supposed or real. Thus, it may opt for Fifo, Lifo, or Hifo, or it may use an average;[16] in some countries, the base stock method is also in use.[17] Where each unit of stock is identified and costed separately, closing value can instead be 'identified cost'. But this may be no more logical than value found from assumed sequences. If a firm at the time of sale holds several like units bought at different prices, its mere choice of unit for appropriation to the sale (accidental or deliberate) may greatly affect accounting figures for closing stock and profit, but cannot affect economic reality.

A factory that uses historical cost also faces the other difficulty mentioned on p. 77, namely, that of selecting the cost *ingredients*. Thus, the firm must decide whether to restrict cost to direct materials, wages, etc., or to add overheads—and, if so, which of the many types to include, and which of the many allocation methods to use. The range of possible combinations is enormous.

Sometimes a firm rejects historical cost in favour of a target or 'standard' cost. But here again it must choose the ingredients; and, if it decides to include overheads, it must assume some given level of output. A standard cost may still be subject to some of the faults that beset historical cost, notably the timelag error on cost measurement and the failure to show holding gains.

Attempts to find current values. A value based on a current market price would seem far more defensible than the conventional methods of preceding paragraphs. But where each manufacturer makes his own differentiated product, market dealings in work-in-progress may be rare, i.e., such assets may have neither a buying nor a sale price; and finished goods may have no buying price.

Accountants are not alone in finding that current value is elusive here. We might innocently suppose that the expert whose job it is to appraise the value of stocks (e.g., to assess compensation for their loss by fire) could come to our rescue. But he, too, cannot make bricks without straw. He will probably tell us that he assesses compensation by whichever method the firm itself uses to value stocks in its own accounts. So all that we should learn from our quest for help is to look with care at the wording of the insurance policy of the firm, and to include loss-of-profits cover.

The notion of current replacement cost is not simple. Where the owner of a factory's stocks would replace it by making it afresh, replacement cost could be of almost any size, according to the circumstances envisaged; the replacement of one unit in slack times might bring almost no extra outlays, whereas the replacement of many units in busy times might bring not only big outlays (overtime pay, etc.), but also general disruption. If a manager had to cost such assets for a decision budget, he would have to weigh all the circumstances of the moment. Such a complete review would be out of the question at a routine stock-taking. Test (a) on p. 121 (price found by everyday dealings in the asset) is of little use here.

Can test (b) come to our rescue, i.e., can we measure the stock's contribution to the firm's 'size' by estimating how much capital is needed to finance all the stocks? Such an estimate would be crude and hypothetical; but it might nonetheless give quite a helpful view of the resources of the firm, and offer an adequate way of dealing with the difficulties. The argument would presumably run thus: to furnish itself with a comparable total stock, a new or deprived firm would have to buy raw materials and also pay wages and overheads during the time period needed for manufacture of the whole stock. The 'replacement cost' of the stock can thus be interpreted as the total expense for that period. An approximate figure could be built up by valuing each item of stock at average total cost, i.e., loading it with all overheads. However, the valuer could assume that the firm would work at the most efficient level of activity, and so he could charge overheads at the low rates of such a level; thus, the rates would somewhat resemble those of full standard costing. Unsatisfactory items that the firm would not replace would be written down to scrap value, etc., often zero.

This method differs from those in common use mainly because of its stress on overheads. It must therefore offend theorists (as it seems to involve allocation of fixed costs) and practical men (as its values are higher and thus less cautious than is normal). But overhead is the core of the problem—and is likely in future to gain in importance with every increase in mechanization, etc. The overhead rate in the electronics industry can already exceed

500 per cent of labour. To value at direct cost may soon be to value almost at zero. Indeed, any discussion of principles should, to be satisfying, deal adequately with the extreme case where *all* the cost is overhead. The method suggested above does at least meet this test.

Long-term contracts

A partly-finished building, ship, etc., is another form of work-in-progress. It is one that is likely to constitute a big part of the firm's 'size'; so the valuation method can greatly affect the year's profit. But here again valuation is hampered by the lack of market dealings.

One can suggest only that the aim should be to use a deprival value, and that the latter should normally be interpreted as replacement cost, at today's prices for the inputs, but with an eye to the snags and savings that hindsight can detect. Overhead should be added, on the same grounds as for factory work-in-progress. Where the contract threatens to end in loss, deprival value's upper limit of net realizable value (p. 129) will serve as a ceiling.

However, accounting here behaves in a way that is quite out of character, and thereby piles on more problems. Where the activities of a firm consist of several large ventures—building contracts, voyages, etc.—the group of ventures that happens to end in a given year may differ greatly in number, size, and profitability from the groups of other years. Thus, successive annual totals of profit on completed ventures may bob up and down capriciously. Such figures give poor information. So there is a strong temptation here to throw the usual rules overboard, and to smooth the figures by recognizing some profit at dates before it is realized by the final delivery of the building, etc. If the firm decides to do this—perhaps by recognizing slices of profit in step with the receipt of progress payments—the accountant must adjust his figures by valuing assets (e.g., unfinished work or debts) at more than the historical cost of the venture to date, and perhaps more than its replacement cost.

Where an accountant acts in this way, he is rejecting the safeguards on which he normally relies. In place of a concept that restricts assets to the solid, realized achievement of the past (see

p. 18), he now embraces one that looks forward, i.e., he values some assets *ex ante* by estimating their future net receipts. Many accountants denounce this inconsistency. Their chief objection is the danger of counting chickens before they are fully hatched. Until completion, the final cost of a long contract—perhaps lasting six or seven years——may be impossible to estimate at all closely, especially if there is a risk of strikes, wage increases, technical pitfalls, etc. For that matter, even after completion the builder may still be liable during a guarantee or maintenance period of perhaps two more years. Therefore, profit estimates must often be upset by later events. Another objection is that one cannot logically impute 'inequalities of profitability' to different stages of work that is 'joint', i.e., is sold as a unity.

It will be interesting to see which of the opposing views wins. The practical grounds for recognizing profit during the contract are strong. Some safeguards are possible, e.g., the accounts can give suitable warning notes.[18] And the idea of showing separate figures for realized and unrealized profit (suggested in Table 4.1) here seems particularly useful. After completion, the unrealized profit would be transferred to realized profit; and in any table of long-term results, the transfer might be spread back over several years. The most logical way to allocate profit to different years is perhaps to use DCF arithmetic, i.e., to calculate each year's increase in the present value of the cash flows of the venture, discounting at its internal rate of return.

Intangibles

Accounting interprets 'tangible assets' broadly, so that the phrase covers not only physical assets but also rights (e.g., claims on debtors) that can be enforced at law. 'Intangibles' is correspondingly restricted.

Should intangibles be looked on as assets? It is hard to suggest rational rules for intangibles. By what tests should one decide whether outlays on advertising, research, etc., give birth to an asset? And, where the existence of the asset has been recognized, at what dates and rates should it be written off?

Much the same problem faces the economic statistician who is compiling figures on national resources. He knows that, where country A invests heavily in physical assets and country B in education, comparison of figures for physical capital alone gives a false picture. But he knows also that to measure human capital is difficult. So he may reasonably decide to find the physical figures only, and leave his readers to allow for B's superior education as best they can.

A simple mind could hardly entertain the notion of intangible assets. In a child's tales, wealth is castles, land, flocks, gold—i.e., physical things. It is a long step forward to realize that the essence of wealth is the prospect of benefits, not their physical source. The accountant is thus showing his maturity if he ceases to use the physical test for deciding whether outlays fall under the heading of 'asset' or 'expense'. The correct test, he then argues, is whether or not the outlay improves the prospects of the firm (when the outlook at the year's end is compared with that at its start). Tangibility has nothing to do with this test; he applies it alike to the cost of a lathe and an advertising campaign.

But physical attributes do help with valuation. Most tangible assets can be traded on the market; they also lend themselves to the notion of deprival. Intangibles are less helpful: in what sense can one speak of the sale or replacement of last year's advertising, and how can a firm deprive itself of the benefit of its preliminary expenses? Physical attributes may at least set limits to the asset's life. And often the valuer can visualize and predict the cash flows of physical assets more surely than those of intangibles. In short, valuation of intangibles is apt to demand superlative judgement plus prophetic gifts that none of us can feel sure of possessing. As like as not, moreover, the decision on whether to 'assetize' expenditure on intangibles (for instance, to capitalize the cost of research and development) will need to be made when the company is going through a bad patch, i.e., when the pressure to improve the profit figures is highest and cool judgement is hardest. Yet bad judgement can here spell disaster, since it may enable a company to report reassuring profits throughout a lean period that ends in bankruptcy (e.g., Rolls-Royce in 1967–71).

The deprival concept is no help here: the notion of depriving a firm of all knowledge won by past research, etc., hardly makes sense. The sale-price concept would have at least the merit of providing a clear if extreme solution, since many intangibles are by their nature incapable of being sold and so would have to be valued at *nil*. Some such complete ban on intangibles (save, perhaps, where they are property in the legal sense, e.g., patents) would provide a workable rule, and might protect the shareholders and creditors of a shaky firm; the ban would also allow the balance sheet to show the 'size of the tools' in an everyday sense. But the ban would be an intolerable constraint on many sound companies during a development stage.

The problem seems likely in the future to get worse rather than better. The trend towards more research, longer incubation periods for new products, etc., will make for more and bigger intangibles.

'Goodwill'. Normally the balance sheet concerns itself with separate asset values, and ignores the going-concern value of the whole. However, if the whole firm changes hands, the buyer's book-keeper may need to make entries for both the total payment and the separate assets. Then the two methods are perforce mixed, and in consequence an awkward balancing figure emerges. Our experience of the physical world suggests that the whole must equal the sum of the parts—that, if our measurement of physical things belies this, we must have gone wrong somewhere, e.g. we may have overlooked one of the parts. But we should be wary about applying this experience to the realm of value. To treat the balancing figure as an extra asset (still more, an asset linked with popularity) is an error. It is not an extra asset;[19] it is the gap between the answers found when two quite different things—in the economic sense—are measured. This is obvious where the whole and the parts are valued on different bases (e.g., the whole firm at its current price and the assets at the historical costs of earlier dates). But even if both the whole and the parts are valued on the same basis, a gap is likely: where, because of market or technical or other difficulties, a set of parts cannot readily be acquired and built up quickly into an effective whole, the market will tend to prefer the whole and to pay more for it. (It is instructive to compare a set of golf clubs with a rare Dresden shepherd and shepherdess.) The extra price is for the extra benefits that the whole will yield.[20] These benefits may spring from a multitude of attributes that jointly breathe life into the parts: to ascribe them to one hidden part is naïve.

Suppose that a connoisseur is willing to pay £10 apiece for separate china figures, and £50 for a matching pair. The extra £30 suggests that he gets extra pleasure from the pair, and not that there is a third figure lurking in the background.

In a balance sheet, the balancing figure should surely be kept apart from the tangible assets, and should be described with some full and clear phrase, e.g. 'Excess of price paid for whole firm as a going-concern over the net sum of the separate asset values'. (In a consolidated balance sheet, words such as 'Excess of price paid for shares in subsidiary over the separate values of the subsidiary's assets' are now accepted usage for describing an analogous figure.) When we instead use 'goodwill', we confuse readers. What is worse, we betray confusion in our own thought.

Balance sheet treatment. In the absence of any clear solution to the problem of intangibles, we must accept that it will be dealt with in various unsatisfying ways. We can at least say that a balance sheet ought to separate tangibles from intangibles in a style that will alert readers to the more arbitrary nature of the values of the intangibles. Perhaps the balance sheet should class as assets only the intangibles that are backed up by legal rights (patents, copyrights, etc.), and should show the rest as deductions from the owners' balances until they are written off, for example:

	£
Assets:	
Copyrights, etc.	—
Net tangible assets	—
Net total	—
Excess of price paid for whole firm as a going-concern over the net sum of the separate asset values	—
	—
	=

Obtained from:	£
Shareholders' capital, retained earnings	—
Less sums spent on research, etc.	—
	———
	—
	═══

Some such layout would seem particularly suitable where the price paid for the going-concern is *less* than the net sum of the assets; a deduction from the total is more informative than arbitrary cuts in the value of one or more fixed assets, or the creation of a capital reserve.

Revaluation of intangibles. If intangibles are (for better or worse) included in a revalued or stabilized balance sheet, how should the figures be updated? Presumably one could think up some special index for, e.g., advertising or research costs. However, on the assumption that such items are better looked on as explanations of past cash outflows than normal assets, the general index would seem more appropriate.

Assets that yield cash directly

In part as a preface to a discussion of liabilities, it may be worth while to spell out the steps in the valuation of the corresponding assets, e.g., holdings of shares and long-term loans, etc. Here these are called 'assets that yield cash directly'.

To find deprival values for such assets, one must again ask how the owner should measure them for his decision-budgets. The occasions when he will draft such budgets may in some cases be rare; but one can, for instance, envisage him getting an offer for his unquoted shares, and asking himself (as a guide to the minimum price to accept) what difference their loss would make to his cash flows.

The benefit of ownership

Suppose that the asset in question is called A_1, and the owner expects his holding to yield $£x$ a year as interest or dividend plus a lump sum of $£y$ at redemption date; that he likes this package so much that he will if deprived of it try to buy a similar one; and that he can buy for £90 000 a holding of another security, A_2, so like A_1 (as regards interest, redemption, risk, etc.) that we can conveniently call its price 'replacement cost'. Plainly, Have and Have Not budgets would show that the value of A_1 is £90 000, since the receipt of £90 000 enables him exactly to make good the loss of A_1. (The face values of A_1 and A_2 are of no relevance.) Deprival value is once again replacement cost.

But sometimes the owner's opinion of A_1 will have fallen since he bought it, so that he is now disinclined to replace it with A_2. Perhaps, indeed, he feels that he ought to have sold A_1 already. If his best plan is to sell as soon as possible, and his holding will fetch £85 000 (£90 000 less the 'dealer's turn', etc.), then this smaller sum is now deprival value.

With many types of cash-yielding assets, the gap between replacement cost and sale price will be less than is suggested in this example, e.g., it will be trifling in a highly-developed market such as that for government securities. But in some circumstances the gap could be greater. Thus, there may be no willing buyers for the obligations of a small company; and one can think of debts whose repayment is so unsure or slow that no factoring firm, etc., would take them save at a high discount—perhaps not on any terms. Further, the gap will be increased if gain on the proceeds is subject to tax. Where there is a big gap, another type of receipts is likely to become more relevant than net realizable value: the receipts to be got by keeping the asset may now seem more desirable than those from prompt sale. In the example, suppose that net sale price is only £60 000, and that the owner neither would deem the asset worth replacing at £90 000, nor would sell at once for £60 000. Here he presumably feels that his receipts from holding the asset for the best future period— say the $£x$ per year and $£y$ at redemption—are worth more than £60 000 spot, though less than £90 000. To find deprival value, he would have to conduct a kind of mental auction sale; the value is the minimum price, say £70 000, at which he would part with the asset. Presumably he hits on £70 000 because this sum would enable him to invest in his current favourite asset B, whose prospective cash flows may differ in size, timing, risk, etc., from A's flows, but nevertheless are the equivalent of the latter in his eyes. Thus, in a sense B is the true replacement of A_1. However, as B may be utterly unlike A_1 in most respects (e.g., the best 'investment' may be the repayment of loan), to talk of the £70 000 as 'replacement cost' might be inconvenient. Perhaps one should say instead that the future receipts from A_1 must be discounted at the owner's appropriate cost-of-capital rate.

The deprival formula

The deprival value of cash-yielding assets can thus be defined by slightly adapting the form used on p. 131. Here the phrase 'the higher of cost savings and net realizable value' is not applicable; the reference to 'cost savings' can be dropped, and 'net realizable value' must be stretched to cover the alternatives of prompt sale or retention (possibly for many years). Thus, the deprival value of cash-yielding assets is the lower of:

(a) (if the owner could and would replace on deprival) replacement cost;
    and
(b) (otherwise) the higher of
    net current sale price,
    and
    the present value (at his appropriate discount rate) of future receipts,
    according to whether his best plan is to sell the asset at once or keep it.

Or:

Deprival value
= lower of

Replacement cost   Net receipts
= higher of

net current   discounted
sale price   future receipts

Difficulties

In practice, it may well be impossible to value cash-yielding assets with any sureness, because the variances between the 'unknown' and the nearest 'known' assets are so great (e.g., the valuer must try to allow for differences in factors such as gearing and cover). Even if the cash flows from both

purport to be fixed sums of money (as with debts, debentures, etc.), there may be variances in timing and risk. Where the size of the flows is also likely to vary (as with equities) the difficulties increase still further.

There are plenty of other problems to test the judgement of the valuer. A simple debt may be subject to unpredictable delays. Loans to associated companies may secure trade benefits (over and above such obvious receipts as interest) that are well-nigh impossible to quantify. Moreover, general price change must tend to affect the owner's discount rate. During inflation, he will expect his equity investments to yield rising money receipts, i.e., to earn at a rate that is influenced by both (a) time and risk in the absence of inflation, and (b) the fall in money's value. He should therefore discount receipts at a rate higher than that appropriate in times of stable prices.[21]

Liabilities

If there is a good case for revaluing the cash-yielding assets, consistency suggests that there must be an equally good case for revaluing the liabilities (and here we shall stretch the word to cover all fixed-money obligations, e.g., preference shares). The aim of a revaluation may be to aid scrutiny of the firm's resources; it may also be to aid income measurement (e.g., by finding unrealized change in value); for both these ends, the negative items would seem just as significant as the positive ones.

'Relief value'

With liabilities, the phrase 'deprival value' may sound inept. We are here concerned with the benefit that the firm would receive *if it were relieved of a burden*; so 'relief value' is perhaps a more suitable term.

There may not be many occasions on which a manager must calculate such a value for decision purposes. But we can imagine him doing so, for instance, when a would-be buyer of one of the firm's departments, etc., offers to relieve the firm of a loan as part of the consideration. How much is such help worth? The switch from positive to negative asset suggests that the valuation formula may be a mirror image of that for positive flows in the left hand column of p. 138.

The measurement of a burden

A long-term liability usually saddles the borrowing firm with a burden such as the payment of £x per year as interest and a lump sum of £y at redemption date. Let us first suppose that the firm's best plan, if it were relieved of the burden, would be to borrow afresh in much the same way, and that it could today raise £90 000 (net of cost) in return for its undertaking to pay £x a year and £y at the given redemption date. By following this plan, it would still face unchanged future cash outflows, but gain £90 000 at once. So the benefit of relief is £90 000, i.e., is the amount of the potential 'replacement loan' that can be serviced with the given future cash flows.

However, the firm may now be unwilling (if relieved) to raise a similar loan—say, because it could gain tax advantages by switching from loan to preference shares, or expects deflation and so no longer wants to owe money; the burden has grown to more than £90 000. Possibly the firm is already planning to get rid of the loan, e.g., by paying off the creditor, or buying up and cancelling loan stock. Let us say that it will, in one way or another, be able to discharge the liability by paying £100 000. To be relieved of the liability by someone else is to be spared paying this £100 000. So here the value of the burden is £100 000, i.e., is the cost of current redemption.

As with cash-yielding assets, possibly the gap between the two kinds of 'market price' may be much less than our examples suppose. But with some forms of liability it can perhaps be wider (e.g., the contract may call for a payment of £120 000 at premature redemption, while other lenders may now demur at putting up more than £80 000 because the firm's credit has sunk); then the firm may be unwilling to pay as much as either:
(a) (if relieved) the future £x per year and final £y for such a small replacement loan as £80 000; or
(b) £120 000 immediately to redeem the existing loan.
So here the loan's 'relief value' is some figure between £80 000 and £120 000. To find it, one must consider what is the maximum that the firm would sacrifice to be quit of the £x and £y outflows; one would presumably have to discount these flows at the firm's appropriate cost-of-capital rate. The answer might be say £105 000.

The valuation formula

If this line of reasoning is right, the relief value of a liability is the higher of:
(a) (if the firm could and would borrow afresh if relieved of the burden)
the biggest sum that it could now borrow in return for a commitment to make the given future payments; and
(b) (if it would not borrow afresh) the lower of
current redemption payment,
and
the discounted future payments (at its appropriate rate of interest),
according to whether its best plan is to repay at once or later.
This may seem simpler if set out as:

The relief value of a liability
= the higher of

Replacement   Net payments to meet the liability
loan   = lower of

current   present value
repurchase   of future
price   payments

—a formula pleasingly symmetrical with that on p. 138. 'Current repurchase price' covers purchases of the firm's loan, etc., in the market, and prompt repayment or redemption.

The valuer's calculations should assume that future payments will be made at the best dates and at the lowest figures that the contract and circumstances permit. True, the firm will hardly contemplate default on its own obligations; but it can sometimes buy them cheaply in the market, or allow inflation to whittle them down in real terms.

Arguments for and against revaluing liabilities

Par values are usually meaningless and deceptive. To replace the par values of liabilities with current values would be helpful in several ways (and certainly would be evidence that the revaluation was wholehearted). Thus, current values are the logical figures to use in studies of capital gearing. Further, they give some evidence of the company's skill at borrowing; for instance, a decline in the market value of the debentures suggests that the managers borrowed at a good moment, and so have served the equity-holders well. (Does loyal service to the equity-holders imply disloyalty to the holders of preference capital, loan, etc.? My feeling is that all holders of fixed-money claims have opted to gamble on the money unit, and must be left to win or lose. To show their holding at current value would at least let them see how their speculation has fared.)

The argument against revaluing money liabilities (and also money assets) is that the gains or losses are common knowledge and sometimes small; if the balance sheet were to set out the few important facts (interest rate, date and terms of redemption, and—best of all—quoted market price), it would tell the reader everything he normally needs in order to form a judgement. Further, the gain or loss on redeemable securities tends to evaporate as redemption date draws near.

Despite these comforting arguments for accounting inertia, the fact remains that good analysts often do find it worth their while to revalue prior charges. An informative balance sheet might well do the same for the general reader.[22]

Example of revaluation of liabilities

Suppose that a company starts (at general index 100) with £4000 of equity capital and £1000 of

TABLE 12.5
BALANCE SHEETS ILLUSTRATING THE REVALUATION OF LIABILITIES

	(1) Ordinary figures £		(2) Stabilized figures £
Assets	5000	$\times \frac{300}{100}$	15 000
Ordinary shareholders:			
Capital	4000	$\times \frac{300}{100}$	12 000
Gain on owing money			2 000
Gain on revaluing liabilities			300
			14 300
Debentures	1000		700
	5000		15 000

debentures, and invests the £5000 in land. In the years that follow, the general index trebles, the land rises in step, but the relief value of the debentures sinks to £700. Trade profit is paid out at once as dividend. The closing balance sheet (ordinary figures) is shown in column (1) of Table 12.5. Even if the debentures had retained their initial value of £1000, the company would have made a gain on owing of £2000; as the debentures have sunk to £700, it has made a further gain of £300. These gains are shown by the stabilized accounts in column (2).

Provisions and allowances

If an old provision, etc., is meant to show that a particular asset is overvalued, presumably it should usually be revised in much the same way as the asset itself (e.g., with that asset's special index). Thus, an accumulated depreciation provision should keep step with change in the gross value of the asset (a matter that chapter 13 will discuss at some length). A provision for maintenance (e.g., of furnaces for making steel) ought to mirror expected costs at the rates likely to obtain when the repairs will be done. Where money assets should not be revalued, neither should provisions for loss on such assets (e.g., bad debts).

Tax provisions and equalization allowances should depend on the best estimate of the sums of money that will be paid, but should presumably be discounted at a rate that allows both for time and the likelihood of future inflation.

Accumulated gains, etc.

If the balance sheet is fully stabilized, then the owners' balances are revalued. The general index seems best for this task (see p. 32). In the stabilized accounts of earlier dates, each year's profit will already have been corrected, at the close of the year when it was earned, for the timelag error on cost; now the retained corrected profits should be updated with the general index.

During inflation, such revaluation would mean that accumulated corrected profits would rise. Suppose a company started with £1000 of capital, and used this to buy land (at general and special indices of 100). In succeeding years, the general index went up to 300. Undistributed trade profit is £220; it came from the rent of the land, and so includes no timelag error. It accumulated during the company's early years, when the general index stood at 110. The corresponding cash was promptly used to buy investments (cost £220), which then appreciated in step with the general index, so that their end-value is £600; but the value of the land did not quite appreciate in step, and rose from £1000 to only £2800.

The closing balance sheet (ordinary figures) is shown in column (1) of Table 12.6. Column (2) shows the stabilized figures; both capital and trade profits are updated, and the £200 real loss on land is made obvious.

Various compromises between columns (1) and (2) are possible. Column (3) shows a rather crude method, often met in practice if assets are revalued. It retains orthodox capital and profit, and thus throws all the surplus on revaluation into an omnibus figure of £2180. This figure has little significance and may mislead.

TABLE 12.6
BALANCE SHEET ILLUSTRATING STABILIZATION OF ACCUMULATED GAINS

	(1) Ordinary figures £		(2) Stabilized figures £ at index 300	(3) Ordinary balance sheet with assets revalued £
Land	1000	$\times \frac{280}{100}$	2800	As (2)
Investments	220	$\times \frac{300}{110}$	600	
	1220		3400	3400
Capital	1000	$\times \frac{300}{100}$	3000	1000
Profit (trade) accumulated	220	$\times \frac{300}{110}$	600	220
Gain on revaluation of assets:				
In money terms: Land				1800
Investments				380
In real terms: Land			− 200	2180
	1220		3400	3400

New legal concepts on profits available for dividends?

Columns (2) and (3) suggest that the shareholders' balances exceed those shown by ordinary accounts, and that the latter figures should be raised. But if some such revaluation becomes usual, important new problems will emerge. In particular, directors and shareholders will begin to ask where the legal ceiling on dividends now lies; 'mixed' totals, like the £220 of the example, will no longer seem convincing. How should the law decide such novel questions?

The answer is plain so far as increase in capital is concerned (£2000 in the example): this is merely a nominal restatement of the original capital, and cannot be distributed without reducing real capital, and thus weakening the traditional safeguards of creditors. Justice suggests that the payment of dividends out of such capital adjustments should be forbidden.

Real appreciation is a less certain matter. It happens in the example to be negative (−£200). Should this be made good out of trade profit? And what if it were instead positive? Most of us are cautious enough to feel a bias against payments from unrealized gains. But practice and legal attitudes could change: the British courts have been eccentric in their dividend decisions, and their attitude on this point has not yet been made clear— 'the judgement in the *Ammonia Soda Co.* case of 1928 suggests, moreover, that an unrealized increase in the value of a fixed asset may in certain circumstances enter into the calculation of divisible profits'.[23] A particularly appropriate circumstance (we may guess) is the careful and systematic revaluation of all assets.

Last, consider the revalued trade profit (£600 in the example). Logic does not suggest any strong reason against treating it all as divisible; it is the measure of old realized trade profits in up-to-date terms (and, in the sense that it contains no element of timelag error, is even conservative). If, however, this view is sound, the directors of innumerable companies can, by revaluing mixed totals of corrected profits, raise their dividend ceiling without impropriety. This opens up a perhaps unnerving prospect—if not of wholesale dividend increases, at least of doubt and upheaval in concepts and case law.

Equity capital

Our approach to revaluation has left equity capital in a rather passive role—as little more than a residual balance. Logic suggests that the normal (often mixed) historical figure should be stabilized with the general index, i.e., raised in the eyes of the owner to the current equivalent of his historical contributions. Company law presumably forbids similar change in ordinary accounts, but could hardly prevent the increase (e.g., the £2000 in Table 12.5) from being shown next to capital as a separate 'valuation adjustment' or 'capital reserve'. From time to time, the balance sheet might then be tidied up by using this surplus for the issue of bonus shares. Other types of equity balances, such as premiums on the shares issued, should also be updated with the general index.

Some ingenious minds have suggested a far more radical attack: if each asset, loan, etc., ought to be restated at its market value, why should the company's own shares too not be restated in a way that reflects the *ex-ante* value of the going-concern (most simply, at their market quotation, so that the total gives the company's 'market capitalization')? Here we have returned to the issue raised at the start of this chapter, i.e., the distinction between the total of the separate (net) assets and the *ex-ante* value of the whole firm. If we accept that the most useful task of the balance sheet is to give information about the 'size of the tools', and not about the going-concern value of the whole firm, then the owner's balances must do no more than reflect the net assets. To mix the two types of value is to invite maximum confusion.

Conclusions on revaluation

Though we may hope that the balance sheet of the future will contain defensible values, we must recognize that the task of finding them will involve the accountant in many new troubles. The notion that assets can be put in a value list seems, on the surface, to be simple enough: but in fact it soon strikes practical and logical obstacles.

This chapter has introduced some of the obstacles (notably ones that arise when the given asset is divorced from market dealings, or would be replaced by something very different). But there are still others. Two of these must be mentioned. They tend to become important where values are interdependent, i.e., where it is misleading to measure the given asset by itself.[24]

First, it sometimes happens that the loss of the one asset would cripple the firm. This is unlikely where the firm's cash inflow is high relative to the asset's replacement cost: given the 'normal circumstances' (plenty of time available, etc.) envisaged by p. 132, a deprived firm would here make itself whole by replacing the asset; and so replacement cost is a suitable measure of value. But if the inflow is low relative to the replacement cost, a deprived firm might decide to close down the whole rather than replace. An example is a costly bridge or tunnel on a moribund railway. Deprival may lead not to replacement but to the line's closure and thus to loss of the net receipts from the whole; so this one asset's deprival value is the present value of the line's future net receipts. But the same may hold for other bridges and tunnels, too. To sum such deprival values is to reach an absurdly high total.

Second, the plant as a whole may be semi-obsolete, and yet its parts—viewed piecemeal—may still be worth replacing. If the chance arose (e.g., if a fire wiped out the plant), the whole would be replaced by an improved set of assets, working on a quite different system. But, in the absence of such a clean sweep, a machine of the improved kind may not fit in, and so the firm must keep up the old system; the loss of an existing machine would lead merely to its replacement by a more or less similar machine. Here each single asset can sensibly be valued at its replacement cost, and yet the sum of such values fails to allow for the general obsolescence.

It seems desirable, where the parts add up to an unwarrantably high total, to remove the excess from the balance sheet. But can one do so by writing down the individual values? There may be no logical way of apportioning the excess between them; we may question even the practice of writing it off from fixed assets, leaving the current assets unscathed. A more defensible plan may be to list the assets at their full values, and then to deduct some comprehensive provision for obsolescence, etc., from their sum, as in the example given in the next column.

The net total should be the price that the firm, if deprived of all the net assets, would be willing to pay for a similar set—a price low enough to enable it to compete with today's most efficient new plants.

The difficulties of finding balance sheet values mainly arise, as earlier pages have said, from the inherent crudeness of all value concepts that are

	£	£
Fixed assets, at deprival values		
A		—
B		—
etc.		—
		—
		—
Current assets, at deprival values		
C		—
D		—
etc.		—
		—
		—
		—
Less Provision for obsolescence		—
		—
Net total		—
		—

not founded on an *ex ante* treatment of composite cash flows. If this glum view is right, we must accept that all concepts for individual assets are beset by faults, and that the balance sheet must often be blinkered and ritualistic. The deprival concept shares the general weakness; but it seems at least to be sufficiently useful and reasonable to merit a trial.

References

1. Edward Ross, *Financial Statements—A Crusade for Current Values*, Pitman, 1969, amplifies the case in vigorous style.

2. Mr H. P. Barker, Parkinson Cowan, Ltd, Annual Report, 1964.

3. See, e.g., R. Turvey, 'Rates of Return, Pricing, and the Public Interest', *Economic Journal*, September 1971, p. 489.

4. See K. MacNeal, 'What's Wrong with Accounting', in *Studies in Accounting Theory*, 2nd ed., (eds) W. T. Baxter and S. Davidson, Sweet & Maxwell; Irwin, 1962, p. 67. This is outspoken on the ill-results of using historical cost (justified on the 'going concern principle of value') instead of current value: 'accepted accounting principles permit new types of exploitation on a scale that makes plain stealing look tame. This exploitation is not crude stealing; it is horse-trading on plush carpets with a background of authentic period furniture; it doesn't give the smartest Indian a chance, nor is it supposed to'.

5. The *Conclusions of the Second Congress* of the European Federation of Financial Analysts' Societies, 1963, p. 7, state that 'capital employed' should include fixed assets at replacement cost and quoted investments at market values. 'Further, it was considered that if the necessary information could be made available, such statistics might assist governments and other organisations in the economic planning of industries and regions. Therefore it would seem to be in the self-interest of governments to require that accounting procedures and the publication of information about the financial status of companies should be of such a standard as to provide the minimum information.'

6. David Solomons, *Divisional Performance: Measurement and Control*, Financial Executives Research Foundation, 1965, p. 123.

7. S. Fabricant, *Capital Consumption and Adjustment*, National Bureau of Economic Research, 1938, surveys the doings of this period.

8. Mr Justice Danckwerts in *Holt* v. *Commissioners of Inland Revenue* [1953] 32 A.T.C. 402.

9. These matters are set out more fully and skilfully by Professor J. C. Bonbright, of Columbia Business School, in his massive and incomparable *Valuation of Property*, Michie, 1965.

10. The size of the brokers' charge or the 'inside dealers' margin' depends on 'the degree of perfection [in] the market in which they operate and on the amount of "processing" or "transformation" performed by them', e.g., transportation, packaging, physical transformation through manufacture, etc. It depends, too, on how far they act as shock-absorbers by varying their quantity of stocks held; thus they may buy when prices are sagging, and sell later when prices rise—'an intertemporal transfer of goods ... fundamentally no different from any geographical transfer'—N. Kaldor, 'The Irrelevance of Equilibrium Economics', *Economic Journal*, December 1972, p. 1248.

11. Raymond J. Chambers, *Accounting, Evaluation, and Economic Behaviour*, Prentice-Hall, 1966, p. 92. This book sets out the case for sale price fully.

12. 'When I say, "My house is worth $10,000 to me", I mean (if I am precise in my use of language) that the retention of the house is worth to me as much as the acquisition of $10,000 in cash would be worth to me. But this is the same thing as saying that the anticipated loss of my ownership interest in the house has an adverse value to me of $10,000. Such negative terms as "anticipated loss", "damage", and "injury", when used as quantitative terms to which dollar signs may be attached, are simply the converse of such positive words as "value", "worth", and "importance"'—J. C. Bonbright, *op. cit.*, p. 72. Professor F. K. Wright seems to hit the nail on the head when he uses "opportunity value" in this context (see 'Towards a General Theory of Depreciation', *Journal of Accounting Research*, Spring, 1964).

13. In his *Valuation of Property*. A. J. Merrett and Allen Sykes, *The Finance and Analysis of Capital Projects*, Longmans, 1963, provide a useful alternative treatment linked with long-term budgets.

14. This 'revenue approach' is amplified and discussed in W. T. Baxter, *Depreciation*, Sweet & Maxwell, 1971, pp. 43 and 101.

15. When the facts warrant, a just compensation law will allow for dramatic circumstances, though perhaps by distinguishing more than one type of loss rather than valuing the asset at an unusually high figure. Professor Bonbright (*op. cit.*, pp. 75–6) takes as illustration an imaginary legal system in which a man deprived of his car sets the damage at $1500: if he should claim for 'a total loss of $1500 due (a) to the necessity of buying another car for $1000 and (b) to missing an important business engagement that would have yielded him a profit of $500, most courts would distinguish between the loss of a car "worth $1000" and the incidental loss of an opportunity to make a profit. They would not be likely to think of the car as having been temporarily worth $1500 to the owner because of its usefulness in preventing the owner from missing his engagement. But unless "value" is defined to mean market value, or else to mean the value that the automobile *would* have to the owner under *hypothetical* conditions, the distinction is invalid.'

16. 'Average' is a vague term. It may mean the running average cost of recent purchases, in which case the closing stock value comes near to Fifo. Or it may mean the average of opening stock and the year's purchases, and then gives a value betwixt Fifo and Lifo. See J. Keith Butters and Powell Niland, *Inventory Accounting and Policies*, Harvard University Press, 1949, pp. 154–5.

17. The base stock method resembles Lifo, in that it too makes perennial use of the prices at the chosen base date, perhaps right back near the firm's start, for valuing the physical volume held at that date (as distinct from later increments). It justifies itself, however, not so much by a flow concept as by analogy with the valuation of fixed assets at their original cost.

18. 'The related note should, therefore, contain details of the amounts of cost, attributable profit, anticipated losses and progress payments received and receivable included in that amount. The amount of profit or loss arising from long term contracts needs to be disclosed, indicating particularly any material profits and losses on contracts treated as completed in prior years and the net amount provided in the year for anticipated losses'—Accounting Standards Steering Committee, *Exposure Draft No. 6*, London, 1972, paragraph 12. Perhaps the average length of outstanding contracts should be stated, too.

The arithmetical distinction between the base-stock method and Lifo hinges on what happens when there are 'decrements' in physical stock. The true base-stock method deducts decrements at replacement cost; where this is high, the net total for the value of the remaining stock is reduced to an even more conservative size, and so is profit—Willard J. Graham, 'Changing Price Levels and Income', *Accounting Review*, January 1949. But there are doctrinal disputes among the devotees of Lifo and of the base stock over the true values of increments and decrements.

19. J. C. Bonbright, *op. cit.*, page 79.

20. The following story was told in *The Times*, 20 February 1973, to illustrate Indian business capacity:

Police in a village saw an Indian had come into some money. He told them he had received it from importing shoes. But you need a licence to do that, the police reminded him; did he have one? No, he admitted. Then surely the shoes must have been seized by the state and sold at public auction? They were, the man said; but in that case, the puzzled policeman asked, how did he benefit?

'Ah', the Indian said, 'I imported 10,000 left shoes into Calcutta, and they were sold at public auction, but no one wanted them, so I got them very cheaply. Then I imported the right shoes into Bombay, and they, too, were sold, but no one wanted them. So I got them cheaply, too. Then I matched the pairs and sold them all at a good profit.'

21. See M. Bromwich, 'Inflation and the Capital Budgeting Process', *Journal of Business Finance*, Autumn 1969.

22. A possible book-keeping scheme for handling gain and loss on prior obligations is given in Edwards and Bell, *The Theory and Measurement of Business Income*, University of California Press, 1960, p. 204. This even shows the variance between actual interest charges and what would be paid on loans raised at current rates.

23. B. S. Yamey, 'The Case Law Relating to Company Dividends' in W. T. Baxter and S. Davidson, *op. cit.*, p. 428. The uncertainties are not dispelled by more recent British cases; *Westburn Sugar Refineries Ltd* v. *I.R.C.* [1960] S.L.T. 297, and *Dimbula Valley (Ceylon) Tea Co. Ltd* v. *Laurie* [1961], ch. 353.

24. H. C. Edey, 'Deprival Value and Financial Accounting', Edey and Yamey (eds.), *Debits, Credits, Finance and Profits*. Sweet & Maxwell, 1974, p. 83.

13. The valuation of depreciating assets

The asset viewed as a store of inputs

Sometimes an asset is best viewed as a quantity of inputs bought ahead of needs. A tank of fuel-oil at a factory is a store of gallons awaiting use: likewise, a machine is a store of service-units (e.g., ton-miles) awaiting use. Such stores are bought in big purchase-lots, and not in driblets, for the sake of convenience, the economies of bulk-buying, etc. Thus, a brand-new lorry may be preferred to a series of shortlived, secondhand ones because it is thought to be more reliable or to cost less per ton-mile.

If a whole purchase-lot is used-up within an accounting period, no problem of balance sheet valuation arises. If some of the lot spills over into later periods, the units still on hand must be valued. The task seems easier where the number of units can be gauged with the simpler physical measures of weight, volume, and so on—e.g., as so many gallons of oil. It seems much less easy where the units cannot be so gauged. Usually 'depreciating asset' means an asset that is subject to this difficulty; thus, we often find it hard to quantify the remaining physical services of a machine, and lack any obvious guide to their value per unit. For valuation theory, however, such assets do not appear to differ much from other stores of input, and the analogy with raw materials, etc., should serve as a useful starting-point.

Where asset values are linked with historical cost, accountants have dealt with depreciation by writing off the cost by one or other of their traditional 'depreciation methods'. The rationale of these methods ('matching cost and revenues') seems crude, and the grounds for choosing a particular method are seldom stated in a clear way. Moreover, the methods produce a limited range of somewhat rigid value patterns. Even if the link with historical cost is retained, there seems no reason why the patterns should not be more flexible. And if assets are instead to be shown at current values, their valuation method must be agile enough to respond to all manner of ups and downs. It must be able to cope, for instance, with the pattern for a cow: this will vary not only with changes in market conditions, but also with age—upsurge in youth, a summit at maturity, and fall thereafter. Deprival value seems admirably suited to give such flexibility.

This chapter will run most easily if it separates value movements due to ageing (with depreciating assets such as machines, from a peak at acquisition to a low point at disposal) from those due to changing market forces. It starts with the former.

Reasons for calculating depreciation

Like other assets, a depreciating asset can be valued by several different concepts, e.g., at replacement cost or sale price; and, if we define annual depreciation cost as the change during a year in one of these values, the cost charge also has a corresponding range of possible sizes. It was suggested on p. 23 that rival income figures should be judged by their informativeness, and that sometimes one figure may be the most informative for purpose A and another for purpose B. In the same way, the rival figures for depreciation cost should be judged by their informativeness, and one may be the best for A and another for B.

Thus, it is helpful to remind ourselves of the occasions when information about depreciation may be wanted:

In final accounts. (a) The cost figures of the *income statement* are sometimes looked on as a test of efficiency. More important, they influence the profit balance, i.e., the guide to the owners' consumption and investment (see p. 23); thus, depreciation charges that err on the high side could result in unduly low dividends and failure to attract the capital needed to expand plant to its best size.

(b) The values for plant, etc., in the *balance sheet* are evidence of the 'size of the tools' and capital maintenance.

In decision budgets. Here depreciation costs may help with, e.g., problems of pricing, and of deciding whether a given job will be worth doing. Depreciated asset values may help with decisions on when to sell and replace the asset.[1] They should therefore be linked in some logical way with replacement and secondhand prices, e.g., if book-value threatens to sink below sale price, this should be a signal that the time for disposal is near.

In calculating tax. Here the procedure depends on legal rules, not economic goals, and so lies beyond the reach of reason.

The well-known methods

For the most part, accountants have been content to write down assets with the help of well-known book-keeping methods,[2] such as:
- the straight-line method;
- the fixed-percentage (more clearly, the 'fixed percentage of the diminishing balance') method; and
- (especially in North America) the sum-of-the-digits method.

Occasionally, other arithmetically simple methods are employed, for instance:
- a fixed annual charge to cover both depreciation and repairs; and
- a charge varying with use—the 'service-unit' method.

Even more rarely, the methods recognize the desirability of discounting, i.e., of allowing for 'interest' at some suitable rate. As we shall see, the case for doing so (in these as in other calculations that deal with cash flows of widely different dates) is strong. The methods that allow for 'interest' include:
- the annuity method; and
- the sinking-fund method.

Is accurate calculation of depreciation worth while?

Accounting textbooks say little about the criteria that should guide one's choice of method. Indeed, accountants have tended by and large to dismiss depreciation as something that does not merit careful measurement. They argue that fixed-asset values have little usefulness; that, regardless of method, the depreciation charges will mount up over the whole life of the asset to the desired total (the net historical cost of the asset); and that accuracy is in any case impossible because it demands knowledge of the future.

They can argue, too, that under certain circumstances the choice of method has little effect on the total depreciation cost of any year. Suppose the firm has four similar assets, each with a four-year life. Their ages are such that one asset is renewed each year. The price of each is £130, less a £30 trade-in allowance. Whichever of the methods is used, the total yearly depreciation cost will be £100, i.e., it must equal the year's net cost of replacement. Take, for instance, the costs for any year by the straight-line and the fixed-percentage methods (respectively, £25 and 30·7% of the diminishing balance):

	Straight-line	*Fixed percentage*
	£	£
Machine 1	25	39·9
2	25	27·7
3	25	19·1
4	25	13·3
Total (= net replacement cost)	100	100

i.e., the total costs of these two very dissimilar patterns are equal—because the costs for all four machines in any one year are the same as the costs for the whole life of any one machine. But this comforting truth usually ceases to hold where there is change in the number or average age of assets, or in their prices. And it does not solve the problem of balance sheet values: a 'high–low' write-off pattern (i.e., a pattern, such as that of the fixed-percentage method, which moves from high charges at the start of life to low charges at the end) gives a smaller total value for the assets than a straight-line pattern, which in turn gives a lower total than a low–high pattern.

It is not unreasonable to decide that, where the investment in depreciating assets is tiny, careful estimates of depreciation are not worth while (though this attitude contrasts surprisingly with the pains that accounting often takes over prepaid expenses and other minutiae). Where the investment is large, the matter must hinge mainly on whether the figures have a useful part to play, and in particular on how far they help with decisions. One must therefore try not only to find the best depreciation method for various assets, but also to consider the types of decision that depend on depreciation data.

Definitions

Before one can come to grips with the main problem, certain preliminary points must be cleared up.

Use-assets and time-assets. The lives of some assets end when the asset is worn out by use. The lives of others are ended by events that time must bring anyway, regardless of use, e.g., the expiry of a lease or the invention of a better asset. Thus, it is convenient to talk of 'use-assets' and 'time-assets'. (It may be that some assets depreciate partly because of time and partly because of use—e.g., my car's life may end when a better model is put on the market, but its trade-in value then may to some extent be affected by its mileage.) Possibly, time is the more usual cause of depreciation, and so the following pages tend to concentrate on time-assets.

If an asset's value depreciates during a year, this fall is normally a cost for purposes of income measurement, i.e., must be charged in the income statement. With use-assets, there is a cause-and-effect link between the use of the asset on a job, etc., and the fall; so the fall is an avoidable cost of the job, and should be shown as such in budgets for the job, as well as in the income statement (ideally with the direct costs). With time-assets, however, use does not cause the fall; time depreciation is therefore not an avoidable cost of the job, and should be left out of decision budgets, but included with other fixed costs in the income statement.

Depreciation and obsolescence. If the word is used in a narrow sense, 'depreciation' is due to physical factors such as wearing-out and to the resulting rise in repair costs, decline in output, etc. Perhaps because our naïve minds often find it hard to accept economic loss that is divorced from physical decline (we shrink from throwing out white elephants if they look 'as good as new'), we tend to use a special word—'obsolescence' instead of 'depreciation'—when value sinks for non-physical reasons. Obsolescence may be due, for instance, to a fall in demand for the product (because, e.g., fashion changes or a better product is invented) or the arrival on the market of a better asset; it may be sudden or slow; and it may be unforeseen or predictable.

This distinction between depreciation and obsolescence can on occasion help understanding. But it does not usually seem to serve much purpose in accounts; and, as the two kinds of decline are often difficult if not impossible to unravel, this chapter treats them in principle as one.

Primary and secondary assets. It was suggested on p. 94 that it is convenient to give the name 'primary asset' to the depreciating asset whose figures are being studied, and 'secondary assets' to the extra net assets that accumulate as a result of providing for its depreciation. As the primary asset falls, the secondary assets rise: together they should maintain the owner's capital. This change-over can be envisaged in terms of Fig. 13.1. Here OC represents the amount of capital invested in the primary asset at the start of its life. OK represents its life-span. Its value falls over the years along some such pattern at CK. But, if secondary assets accumulate in the quantities suggested by the area CC'K, the owner's capital is maintained.

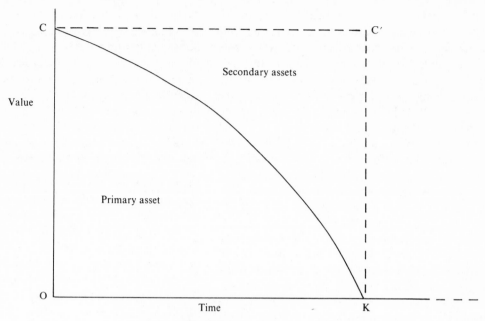

Fig. 13.1
Depreciation and the firm's asset structure

Secondary assets may at first take the form of cash. But in time this cash will tend to enrich the whole net asset structure; for instance, it may be used to buy more stocks or even other depreciating assets, or to repay interest-bearing loans. In this way, the secondary growth normally becomes part and parcel of the general structure, and (though their total size is measured by the cumulative depreciation provision) the secondary assets cannot be identified as such. But occasionally they are put aside as earmarked financial securities, with some such name as 'sinking-fund' investments'.

Deprival budgets for depreciating assets

Deprival value depends on the difference between two cash budgets—one for the figures if the owner is left in possession, and the other for the figures if he is deprived (see p.126). We shall continue to call the former the Have budget, and the latter the Have Not budget. It will be convenient also to call the existing asset Old, and its potential replacement New.

Relevant cash flows for deprival budgets. Which cash items should be put in the budgets for depreciating assets? We are concerned to find the *contrast* between the two sets of figures; as usual therefore figures that are common to both sets—*in date as well as size*, i.e., after discounting—are irrelevant and can be left out. The well-known book-keeping methods put most of their stress on initial price and scrap proceeds; and certainly these in most instances affect the contrast, and then should be included. But many other items may be just as relevant. The obvious example is repair cost. If this increases because of the asset's ageing (i.e., because of 'wearing out' through time or use), then it too will affect the contrast. If, on the other hand, it would not be changed by a switch from Old to New, it can be ignored. Receipts may in some cases be as relevant as outflows. For instance, they will vary where an old asset loses customer-appeal or works only by fits and starts; the rent of apartments may fall as they grow old and dingy; and a plane or car may cease to attract passengers when it becomes comparatively slow and unreliable. Often, however, receipts cannot affect the contrast, particularly if the given asset is only one link in the productive chain: as one asset in an assembly-line grows old, the owner suffers not because his receipts dwindle, but because he has to pay for higher repairs to that asset and finally for a replacement. For many assets, then, the budgets can be confined to a few outflows.

'Interest' and deprival budgets. In any budgets that stretch over long tracts of time, discounting of the figures may greatly increase accuracy. The figures in the Have and Have Not budgets for depreciating assets will often become more helpful if they are reduced to present values; and this discounting process is essential while we are exploring theory. The nature of the 'interest' rate will be discussed in later paragraphs.

Assumption of knowledge of future. If value depends on budgets, i.e., is forward-looking, serious discussion of our subject is impossible unless we concede that some estimate, however rough, can be made of the cash flows for the asset's whole life, and sometimes indeed for longer periods. Even the usual rule-of-thumb methods use estimates of life-span and scrap proceeds; and, in fact, they rely also on sweeping assumptions about the future—all the more dangerous because they have never been spelled out.

How the earnings of the other assets affect the depreciating asset's value

If I today incur a liability of £10 due several years hence, I can meet it by depositing a smaller sum, say £7, at interest. Provided I resolve not to treat each future year's receipt of interest as spendable income but to let it accumulate, I can regard the cost of my transaction as being only £7; the remoteness of the payment date lessens my burden. Similarly, if I decide to provide for a £10 outlay due 10 years hence by laying aside equal annual instalments at interest, each instalment's size is less than £1 p.a. because these charges are supplemented by their interest earnings.

Patterns where the secondary assets form an external fund. In a full analysis of depreciation, the same reasoning applies. One can see this most clearly where the secondary assets are held as a segregated group of interest-yielding investments, and this external 'fund' is each year enlarged by both the year's instalment and the interest on

earlier instalments. The size of the instalment (i.e., the constant yearly figure that will with compound interest build up the fund to the desired total by the end of the asset's life) can be found from the $(s_{\overline{n}|})^{-1}$ column of interest tables; and, thanks to the interest, is less than the straight-line charge that would accumulate to the desired total. In the first year, the depreciation charge is the same in size as the instalment. In later years, it is best thought of as the instalment plus the year's interest; and, as the fund grows yearly, interest receipts tend to grow fast—so that the charges are tilted in a low–high pattern. This is illustrated in Fig. 13.2. Time is measured along the OX axis, and the annual revenues (net of all costs save primary depreciation) and depreciation charges on the OY axis. SL traces the fixed annual charges of the straight-line method, and DF the instalments to the external fund. The revenues of the primary asset are shown by, say, RP (here representing a constant annual sum). Total revenue starts at BR; but it is supplemented in later years by the interest, and thus has a low–high pattern such as RT (where interest is PT in the final year). The total yearly additions to the depreciation fund (the same thing as the write-offs from the asset's net value) follow the parallel pattern DD'. Net income (primary plus secondary) for any year is represented by the distance between DD' and RT, and is here constant over the life. If the life of the asset is long and the rate of the secondary earnings is high, DF lies far below SL; the diagram shows the gap where the asset's life is 20 years and the interest rate is 15 per cent.

Where, because of secondary earnings, the additions to a fund rise yearly like DD', the fund itself grows at an increasing pace. This explains the shape chosen in Fig. 13.1 for CKC', the secondary assets; the rising supplements of interest must make CK concave to O. But CK traces also the value of the primary asset; so this must here have a humped pattern. The secondary earnings thus affect both the annual charges and the value of the primary asset.

It is not fanciful to think that the value pattern of a depreciating asset tends to hump. The idea is borne out by the market-price patterns of other 'wasting assets' such as annuities and leases. Thanks

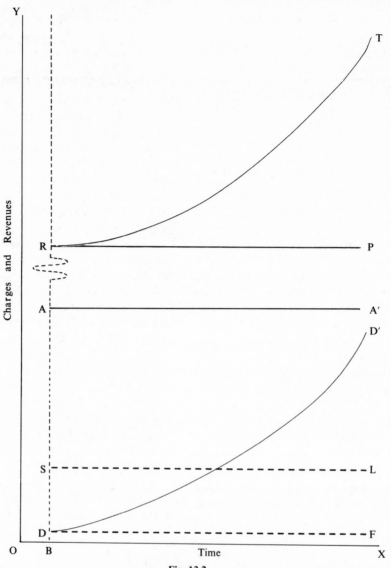

Fig. 13.2
Annual depreciation charges and revenues

to the pull of interest, their values fall slowly in early life and fast later.

External funds are rare (because most firms think their secondary assets will earn more inside than outside the business). Where they are used, they are often called 'sinking funds'; and unfortunately the sinking-fund method of book-keeping obscures the true pattern of yearly cost by charging only a low constant sum (DF) in the income statement, and putting secondary interest direct to a fund account.

Patterns where secondary assets stay in the firm. Where, as is usual, the secondary assets are not segregated as an external fund but form part of the firm's own working structure, the secondary earnings are less obvious. But they must nevertheless exist. If the depreciation provision is used to repay loans, etc., its 'earnings' are the resulting fall in interest charges. If it is used to buy more stocks of merchandise, its earnings are the rise in gross profit. If it is used to buy more machinery to replace hand labour, its earnings are the fall in

150

wages. And so on. One way or another, profit before depreciation should again tend to rise each year (see RT) throughout the life of the primary asset. And accurate depreciation charges again start below the straight-line charge, and rise each year (see DD'). In the absence of disturbing factors such as increasing maintenance costs, value must follow a humped pattern such as CK in Fig. 13.1. The great attraction of the annuity method (described below) is that its net write-offs rise each year and its value pattern is humped.

The growth of the secondary assets is thus part and parcel of the depreciating asset's story. Their earnings enter into its cash flow just as surely as, say, the scrap receipt; and so—rather surprisingly—these seemingly remote secondary flows influence the depreciation calculation. The 'interest' of the annuity method should presumably be interpreted as reflecting these expected secondary earnings (and not the rate of return from the primary asset).

Full service charge. One more cost-curve claims attention. To find the whole yearly sacrifice of investing in an asset, the owner must allow for the cost of the capital sunk in the asset. As we have seen, this finance may be got from loans, etc., or by dipping into existing funds. Either way, the investment brings yearly sacrifice—extra payments of interest and dividend, or earnings forgone on other potential investments squeezed out by this one. To be worth while, the earnings of a primary asset must be high enough at least to recoup not only depreciation and any repairs, etc., but also

those costs of capital. Such minimum adequate earnings could under stable conditions follow a horizontal pattern like AA' in Fig. 13.2. Thus, if the asset is to be bought at date B for hiring out, the expected yearly rent must be at least BA; in the first year, DA meets the cost-of-capital and BD the depreciation cost; in later years, cost-of-capital shrinks (as the purchase loan is repaid or secondary assets accumulate) and depreciation cost rises. If the asset is instead used inside the firm, its minimum worthwhile earnings must also cover BA, the whole yearly cost of 'servicing' the investment. We shall call this whole cost (traced over the years by AA') the *full service charge*. Later pages contain arithmetical examples and supporting argument on these patterns of depreciation and value.

The perpetuity approach

The nature of depreciation: the worsening of a cash prospect

When a man decides to own a depreciating asset, he is involving himself in a new series of future cash flows. The flows governing deprival value (see p. 48) are those whose present values affect the contrast between the Have and Have Not budgets—notably the flows that vary because of the ageing of the asset. They probably include a price paid at once, and varying repair charges, etc., paid at later dates; they may also include some varying receipts, such as final scrap proceeds. Moreover, when the first asset's life is over, the owner is

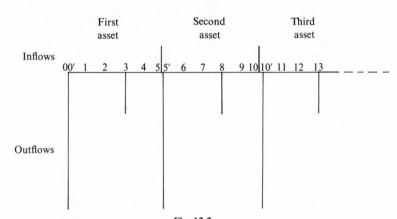

Fig. 13.3
Example of the cash-flow series of successive depreciating assets

151

likely to replace it with a second, bringing much the same set of flows. And so on. In the absence of special circumstances, his decision involves him in sets of flows that stretch to his time-horizon. He can estimate their size by treating them as a perpetuity.

As an example, suppose the flows are the initial price of £100, and £30 for an overhaul at the end of year 3; and that the asset will be sold for £20 (at the end of year 5). Suppose further that it will at once be replaced by an identical asset (at 5'), and the same series of flows will thereafter be repeated for life after life. The flows can be shown as in Fig. 13.3: time runs from left to right, inflows are above the horizontal line, and outflows are below it.

At date 0, just before buying the asset, the man faces the whole range of future flows. Using v^x for the present value of £1 due at the end of x years, we may express the prospect as:

$$(£100 + v^3£30 - v^5£20) + (v^5£100 + v^8£30$$
$$- v^{10}£20) + \ldots$$

A moment later (at 0'), when he has paid the £100 price, this prospect becomes lighter by £100, i.e., it is now only:

$$(v^3£30 - v^5£20) + (v^5£100 + v^8£30$$
$$- v^{10}£20) + \ldots$$

This second series constitutes his Have budget at 0'. The first shows the flows that would face him if he were deprived, i.e., it constitutes his Have Not budget at any date. Deprival value at 0' is the difference between these two present values, i.e., it measures the contrast between the two prospects; not unexpectedly, the difference between the Have and Have Not budgets (i.e., deprival value) is now £100.

However, as time goes by the prospect grows worse again as the future outlays loom nearer and their present values grow bigger. At date 1, the Have series is:

$$(v^2£30 - v^4£20) + (v^4£100 + v^7£30$$
$$- v^9£100) + \ldots$$

The present value of the payments has risen because they are now more imminent. The gap between this

worsening Have and the unchanged Have Not budgets has shrunk slightly; value has fallen. At date 2 it has shrunk further. It widens slightly after the £30 repair outlay has been made, but otherwise gets steadily smaller—until the asset is scrapped at year 5, and value sinks back to *nil*. Thereafter, the same rhythm is repeated over each successive life. Deprival value at any date can be found by contrasting Have and Have Not series of future cash flows in perpetuity as seen from that date. Depreciation cost for the period between two dates is the decline in value during the period, i.e., it is the contrast between contrasts.

This perpetuity approach enables one to formulate a concept of depreciation that seems not unsatisfactory. The next few pages will try to explain it more fully. Its arithmetic is less simple than that normally employed in accounting, but is not too hard. And, once the approach is understood, the concept (and its arithmetic) often can be allowed to sink into the background. So long as conditions are stable, it may be looked on more as a touchstone for choosing between the simpler methods than as a method in its own right. But when conditions cease to be stable, one should again use the perpetuity approach for guidance.

In the interests of easy understanding, the next few pages will assume technology and prices to be constant, so that ageing is the sole reason for writing down the asset.

Present values and annual equivalents

One can boil down a long series of cash flows for an asset to equivalent forms that are much easier to deal with. Some of these forms are:

(1) Present value at purchase date of a complete set of flows for one asset's whole life[3]—in the example above (£100 + v^3£30 − v^5£20).

(2) Annual equivalent of form 1, i.e., the figure that was called (on p. 150) the full-service charge.[4] As is suggested in Fig. 13.2, cost-of-capital must typically be a big part of the charge; with rates of not less than 8 per cent, and lives of 20 years or more, one can say not too inaccurately that cost-of-capital for most of the life exceeds depreciation.[5]

(3) Present value of the whole range of future flows in perpetuity—the Have Not budget. This can

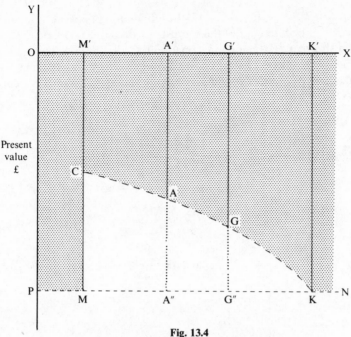

Fig. 13.4
Perpetuity approach to value of a depreciating asset

be found by discounting either form 1 or 2 above in perpetuity.[6] With long lives and stiff discount rates, it is apt to prove not much more than the price of the first asset.

Diagrammatic treatment of perpetuity approach to Have and Have Not flows

The idea of the perpetual flows can perhaps be best developed in diagrams. In Fig. 13.4, time is measured on OX, and the present value of a perpetuity of future flows on OY. If we take as example an asset whose relevant cash flows are dominated by payments, so that they can on balance be thought of as a burden rather than a benefit, the present value is negative and can conveniently be measured below OX. Thus, at date O the burden of deciding to start owning a series of assets in perpetuity (see form 3 above) can be shown as PO. At date M', it is MM'. At date K', it is KK'. PMKN gives the Have Not budget at any date; where it assumes unchanging prices, lives, etc., it is a horizontal straight line.

For simplicity, the diagram assumes too that the cash series has only one relevant flow per asset,

the initial price. Suppose the firm decides at date M' henceforth to own this kind of asset, and pays for the first one; its life is M'K'. The present value of the future payments thereafter shrinks, from MM' to CM' if MC is the price. But the passage of time brings the replacement prices of subsequent assets nearer, and so their present value lengthens again—to AA' at date A', to GG' at date G', and finally (when the life ends at date K') back to KK'. The curve CAGK represents the Have budget.

Deprival value is shown by vertical distance between CK and MK. To measure it at (say) date G', one must compare G''G' (the Have Not burden that at once faces a deprived owner) with GG' (the lesser Have burden, found by discounting the full burden KK' of the normal replacement date K'): the difference is G''G, and accordingly this measures the deprival value then. In the same way, A''A is the deprival value at A', and MC (= price) is the deprival value at M'. As there are here no complicating factors (such as varying repair outlays and a scrap value), the complete value curve for the whole life of the one machine follows the fairly simple pattern MCAK.

153

Possible value patterns

The unshaded area MCAK can be lifted out of the perpetuity framework and shown alone, in a much simpler diagram, as in Fig. 13.5a; the asset's life is represented by the horizontal MK, and its value (the difference between Have and Have Not present values in Fig. 13.4) by the vertical distances between CAK and MK.

The new diagram provides an easy way of showing the life-pattern of a depreciating asset. It

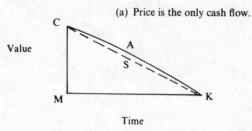
(a) Price is the only cash flow.

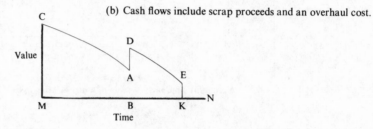
(b) Cash flows include scrap proceeds and an overhaul cost.

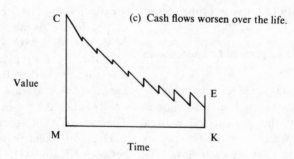
(c) Cash flows worsen over the life.

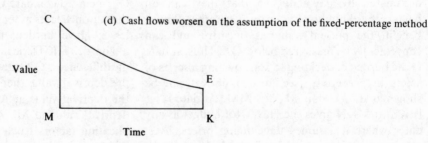
(d) Cash flows worsen on the assumption of the fixed-percentage method

Fig. 13.5
Some possible value patterns of depreciating assets

154

has the advantage of simplicity, but fails to indicate the rationale of the value curve. The diagram shows also the pattern of the straight-line method MCSK.

Where price is the only cash flow. CAK in Figs. 13.4 and 13.5a are the same kind of curve as that produced by the annuity method. This suggests the annuity method to be the correct one to use under the conditions assumed in those diagrams, namely, that the relevant cash flows contain no items (such as rising repairs) that vary because of ageing, and that the cost-of-capital is not negligible.

With a lowering of cost-of-capital rates, the curve CAK (concave to M) would flatten out and look more like the straight line CSK. This suggests that the straight-line method is the correct one if repairs, etc. do not vary with ageing and the cost-of-capital rate is negligible. It suggests, too, that the annuity method is best thought of, not as an additional method on the familiar list (see p. 146) but rather as a more careful version of the straight-line method, i.e., one that allows for the same cash flows but uses their discounted equivalents. Each of the other methods (e.g. fixed percentage) can also be provided with a more careful version, i.e., they can be adapted to allow for interest, to fit the assumptions of the perpetuity approach.

Where the cash flows include scrap proceeds and an overhaul cost. The perpetuity approach can still be applied, and produces fresh value curves, when the facts are more complex than is assumed in Fig. 13.4.

Consider an instance where the cash flow of each successive asset ends with scrap receipts, and contains a varying item (such as the outlay for a major overhaul) some two-thirds through the life—as in the example on p. 151). Then the curves must be redrawn as in Fig. 13.5b. It was explained on p. 152 how the owner's cash budget becomes brighter after he has paid the initial price; his payment improves the Have vista of Fig. 13.4 and so creates the value MC. In the same way, his Have budget improves after he has made any other useful outlay, and this payment too must push up the value curve (e.g., a car is worth more after it has been reconditioned); hence the value rise at B after the payment of AD. Conversely, the vista darkens when the owner can no longer look forward to getting the final sale receipts; thus the final drop in value takes place at K, when the owner receives the scrap price KE. The value curve for the whole life is now MCADEK—falling until date B, then restored by AD at the overhaul, then falling to scrap level just before date K, and thereafter to zero. CA and DE are concave to M, because they allow for cost-of-capital; they would be straight lines in a less careful version that ignored this cost.

Where the cash flows worsen from year to year. With imagination, one can perhaps see what could happen to CADE if a series of rising yearly repair outlays, stretching over the whole life, is substituted for the one big overhaul. This pattern of worsening cash flows tends to result in some such saw-like pattern as CEK in Fig. 13.5c. Note that CE now sags down in the middle; depreciation cost is big in the early years of light repairs, and small when the repairs grow heavy.

Figure 13.5c for simplicity ignores cost-of-capital. The more careful version, allowing for this cost, would be subject to conflict between two tendencies—the 'sag' (due to rising repairs and the 'hump' due to cost-of-capital. The outcome of the conflict must vary from case to case, but perhaps the straight-line method can often be justified as a simple approximation to the net result.

Where the cash flows worsen as assumed by the fixed-percentage method. The fixed-percentage (or exponential) method also produces a sagging value curve. It is best thought of as a simplified version of the curve in Fig. 13.5c (smoothed by linking the tops of the saw-teeth), i.e., it suits a low–high outlay pattern. So accountants are right in saying that the fixed-percentage method caters for rising repairs. But, of course, a curve begotten by a general mathematical formula (such as the example in Fig. 13.5d) need not be a close fit for a given low–high pattern. A curve specially tailored to each asset would be more likely to be exact, and could allow too for cost-of-capital.

Bespoke methods. There seems no good reason, especially where a firm knows from experience what the cash-flow pattern of a given asset is likely to be, why it should not tailor a depreciation formula specially for that asset.

Something approaching this is already done if the firm uses the method that charges a fixed annual provision to cover both depreciation and repairs. But this method should be extended to allow for other kinds of variation in cash flows due to age, for cost-of-capital, and (with use-assets) for physical usage during each year. The total cost of each unit of input from the asset is presumably (on our assumption of constant prices, etc.) the same,[7] i.e., depreciation complements the year's cash flows, and depreciation plus repairs, etc., for each unit is constant. A simple example is given below.

Arithmetic of deprival value

The yearly figures for asset value and depreciation cost over the whole life can be got from a table of Have and Have Not budgets. These can compare present values of perpetuities, as is suggested on p. 151; more conveniently, they can instead compare annual sums—the actual flows for each year of Old's remaining life, and New's full service charge (see form 2 on p. 152 above). The second procedure seems preferable here, since it can readily be used also with the simpler approach that ignores cost-of-capital.

As an example, let us use the figures of p. 151 and Fig. 13.5b, i.e., a price of £100 for a time-asset, an overhaul at the end of year 3 costing £30, and £20 of receipts when the asset is scrapped at the end of year 5. The most suitable of the traditional methods (fixed annual charge to cover depreciation and repairs) deducts $\frac{1}{5}$ (£100 + £30 − £20) = £22 each year and 'capitalizes' the repair, so that book-values run £100, £78, £56, £64, £42, and £20; it justifies itself by historical-cost arguments.

Simpler approach—cost-of-capital ignored. When it ignores cost-of-capital, the deprival value approach will reach the same values (provided the cash flows of the replacement are expected also to be £100 + £30 − £20); but it justifies itself by comparing future flows. At the end of year 2, for instance, the owner expects to pay £30 in year 3 and to get back £20 in year 5, so his Have budget for the remaining 3-year life adds up to a £10 outflow. But, if he were deprived now, he would have to pay on average £22 a year for the replacement, so

his Have Not budget for the 3 years adds up to £66. Thus, the value is £66–£10, i.e., is again £56. The Have and Have Not budgets at the close of each year can be combined into one table (Table 13.1).

TABLE 13.1
SIMPLE CALCULATION OF DEPRIVAL VALUE OF A DEPRECIATING ASSET

Year of life	0	1	2	3	4	5
	£	£	£	£	£	£
Have budget						
(i) Outlays on Old	100	—	—	30	—	—
(ii) Receipt from Old	—	—	—	—	—	20
Have Not budget						
(iii) New's average outlay	—	22	22	22	22	22
Net benefit of owning for (iv) year (= write-off at year-end)		22	22	−8	22	42
Deprival value (= future (v) years' net benefits)	100	78	56	64	42	—

Line (iv) in Table 13.1 for the *net benefit of owning* shows the extra cash outlay for each year that would face a deprived owner, and thus the advantage of ownership during a year. This benefit evaporates by the end of the year, and so must be written off. If the repair is (the common practice) debited in the income statement, (iv) also gives the depreciation charges; if it is added to the asset's value, (iii) gives the depreciation charges. The cost of depreciation and repairs is constant. At any year-end, the sum of the remaining years' benefits is *deprival value*, shown on (v)—e.g., at the end of year 2, deprival value is −£8 + £22 + £22 + £20 = £56.

If the asset is instead a use-asset, the £110 of total net outlay would be divided over all the units of expected total physical use to find an average cost per unit, and then spread across line (iii) in proportion to annual use.

Approach that allows for cost-of-capital. Let us next redraft Table 13.1 in a way that recognizes cost-of-capital, i.e., provides the simple method with its more careful version. For emphasis, we shall take the rather high rate of 25 per cent per year. First, we work out the values explained on p. 152;
(1) The present value of the flows for one whole life[8] is £108·8.

(2) The full service charge[9] is £40·46.

(3) The full burden in perpetuity (not necessary for this calculation, but interesting)[10] is only £161·8.

Depreciation cost and the asset's value for each year are worked out in the budgets of Table 13.2. The 'cost-of-capital' figure for each year is calculated on the asset's opening value for that year, as shown at the foot of the preceding column. The net benefits of owning during any year is again the year's cost avoided thanks to ownership, i.e., is the excess of the full service charge (perhaps best thought of as a rental that would be paid by a deprived owner) over the outlays of an undeprived owner, e.g., in year 1, £40·46 − £25 = £15·46; the sum of the future net benefits after any date again gives the asset's value at that date. Here the bottom line gives values higher than those in Table 13.1, i.e., it shows how cost-of-capital humps up the value pattern, as on CA and DE in Fig. 13.5b.

TABLE 13.2

FIGURES TO ILLUSTRATE THE PERPETUITY APPROACH

Year	0	1	2	3	4	5
	£	£	£	£	£	£
Have budget						
Outlay	100			30		
Receipt						− 20
Cost-of-capital		25	21·14	16·30	17·77	12·09
		25	21·14	46·30	17·77	− 7·91
Have Not budget						
Full service charge, see para. 2 (above)		40·46	40·46	40·46	40·46	40·46
Net *benefit of owning* per year		15·46	19·32	− 5·84	22·69	48·37
Deprival value (= future net benefits)	100	84·54	65·22	71·06	48·37	—

Accounting for cost-of-capital

The book-keeping of the annuity method can be made to cope with depreciation and value patterns like those in Table 13.2. The best way to master its entries is to draft a set of final accounts that tell the complete life-story of a depreciating asset. The chosen life should be short (say, three years); and the accounts should cover the fortunes of the whole firm—so that they illustrate and confirm what earlier pages have said about the interaction of general earnings with depreciation patterns.

Table 13.3 contains such an example. The primary asset, a machine used in the firm's manufacturing department, costs £100; it has a life of 3 years and no scrap value. The net revenue from manufacturing, before allowing for depreciation, is £80 per annum. (Following the usual convention, we assume cash movements to take place at the end of the year.) On its other assets—for simplicity here assumed to be interest-earning securities—the firm can earn 20 per cent. All profits are paid out as dividend. At 20 per cent (consult interest tables), £100 will buy a 3-year annuity of £47·5, i.e., this is the full service charge on the £100 machine.

Balance sheets. At each year-end, £47·5 of depreciation is subtracted from the primary asset's opening value. But, for the reasons given below, the latter is also increased (here at 20 per cent p.a.). So the net write-offs are less than £47·5; moreover they have a low–high pattern—£27·5, £33, and £39·5—that gives the hump to the values of the asset.

The notion that an asset can be subject to both depreciation and increase is unfamiliar. The easiest way to explain it is perhaps to use a backward-looking argument, and say that the full cost of the asset to date consists not only of the initial investment but also of cost-of-capital; so this invisible cost should each year be added to the asset's value, as 'interest' on the opening balance for the year, and thus increases the value. The forward-looking argument justifies the increase in a different way. A man who badly needs money for profitable ventures, i.e., who has a high cost-of-capital rate, recoils from imminent outlays. He is relatively indifferent to remote ones: a small provision now will take care of them, thanks to the high growth rate. He thus deems an asset's replacement a matter of small concern in the early years, and of great concern in the final years. In other words, depreciation is small at first and big later, and the value of the asset sinks slowly at first and fast later; the humped-value pattern (CAK in Fig. 13.5a) is not just a quirk of book-keeping, but matches the facts:

TABLE 13.3

EXAMPLE OF THE ANNUITY METHOD

Year	0 £	1 £	2 £	3 £
Balance sheet				
Primary asset				
Balance brought forward	100	100	72·5	39·5
Less Write-off:				
Full charge		47·5	47·5	47·5
Less Value increase				
(= 20 per cent cost-of-capital)		20	14·5	8
Net		27·5	33	39·5
Carried forward		72·5	39·5	—
Secondary assets		27·5	60·5	100
	100	100	100	100
Capital	100	100	100	100
Income statement				
Manufacturing section				
Revenue		80	80	80
Less depreciation and cost-of-capital				
Full service charge		47·5	47·5	47·5
Manufacturing profit		32·5	32·5	32·5
General section				
Interest from secondary assets		—	5·5	12
Cost-of-capital (added to primary asset)		20	14·5	8
Total		20	20	20
Total profit (= dividend)		52·5	52·5	52·5

The secondary assets are retained in quantities that just offset the fall in the primary asset. In this way, the firm maintains its wealth at £100 throughout.

Income statements. The manufacturing department is each year debited with the £47·5 full service charge (i.e., the net write-off plus cost-of-capital—and, where wanted, a provision for average repairs, etc.); manufacturing profit is constant. The secondary receipts (20 per cent of the secondary assets) grow at a compound rate—£0, £5·5, £12. They thus tend to give total profit a low–high pattern over the life. At replacement date, however, secondary assets and their earnings will vanish; and the cycle will be repeated in each successive life. A thoughtful owner, anxious to use income figures as a guide to consumption, investment, etc., must look askance at reported profits that go up and down in a 3-year cycle, when conditions really are stable. A constant figure will here give him the most helpful information about his maintainable consumption etc., i.e., is the 'truest' income. The annuity method makes for a constant income, by offsetting the rise in secondary earnings with the falls in addition to the primary asset (£20, £14·5, £8—the cross-entries for the value increase). In this simple example, profit stays at £52 every year.

Results of recognizing cost-of-capital

Some firms that own premises, wagons, etc., charge each department with a suitable notional rent for the use of these assets. In consequence, each department's section of the income statement is made more searching, and its manager's demands for extra resources can be checked; further, the cost of ownership can be compared with the likely cost of renting. As the charges are also credited to some non-departmental section of the income statement (e.g., interest), their net effect on the profit of the whole firm is *nil*.

Where the depreciation method allows for cost-of-capital, it too charges each department with notional yearly rent that covers the full sacrifice of owning a depreciating asset (see AA′ in Fig. 13.2), cost-of-capital as well as the asset's decline in value over the year. Such a full service charge makes the departmental section of the income statement a far more rigorous test of performance, and helps to show whether the decision to acquire an asset has proved sound. Moreover, as Table 13.3 shows, the method offsets the low–high secondary earnings, and so makes for constant profits.

Cost-of-capital is seldom recognized when practical men calculate depreciation. This is not unreasonable if the rate is low or the life is short. But cost-of-capital alters the figures materially if the rate is high or the life is long (as they often are); its recognition then gives useful extra information about asset values, income, and costs.

Size of the cost-of-capital rate

It may not be easy to tell exactly what rate of cost-of-capital should be used for the annuity method, and the rate may change over time. We here face the old and fundamental problem of explaining why we prefer £1 now to £1 later.

If a firm could finance itself wholly, and without limit, with loans at x per cent interest, then x per cent would be the cost-of-capital rate; and if the depreciation provisions were used to retire the loans at par, then x per cent would be the rate for depreciation arithmetic. But finance is in real life usually obtained from some mix of equity and other capital, loans, etc.; so the cost-of-capital is often calculated as the average rate on the various sources of finance, weighted by their respective market values.[11]

In circumstances less simple than those assumed above, the cost-of-capital rate would seem still to have relevance. Suppose that the firm will not repay existing borrowings, but will use all new resources (including depreciation provisions) to buy assets. Here the cost-of-capital rate presumably serves as the cut-off rate by which the firm tests whether new projects are worth while; so it tends to show the minimum earnings rate for new assets, and thus at least the minimum secondary earnings.

This reasoning gives a rough guide to the size of the rate; and probably precision is here not of first importance, i.e., an approximate allowance yields far more information than no allowance. Further, the reasoning explains why phrases such as 'cost-of-capital' or 'secondary earnings' are more helpful than 'interest'—for instance, they suggest the high rates appropriate to business projects rather than the lower rates earned on less risky investments.

Optimum life-span

The preceding pages assume that the owner has found out the optimum life, i.e., he knows which life-span will best suit his pocket. How does he find the right number of years?[12]

Let us assume the relevant cash flows of this asset and its replacements to be dominated by the outlays (initial price, repairs, etc.) so that their present value can be pictured as a burden (PN in Fig. 13.4). If initial prices were the main thing to be considered, then the burden would be lightened (i.e., PN would be raised) by keeping each asset longer. But, in fact, a longer life must at some point entail disadvantages such as higher repairs and lower resale values. These will make for a heavier burden (i.e., push PN down). Thus, the owner must weigh two conflicting forces and try to find the compromise that minimizes his burden. By drafting alternative budgets for series of different life-spans—i.e., by comparing perpetuities of, say, 10-year lives, 11-year lives, 12-year lives, and so on—he can discover which life gives the lowest burden. His arithmetic can take the form of trial-and-error calculations of either present values of perpetual burdens (form 3 on p. 152) or their yearly equivalents (full service charges—form 2 on p. 152). Or he may find it simpler in some types of calculation to remember that the increasing rate of yearly outlays (repairs plus fall in scrap value) must in the last year of the optimum life rise to the level of the full service charge of the replacement. For instance, the owner of an old television set uses this approach if he works out that it will now come cheaper to hire a new set than to pay the rising repair bills on the old one.

Arithmetic

Let us use a simple method that ignores cost-of-capital. At the start of the life, the owner should here draft a table of alternative budgets to find which life-span gives (as a crude approximation to the full service charge) the least average annual cost. Suppose the price is £1000, and he expects that the repair costs and scrap values will be:

Year	1 £	2 £	3 £	4 £	5 £	6 £
Repairs	—	100	100	150	300	450
Scrap receipts if asset is sold at end of year	690	540	420	350	300	270

The alternative budgets for the various possible life-spans run:

TABLE 13.4

ALTERNATIVE BUDGETS TO FIND OPTIMUM LIFE

Life-span, years:	1 £	2 £	3 £	4 £	5 £	6 £
Cash outflows						
Year 0	1000	1000	1000	1000	1000	1000
1	—	—	—	—	—	—
2		100	100	100	100	100
3			100	100	100	100
4				150	150	150
5					300	300
6						450
	1000	1100	1200	1350	1650	2100
Cash inflow (scrap)	690	540	420	350	300	270
Net outflow	310	560	780	1000	1350	1830
Average per year	310	280	260	250	270	305

So the minimum rate of yearly cost (£250) is achieved if this asset is kept for 4 years.

When my cash position is so tight that I am desperately anxious to husband every penny, I try to put off big payments until later, even if this costs me extra small payments now. Recognition of cost-of-capital likewise makes an owner tend to put off replacement and pay instead for more repairs, etc.

If the table allowed for cost-of-capital (i.e., used discounted figures), the lowest yearly 'average' (now modified to the full service charge) would tend to shift to the right; thus it might shift to the foot of the 5-year column, i.e., show the optimum life to be a year longer than the undiscounted figures suggest.[13]

160

Revaluation of depreciating assets

So far, the argument has assumed that the cash flows of the asset will continue as first predicted, and that its replacement will also have these same flows. But, in fact, they are likely to alter, because of change in prices, technology, etc.

As earlier chapters explained, revaluation problems should be analysed in three steps, by considering (1) general price change alone; (2) price change of the given asset alone, i.e., special change when general prices are stable; and (3) the combination of general and real changes.[14] With depreciating assets, it is easiest to start with (2).

Special price change when general prices are stable

The phrase 'special price change' here means change per unit of input; it thus occurs when a better New is marketed at the same price, as well as where New's price moves in a more obvious way. After the change, the deprival budgets (such as those in Table 13.1) must be revised to match the new expectations.

Budget revision after price change. In the Have budgets, the future cash flows of the existing asset (notably scrap value) may need alteration. Some or all of the flows of the new asset will change, and so the yearly cost figures (average cost or full service charge) in the Have Not budget must change, too. As a result, the deprival values of the old asset may go up or down, in both the current and later years.

The figures in Table 13.4 can be used to illustrate such a change:

Year	0	1	2	3	4 (before scrapping)
	£	£	£	£	£
Have flows	1000	—	100	100	150
Have Not average flow	—	250	250	250	250
Net benefit for year		250	150	150	100
Deprival value	1000	750	600	450	350

When the asset to be valued (=Old) is bought, 4 years seems to be its optimum life and £250 its average annual cost; its expected value pattern appears at this starting date to be £1000, £750, £600, £450, and £350.

Now, suppose that another model (New) is invented unexpectedly at the close of year 2. The improvements in New seem likely to reduce the price, the running costs, and the scrap value of the replacement by 20 per cent (and so the average annual charge in the Have Not budget drops to £200). In sympathy, Old's resale value at year 4, hitherto £350, drops to, say, £280 (but its repair costs are not changed). Table 13.5 on p. 162 shows how Old's value pattern is recalculated.

At the end of year 2, but before New's advent is announced, Old is worth £600, and the year's write-down is £150. But when New's attractions become known, the gap between the Have and Have Not budget shrinks, and Old's value drops sharply by a further £170 to £430. This windfall loss is a good example of how technical improvement brings obsolescence; owners of assets may well look askance at the onward march of technology. Note that Old's own prospects are almost unchanged; but it suffers in comparison with New, and so the future net benefits of ownership fall. Here again the figures stress the *relative* nature of value.

Diagrammatic treatment of value change. Curves such as those in Fig. 13.5 can be readily adapted for price changes. Figure 13.6 shows some of the possibilities. Let us start with downward movement in the value of an old asset (perhaps due, as in the arithmetical example above, to the appearance of a new asset the price and upkeep costs of which are lower, but here with a somewhat different impact and timing). Old's value curve was expected to be CFK'K (the path of which reflects rising repairs). New appears unexpectedly at date E. At once the relative advantage of possessing Old is lessened. Old's value curve falls vertically from F. If the comparison of Old with New gives New a moderate advantage only, the drop may be to a point such as G, and the revised curve may be CFGL'L, i.e., the optimum life is here shortened to L.[15] But many other effects are possible. As we

TABLE 13.5

SIMPLE CALCULATION OF DEPRIVAL VALUE, WITH SPECIAL PRICE CHANGE

Budgets at end of year:	1	2 Before price change	2 After price change	3	4 Before scrapping
	£	£	£	£	£
Have budget					
Old's future outlays:					
Year 2	100				
Year 3	100	100	100		
Year 4	150	150	150	150	
	−350	−350	−280	−280	−280
	—	−100	−30	−130	−280
Have Not budget	(pre-change model)		(post-change model)		
Replacement's expected costs (as an average yearly charge)					
Year 2	250				
Year 3	250	250	200		
Year 4	250	250	200	200	—
	750	500	400	200	—
Deprival value (= expected net benefits)	750	600	430	330	280
Annual write-off					
Foreseen	250	150		100	50
Unforeseen ('obsolescence')			170		

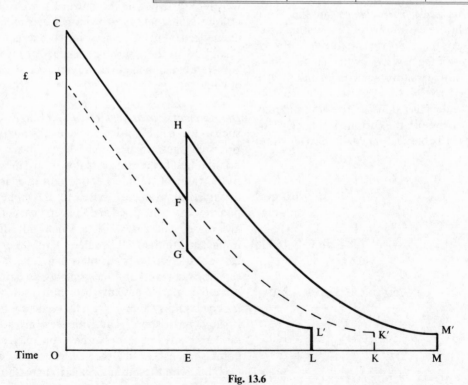

Fig. 13.6

Some possible effects of price change on a depreciating asset's value

have seen, Old's value and life depend on the gap between Old's future annual outlays and New's full service charge. If at E the former already exceed the latter, Old will be scrapped at once (i.e., L coincides with E) as its value is less than its scrap price. If they remain lower until K, Old's earlier life estimate still holds (i.e., L coincides with K) though its value curve is beneath FK'.

If New's price, etc., are above Old's, the book-value should be raised, and Old's life tends to be extended. Its revised value pattern may, for instance, be CFHM'M.

Gradual value change. Change in value often takes place gradually rather than with the one violent jump of Fig. 13.6. Moreover, it may to some extent be foreseen.

Gradual price change will result in a series of small movements instead of steep jumps such as GF and FH. And, when changes in a future year are foreseen, the revised Have Not budgets must at once tend to affect deprival value, i.e., to spread the value changes back towards early life. Realistic value patterns should probably follow gentle curves from C to L' or M'. This is one of the situations in which depreciation and obsolescence are almost indistinguishable.

Accounting entries. When price change affects the value of a depreciating asset, advocates of current value will alter the balance sheet figures. Thus, the semi-obsolete asset in the example in Table 13.5 must be written down to £430. For most depreciating assets, however, a balance sheet normally gives three figures: (a) the original (gross) cost, (b) cumulative depreciation, and (c) a net value—and these figures are useful, in that they enable readers to form some picture of the age of the plant. Consistency demands that a revalued asset also should be provided with (a) and (b) as well as (c). But how does one now define and measure (a) (i.e., what is a suitable substitute for the asset's original cost in a revalued balance sheet)? In the example, three figures suggest themselves for the balance sheet of year 2:
(1) The current price of another asset (new, i.e., at the start of its life) of the Old type.
(2) The current price of whatever other asset (new) would in fact be the replacement.

(3) A notional price. Suppose that another asset of the Old type was bought (new) at the end of year 2, just before New appeared; and that, following New's appearance, its £1000 price was at once written down to allow for its obsolescence. By the reasoning of pp. 161–2, the written-down value (i.e., deprival value of a brand-new asset) would be £730. This seems a suitable notional price (and is represented by OP in Fig. 13.6).

These three possible sets of figures could read:

	(1) £	(2) £	(3) £
Depreciating asset's value:			
(a) Gross			
Price, Old	1000		
Price, New		800	
Notional price, Old			730
(b) Cumulative depreciation	570	370	300
(c) Net value	430	430	430

Method 3 (above), putting gross value at £730, seems least unsatisfactory.

In following years, the special-index man will base depreciation charges on the revised value. Chapter 8 argued however that, where there is real gain on assets that are later used-up as inputs, the gain cannot change total profit for the whole period; income statements should not charge for its exit unless they also take credit for its entry. If this argument is sound, depreciation charges should remain at historical cost; or, if they are raised to current level, the extra charge should be offset by yearly transfers from the holding gain (as in the example in Table 10.3). As was pointed out on p. 98, even special charges may well fail to accumulate to the whole replacement price of the next asset.

Where revaluation results instead in a fall (such as the £170 in the example on p. 162), logic suggests the use of corresponding entries with debits and credits reversed. Many accountants will however prefer a prompt charge against current income— partly from caution, partly because of the difficulty of defining and pinpointing the later realization times (see p. 18).

Where a machine normally stands idle, it may not merit replacement, and thus its replacement cost is irrelevant. As it has not been junked, despite the nuisance of its claims on space, etc., it must hold promise of some value in use (say, as a standby in case newer assets break down or are overstretched) and so sale price is irrelevant, too. Here deprival value is probably the replacement cost of the potential value in use. Perhaps it is best thought of as what the firm would be willing to pay as a kind of once-and-for-all insurance premium to keep the reserve capacity available. This premium might be assessed by considering the cost of buying or hiring a suitable alternative asset, and then reducing this cost by a probability factor to allow for the chance that it will never be incurred.

General price change

If general and special prices move to much the same extent, and are expected to go on doing so, the current value of assets can be found by adjusting historical cost with the general index; a gain or loss on revaluation then appears in ordinary accounts but not in stabilized accounts. Here adjustment with the general index also cures the timelag error on annual cost (see chapter 10), and thus gives the most defensible net profit figure.

But general price change cannot affect the real values of non-money items. If our accounts and tables used stabilized figures (all in £s of, say, the close of the final year) for the whole period, they would show that general change does not alter real value patterns and optimum life.

Where our assumed real stability does not stretch into the future (e.g., where New will need less repairing), deprival value may diverge from adjusted historical cost. Here we have the 'mixture' situation treated below.

Mixture of differing special and general price changes

If real change is superimposed on money change, the approach of Table 13.5 again yields current deprival values. Often the real change will be downwards (because of technological improvement) and the money change will be upwards (because of inflation).

Stabilized accounts should try to unravel the real from the illusory (money) value movements. Thus, the balance sheet should show the real appreciation, as revaluation surplus with some such label as 'real holding gain (unrealized)', in the way illustrated on p. 33.

The special-index man would have us gear the depreciation charge and income measurement to the special value of the asset. The general-index man is satisfied with net charges that maintain real capital—a goal at once more practicable and defensible. The accounts in Table 10.4 and Table 10.5 both illustrate these matters in the year of change; appendix 2 of this chapter has a more ambitious study of the whole life of an asset.

A table of stabilized figures for a long period will show that, when there is a mixture of real and money price changes, the former affects real value and optimum life, but the latter does not.

Conclusions

This chapter helps to clarify the earlier tentative definitions of deprival value—on p. 131 (stocks) and p. 139 (assets that yield interest, etc.). The cash flows of a depreciating asset tend to be more complex than those of other assets; over its whole life, too, the type of ownership benefit reflected by deprival value may well shift, say from replacement cost to (near the end) sale receipts.

Deprival and other values over the whole life

It was suggested on p. 145 that a depreciating asset should be looked on as a store of input-units, to be consumed by time or use, bought in bulk at the lowest unit-cost. Suppose that the lowest unit-cost for ton-miles is obtained by buying brand-new lorries yielding x ton-miles over optimum life; and that, when a certain ageing lorry (= Old) is valued, it will still yield $x/3$ ton-miles. Thanks to this store, the owner is normally spared the present need to replace $x/3$ units (i.e., to pay a replacement price, in the special sense illustrated in Table 13.1); on the other hand, he will have to pay for

Old's future repairs, etc. The benefit of ownership (= deprival value) is here a *net* future outflow avoided.

The benefit shrinks as time or use eat up the store of units, and thus lessen the gap between the Have and Have Not prospects (e.g., in Fig. 13.4, from A"A to G"G in the period A'G'). It may be changed too by change in the estimates of future cash flows, notably New's price, etc. And eventually the date will be reached at which Old ceases to obviate a need for replacement outlay—probably because replacement is so near, but perhaps because replacement no longer seems desirable (say, because New's price has soared). Henceforth, Old's value no longer hinges on New's figures (which should be dropped from the Have Not budget), but on the best contribution that Old can still make. Often this is Old's sale price (i.e., Old should be sold at once). But sometimes it is Old's discounted future net receipts—e.g., where Old is a taxi—or cost savings (see Table 12.3).

We can perhaps generalize by defining deprival value as the worsening of cash flows that would follow the asset's loss; if we want to spell out the main possibilities, we need some such formula as:

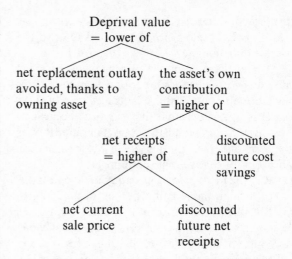

Diagram covering whole life. To make the matter more vivid, a diagram should trace several kinds of values over the whole life of the asset. Figure 13.7 measures time along OX and values up OY. It assumes that the cheapest input-units come from an asset (new or secondhand) whose future life at purchase date O is OK; its price is OR. Preliminary capital budgets show such an asset to be worth buying because its contribution OF

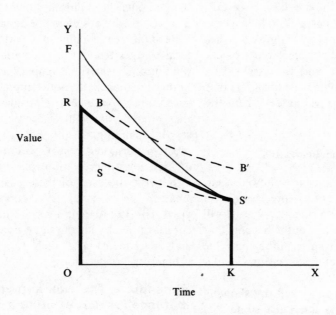

Fig. 13.7

Various values of a depreciating asset

165

(the present value of its net cost savings or revenues, and of its final sale proceeds) exceeds OR; so the asset is duly bought.

At later dates, various different forms of value may suggest themselves for appraising the remaining store of inputs. Table 13.7 traces four of these patterns. It assumes that they sag (say, because of low–high repairs), and that they fall smoothly as the asset ages (i.e., are not jerked by, for instance, abrupt price change). The patterns are

(1) RS′, the net *replacement* outlay avoided thanks to owning the remaining stock of input units.
(2) BB′, the *buying* price of a similar ageing, i.e., used, asset. Because RS′ represents the cheapest source of inputs, BB′ must lie above RS′. For the same reason, BB′ is irrelevant to deprival value.
(3) SS′, the *sale* price of a similar ageing asset. SS′ lies below BB′ (because of transfer costs, specificity, etc.—see p. 123). As long as the asset is worth keeping, SS′ does not rise above RR′; if it did, the firm would gain by selling and buying a replacement for OR.
(4) FS′, the discounted future contribution. This falls until, at date K, the asset should be replaced and so the highest contribution is the sale price KS′.

Deprival value starts as the purchase price OR. It then follows replacement cost RS′ so long as the asset merits replacement, i.e., so long as RS′ lies below FS′. When the two curves meet, replacement cost ceases to be relevant, and the asset's best contribution (here from prompt sale for KS′) takes over. So the pattern of deprival value is here the heavy line ORS′K.

The benefits of sound depreciation values

If the suggestions of this chapter are followed, then:

(1) The balance sheet value of a depreciating asset will be closely linked with current prices. It will also reflect managers' views of the benefits that the asset still can yield as input; the same value will tie in with many kinds of decision calculation on the best use of the asset.
(2) The stabilized balance sheet will (by showing real holding gain on the asset) give some idea of management's skill in buying assets when they are cheap.

(3) The income in corrected accounts will, after price change, be free from the distortion of the timelag error.
(4) If cost-of-capital is recognized, the firm's operating divisions, etc., will be charged with an expense that may be important yet is normally neglected.
(5) In successive income statements, the total net charges for the asset—depreciation, varying repairs, etc., and cost-of-capital, less real gain realized—will work out as a constant real amount per unit of time or use. This will smooth out some spurious fluctuations in the income pattern—and thereby give better information for decisions on, e.g., dividends, further investment in fixed assets, and (at least with use-assets) pricing of the product. It will also give an improved check on the worthwhileness of past decisions to buy assets.

As an example of the harm done by inept methods, consider the firm that charges its branches with straight-line depreciation on delivery vans (with a low–high repair pattern). As a van ages, a branch manager will see his combined depreciation and repair charges rising, and will start to press for the renewal of the van—before its optimum life has run out; should his argument be accepted, the firm as a whole suffers. If depreciation cost is instead tapered in a high–low pattern, the branch's total charges tend to be constant throughout the optimum life (see the example on p. 156) and the branch manager is not tempted to press for premature replacement. Consider, too, the firm that expands its plant for some years, and then stops expanding. If the plant has a low–high repair pattern, and cost-of-capital is unimportant, a high–low depreciation pattern is desirable. Otherwise, the total of these charges will be too small in the early years and too high in the late years, and the income figures will at first be too cheerful (thereby encouraging excessive dividends and investment) and then too gloomy (again prompting bad decisions).

Appendix 1: The well-known accounting methods for depreciating assets

In outline, the well-known accounting methods for depreciating assets are as follows. The original cost of the asset is C, expected resale ('scrap' or 'salvage') value S, and life-span n years.

Straight-line. Here the depreciation charge is $(1/n)(C - S)$ in all years. For example, if the asset costs £1250 and will fetch £50 after a 3-year life, the charge is £400 p.a.; the book-values for successive year-ends run £1250, £850, £450, and £50.

Fixed percentage. The diminishing balances are written down by a rate r (a fraction of 1) found from

$$r = 1 - \sqrt[n]{\frac{S}{C}}$$

or $n \log (1 - r) = \log S - \log C$.

In the example, the rate is 0·658; the charges run £822, £282, and £96; the book-values £1250, £428, £146, and £50.

Sum-of-the-digits. The years are represented by the digits $1, 2, 3, \ldots, n$. The fractions of $(C - S)$ charged in years $1, 2, 3, \ldots, n$ are the digits in reverse order, divided by their sum. In the example, the fractions are

$$\frac{3}{1 + 2 + 3} \text{ in year 1,}$$

$$\frac{2}{1 + 2 + 3} \text{ in year 2,}$$

and

$$\frac{1}{1 + 2 + 3} \text{ in year 3;}$$

the charges run £600, £400, and £200; the book-values £1250, £650, £250, and £50.

Fixed annual charge to cover depreciation and repairs. Let R = total expected repairs during life. The charge is $(1/n)(C - S + R)$ in all years, and repair outlays are added to the value of the asset. In the example, suppose R consists of a £300 overhaul in year 2. The charge is £500 p.a.; the book-values £1,250, £750, £550, and £50.

Service-unit. $(C - S)$ is divided by the expected total of units during the life; the unit-cost is multiplied by the number of units 'consumed' in a year, to give that year's depreciation charge. In the example, suppose the asset is a car, expected to run 100 000 miles; unit-cost is thus £0·012 per mile.

Yearly mileage is 25 000 in year 1, 60 000 in year 2, 15 000 in year 3. The charges are £300, £720, and £180; the book-values £1250, £950, £230, and £50.

Annuity and sinking-fund methods. These defy nutshell description, but are examined in this chapter. The sinking-fund method debits the income statement with seemingly small (by straight-line standards) constant yearly charges, but in fact augments these with the compound interest on the earlier charges; so $(C - S)$ is reached by rising yearly steps. The annuity method accumulates $(C - S)$ by the same steps; it uses various cross-entries the net effect of which is to subtract rising annual sums from revenue.

Appendix 2: Price change throughout the depreciating asset's life

It is not easy to squeeze a complete example into a small table. The figures should cover many kinds of events, and illustrate many alternative modes of treatment. But the following example shows at least the mixture of general and real change. It assumes a short life (only three years), and its solution in Table 13.6 gives three versions of each year's accounts:

(a) Ordinary accounts.

(b) Stabilized accounts, in £ of 31 December of each year. The assets are revalued at their current prices. The depreciation charge is based on the resulting end-of-year value; but the real holding gain in this charge is also brought in as extra income, so the net profit is the figure that would be found by general-index adjustment (p. 164).

(c) As (b), but the depreciation charge is based on *mid-year* special values (adjusted between July and December with the general index). It was argued on p. 100 that this is the best measure of a year's current input cost. As the fall in the charge (compared with (b)) is matched by a fall in the credit for real holding gain, profit stays the same as in (b).

Data of example

The firm has a capital of £3000, with which it buys the primary asset on 1 January, year 1. The asset has no scrap value at the end of its 3-year life. The primary revenue is £1540 in year 1, and rises with the general index. Secondary assets appreciate with the general index (which implies that net money-assets are *nil*), but otherwise have no earnings. The straight-line method is appropriate. All profits are paid out as dividends. The general index rises over the three years from 100 to 160, and the special index from 100 to 200; each year's average and end-figures are shown near the top of Table 13.6:

TABLE 13.6

LIFE–HISTORY OF A DEPRECIATING ASSET SUBJECT TO PRICE CHANGE

	Year 1 (a) Ordinary accounts £	Year 1 (b) Stabilized accounts £ of 31 December	Year 1 (c) As (b), but input at mid-year price	Year 2 (a) Ordinary accounts £	Year 2 (b) Stabilized accounts £ of 31 December	Year 2 (c) As (b), but input at mid-year price	Year 3 (a) Ordinary accounts £	Year 3 (b) Stabilized accounts £ of 31 December	Year 3 (c) As (b), but input at mid-year price
General index: Average	110			126			147		
End	120			140			160		
Special index: Average	115			136			160		
End	130			145			200		
Income Statement									
Sales, *less* Current costs	1540	*1680*	*1680*	1764	*1960*	*1960*	2058	*2240*	*2240*
Depreciation									
Historical cost	1000			1000			1000		
Replacement cost									
End of year		*1300*			*1450*			*2000*	
Mid-year			*1255*			*1511*			*1742*
Current operating profit		*380*	*425*		*510*	*449*		*240*	*498*
Real holding gain realized		*100*	*55*		*50*	*111*		*400*	*142*
Net profit	540	*480*	*480*	764	*560*	*560*	1058	*640*	*640*
Less Dividend	540	*589*	*589*	764	*849*	*849*	1058	*1152*	*1152*
Deficit: for year	—	*(109)*	*(109)*	—	*(289)*	*(289)*	—	*(512)*	*(512)*
Deficit: brought forward	—	*—*	*—*	—	*(127)*	*(127)*	—	*(475)*	*(475)*
Deficit: total	—	*(109)*	*(109)*	—	*(416)*	*(416)*	—	*(987)*	*(987)*
Balance Sheet									
Primary asset (cost, new)	3000	*3900*		3000	*4350*		3000	*6000*	
less Depreciation	1000	*1300*	as (b)	2000	*2900*	as (b)	3000	*6000*	as (b)
	2000	*2600*		1000	*1450*		—	*—*	
Secondary assets									
Of year 1	1000	*1091*		1000	*1273*		1000	*1455*	
2				1000	*1111*		1000	*1270*	
3							1000	*1088*	
				2000	*2384*		3000	*3813*	
	3000	*3691*		3000	*3834*		3000	*3813*	
Capital (nominal)	3000	*3600*		3000	*4200*		3000	*4800*	
Real holding gain (unrealized)									
on primary asset	—	*200*		—	*50*		—	*—*	
Profit deficit	—	*(109)*		—	*(416)*		—	*(987)*	
	3000	*3691*		3000	*3834*		3000	*3813*	

Solution

The ordinary accounts of columns (1a), (2a), and (3a) tell the usual story of rising profits. Because these uncorrected sums are paid out as dividends, real wealth is eroded: the secondary assets at the end of year 3, shown at their cost of £3000 though worth £3813 if revalued,[16] are less than the real opening wealth (£3000 at the start of the three years = £4800 at the end), let alone the replacement price of £6000.

The stabilized income statements reveal the rising yearly deficits. The stabilized balance sheets value all the assets at current prices, and show the real holding gain on the primary asset—written off as the asset is consumed. The depreciation charges of version (b) tie in with the December values, but not with the replacement costs of the dates when inputs are consumed; the versions in (c) are geared to those dates, and so give a better view of the year's costs.[17] Where the main aim is comparison over the years, the stabilized accounts should be restated in a common £, say that of 1 January, year 1.

If the owners had instead restricted dividends to the profit figures of (b) and (c) (i.e., if they had used the general-index concept of capital maintenance), there would be no deficits and the value of the secondary assets would in the end have risen to £3813 plus £987, i.e., to £4800. This sum falls short of replacement cost (£6000), but maintains real capital.

If the owners had preferred the special-index view of capital maintenance, they would have reduced profits and dividends further, by not crediting real holding gain realized to the income statement. Their resulting savings would in the end have raised the secondary assets[18] to £5390. So, even if they follow the precepts of the special-index man faithfully, their funds still fall short of replacement price. To reach the latter, they would in years 2 and 3 need to top up the accumulated provision (see p. 98).

References

1. W. A. Lewis, 'Depreciation and Obsolescence as Factors in Costing' in J. L. Meig (ed.), *Depreciation and Replacement Policy*, North-Holland, 1961, is helpful on these and other relevant matters.

2. These are briefly described in Appendix 1 of this chapter (p. 167).

3. Let

V_0 = initial price;
i = relevant cost-of-capital rate;
v = present value factor—that is $1/(1 + i)$;
k = number of years in the whole life;
$0(k)$ = sum of the present values of the relevant cash flows, e.g., variable repair outlays, during the life;
Sv^k = present value of the scrap proceeds.

Then A, the present value of all these flows, is found from:

$$A = V_0 + 0(k) - Sv^k \qquad (1)$$

For fuller treatment, see A. J. Merrett and Allen Sykes, *The Finance and Analysis of Capital Projects*, Longmans, 1963, Chapters 1, 18, and 19.

4. This yearly charge or rental U is found from:

$$U = A \times \frac{i}{1 - v^k} \qquad (2)$$

5. A good rule-of-thumb for finding the approximate charge is to add together:
(a) the straight-line depreciation charge;
(b) interest for a year on two-thirds of the asset's price; and
(c) yearly average of any relevant repairs.

6. P, the perpetuity, is found from:

$$P = \frac{A}{1 - v^k} \qquad (3)$$

or from:

$$P = \frac{U}{i} \qquad (4)$$

7. W. T. Baxter, *Depreciation*, Sweet & Maxwell, 1971, argues the point on p. 39; p. 80 gives an arithmetical example, and p. 113 superimposes cost-of-capital. To find a value pattern, the accountant must take the following steps:
(1) At the start of life, find the full service charge (see form 2 on p. 152)—a constant per unit of time (or of use, if the asset is a use-asset).
(2) Each year, increase the value of the asset by debiting it with:
(a) the varying outlays (e.g., overhaul costs);
(b) 'appreciation'—at the cost-of-capital rate on the opening balance;
and reduce it by crediting:
(c) the full service charge—with time-assets, a constant each year; with use-assets, a constant per unit of use;
(d) any receipts varying because of the age of the asset.

8. From eqn (1) in ref. 3 (above):

$$A = £100 + 30v^3 + 20v^5 = 108 \cdot 8064.$$

9. From eqn (2) in ref. 4 (above):

$$U = 108 \cdot 8064 \times \frac{0 \cdot 25}{1 - 0 \cdot 32768} = 40 \cdot 4593.$$

10. From eqn (4) in reference 6 (above):

$$P = \frac{40 \cdot 4593}{0 \cdot 25} = 161 \cdot 83.$$

11. See E. Solomon, *The Theory of Financial Management*, Columbia University Press, 1963.

12. K. N. Bhaskar, 'Optimal Asset Lives',

13. See W. T. Baxter, *Depreciation, op. cit.*, p. 14.

14. Compound interest formulae for the analyses are given in W. T. Baxter and N. Carrier, 'Depreciation, Replacement Cost, and Cost-of-Capital', *Journal of Accounting Research*, Spring 1971.

15. An asset should be replaced when its yearly outlay pattern (repairs, etc.) climbs above its successor's annual cost (full service charge). Here the latter sinks at New's advent. So the two patterns may now intersect in an earlier year.

16.
$$\text{Provision of mid-year 1} = 1000 \times \tfrac{160}{110} = 1454 \cdot 5$$
$$\text{Provision of mid-year 2} = 1000 \times \tfrac{160}{126} = 1269 \cdot 8$$
$$\text{Provision of mid-year 3} = 1000 \times \tfrac{160}{147} = 1088 \cdot 4$$
$$\overline{3812 \cdot 7}$$

17. For instance, during year 1 the average current cost of input is only £1000 × 115 = £1150. For stabilization in end-£s, this is raised with the general-index factor $\tfrac{120}{110}$ to £1255 (column (1c)).

18. Extra provision, version (b), by end of life:

		£
Year 1 £100 × $\tfrac{160}{120}$ =		133
2 50 × $\tfrac{160}{140}$ =		57
3 400 × $\tfrac{160}{160}$ =		400
		590
General-index provision		4800
		5390

14. Revaluation mechanics

Let us now pass from the theory to the ways and means of carrying out a revaluation. We shall assume that deprival value is the concept to be used; but the steps will often be much the same for other concepts.

Outside *versus* inside appraisal

In a big firm, a revaluation (particularly the first one) must involve much extra work. How is it to be done most easily? One way is to hand over the task to a professional appraiser. This avoids burden on the firm's own staff, and ensures that the figures are independent. On the other hand, one may perhaps feel that the appraiser's principles and assumptions are uncertain; that his fee is stiff; and, with specialized plant, that no outsider (however expert) is likely to know all the facts.

There is thus a lot to be said for letting the firm's own staff do some or all of the valuing. But a number of questions must first be weighed. Are the firm's engineers, accountants, etc., familiar with market prices and installation costs—say, because they frequently buy replacements? Is an adequate plant register kept already? Are the bits of plant relatively few in number, though possibly big in size and value? (Compare the chemical industry with mechanical engineering.) Do the bits of plant fall into like groups, each of which can be reappraised collectively, perhaps with a group index? Are such indices already being made, either by an outside body or the firm's own engineers?

Administrative steps for internal appraisal

If the answers to such questions above suggest that the firm's staff can do the revaluing, the next step is to draft the rules. The obvious plan is to set up a central working party of engineers and accountants (in a scattered firm, drawn from representative plants) to do the drafting and to plan the campaign. (The engineers may be accustomed to working on very similar committees to review asset lives, etc.) The auditors should probably be represented too, since the working party's decisions will affect the principles on which the published accounts are drafted. And, if the auditing firm has a management-consultancy section, the latter may be a useful source of extra labour, ideas, and criticism. Perhaps, this is an important new field for management-consultants.

A set of common rules will be particularly useful in firms with scattered branches. In such firms, it may be sensible for each branch to set up its own committee also, to plan the operation in detail and to allow for local conditions.

The task of the committees is apt to be heavy, and may demand many meetings. So the firm must allow plenty of time for each revaluation. The aim should not be to allot values just at the balance sheet date, but rather to spread this work over the least busy months of the preceding year. Unless something very untoward happens, fixed-asset values found on average, say, at mid-year will still be adequate for the end of the year; at worst, the total can be adjusted by the six-months' change in some suitable omnibus index. The volume of clerical labour is also likely to be big—though, if revaluation becomes an annual task, the detail could be reduced to a routine and then put onto a computer. As has been said, the assets should so far as possible be classed into groups that can be reappraised collectively.

One of the early steps for the committees is to consider whether the prices of each asset group have changed enough since the last review to warrant any revision. Unless the change exceeds, say, 5 per cent, the group may sensibly be left alone for another year; over the years, all the assets will be covered in leapfrog style.

Revaluation by index *versus* direct appraisal

Much effort is spared when old values (historical cost or an earlier revaluation) can be raised with an index. A suitable index for each asset group may already be to hand (e.g., prepared by the firm's own engineers, or an economic advisory service); or, if the firm's scale of working is so big that new machines are bought frequently, their prices may provide the material for building an index and keeping it up to date. Otherwise, the committee must try to get quotations from outside suppliers or cost estimates from the firm's own construction department, and then use such data to build the index.

As a shortcut, sometimes it is justifiable to apply a composite index to a group of rather dissimilar items. This index might be a weighted average of other indices. For instance, a steelmaker's stocks may consist of raw materials (perhaps one-quarter of total value), finished goods (one-half), and miscellaneous (one-quarter); then the raw-materials index of the trade, its wholesale index, and basic-materials index can be blended in a 1:2:1 ratio.

Indices cannot do their job properly if an asset's historical cost has been written down too much or too little—for example, where the future life of a machine has been underestimated. (In the extreme case where active assets have been written off completely, their revised values will still be *nil* after the indices have been applied.) Thus, there are doubly-strong grounds for first adjusting historical cost if it seems too cautious or hopeful by orthodox standards.

While one should not be too fussy about the accuracy of indices, it may be that no index can adequately cover the diverging prices of very different—perhaps highly specialized—kinds of machines. Then special indices must perforce be discarded in favour of more direct estimates. If these are hard to make or of dubious accuracy, approximate revaluation with the general index may be defensible.

It is wise to concentrate on the more expensive assets, and to spare effort on the less costly. Thus, machines might be split into two value groups—those worth over (say) £2000, and cheaper ones. The former deserve some care; the latter (probably far more numerous, but not of such great total value) can be valued more roughly, perhaps with indices found by revaluing the costlier group.

In countries where steep inflation has led to legal recognition and control of revaluation, the permitted method seems generally to be linked to official indices. Thus, the French regulations at one stage stated that any other form of revaluation would 'give rise to so many varying standards that there would be no satisfactory degree of justice for all'.[1] If the new values are to govern tax allowances for depreciation, clearly the case for official indices becomes very strong—though our theory suggests (chapter 8) that a single index, of general consumption prices, ought to be used here by all tax-payers.

Constituents of deprival value

Chapter 12 defined deprival value in terms of three possible constituents: replacement cost, resale value, and cost saving in use. Sometimes the valuer will at once be able to see that only one of these is relevant in the given circumstances (e.g., replacement cost is markedly lower than others), and then the others can be ignored or estimated in summary fashion. On occasion, however, two or all three will have to be considered, particularly where other people (e.g., the auditors) must be convinced that the chosen constituent is the right one. A possible schedule of figures is given below (see p. 173) as an illustration to stock inventories.

But, if we may judge from the many demands for more and more supplementary information,[2] the day may come when published reports will have to include schedules of sale values. Then the accountant will have to find these values for all the assets. His task will not be difficult so far as the firm's own merchandise is concerned: members of the sales staff should usually be excellent judges of sales price, and of the future outlays on delivery, etc. With some fixed assets, however, members of the firm's own staff are perhaps less likely to be expert on resale value. The latter may be trivial (old machines) or great (buildings). Sometimes the lists of sale prices published by secondhand dealers, or advertisements, will be helpful; but such prices will of course tend to be swollen by brokers' charges, etc. A deduction must be made also for likely dismantling and delivery costs, and for time discount if the sale proceeds will not be received promptly.

Programme for various assets

Machinery, furniture, etc. In the main, the revaluation of machines, etc., will have to be done by engineers or other experts. Their work is made easier if they are given suitable schedules to fill in. The schedules list the plant in each department— for example, giving each asset one horizontal line, cut vertically by columns for the relevant data, including say:
(a) Description of the asset, its number, etc.
(b) Date of purchase.
(c) Historical book-values—gross (including installation cost), depreciation (to preceding year-end), and net.
(d) Depreciation method.
(e) Price of potential replacement, and whether it is a different and better model.

(f) Amounts by which (c) should be changed to allow for change in the replacement. (Here the issues raised in chapter 13 become important; possibly a long calculation, like that in the table on p. 161, will have to be made to find these values, the new optimum life, etc. But a shortcut may give acceptable approximations: experience with the long calculations may show that there are, in some conditions at least, suitable factors by which values in (c) (for asset after asset) can be updated.)
Further columns will record the remaining optimum life, the year's write-off, closing book-values, and other matters of interest. The accounting staff are probably better fitted than the engineers to do the arithmetic on this schedule, but the engineers should approve the final figures in each line and the totals.

Land and buildings. If the firm has its own property department, this will be able to value the land and buildings. Even if there is no such department, other members of the staff may be able to cope with at least minor changes, perhaps using local indices of building costs. Otherwise, an outside appraiser must be asked to find the new figures. Land values should presumably be related to recent sale prices in the area, and should allow for improvements such as nearby roads and drains.

A merchant's stocks. The routine and checks for inventories are well established. However, we now want deprival values as well as conventional 'lower of cost or market' values; so an extra figure is needed on each line. A simple example might run:

Item	(1) Historical cost £	(2) Replacement cost £	(3) Net realizable value £	(4) Lower of cost or market £	(5) Deprival value £
1	10	12	13	10	12
2	10	9	11	9	9
3	10	12	11	10	11
	30	33	35	29	32

The deprival test puts the appreciation (ignoring general price change) at £32–£30, i.e., £2. This gain might reasonably be separated from realized profit in the income statement, and classed with un-realized profit.

A manufacturer's stocks, etc. The inventory sheets may contain much the same information as those of a merchant. But the 'net realizable value' of work-in-progress is its future contribution (see p. 131), that is:

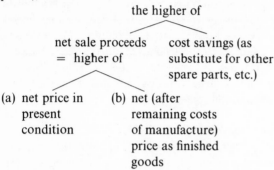

the higher of

net sale proceeds = higher of   cost savings (as substitute for other spare parts, etc.)

(a) net price in present condition   (b) net (after remaining costs of manufacture) price as finished goods

These values may seem troublesome to calculate, and (save for items that have become obsolete, etc.) obviously less relevant than replacement cost. So it may normally be good sense not to bother about them, i.e., to value satisfactory goods at replacement cost, and unsatisfactory ones at or near to zero.

Where a firm uses standard costs to value its finished goods or tools made in its own workshops, etc., the revaluation may be done by bringing the standards up to date. Indeed, this revision will presumably take place in any case. The labour and material ingredients can usually be changed with the help of indices.[3] But improvements in technology—which lower costs—demand more direct appraisal.

Checks on revaluation

After the new values have been found, they may be checked by the auditor (and presumably such a check is obligatory for figures that will appear in the published accounts). However, one of the company's own officials is perhaps more likely, thanks to a closer knowledge of the particular assets, to be a skilled critic. In particular, if the company has an internal auditor, he is the obvious man to make a searching check.

It will be simple enough for the auditor to verify the arithmetic. But it is probably much more important for him to browse quietly over the results. Do the totals look sensible? How have the figures for the various asset groups and the bigger items behaved? How do the changes compare with those of earlier revaluations? The auditor must try to make sure that the instructions have been understood, and that their spirit has been observed. Admittedly, the values must be partly a matter of personal judgement. But consistency is important, and so the rules of the committee must prevail over individual views; the auditor must be on the alert for, say, the engineer with a bee in his bonnet where obsolescence is concerned. Perhaps his best plan is to discuss sample figures with each valuer, watching for signs of an unduly eccentric approach. He can get a useful starting-point by comparing the percentage write-ups for similar machines in different departments, etc., and by discussing the trends of published prices and indices.

When stock is being valued for ordinary year-end inventories, it may be to everyone's advantage to produce high values; and so the auditor must be on his guard for an upward bias. The same may not hold so strongly when plant is revalued. High plant values mean high depreciation charges—which may inject gloom into statements of costs and profits, and perhaps lead to unwelcome pricing problems. The auditor may, on occasion, have to contend with bias towards low values.

Revaluation and figures in ledger and balance sheet

When the task of revaluing is over, the new figures must be entered suitably in the ledger and balance sheet. Some interesting problems then arise.

For many reasons, it may at present seem desirable that orthodox historical cost should not be squeezed out of the ledger. If it is retained, the extra value given to an asset should be kept apart from historical cost—say, in a second column of the asset account, or in a new kind of account ('asset X—valuation adjustment account')[4].

Obviously, where the new values are put into the ordinary accounts, it is important that the wording of the balance sheet should stress and explain the revaluation. The basis ought to be explained (at least in the first year of any new system) and the exact amount of write-up should be stated. All consequential movements in the owners' balances, etc., should be set out in full, with the revaluation surplus carefully distinguished from ordinary profit. Often, the surplus on fixed assets is added permanently to a capital adjustment account; however, it may in large part be well fitted for addition to the legal capital via the issue of bonus shares.[5] A simple example of a revalued balance sheet was given in Table 13.6. Where revaluation is not an annual event, the balance sheets of later years may have to describe the asset figures with some such wording as 'Revalued at (deprival value, etc.) at (date), plus later additions at cost'. The mixture of methods looks clumsy, but may do little harm where the period between revaluations is not long.

Some accountants hold that, where tax would be payable on capital gains if the asset were sold, part of the revaluation surplus should be labelled as a provision for the potential liability.[6] But such a rule begs too many questions to be readily acceptable. What happens if revaluation results in a loss? What happens where the firm has no intention of selling the assets, e.g., where they are machines that will be consumed as input? What happens where the chosen valuation concept is not that of sale price? If, for instance, deprival value is used, it must normally hinge on replacement cost, and then must turn a blind eye to both sale proceeds and tax on them. Where sale price is the relevant figure, presumably the Have budget should allow for tax on, say, capital gains, i.e., the surplus is already a net sum.

References

1. M. Norman and H. A. Astbury, 'Fiscal Measures in France', *The Accountant*, 12 March 1955.

2. On the uses of supplementary data, see H. C. Edey, 'Accounting Principles and Business Reality', *The Accountant*, 24 and 31 August 1963.

3. Various devices serve to make this revision less troublesome. The digits selected for the code numbers of spare parts can show which materials are used; and the total costs of an assembly can be sub-totalled to show the costs of each different material and type of labour.

4. The entries for the latter method are illustrated in E. O. Edwards and P. W. Bell, *The Theory and Measurement of Business Income*, University of California Press, 1960. See also A. Goudeket, 'An Application of Replacement Cost Theory', *Journal of Accountancy*, July 1960.

5. Some British experience is analysed in E. B. Butter and H. Hart, 'Revaluation in Business Decisions and Measures of Capital', *Accountancy*, June 1963.

6. Institute of Chartered Accountants of England and Wales, *Recommendations on Accounting Prihciples*, N. 27.

15. Conclusions

Earlier chapters have covered many topics—some concerning principles, others techniques. This final chapter must try to put the topics into perspective and to sum up.

Because ordinary accounting is in the main a historical record, it is an imperfect means for giving current information. Even when general prices remain tolerably steady, its defects evoke proposals for improvement. With inflation, the defects become much worse, and the proposals more radical. But (as is pointed out on p. 26) the reform proposals conflict both in their aims and degree of completeness. Thus, accounting now faces a wide choice of possibilities: it must decide between rival principles, and also whether to patch up here and there or adopt a complete package.

Accounting Standards

In 1974, the Accounting Standards Steering Committee—representing the main bodies of British accountants—published *Accounting for changes in the purchasing power of money* as its provisional statement of accounting practice No. 7 (the 'provisional' from deference to a government committee set up at that time to consider the same topic). From the many reform possibilities, the committee opted for full stabilization, in end £s, with the general index, i.e., for current purchasing power (CPP) accounts. SSAP 7 calls on quoted companies to back up their ordinary published accounts with the stabilized figures, and further to explain the gap between the ordinary and the stabilized profits, i.e., to enumerate the timelag error on cost-of-

goods and depreciation; the money gain or loss; and (an awkward item) the differences between the actual sales, costs, etc., and their end-year equivalents (compare columns (1) and (2) with (3) in Table 7.7 on p. 57). SSAP 7 is reprinted at the end of this book.

In America, the position now seems to be very like that in Britain. The American Institute of Certified Public Accountants has recommended to the Financial Accounting Standards Board that published annual accounts should include supplementary data to show the effects of general price change.

However, official standards do not by any means bring the argument to a full stop. They may well prove to be only educative stepping-stones, with faults that must sooner or later lead to revisions (e.g., their rejection of special values for assets seems an obvious weakness). They are mandatory—perhaps too strong a word—only in their own country, for big companies and for published reports. The huge majority of accounts lie outside their reach. Thus, accountants still must decide whether reform is worth while, and which method is best.

The two main areas of weakness are income measurement (especially in times of general price change), and asset valuation (whether general prices are changing or not). The two kinds of defect are quite different. In the income statement, the use of historical cost during inflation leads to the fabrication of profits where none exist—much as if every statement contains an arithmetical blunder that boosts profit. In the balance sheet, historical figures ignore gain that exists in reality.

Income statement

Income statements are apt to deduct costs of one date from revenues of another. The curing of this time-lag error seems to be the most urgent need in the field of income measurement.

Consequences of the timelag error

If the error has a marked effect on income figures (as it probably has in certain kinds of firm, especially when the rate of inflation has been high), then they fail in their functions as guides to consumption, investment, and efficiency. During inflation, an owner may suppose that his capital is intact, whereas in fact it is diminished (particularly as dividends and tax tend to be functions of uncorrected profit). Investors can be misled about the relative profits of firms A and B, or industries C and D, so new resources may be misdirected. Manager E can be made to seem more efficient than manager F, and method G than method H. Thus, decisions on efficiency may be warped. 'Make or buy' budgets, for instance, will tend to compare 'make' figures that are historical costs with 'buy' figures that are current prices. Decisions on sale price may be made wrongly if cost figures are historical; and, even if the firm's own accountant is enlightened on this point, the accountants of competing firms may not be.

Conceivably a gifted manager or analyst knows intuitively of the existence of the error and tries to allow for it in his calculations. We can only guess how far he succeeds. Its seems not unreasonable to think that the lush figures of the income statement make for general inefficiency in our economy.

Tax

These arguments are strengthened when tax is brought into the picture. As was pointed out on p. 57, the error in the income statement leads to an extra tax—never envisaged by the legislature—on those who hold stocks or depreciating assets, or make capital gains. Particularly if dividends as well as tax are linked with uncorrected profit, seemingly prosperous firms may fail (in real terms) to expand or even maintain their wealth, and so may suddenly face cash shortages when assets have to be replaced. Fortunately for themselves, many such firms have tended so far to find borrowing easy, and have to some degree been able to make do with loans; but this source may be drying up as lenders awake to their negative interest earnings during inflation.

Given high enough rates of tax and inflation, the extra tax could in some types of firm exceed corrected income, and thus constitute a (real) capital levy. Though this bogey has probably been exaggerated, often tax must tend to bite deeply into business savings. In most economies, these savings are now a major source of fresh capital, so that the diversion of the flow is a grave matter.

However, even if firms have the cash to finance new investment, the extra tax must presumably act as a disincentive to the holding of stocks and depreciating assets. Thus (to quote President Eisenhower), illiberal treatment of depreciation 'discourages long-range investment on which the risks cannot be clearly foreseen. It discourages the early replacement of old equipment with new and improved equipment, and it makes it more difficult to secure financing for capital investment, particularly for small business organizations'.[1] It does not seem too fanciful to suppose that countries whose level of national investment has been low (e.g., the UK) may have been held back in part by this extra tax, levied at the high rates that are common.

Those who bear this extra tax must feel (so far as they realize what is happening) that it is not only harmful but grossly inequitable. They certainly have a case. But here we are on difficult ground. Perhaps one should not stress equity too much when taxes are concerned. Why, for instance, should beer be taxed and not cider? Moreover, it is sometimes argued that the extra tax is only one of the many ill-results of inflation; and that, when owners of money assets are hit even worse, it would be absurd to remit the extra tax. Various counter-arguments suggest themselves. It seems not unreasonable to hold that we are here dealing with two quite different and unconnected matters: loss on money is a sober reality, and will be prevented only when we learn how to prevent inflation; whereas the error is merely an arithmetical blunder that can be righted readily. When doctors cannot cure patient A but can cure B, must they in fairness let both die? Again, one can hardly argue that it is just to tax firms on the timelag error since they pay no tax on their gain on owing. The two quantities may be far from equal and opposite (e.g., a firm with a big error may also make a big loss on owning money). And:

the ownership of productive assets carries with it many risks which are not shared, or are shared in a much smaller degree, by owners of claims fixed in terms of money. To require the owners of productive assets to carry in addition to the risk peculiar to the function of entrepreneurship, the risks which are proper to rentiers, is not only unjust but likely to have undesirable social results. In particular, it makes the ownership of productive assets relatively less attractive in times of rising prices than the ownership of non-productive assets, and may well make the hoarding of goods a better hedge against inflation than a share in the ownership of a productive enterprise.[2]

The trade cycle

As chapter 11 explained, the timelag error may have other and still worse consequences. It makes for high profit figures in times of general price increase, which in the past at least have tended to coincide with the upswing of a trade cycle; it may thus raise the expectations of businessmen and inject undue optimism into their investment budgets, and so add fuel to the boom. Conversely, when prices are falling on the down-swing, it depresses the profit figures, and so may have bred extra pessimism and checked investment. If this view is right, accounting malpractice has aggravated the ills of boom and slump: reform is an urgent social duty.

Case against correction of the timelag error

Proposals for correction have been opposed on many grounds. One of the more respectable arguments is utterly defeatist: all accounting measures of income are necessarily so poor that it is wiser to give up the whole attempt than do any patching. This is the view for instance of whole-hearted advocates of 'cash-flow accounting'. The starting-point of the argument is, of course, sound enough—any measure of income must leave much to be desired. But it is one thing to say that a measure is imperfect, and quite another that it is useless or worse than useless. The notion of

income is essential for our day to day affairs; we seem sure to go on using it and demanding guidance on its size. We may accept all the caveats about the limitations of the accounting figure, and still feel that on balance it is helpful. Its improvement seems more desirable than its abolition.

Another line of argument suggests that the readers of accounts will be happier with the familiar error than an unfamiliar cure. Thus, one economist writes, no doubt with tongue in cheek:

There is something to be said also for a certain naïvete and simplicity in accounting practice. If accounts are bound to be untruths anyhow, as I have argued, there is much to be said for the simple untruth as against a complicated untruth, for if the untruth is simple, it seems to me that we have a fair chance of knowing what kind of untruth it is. A known untruth is much better than a lie, and provided that the accounting rituals are well known and understood, accounting may be untrue but it is not lies; it does not deceive because we know that it does not tell the truth, and we are able to make our own adjustment in each individual case, using the results of the accountant as evidence rather than as definitive information.[3]

The trouble is, of course, that a great many people do not know that accounting does not tell the truth, and that we are not able to make adequate adjustments unless we have more skill and information than is common.

Some critics argue that general indices are too clumsy to provide an adequate cure. Chapter 2 concedes that any published index is indeed unlikely to match the consumption of a given shareholder, etc., with much precision. While the statisticians will no doubt be able to improve their figures somewhat if the need is made clear to them, the criticism will always have some truth. But the point remains that almost any general index will serve most of us better than does the assumption of constant prices.

Other critics have doubted whether it is in the public interest to cure the error. If accountants raise cost figures during inflation, the argument runs, some firms will put up prices (i.e., they will price their goods on the basis of current instead of historical costs); as a result, prices will rise faster than they would otherwise have done, and the inflation will be made worse. There are various answers to this argument. One is that a delayed rise in prices may do harm rather than good, in that it fosters a shopping spree just when demand ought to be checked. Another surely is that truth must always serve the public interest better than deception: the prime duty of the man who prepares any form of statistics is to make them as accurate as he can, regardless of seemingly bad consequences.

A more usual line of argument is, of course, that the trouble and cost of any cure outweigh the benefits. This book has already tried to show that correction is not excessively difficult. A simple form need not be unduly troublesome or costly: an accounting witness told a government committee that he had done the necessary work for his own group of companies without much extra labour; with ordinary depreciation calculations that took about 1000 man-hours, the extra charge called for a further 10 hours.[4]

Choice of cure

The cure for the error can be either the 'first-aid' cost adjustment of the income statement (see chapters 7–10), or part of some full-stabilization package for both income statement and balance sheet.

The first-aid is by no means to be despised. It demands a minimum of change in the normal figures and methods. It seems specially appropriate where the timelag error is confined to a few items in the income statement; also, it is useful for calculating many forms of gain and loss besides annual profit (e.g., capital gains). Most readers of accounts are likely to feel more at home with figures that are still, for the most part, of the familiar kind—though, admittedly, the new-fangled charges may at first need a lot of explaining. And this mild reform would play a useful educational role in preparing opinion for more complete measures.

But full stabilization seems preferable, at least for the large and sophisticated firm. Besides curing the timelag, it brings improvement in other areas, and leaves fewer inconsistencies; for instance, its income statement dovetails neatly with its balance sheet. It can deal with the various forms of real gain and loss, notably those on holding money. And, as stabilized accounts can be readily updated, comparison between the results of different periods is easy.

As was said on p. 176, in the end the arguments for full stabilization seemed persuasive to the British accounting bodies.

Asset revaluation

Case for revaluation

Chapter 12 set out the main arguments for revaluation. If balance sheets have any meaning to their readers, it must surely be as a guide to the size and nature of the assets and liabilities; and current value must give a clearer picture than historical cost. The latter does not necessarily bear much relation to the former. This becomes particularly obvious after a marked change in general prices; today most balance sheets give an antiquated picture of the firm. But the principle holds even where the change is confined to one or two special items.

Usually, the most important kind of reader is the investor, actual or potential; the balance sheet is the firm's 'invitation to the financial market to participate in the profit'.[5] To be sure, investors would prefer an invitation in the form of a forward-looking valuation of the firm as a whole (see p. 116). But, unless and until directors become more reliable prophets, investors must be content with the balance sheet, and use it to form their own judgements. The better the balance sheet, the better the judgements.

Takeovers provide strong evidence that historical values are in some circumstances harmful to shareholders. And there are many other ways in which historical values may have distorted investment decisions. For instance, they lead to higher income: asset ratios (especially when reinforced by the timelag error), and so paint a spurious picture of a firm or industry with old assets.

Other important groups of readers are creditors and managers. The former would plainly prefer current to out-dated values. If managers lack current values, they are likely to be misled in several ways, for instance when they study the rates of return on the assets of different departments, or make decisions that lead to the using-up of existing stores and machines.

The fact that the owners' balances (retained earnings, etc.) are 'mixed' historical totals—see p. 14—means that they too give muddled information. They fail, for instance, to show whether the owners' real capital has been maintained after price change. Still less do they analyse the various forms of realized and unrealized appreciation over the years; in particular, they ignore a figure that is immensely important during inflation, the loss or gain on the net money assets.

Arguments against revaluation

The case against revaluation can be pitched at two different levels. One level is a matter of technicalities, expense, and trouble. The unfamiliar task of special revaluation would be costly and impose strain on staff, particularly at the first round. The book-keeping would become a somewhat lengthier and more laborious process, e.g., each asset might be given a valuation adjustment account as well as the historical cost account (p. 174). The changes would sometimes open the door wider to biased or dishonest statements; certainly, they would call for extra internal checks and new auditing standards. And the advocate of reform must admit that, where the new systems have been tried out, sometimes they have later been abandoned: 'both the German and the French examples are instructive in that they demonstrate the tendency to return to historical cost accounting after the inflationary blizzard has passed'.[6]

Such arguments were tested in chapter 14, which tried to show that, once the new system has grown familiar, the routine should not be too demanding. When one recalls how readily accountants have been able to adapt themselves when other new methods became desirable (e.g., to deal with complicated change in tax or costing), there does not seem to be much doubt about their ability to deal with revaluation techniques. We can admit that the new system will cost more; the investors and managers who demand better information will in the main be ready to accept this price.

The other level of objection relates to principle. Some of the critics might put their thoughts as follows. We can value the whole firm and its shares in a way that satisfies logic, by discounting expected cash flows. The separate assets are another matter. The quest for the 'size of the tools' may spring from an ingrained habit of mind, and yet not be altogether logical; perhaps their size is something that cannot be measured in a satisfactory way:

> The constituent parts of a value have no independent value of their own; all valuation formulas lack real content, and cannot be proved to be either correct or incorrect. Single assets and all other parts of the entity are valuable only as parts of this entity, and their value cannot change save with changes in the entity's value.[7]

Once such ideas have dawned on him, the critic of accounting may well feel that there is no point in tinkering with a document that is so inherently unsound. If he likes stretching theory to the extreme, he will argue that the balance sheet, like the income statement, is beyond reform and should be dropped from reports. In its place might come statements of past and expected cash flows, and lists showing the physical measurements of the assets, etc.—to be interpreted in the light of each analyst's judgement and interests.

Perhaps we shall in the end accept such counsels of despair. But it seems good sense first to find out whether we cannot turn the balance sheet into something more defensible. We may entirely concede that its value concepts must be arbitrary and its description of the whole firm is blurred; and yet we may feel that this imperfect picture is far better than no picture. We can argue too that, if analysts are given not balance sheets but schedules of statistics, they will probably have to use such data to make their private calculations of profits and asset values, i.e., to construct their own income statements and balance sheets: and that this work can be done more easily and knowledgeably by the firm's accountants.

Development in the future

The arguments for reforming accounts seem at last to be winning wide support: we can reasonably expect that new methods will soon become more usual, if not indeed compulsory, in the more developed countries. Which of the possible reforms should accountants adopt, and what other decisions must they make?

Stages of future development

It does not seem likely or desirable that the time-honoured statements will, in the first instance, be swept away completely. More probably, the main published accounts will continue to show historical costs, and improved figures will be given as supplementary statements (as in the reports of quoted British companies from 1974). A cautious first step of this kind has much to commend it. If the improved statements work well and become widely understood, in time the traditional ones may be allowed to disappear.

It is not easy to decide whether the new statements should at first be content with half-measures such as fixed-asset revaluation and the correction of the timelag error, or whether they should at one stride go all the way to full stabilization. The latter may well seem too big a change. But the compromises are apt to be very awkward (e.g., corrected depreciation cost does not tie in with historical-asset values), and to leave many questions unanswered (e.g., on the size of the gain or loss on money assets). And young people, at least, do not seem to find stabilization too big a mouthful.

Any company with enough enterprise has, of course, scope for reform in its own reports: thus Philips' Lamps has already achieved distinction as a pioneer. But reform is not likely to become general unless there is outside encouragement. Accounting societies may well give a lead (as in the UK), and stock exchanges are in a position to apply strong pressure. The most alluring carrot would be a government decision to forgo tax on the error where firms cure it in their published accounts. But we must hope that any outside regulation will not take the form of a straitjacket; a rigid standard may bring ossification, whereas we need scope for much debate and experiment.

Other decisions

Whatever the decision on the steps by which the new statements are introduced, further decisions must be made on the valuation methods to be used. We must, in particular, choose between the general-index and special-revaluation approaches. This book has suggested that our decision should vary according to the type of calculation (see chapters 7 and 8). Asset values should be found by special revaluation, as should costs in decision budgets, etc. But income is better based on the general index, i.e., the latter gives the better cure for the timelag error. If the costs of the income statement are instead corrected with the special index, the real appreciation should be entered as an extra gain, thus restoring the net balance to the level of the general-index approach (p. 74).

Other decisions must be made on income concepts. How, for instance, should unrealized appreciation be treated? Chapter 4 argued that it may usefully be shown as one form of income, but that it should be clearly distinguished from realized income. The distinction must, however, sometimes depend on conventions such as the Fife assumption; and for some kinds of gain (e.g., on owing money) accounting has not yet even begun to formulate the conventions.

If we accept that asset values must be found by the special approach, we still have to choose the precise form of value, e.g., replacement cost or sale price, that will be most helpful to readers (whether general prices are changing or stable). Chapter 12 argued that none of the more usual bases is adequate, and that an unfamiliar one, deprival value, should be introduced. This would at least be useful for management decisions as well as published accounts; and, as its rules are dictated by a severe logic, it could be applied with some consistency in different firms.

Future problems

When the reform proposals are put into effect, no doubt time will show them to be less than perfect; experience will confirm the limitations that are already obvious, and will show up plenty of new ones. The usual process of adaptation and improvement will then take place. The technical problems will resolve themselves without much trouble. But the technicalities will be only the beginning. Once we set about reforming accounts in earnest, we shall become aware of problems of principle that have so far lain dormant. As earlier pages have suggested, the final test of the accountant's figures is probably their power to give information. But this at once raises further points. Who is to be informed—i.e., owners or potential owners or managers? And what if their needs differ? Many of us have tried to focus these issues by assuming that the figures will be used as guides for decisions, and as a post-mortem check on past decisions. This must often be true. But is human curiosity aroused only by the need to make decisions? Many people like to know all sorts of odd things that hardly seem to have much bearing on their decision-making (e.g. facts of astronomy or history, or which team won the cup in 1948). Indeed, such curiosity is one of the signs of a lively mind. Why should people not want to know about the size and growth of firms too, and by what tests should we choose the best figures?

In the meantime, the only simple solution to these problems must lie in an assumption that the many different users of published reports can be thought of in terms of an 'average' person, i.e., someone whose needs can be deemed typical. This notion is, of course, the justification for correcting income with the general index (a procedure that presumes a typical pattern of personal expenditure), and for measuring assets at deprival value (which presumes that the figure best suited for decisions inside the firm will meet the needs also of most outsiders).

These problems, and no doubt many others that we cannot yet even imagine, will confront us as soon as we set about the task of improving on historical cost accounts. Reform will not make for easy and thoughtless lives. But it now seems almost inevitable. Opinion both within and without the accounting profession increasingly expects it, and is likely to grow more insistent with each surge in prices. And men whose chosen life-work is to make difficult measurements can hardly rest content with poor results; because we take pride in our work, we should welcome this chance to experiment and improve.

Appendix: Example of full stabilization

Below is an example that illustrates most of the points aired in earlier chapters, with details of the kind of workings needed in practice. It starts with the ordinary accounts of a manufacturing firm, then shows how these can be translated into two alternative stabilized versions:

(a) historical cost adjusted with the general index; and

(b) as (a), with special-index adjustment for assets and costs.

Data

A company started at 31 December 19x0. Prices were fairly steady throughout 19x1, but rose during 19x2. The ordinary balance sheets at the end of 19x1 and 19x2 are shown opposite. The income account of 19x2 runs:

	£	£
Sales		6060
Less Opening Stock	970	
Purchases	2475	
	3445	
Less Closing Stock	1309	
Cost of raw materials used	2136	
Expenses and wages	1025	
Depreciation	660	
		3821
Profit before tax		2239
Less Tax		300
Profit after tax		1939
Less Dividends		1100
Unappropriated profit for 19x2		839
Unappropriated profit for 19x1		870
		1709

The following pages show one way (worksheets in ledger form) of finding stabilized figures for 19x2.

The relevant indices, adjusted to 100 at the company's start, are set out below. Where the timelag error on cost-of-goods is to be corrected with great accuracy, index data for, say, each month are necessary—not only for the given year itself, but also for the preceding turnover period during which opening stock is bought. Thus, as the turnover period in this example is six months, for great accuracy the July 19x1 purchase costs would be raised to the January 19x2 level, the August 19x1 costs to the February 19x2 level, and so on; in all, adjustments would be made to eighteen lots of purchases. But sufficient accuracy is here achieved if the incoming stock is treated in three lots:

19x1. July to December—opening stock, regarded as bought on 30 September 19x1.

19x2. January to June—first half-year's purchases, regarded as bought on 31 March 19x2. July to December—second half-year's purchases (= closing stock), regarded as bought on 30 September 19x2.

The other costs, and the sales, are each treated as single transactions at 30 June 19x2.

There is some convenience in working with one early stabilization base in all years.[8] So the figures are here stabilized in the £ of January 19x1, i.e., the start of the business.

Workings in ledger form

With simple data, it is feasible to find the answers with some preliminary calculations and then worksheets. But a better plan probably is to use ledger accounts (as on pp 186–9). These accounts can helpfully have parallel columns for the stabilized figures. Each transaction is then stabilized with the aid of the general index factor of the given date. This arrangement cuts out any need for special calculation of the loss on money, as the figure emerges automatically; it likewise corrects (by the general index criterion) all timelag errors on cost. If special adjustment is wanted, it can readily be superimposed by adding extra accounts—e.g., (7a)

Balance sheets

	19x1 £	19x2 £		19x1 £	19x2 £
Ordinary capital	10 000	10 000	Plant—cost	5 400	6 560
Gain on sale of investment		1 300	*Less* Depreciation	600	1 260
Trade profit	870	1 709			
10 per cent preference capital	2 000	2 000		4 800	5 300
Creditors and provisions	1 100	1 300	Investment	5 000	—
			Stock of raw materials (Fifo)	970	1 309
			Debtors and cash	3 200	9 700
	13 970	16 309		13 970	16 309

Indices

		General	Stock	Plant
19x1				
1 Jan.	Raised capital, bought batch I of plant, etc.	100	100	100
30 Sept.	Bought opening stock 19x2, 100 tons, £970	100	97	100
31 Dec.		100	100	100
19x2				
31 Mar.	Bought 110 tons stock for £1166; and batch II of plant for £1160	105	106	107
30 June	Investment sold for £6300; paid creditors and tax £1100; average date of sales, expenses, etc.	110	112	116
30 Sept.	Bought closing stock, 110 tons, £1309	115	119	126
31 Dec.	Provision made for tax £300, and dividends £1100	120	125	130

and (7b)—to deal with the differences, real gain and loss.

Opening figures

Because the general index was stable throughout 19x1, the figures for that year need little adjustment, i.e., most of the opening balances for 19x2 are the same in the ordinary and stabilized columns. The exception is the £970 opening stock, whose index stood at 97 at its average purchase date (September 19x1), and rose to 100 by December 19x1, so that real appreciation was already £30. If the firm wants to record such gain, the £30 will be shown in the accounts numbered:

(11a), i.e., as a debit to an account for this addition to the asset's real value; and

(11b), i.e., as a credit to an account for the 'surplus' or unrealized holding gain.

Transactions during the year—the timelag error on costs

The trading transactions that are free from timelag are straightforward. Their figures are converted into stabilized equivalents with the mid-year factor of $\frac{100}{110}$. Thus the £1025 of expenses, notionally incurred at mid-year, are debited to the profit and loss account at £1025 in the ordinary column, and at $\frac{100}{110} \times £1025 = £932$ in the stabilized column.

But other factors must be used for costs subject to the timelag error. A simple example is provided by the sale of the investment.

Sale of investment. This asset costs £5000 when the index was at 100 (see account (9)). Sale proceeds are £6300 in June 19x2 when the index is at 110. So the nominal profit is £1300. But, if the timelag error is corrected, in £ of June the cost becomes $\frac{110}{100} \times 5000 = 5500$, and the corrected profit (by the standard of the general index—see p. 67) falls to only £800—or, in £ of 1 January, to $800 \times \frac{100}{110} = 727$. The latter figure emerges readily from the stabilization process. Suitable entries might be those shown in accounts (9) and (10).

Raw materials used. Here too the stabilized figures automatically get rid (by the general index standard) of the timelag error. Further, if we want the stabilized profit and loss account to charge cost-of-materials-used at replacement level, we need some such calculation as that below. It shows the real appreciation on each of the two lots used, during their six-month's turnover[9]—in all, $£_{xo}68$. This is added to cost in the profit and loss account (2); the credit is put to an account for real holding gain (11b). But then, if one accepts that income should be based on general (not special) price change (see p. 74), this £68 real gain must be brought back as a credit to the profit and loss account.

	(1) Historical cost £	(2) Factor to adjust (1)	(3) (1) stabilized in £ of 1 Jan 19x1	(4) Replacement cost £	(5) Factor to adjust (4)	(6) (4) stabilized in £ of 1 Jan 19x1
Material used						
Lot 1. (opening stock = purchases, second half 19x1)						
Cost, 30 September 19x1	970	$\times\frac{100}{100}$	= 970			
Replacement cost, 31 March 19x2		$\times\frac{106}{97}$		= 1060	$\times\frac{100}{105}$	= 1010
Lot 2. (purchases, first half 19x2)						
Cost, 31 March 19x2	1166	$\times\frac{100}{105}$	= 1110			
Replacement cost, 30 September 19x2		$\times\frac{119}{106}$		= 1309	$\times\frac{100}{115}$	= 1138
Cost-of-materials-used	2136		2080			2148
Real holding gain (£2148 − £2080)						68
Material in closing stock						
Lot 3. (purchases, second half 19x2)						
Cost, 30 September 19x2	1309	$\times\frac{100}{115}$	= 1138			
Replacement cost, 31 December 19x2		$\times\frac{125}{119}$		= 1375	$\times\frac{100}{120}$	= 1146
Real holding gain (£1146 − £1138)						8

Replacement cost charges for the year's depreciation. To offset the timelag error, the charge for an asset that is used up should in strict logic be its price at the date when the output is sold (and not at some later date of general revaluation, such as the end of the year). So depreciation cost, like the cost of materials, should be tied to the indices of the sale dates—say mid-year on average (see p. 100). The extra charges are found thus:

	(1) Historical cost	(2) Factor to adjust (1)	(3) (1) stabilized in £ of 1 Jan. 19x1	(4) Replacement cost	(5) Factor to adjust (4)	(6) (4) stabilized in £ of 1 Jan. 19x1
Batch 1. From January 19x1 to June 19x2	600	$\times\frac{100}{100}$ =	600			
		$\times\frac{116}{100}$ =		696	$\times\frac{100}{110}$ =	633
Batch 2. From April 19x2 to June 19x2	60	$\times\frac{100}{105}$ =	57			
		$\times\frac{116}{107}$ =		65	$\times\frac{100}{110}$ =	59
	660		657			692
Real holding gain (= (6) − (3)) in opening £, on plant consumed during year						35

Use of the stabilized figures of column (3) will cut out the timelag error (by the general index standard). If, further, one wants to raise the depreciation charge to replacement cost, the £35 of real appreciation (column (6)) must be added to the depreciation charge in the profit and loss account (2); the credit is in an account for extra cumulative depreciation (8a), that will (at the end of the asset's life) serve to write down the real additions to the asset's value in (7a). But, if one accepts that the timelag error on income should be corrected with the general index only, the £35 must be brought back as a credit to the profit and loss account (2); the debit is in the real gain account (7b), where it starts the process of writing off (over the asset's whole life) all the revaluation gain.

End of year adjustments

Stock revaluation. If assets are to be shown at end values, there is some case for raising closing stock from its value at purchase date (September) to that at December. This final burst of real appreciation is £8 (see table for material, p. 184). As the accounts for real appreciation—(11a) and (11b)—still have balances (the appreciation on opening stock) of £30, these must be reduced with a cross-entry of £22.

Revaluation of plant and of the depreciation provision. To show the plant and cumulative depreciation in stabilized figures, the needed values are:

	(1) Historical cost £	(2) Factor to adjust (1)	(3) (1) stabilized in £ of 1 Jan. 19x1	(4) Replacement cost at Dec. 19x2 £	(5) Factor to adjust (4)	(6) (4) stabilized in £ of 1 Jan. 19x1
Machinery						
Batch 1	5400	$\times\frac{100}{100}$ =	5400			
		$\times\frac{130}{100}$ =		7020	$\times\frac{100}{120}$ =	5850
Batch 2	1160	$\times\frac{100}{105}$ =	1105			
		$\times\frac{130}{107}$ =		1409	$\times\frac{100}{120}$ =	1174
	6560		6505	8429		7024
Real holding gain (= (6) − (3))						519
Cumulative depreciation						
Batch 1. $\frac{1200}{5400}$ of above values	1200		1200	1560		1300
Batch 2. $\frac{60}{1160}$ of above values	60		57	73		61
	1260		1257	1633		1361
Part needed to offset real holding gain (= (6) − (3))						104
Extra charge already in 19x2 profit and loss account						35
Extra adjustment needed at end of year						69

The real increase in the value of plant (column (6)) can conveniently be kept in a second plant account (7a), which will thus be debited with £519 in the stabilized column. This figure can be credited to an account for unrealized appreciation on asset revaluation (7b).

If the gross plant value is raised, the cumulative depreciation (i.e., the total for both 19x1 and 19x2) must be raised also—by £104, as the lower part of column (6) in the table above shows. The increase can conveniently be credited to the second depreciation provision account (8a), for off-setting real appreciation. But this has already been credited with the 19x2 replacement cost charge of £35; so the net sum now needed is only £69. This figure can be used to produce a *net* surplus on revaluation (as seems sensible) by debiting it to (7b).

Appropriations and the timelag error. For complete consistency, closing appropriations for tax, divi-dend, etc., must be adjusted to allow for the timelag between the end of 19x2 and the estimated payment dates thereafter, i.e., must be reduced to show that the later payments are made less onerous by inflation. But this would assume knowledge of the future rate of inflation. Here the amounts are treated instead as if payment will be made at once, i.e., are stabilized with the December 19x2 factor of $\frac{100}{120}$. (In the ordinary profit and loss account, these charges—for payments after average revenue date—must create a timelag error that tends to make accounting profit *less* than corrected profit.)

Loss on holding money. The £9800 closing balance in the ordinary column of the cash, etc., account (5) turns into £8167 when stabilized with the December general index factor of $\frac{100}{120}$. This is not enough to balance the stabilized columns. The shortfall, £984, is the decline in the value of the cash, etc., during 19x2; so £984 should be credited as a

LEDGER

			Stabilized £x0	Ordinary £				Stabilized £x0	Ordinary £
(1)					Ordinary Capital				
					19x1				
					Jan. Balance	b/f		10 000	10 000
(2)					Profit and Loss				
19x2					19x2				
	Opening stock—			970	Cash sales	(5)		5 509	6 060
	historical cost	(11)	970		Real gain realized;				
	Purchases				Cost-of-				
	March	(5)	1 110	1 166	materials	(11b)		68	
	September	(5)	1 138	1 309	Depreciation	(7b)		35	
			2 248	2 475				103	
			3 218	3 445					
	Less Closing stock—	(11)							
	historical cost	(11)	1 138	1 309					
			2 080						
	Replacement cost								
	charge	(11a)	68						
	Cost-of-materials-used		2 148	2 136					
	Expenses	(5)	932	1 025					
	Depreciation								
	HC	(8)	657	660					
	addition, real	(8a)	35						
			692						
	Profit	c/d	1 840	2 239					
			5 612	6 060				5 612	6 060

186

(2) continued			Stabilized £x0	Ordinary £				Stabilized £x0	Ordinary £
Tax		(4)	250	300	Profit		b/d	1 840	2 239
Dividend		(4)	917	1 100					
Balance		c/d	673	839					
			1 840	2 239					
					Balance 19x2		b/d	673	839
					Balance 19x1		b/f	870	870
					Balance		c/f	1 543	1 709

(3) *Preference Capital*

19x2			Stabilized £x0	Ordinary £	19x1			Stabilized £x0	Ordinary £
Dec. Balance		c/d	1 667	2 000	Jan. Balance		b/d	2 000	2 000
Balance-gain on owing		(6)	333						
			2 000	2 000					
					19x3				
					Jan. Balance		b/d	1 667	2 000

(4) *Creditors and Provisions*

19x2			Stabilized £x0	Ordinary £	19x2			Stabilized £x0	Ordinary £
June Cash		(5)	1 000	1 100	Jan. Balance		b/d	1 100	1 100
Dec. Balance		c/d	1 167	1 400	Dec. Tax		(2)	250	300
Dec. Balance-gain on owing		(6)	100		Dividend		(2)	917	1 100
			2 267	2 500				2 267	2 500
					19x3				
					Jan. Balance		b/d	1 167	1 400

(5) *Cash, debtors, etc.*

19x2			Stabilized £x0	Ordinary £	19x2			Stabilized £x0	Ordinary £
Jan. Balance		b/d	3 200	3 200	Mar. Purchases		(2)	1 110	1 166
June Investment		(9)	5 727	6 300	Plant		(7)	1 105	1 160
Sales		(2)	5 509	6 060	June Creditors		(4)	1 000	1 100
					Expenses		(2)	932	1 025
					Oct. Purchases		(2)	1 138	1 309
					Dec. Balance		c/d	8 167	9 800
					Balance—loss on holding money		(6)	984	
			14 436	15 560				14 436	15 560
19x3									
Jan. Balance		b/d	8 167	9 800					

(6) *Loss and Gain on Money*

19x2			Stabilized £x0	Ordinary £	19x2			Stabilized £x0	Ordinary £
Dec. Cash		(5)	984		Dec. Preference capital		(3)	333	
					Creditors		(4)	100	
					Balance		c/d	551	
			984					984	
19x3									
Jan. Balance		b/d	551						

			Stabilized £x0	Ordinary £					Stabilized £x0	Ordinary £

(7)

Plant—Historical Cost

			Stabilized £x0	Ordinary £					Stabilized £x0	Ordinary £
19x2										
Jan.	Balance	b/d	5 400	5 400						
Mar.	Cash	(5)	1 105	1 160						
	Balance	c/f	6 505	6 560						

(7a)

Plant—Addition (Real)

			Stabilized £x0	Ordinary £
19x2				
Dec.	Real gain on revaluation (7b)		519	

(7b)

Real Gain on Revaluation of Plant

			Stabilized £x0	Ordinary £					Stabilized £x0	Ordinary £
19x2						19x2				
June	Profit and loss	(2)	35			Dec.	Addition to value	(7a)	519	
Dec.	Cumulative depreciation (real)	(8a)	69							
	Balance	c/d	415							
			519							
						19x3				
						Jan.	Balance	b/d	415	

(8)

Cumulative Depreciation Provision—Historical

			Stabilized £x0	Ordinary £					Stabilized £x0	Ordinary £
						19x2				
						Jan.	Balance	b/d	600	600
						Dec.	Profit and Loss	(2)	657	660
							Balance	c/f	1 257	1 260

(8a)

Cumulative Depreciation Provision—Real Addition

			Stabilized £x0	Ordinary £					Stabilized £x0	Ordinary £
						19x2				
						June	Profit and Loss	(2)	35	
						Dec.	Real gain	(7b)	69	
							Balance	c/f	104	

(9)

Investment

			Stabilized £x0	Ordinary £					Stabilized £x0	Ordinary £
19x1						19x2				
Jan.	Balance	b/d	5 000	5 000		June	Cash	(5)	5 727	6 300
19x2										
June	Gain on sale	(10)	727	1 300						
			5 727	6 300						

(10)

Gain on Sale of Investment

			Stabilized £x0	Ordinary £					Stabilized £x0	Ordinary £
						19x2				
						June	Investment	(9)	727	1 300

(11)

Stock—Historical Cost

			Stabilized £x0	Ordinary £					Stabilized £x0	Ordinary £
19x1						19x2				
Oct.	Profit and loss	(2)	970	970		Jan.	Profit and loss	(2)	970	970
19x2										
Oct.	Profit and loss	(2)	1 138	1 309						

			Stabilized £x0	Ordinary £					Stabilized £x0	Ordinary £
(11a)										
				Stock—Addition to real value at year end						
19x1					19x2					
Dec.	Real gain	(11b)	3		Dec.	Real gain	(11b)	22	
						Balance	c/d	8	
			30					30	
19x3									
Jan.	Balance	b/d	8						

			Stabilized £x0	Ordinary £					Stabilized £x0	Ordinary £
(11b)										
				Real Gain on Stock Held						
19x2					19x1					
June	Profit and loss	(2)	68		Dec.	Real gain	(11b)	30	
Dec.	Addition to value	(11a)	22		19x2				
	Balance	c/d	8		June	Profit and Loss	(2)	68	
			98					98	
					19x3				
					Jan.	Balance	b/d	8	

balancing figure, and carried down to an account—(6)—for loss and gain on holding money.

Analogous differences emerge on the other money accounts, preference capital (3) and creditors (4). When all these differences are carried to (6), their net total is seen to be a loss of £$_{xo}$551. An ordinary ledger, as p. 47 explained, cannot easily be made to accommodate such gain and loss, and so the ordinary columns of (6) are here left blank.

Preference share values. If the value of the preference shares has diverged much from the figure obtained by general index stabilization in account (3), the new value should be found with the help of a real adjustment account (see the example for debentures on p. 140). Here the divergence is assumed to be immaterial.

Income statement and balance sheet

The final accounts follow on p. 190, with four columns:
(1) Ordinary figures.
(2) Stabilized figures, *general* index adjustment, in £ of 1 January 19x1.
(3) As column (2), with *special* index adjustment
(4) As column (3), in £ of 31 December 19x2. Though the stabilization columns in the ledger are best geared to some permanent base date (here 19x1), published reports, etc., are more likely to be comprehensible if their stabilized figures are those of the end of the year in question. Column (4) illustrates this alternative. Its figures are found by multiplying those in (3) by the general index factor of $\frac{120}{100}$. Similarly, in any later year current figures and comparative figures for earlier years can be calculated readily from the ledger's stabilized columns.

The stabilized columns analyse the position of the ordinary shareholders far more fully than the conventional figures on p. 182. The revised figures show that the fortunes of the company have been mixed. The ordinary figure for 19x2 operating profit sinks somewhat when stabilized; but that for the profit brought forward from 19x1 does not, as it was earned in money of a superior vintage. The gain on the sale of the investment is much less than the original accounts say. The policy of holding big sums of money has been costly; but the real (if unrealized) gains on the values of the other assets go far to offset this error.

Income statement, 19x2

	(1) Ordinary Accounts £	(2) General Index £ Jan. 19x1	(3) Special Indices £ Jan. 19x1	(4) £ Dec. 19x2
Sales	6060	5509	5509	6611
Less				
Opening stock	970	970	970	1164
Purchases	2475	2248	2248	2698
	3445	3218	3218	3862
Less Closing stock	1309	1138	1138	1366
			2080	2496
Replacement cost charge			68	81
Cost of raw materials used	2136	2080	2148	2577
Expenses	1025	932	932	1118
Depreciation	660	657	692	830
	3821	3669	3772	4525
Current operating profit			1737	2086
Real appreciation (realized)			103	122
Profit before tax	2239	1840	1840	2208
Less Tax	300	250	250	300
	1939	1590	1590	1908
Less Dividend	1100	917	917	1100
Retained earnings				
19x2	839	673	673	808
Brought forward	870	870	870	1044
	1709	1543	1543	1852

		(1) Ordinary Accounts	(2) Stabilized Accounts General Index	(3) Stabilized Accounts Special Indices	(4)
		£	£ Jan. 19x1	£ Jan. 19x1	£ Dec. 19x2
Balance sheet, end 19x2					
Plant, cost (new)	(7) (7a)	6 560	6 505	7 024	8 429
Less Depreciation	(8) (8a)	1 260	1 257	1 361	1 633
		5 300	5 248	5 663	6 796
Stock	(11) (11a)	1 309	1 138	1 146	1 375
Debtors and cash	(5)	9 800	8 167	8 167	9 800
		16 409	14 553	14 976	17 971
Ordinary shareholders:					
Capital	(1)	10 000	10 000	10 000	12 000
Surplus on revaluing assets	(7b) (11b)			423	508
Loss on holding money	(6)		−551	−551	−661
Gain on sale of investment	(10)	1 300	727	727	872
Trade profit	(2)	1 709	1 543	1 543	1 852
		13 009	11 719	12 142	14 571
Preference capital	(3)	2 000	1 667	1 667	2 000
Creditors and provisions	(4)	1 400	1 167	1 167	1 400
		16 409	14 553	14 976	17 971

References

1. *New York Times*, 22 January 1954.
2. F. W. Paish, in minutes of evidence, Royal Commission on the Taxation of Profits and Income, 1952, p. 227.
3. K. E. Boulding, 'Economics and Accounting: the Uncongenial Twins', in *Studies in Accounting Theory* (eds.) W. T. Baxter and S. Davidson, Sweet & Maxwell; Irwin, 1962, p. 55.
4. Mr Harry Norris to the Millard Tucker Committee on the Taxation of Trading Profits, April 1950.
5. J. Lehtovuori, *The Foundations of Accounting*, Helsinki School of Economics, 1972.

6. R. H. Parker, 'Some International Aspects of Accounting', *Journal of Business Finance*, **3**, 4, 1971.
7. A free rendering of M. Saario, *The Realisation Principle and the Depreciation of Fixed Assets*, Liiketaloustieteellisen Tutkimuslaitoksen Julkaisuja, 6, 1945, p. 295.
8. M. I. Epps, 'Realistic Accounting under South American Inflation', *Journal of Accountancy*, January 1961, p. 74.
9. Or it could calculate the real appreciation on the 100 tons held for the whole stock year (October–September), $£_{xo}65$, plus that on the 10 tons held for the second half of the stock year (March–September), $£_{xo}3$—in all, $£_{xo}68$.

Selected bibliography

Books

Abramovitz, M., *Inventories and Business Cycles*. New York: National Bureau of Economic Research, 1950.

Alexander, S. S., Bronfenbrenner, M., Fabricant, S., and Warburton, C., *Five Monographs on Business Income*. New York: American Institute of Accountants, 1950.

American Institute of Certified Public Accountants, *Restatement and Revision of Accounting Research Bulletins*, Accounting Research Bulletin No. 43 (issued by Committee on Accounting Procedure). New York: American Institute of Accountants, 1953.

American Institute of Certified Public Accountants *Reporting the Financial Effects of Price-level Changes*, Research Study No. 6. New York: American Institute of Accountants, 1963.

Association of Certified and Corporate Accountants, Taxation and Research Committee, *Accounting for Inflation*. London: Gee, 1952.

Barger, Harold, *The Management of Money*. Chicago: Rand McNally, 1964.

Barker, Ernest, *Church, State and Study*. London: Methuen, 1930.

Baxter, W. T., *Depreciation*, London: Sweet & Maxwell, 1971.

Baxter, W. T., and Davidson, S. (eds.), *Studies in Accounting Theory*, 2nd edition. London: Sweet & Maxwell; Chicago: Irwin, 1962.

Bonbright, J. C., *Valuation of Property*. New York: McGraw-Hill, 1937; (reprinted) Charlotteville, Virginia: Michie Company, 1965.

Boulding, K. E., 'Economics and Accounting: the Uncongenial Twins', in *Studies in Accounting Theory*, 2nd edition, Baxter, W. T., and Davidson, S. (eds.). London: Sweet & Maxwell;; Chicago: Irwin, 1962.

Brown, E. Cary, *Effects of Taxation: Depreciation Adjustments for Price Changes*. Boston: Harvard School of Business Administration, 1952.

Burns, A. F., and Mitchell, W. C., *Measuring Business Cycles*. New York: National Bureau of Economic Research, 1946.

Burns, A. R., *Money and Monetary Policy in Early Times*. London: Kegan Paul, 1927.

Butters, J. Keith, and Niland, Powell, *Inventory Accounting and Policies*. Boston: Harvard University Press, 1949.

Central Statistical Office, UK, *Annual Abstract of Statistics*.

Central Statistical Office, UK, *National Income and Expenditure*.

Chambers, Raymond, J., *Accounting, Evaluation, and Economic Behavior*. Englewood Cliffs, N.J.: Prentice-Hall, 1966.

Cheshire, G. C., *Private International Law*. London: Butterworth, 1965.

Davidson, S., 'Depreciation, Income Taxes, and Growth', in *Studies in Accounting Theory*, 2nd edition. Baxter, W. T., and Davidson, S. (eds). London: Sweet & Maxwell and Chicago: Irwin, 1962.

Davis, J. M., *Currency and Banking in the Province of Massachusetts Bay*. New York: 1901.

Department of Trade and Industry, UK, *Trade and Industry*.

Edey, H. C., 'Deprival Value and Financial Accounting', in H. C. Edey and B. S. Yamey (eds), *Debits, Credits, Finance and Profits*. London: Sweet & Maxwell, 1974.

Edwards, E. O., and Bell, P. W., *The Theory and Measurement of Business Income*. Berkeley: University of California Press, 1960.

Encyclopedia of Forms and Precedents, Vol. 11, 'Landlord and Tenant', 4th edition. London: Butterworth, 1965.

Fabricant, S., *Capital Consumption and Adjustment*. New York: National Bureau of Economic Research, 1938.

Gynther, R. S., *Accounting for Price Level Changes: Theory and Procedure*. Oxford: Pergamon Press, 1966.

Haberler, G., *Prosperity and Depression*. New York: Columbia University Press, 1941.

Haldane, J. B. S., *My Friend Mr Leakey*. London: Penguin Books, 1971.

Hansen, P., *The Accounting Concept of Profit: An Analysis and Evaluation in the Light of the Economic Theory of Income and Capital*. Amsterdam: North Holland Publishing Co., 1962.

Hendriksen, Eldon, S., *Accounting Theory*. Homewood, Illinois: Irwin, 1965.

Hicks, J. R., *Value and Capital*. Oxford: Oxford University Press, 1946.

Honko, J., *Yrityksen Vuositulos* (The Annual Income of an Enterprise and Its Determination: a study from the standpoint of accounting and economics). Helsinki: Liiketaloustieteellisen Tutkimuslaitoksen Julkaisuja, 25, 1959.

Ijiri, Y., *The Foundations of Accounting Measurement*. Englewood Cliffs, N.J.: Prentice-Hall, 1967.

IMF, *International Financial Statistics*.

Jones, Ralph, C., *Case Studies of Four Companies*. Urbana, Illinois: American Accounting Association, 1955.

Jones, Ralph, C., *Effects of Price Level Changes on Business Income, Capital and Taxes*, Urbana, Illinois: American Accounting Association, 1956.

Kirkman, P. R. A., *Accounting Under Inflationary Conditions.* London: Allen & Unwin, 1974.

Lacey, K., *Profit Measurement and Price Changes.* London: Pitman, 1952.

Lehtovuori, J., *Kirjanpidon Perusteet (The Foundations of Accounting).* Helsinki: Helsinki School of Economics, 1972.

Lewis, W. A., 'Depreciation and Obsolescence as Factors in Costing', in *Depreciation and Replacement Policy*, Meij, L. J. (ed.). Amsterdam: North-Holland Publishing Co., 1961.

Macaulay, T. B., *History of England.* London: Longmans, 1898.

MacNeal, K., 'What's Wrong with Accounting', in *Studies in Accounting Theory*, 2nd edition, Baxter, W. T. and Davison, S. (eds.). London: Sweet & Maxwell; Chicago: Irwin, 1962.

Mason, Perry, *Price Level Changes and Financial Statements: Basic Concepts and Methods.* Columbus, Ohio: American Accounting Association, 1956.

Mathews, R., and Grant, J. M., *Inflation and Company Finance.* Sydney: The Law Book Company of Australasia, 1958.

Meij, J. L. (ed.), *Depreciation and Replacement Policy.* Amsterdam: North Holland Publishing Company, 1961.

Merrett, A. J., and Sykes, Allen, *The Finance and Analysis of Capital Projects.* London and New York: Longmans, 1963.

Mills, F. C., *The Behaviour of Prices.* New York: National Bureau of Economic Research, 1927.

Paish, F. W., *Business Finance.* London: Pitman, 1953.

Paton, W. A., *Accounting Theory.* New York: Ronald Press, 1922.

Paton, W. A., *Corporate Profits.* Homewood, Illinois: Irwin, 1965.

Ray, Delmas D., *Accounting and Business Fluctuations.* Gainsville: University of Florida, 1960.

Robbins, L., *The Nature and Significance of Economic Science.* London: Macmillan, 1949.

Rosen, L. S., *Current Value Accounting and Price-Level Restatements.* Toronto: Canadian Institute of Chartered Accountants, 1972.

Ross, Howard, *Financial Statements—A Crusade for Current Values.* Toronto: Pitman, 1969.

Saario, M., *Realisointiperiaate Ja Käyttöomaisuuden Poistot Tuloslaskennassa (The Realisation Principle and the Depreciation of Fixed Assets).* Helsinki, Liiketaloustieteellisen Tutkimuslaitoksen Julkaisuja, 6, 1945.

Schiff, Erich, *Kapitalbildung und Kapitalaufzehrung im Konjunkturverlauf.* Vienna: Wiener Institut für Wirtschafts und Konjunkturforschung, 1933.

Solomon, E., *The Theory of Financial Management.* New York: Columbia University Press, 1963.

Solomons, David, *Divisional Performance: Measurement and Control.* New York: Financial Executives Research Foundation, 1965.

Sprouse, R. T., and Moonitz, M., *A Tentative Set of Broad Accounting Principles for Business Enterprises.* New York: American Institute of Certified Public Accountants, 1962.

Sweeney, Henry Whitcomb, *Stabilized Accounting.* New York: Harper & Bros, 1936, republished by Holt, Rinehart & Winston, 1964.

Terborgh, George, *Business Investment Policy—a MAPI Study and Manual*, Washington: Machinery and Allied Products Institute, 1958.

US Steel, *Annual Report*, 1947.

Wilk, L. A., *Accounting for Inflation.* London: Sweet & Maxwell, 1960.

Williams, W. J. (ed.), *Encyclopaedia of Forms and Precedents*, 3rd edition. London: Butterworth & Co., 1962.

Yamey, B. S., 'Some Topics in the History of Financial Accounting in England, 1500–1900' and 'The Case Law Relating to Company Dividends', in *Studies in Accounting Theory*, 2nd edition, Baxter, W. T. and Davidson, S. (eds.). London: Sweet & Maxwell; Chicago; Irwin, 1962.

Articles and Monographs

Accounting Standards Steering Committee, 'Accounting for Changes in the Purchasing Power of Money', provisional statement of standard accounting practice no. 7, May 1974.

Accounting Standards Steering Committee, *Exposure Draft No. 8*, 'Accounting for Changes in the Purchasing Power of Money', London, 1973.

Arthur Andersen & Co., *Memorandum on Price-Level Depreciation*, Chicago. July, 1959.

Barker, H. P., *Parkinson Cowan Report*, July 1964.

Baxter, W. T., 'Inflation and the Accounts of Steel Companies', *Accountancy*, May and June 1959.

Baxter, W. T., 'Inflation and Partnership Rights', *The Accountant's Magazine*, February, 1962.

Baxter, W. T., and Carrier, N., 'Depreciation, Replacement Price, and Cost-of-Capital', *Journal of Accounting Research*, Spring 1971.

Baxter, W. I., and Yamey, B. S., 'Theory of Foreign Branch Accounts', *Accounting Research*, April 1951.

Bhaskar, K. N., 'Optimal Asset Lives', *Accounting and Business Research*, Autumn 1973.

Bierman, H., Jr., 'Discounted Cash Flows, Price Level Adjustments and Expectations', *The Accounting Review*, October 1971.

Bird, R. M., 'Depreciation Allowances and Countercyclical Policy', *Canadian Tax Journal*, May–June and July–August 1963.

Bird, Roland, 'The Use of Published Accounts, II: The Viewpoint of an Economist', *The Accountant*, 3 February 1951.

Bromwich, M., 'Inflation of the Capital Budgeting Process', *Journal of Business Finance*, Autumn 1969.

Brown, E. H. Phelps, and Hopkins, Sheila V., 'Seven Centuries of the Prices of Consumables, Compared with Builders' Wage-rates', *Economica*, November 1956.

Butter, E. B., and Hart, H., 'Revaluation in Business Decisions and Measures of Capital', *Accountancy*, June 1963.

Chambers, R. J., 'Second Thoughts on Continuously Contemporary Accounting', *Abacus*, September 1970.

Domar, E. D., 'The Case for Accelerated Depreciation', *Quarterly Journal of Economics*, February 1953.

Domar, E. D., 'Depreciation, Replacement and Growth', *Economic Journal*, March 1953.

Drake, David F., and Dopuch, Nicholas, 'On the Case for Dichotomizing Income', *Journal of Accounting Research*, Autumn 1965.

Edey, H. C., 'Valuation of Stock in Trade for Income Tax Purposes', *British Tax Review*, June 1956.

Edey, H. C., 'Income and the Valuation of Stock-in-Trade', *The British Tax Review*, May–June 1962.

Edey, H. C., 'Accounting Principles and Business Reality', *The Accountant*, 24 and 31 August 1963.

Eisenhower, President D., Budget message to Congress, 21 January, 1954; reported in the *New York Times*, January 1954, 14:4.

Epps, M. I., 'Realistic Accounting under South American Inflation', *Journal of Accountancy*, January 1961.

Goudeket, A., 'An Application of Replacement Cost Theory', *Journal of Accountancy*, July 1960.

Graham, Willard J., 'Changing Price Levels and Income', *Accounting Review*, January 1949.

Hellyar, C. D., 'The Lifo Method of Stock Valuation', *The Accountant*, 14 June 1952.

Institute of Chartered Accountants in England and Wales, Recommendations on Accounting Principles, XII (1949), XV (1952) and N27.

Institute of Chartered Accountants in England and Wales, Research Foundation, 'Accounting for Stewardship in a Period of Inflation', 1968.

Institute of Chartered Accountants in England and Wales, *Accounting for Inflation: A Working Guide to the Accounting Procedures*, parts 1 and 2, London, 1973.

Jones, Ralph C., 'Effect of Inflation on Capital and Profits: The Record of Nine Steel Companies', *Journal of Accountancy*, January 1949.

Kaldor, N., 'The Irrelevance of Equilibrium Economics', *Economic Journal*, December 1972.

Lawson, G. H., 'Cash Flow Accounting', *The Accountant*, 28 October and 4 November 1971.

Lipsey, R. G., 'Does Money Always Depreciate?', *Lloyds Bank Review*, October 1960.

Merrett, A. J., 'The Capital Gains Tax', *Lloyds Bank Review*, October 1965.

Norman, N., and Astbury, H. A., 'Fiscal Measures in France', *The Accountant*, 12 March 1955.

Norris, H., 'Depreciation Allocations in Relation to Financial Capital, Real Capital and Productive Capacity', *Accounting Research*, July 1949.

Paish, F., 'Capital and Income', *Economica*, July 1940.

Paish, F., 'Memorandum' in *Minutes of Evidence*, Royal Commission on the Taxation of Profits and Income, 1952.

Parker, R. H., 'Some International Aspects of Accounting', *Journal of Business Finance*, **3**, 4, 1971.

Phillips, A. W., 'Stabilisation Policy in a Closed Economy', *Economic Journal*, June 1954.

Phillips, A. W., 'Employment, Inflation and Growth', *Economica*, February 1962.

Prest, A. R., 'National Income of the United Kingdom', *Economic Journal*, March 1948.

Solomons, D., 'Economic and Accounting Concepts of Income', *Accounting Review*, July 1961.

Stamp, Edward, 'Income and Value Determination and Changing Price-levels: an Essay towards a Theory', *The Accountant's Magazine*, June 1971.

Trumbull, W. J., 'Price Level Depreciation and Replacement Cost', *Accounting Review*, January, 1958.

Turvey, Ralph, 'The Effect of Price-level Changes on Real Private Wealth in the United Kingdom, 1954–60', *Economica*, May 1962.

Turvey, Ralph, 'Rates of Return, Pricing, and the Public Interest', *Economic Journal*, September 1971.

Wright, F. K., 'Towards a General Theory of Depreciation', *Journal of Accounting Research*, Spring, 1964.

Wright, F. K., 'Measuring Asset Services: A Linear Programming Approach', *Journal of Accounting Research*, Autumn 1968.

Wright, F. K., 'A Theory of Financial Accounting', *Journal of Business Finance*, Autumn 1970.

Zannetos, Z. S., 'Involuntary Liquidations of Lifo Inventories', *Accounting Research*, October 1954.

Accounting for changes in the purchasing power of money

Provisional statement
of standard accounting practice No. 7

May 1974

The Institute of Chartered Accountants in
England and Wales

STATEMENTS OF STANDARD ACCOUNTING PRACTICE

ACCOUNTING FOR CHANGES IN THE PURCHASING POWER OF MONEY

Contents

STATEMENTS OF STANDARD ACCOUNTING PRACTICE

7. *Accounting for changes in the purchasing power of money* (*issued May 1974*)

© The Institute of Chartered Accountants in England and Wales.

NOTE ON THE STATUS OF THIS STATEMENT

The Statement which follows differs from conventional statements of standard accounting practice in that it is 'provisional': that is, it does not involve a binding obligation to disclose and explain in annual accounts departures from the procedures contained in it, nor does it oblige auditors to mention such departures in their report. However, there is general recognition that financial statements adjusted for the effects of inflation are essential for efficient management and it is in the interest of shareholders that they should be provided with that information by the directors.

It is believed that the procedures outlined in this Statement will receive substantial support from major companies.

In this Statement references to 'standard' mean 'provisional standard' throughout.

FOREWORD

An Exposure Draft ACCOUNTING FOR CHANGES IN THE PURCHASING POWER OF MONEY (ED8) was issued on 17th January 1973 for comment by 31st July 1973. In July 1973 the then Secretary of State for Trade and Industry announced that an independent Committee of Enquiry was to be set up to consider the various methods of adjusting company accounts and whether, and if so how, company accounts should allow for changes in costs and prices. The terms of reference of the Committee require it to have regard to the proposals put forward by the Accounting Standards Steering Committee and to take into account the wider implications of inflation accounting.

Since it would obviously be some time before the Committee of Enquiry could report and before its recommendations could be considered by Government, the ASSC decided to proceed with its work and prepare a Provisional Standard for approval by the Councils of the professional bodies represented on the ASSC. This decision was reported to and noted by the Government. The Provisional Standard is attached.

It is recommended that all listed companies, and others where possible, should follow the Provisional Standard as soon as possible.

The ASSC was greatly assisted in its work by the CBI, which set up a Committee under the chairmanship of Sir David Barran to report on the subject. This Committee made two reports and supported the proposals of the ASSC. Its final report, dated September 1973, concluded:

PROVISIONAL

STATEMENTS OF STANDARD ACCOUNTING PRACTICE

Accounting for changes in the
purchasing power of money

'The Committee is of the opinion that the objective of inflation accounting should be to encourage the widest possible adoption of the proposals of the ASSC as set out in Exposure Draft 8. It may well be that UK quoted companies will not wait for the standard to become mandatory before producing supplementary statements. The Committee hopes that the Government announcement will not delay the introduction of inflation accounting.'

One of the bodies commenting on the Exposure Draft, namely the Society of Investment Analysts, has reservations shared by a number of other commentators, on the method to be used, believing that, in many cases, a replacement cost approach would be preferable. The Society, however, confirms its support for the principle that company accounts should reflect the impact of inflation as an urgent requirement.

PART 1 – EXPLANATORY NOTE

Introduction

1   Inflation, which is the decline in the purchasing power of money as the general price level of goods and services rises, affects most aspects of economic life, including investment decisions, wage negotiations, pricing policies, international trade and government taxation policy.

2   When the annual rate of inflation appears low, there is a tendency for business undertakings to regard the problem as not serious enough to warrant any action. Nevertheless, over a period of years even a modest rate of progressive inflation can have a significant cumulative effect if there are assets and liabilities with lives extending over a number of years. When the annual rate of inflation rises to a persistently significant level, business undertakings become more aware of the problem and there is a demand, such as we are experiencing now, for action.

3   It is important that managements and other users of financial accounts should be in a position to appreciate the effects of inflation on the businesses with which they are concerned – for example, the effects on costs, profits, distribution policies, dividend cover, the exercise of borrowing powers, returns on funds and future cash needs. The purpose of this Statement is the limited one of establishing a standard practice for demonstrating the effect of changes in the purchasing power of money on accounts prepared on the basis of existing conventions. It does not suggest the abandonment of the historical cost convention, but simply that historical costs should be converted from an aggregation of historical pounds of many different purchasing powers into approximate figures of current purchasing power and that this information should be given in a supplement to the basic accounts prepared on the historical cost basis.

Scope

4   While it is desirable that all companies should provide information on the effects of inflation it is recognized that:
   (a) such information is probably of greater significance in the case of listed companies;

STATEMENTS OF STANDARD ACCOUNTING PRACTICE

*Accounting for changes in the
purchasing power of money*

(b) the work involved in producing the information, although not great, may be proportionally heavier for smaller companies;

(c) there is a need to phase the work of introducing inflation adjusted accounts, which is likely to be greater initially than when once established, so as not to overload the accounting resources of companies generally.

Accordingly, the practice described in this Statement, whilst recommended for all companies, is to be regarded as standard initially only for the annual accounts of listed companies.

The first presentation of the supplementary statement required by this Standard   5
or of figures derived therefrom, should be in the company's annual accounts. Interim accounts or the preliminary announcement of the results for the year are not suitable places for the first presentation of such figures as they do not provide an adequate opportunity to explain their significance. While the Standard applies only to the annual accounts of listed companies it is desirable, where practical and as the relevant figures become available, that the practice of providing this supplementary information should be extended to include other financial statements such as interim accounts, preliminary announcements of figures for the year, ten year summaries, profit forecasts and prospectuses.

The historical cost convention

The annual accounts of companies are prepared substantially on the basis of the   6
historical cost of the items dealt with. In addition, some companies periodically revalue some of their assets to current values. The effect is that items are recorded in terms of the purchasing power of the pound at the date when the asset was acquired or revalued, the liability was incurred, or the capital obtained.

This convention has the advantage that the recorded historical cost is derived   7
from factual monetary transactions, and its use helps to limit the number of matters within the accounts which are subject to the exercise of judgement. However, that advantage is impaired where the purchasing power of the monetary unit used changes significantly over a period of years. The need to show the effect of inflation on conventional accounts has become of pressing importance.

The need for supplementary information

The purchasing power of the pound, in common with other currencies, has altered   8
materially, and in recent years the rate of change has increased. There is clearly a need to reflect the effects of such changes in accounting statements but there is debate about the best method of achieving this object.

It has been suggested that readers of annual accounts can make sufficient and   9
suitable mental adjustments for the effects of changes in the purchasing power of the pound. Such adjustments, however, can be no more than crude estimates because:

(a) the rate of change in the purchasing power of money has not been constant;

(b) the effect of change in the purchasing power of money will vary between companies according to:

STATEMENTS OF STANDARD ACCOUNTING PRACTICE

Accounting for changes in the
purchasing power of money

> (i) individual ratios of monetary to non-monetary items (for an explanation of these terms see paragraphs 14 to 19 below), and
> (ii) different patterns over the course of time in the acquisition of assets, incurring of liabilities and raising of capital.

10   Most users of annual accounts outside a company will not be in a position to make the required adjustments for themselves. Only the directors of a company are in a position to provide suitable information to enable users of accounts to understand the effects of inflation on the results and financial position.

The proposed method compared with other methods

11   The method proposed in this Statement (the 'current purchasing power' or 'CPP' method) is concerned with removing the distorting effects of changes in the general purchasing power of money on accounts prepared in accordance with established practice. It does not deal with changes in the relative values of non-monetary assets (which occur also in the absence of inflation). It should therefore be distinguished from methods of 'replacement cost' or 'current value' accounting which deal with a mixture of changes in relative values and changes due to movements in the general price level. (Detailed comment on the differences between CPP and replacement cost accounting is given in Appendix 1.)

Summary of the principal aspects of the statement of standard accounting practice

12   The main features of the standard are:

> (*a*) companies will continue to keep their records and present their *basic* annual accounts in historical pounds, i.e. in terms of the value of the pound at the time of each transaction or revaluation;
> (*b*) in addition, all listed companies should present to their shareholders a *supplementary* statement in terms of the value of the pound at the end of the period to which the accounts relate;
> (*c*) the conversion of the figures in the *basic* accounts into the figures in the *supplementary* statement should be by means of a general index of the purchasing power of the pound;
> (*d*) the standard requires the directors to provide in a note to the supplementary statement an explanation of the basis on which it has been prepared and it is desirable that directors should comment on the significance of the figures.

13   The form of the supplementary statement is a matter for the directors of the company to decide, provided that they conform to the standard accounting practice (part 3 below). There are a number of ways in which the information required may be shown. An example of a possible presentation is given in Appendix 2. This example includes some ratios as the effect of changes in the purchasing power of the pound on them may be even more significant than on the underlying absolute figures.

Monetary and non-monetary items

14   In converting the figures in the basic historical cost accounts into those in the supplementary current purchasing power statement a distinction is drawn between:

> (*a*) monetary items, and
> (*b*) non-monetary items.

STATEMENTS OF STANDARD ACCOUNTING PRACTICE

Accounting for changes in the purchasing power of money

Monetary items are those whose amounts are fixed by contract or otherwise in terms of numbers of pounds, regardless of changes in general price levels. Examples of monetary items are cash, debtors, creditors and loan capital. Holders of monetary assets lose general purchasing power during a period of inflation to the extent that any income from the assets does not adequately compensate for the loss; the converse applies to those having monetary liabilities. A company with a material excess on average over the year of long- and short-term debt (e.g. debentures and creditors) over debtors and cash will show, in its supplementary current purchasing power statement, a gain in purchasing power during the year. This is a real gain to the equity shareholders in purchasing power but it has to be appreciated that there may be circumstances in which it will be accompanied by a dangerously illiquid situation or by excessively high gearing, and for this reason any such gain should be shown as a separate figure.   15

It has been argued that the gain on long-term borrowing should not be shown as profit in the supplementary statement because it might not be possible to distribute it without raising additional finance. This argument, however, confuses the measurement of profitability with the measurement of liquidity. Even in the absence of inflation, the whole of a company's profit may not be distributable without raising additional finance, for example because it has been invested in, or earmarked for investment in, non-liquid assets.   16

Moreover, it is inconsistent to exclude such gains when profit has been debited with the cost of borrowing (which must be assumed to reflect anticipation of inflation by the lender during the currency of the loan), and with depreciation on the converted cost of fixed assets.   17

Non-monetary items include such assets as stock, plant and buildings. The retention of the historical cost concept (see paragraphs 6 and 7) requires that holders of non-monetary assets are assumed neither to gain nor to lose purchasing power by reason only of changes in the purchasing power of the pound (but see paragraphs 21 and 22 below).   18

The owners of a company's equity capital have the residual claim on its net monetary and non-monetary assets. The equity interest is therefore neither a monetary nor a non-monetary item.   19

The conversion process

In converting from basic historical cost accounts to supplementary current purchasing power statements for any particular period: 20

(a) monetary items in the balance sheet at the end of the period remain the same;

(b) non-monetary items are increased in proportion to the inflation that has occurred since their acquisition or revaluation (and conversely, reduced in times of deflation).

In the conversion process, after increasing non-monetary items by the amount of inflation, it is necessary to apply the test of lower of cost (expressed in pounds of current purchasing power) and net realizable value to relevant current assets, e.g. stocks, and further to adjust the figures if necessary. Similarly, after restating fixed assets in terms of pounds of current purchasing power, the question of the   21

STATEMENTS OF STANDARD ACCOUNTING PRACTICE

Accounting for changes in the purchasing power of money

value to the business needs to be reviewed in that context and provision made if necessary. Other matters that will need to be considered include the adequacy of the charge for depreciation on freehold and long leasehold properties, and whether it may be necessary to include in the deferred tax account in the supplementary statement, an amount for the corporation tax (in the Republic of Ireland income tax and corporation profits tax) on any chargeable gain which would arise on a sale of the assets at the date of the balance sheet at the amount shown in the supplementary statement.

22　In applying these tests, and during the whole process of conversion, it is important to balance the effort involved against the materiality of the figures concerned. The supplementary current purchasing power statement can be no more than an approximation, and it is pointless to strive for over-elaborate precision.

Index to be used

23　In the United Kingdom there are a number of indices which might be taken as indicators of changes in the general purchasing power of the pound. For the post-war years they include the following:

　　(a) the gross domestic product (GDP) deflator;
　　(b) the total final expenditure (TFE) deflator;
　　(c) the consumers' expenditure deflator (CED) (formerly referred to as the consumer price index);
　　(d) the general index of retail prices (RPI).

24　The choice between these indicators is in principle quite finely balanced. The first reflects changes in total home costs and the second changes in the prices of total final output (including investment goods and exports). But changes in the purchasing power of the pound are, as in this Statement, more often conceived in relation to the purchasing power of money spent by individuals on the goods and services purchased for their own personal use and for this reason indicators of the third or fourth type are considered to be more appropriate. The RPI has certain practical advantages over the CED: unlike the CED it is not subject to retrospective revision and it is available monthly by about the middle of the following month (the CED is an annual index available in March of the following year). For these reasons it has been decided that for periods covered by the RPI in its present form (i.e. since the beginning of 1962) the indicator to be used should be the RPI.

25　On the basis of a recommendation from the Central Statistical Office the use of the following indices is specified for the relevant periods:

　　– for periods up to end 1938, the Ministry of Labour cost of living index;
　　– for periods between end 1938 and end 1961, the consumers' expenditure deflator;
　　– for periods from 1962 onwards, the general index of retail prices.

Figures for these indices spliced together to form a continuous series will be found in Appendix 4. The figures quoted are annual averages and as the financial year-ends of companies vary an index number will be required for each month end. An adequate approximation can be obtained by using an appropriate index of retail prices to adjust the annual index. Appropriate retail price indices for each month from December 1914 to December 1966 will be found in *Method of Construction and Calculation of the Index of Retail Prices* (Department of Employment

STATEMENTS OF STANDARD ACCOUNTING PRACTICE

*Accounting for changes in the
purchasing power of money*

and Productivity, HMSO). Figures for later months may be obtained direct from the Central Statistical Office, or from the *Monthly Digest of Statistics* (obtainable from HMSO), or *Trade and Industry* (published by the Department of Trade and Industry and also obtainable from HMSO).

In the Republic of Ireland the general index of retail prices should be taken to refer   26
to the quarterly Consumer Price Index compiled by the Central Statistics Office, Dublin. The four separate index series, which have been compiled since 1922, have been linked together to form a continuous annual average series (base January 1974=100). The Irish Consumer Price Index may be obtained directly from the Central Statistics Office, Dublin or from the *Irish Statistical Bulletin* (obtainable from the Government Publications Office, G.P.O. Arcade, Dublin 1). The method of calculating the current index (base November 1968=100) is described in the *Irish Statistical Bulletin*, March 1969. Where a company's year-end falls at a date other than that to which the index is compiled, it will be necessary to interpolate or extrapolate the values of the index to approximate to the value at the company's year-end.

Overseas subsidiaries and associates

It is possible that some companies may experience difficulties in obtaining the   27
information necessary to produce the current purchasing power supplementary statements from some of their overseas subsidiaries or associates. In such cases, directors will have to weigh the materiality of the items concerned against the cost of obtaining the necessary information. The reasons for the treatment adopted and the magnitude of the items involved, should be disclosed in a note to the supplementary statement.

PART 2 – DEFINITION OF TERMS

Monetary items are assets, liabilities, or capital, the amounts of which are fixed   28
by contract or statute in terms of numbers of pounds regardless of changes in the purchasing power of the pound.

Non-monetary items are all items which are not monetary items, with the exception   29
of the total equity interest (i.e. share capital, reserves and retained profits). The total equity interest is neither a monetary nor a non-monetary item.

Conversion is the process of translating figures from historical pounds to pounds   30
of current purchasing power.

Updating is the process of translating figures of an earlier accounting period from   31
pounds of current purchasing power at one date to pounds of current purchasing power at another, later, date.

Basic accounts are those prepared substantially in accordance with established   32
conventions on the basis of historical cost and include those in which some or all fixed assets have been revalued and/or some or all current assets are shown at estimated realizable value.

STATEMENTS OF STANDARD ACCOUNTING PRACTICE

Accounting for changes in the purchasing power of money

33   *A listed company* is one which has some or all of its securities admitted to the official list of a recognized stock exchange. A recognized stock exchange has the meaning given to it by the Companies Act 1967 (i.e. 'any body of persons which is for the time being a recognized stock exchange for the purposes of the Prevention of Fraud (Investments) Act 1958') together with the Belfast Stock Exchange, which is recognized under the Northern Ireland Prevention of Fraud (Investments) Act 1940, and any stock exchange prescribed by the Minister for Industry and Commerce of the Republic of Ireland under the Companies Act 1963 (at present this is the Stock Exchange – Irish).

PART 3 – PROVISIONAL STANDARD ACCOUNTING PRACTICE*

Scope of this Statement

34   This accounting standard applies to the published annual accounts of listed companies. But the method of presenting the effects of changes in the purchasing power of money which is described is capable of application to every type of business, and its general adoption is recommended as good practice in the interests of more informative reporting.

Accounts to be restated in a supplement

35   All accounts laid before the members of listed companies in general meeting should be supported by a supplementary statement showing in terms of pounds of purchasing power at the end of the year to which the accounts relate the financial position at that date and the results for the year.

36   The supplementary statement should be prepared by converting the basic accounts by the application of a general index of prices as described in paragraph 40. The supplementary statement need not give a converted figure for each item in the basic accounts but may be in reasonably summarized form. The supplementary statement should contain separate figures, if material, for depreciation and for the loss or gain on holding monetary items (i.e. the net loss or gain in purchasing power resulting from the effects of inflation on the company's net monetary assets or liabilities).

37   In the case of a listed holding company presenting group accounts in the form of consolidated accounts, the supplementary statement need deal only with the consolidated accounts.

38   The supplementary statement should contain a note outlining the method of conversion used including the treatment of accounts originally prepared in foreign currencies.

39   The auditors should report on the supplementary statement.

*See the opening Note for explanation of 'provisional'.

STATEMENTS OF STANDARD ACCOUNTING PRACTICE

Accounting for changes in the
purchasing power of money

Index to be used
The index to be used in the conversion process should be:　　　　　40

(*a*) In the United Kingdom
– for periods up to end 1938, the Ministry of Labour cost-of-living index;
– for periods between end 1938 and end 1961, the consumers' expenditure deflator;
– for periods from 1962 onwards, the general index of retail prices based on January 1974=100;
(*b*) In the Republic of Ireland the official Consumer Price Index.

The figure for the index at the beginning and end of the accounting period and　　41
the date of the base of the index should be shown in a note to the supplementary statement.

Corresponding amounts
In all supplementary statements, except the first, prepared in accordance with this　42
Standard, all corresponding amounts shown for the preceding year should be 'updated' (see definition paragraph 31) so that they are restated in terms of the purchasing power of the pound at the end of the year under review.

It is not necessary to provide corresponding amounts in the first supplementary　　43
statement produced in accordance with this Standard, but their provision is recommended.

Date from which effective
While this Standard is provisional and not of binding effect, it should nevertheless　44
be regarded as persuasive in content and the member bodies of the ASSC strongly recommend its adoption in accounts as soon as possible and preferably not later than the first accounting period beginning after 30th June 1974.

APPENDICES

These appendices are for general guidance and do not form part of the provisional statement of standard accounting practice.

Appendix 1 STATEMENTS OF STANDARD ACCOUNTING PRACTICE

*Accounting for changes in the
purchasing power of money*

Appendix 1

*This appendix is for general guidance and does not form part of the Provisional
Statement of Standard Accounting Practice.*

CURRENT PURCHASING POWER ACCOUNTING AND REPLACEMENT COST

The basis of current purchasing power accounting

1 Current purchasing power (CPP) accounting is concerned with removing the
effects that changes in the general purchasing power of money have on accounts
prepared in accordance with ordinary accounting practice. It looks at the undertaking from the point of view of the purchasing power invested in it by its owners
and of the maintenance of that purchasing power, but otherwise it accepts the
existing conventions of financial accounting.

2 It has been suggested that more radical changes are needed and that, in particular,
better information would be provided in relation to the use and control of assets,
especially for management, if some form of replacement cost accounting were
instituted. Replacement cost accounting and inflation accounting are, however,
different concepts. They are not mutually exclusive. Replacement cost accounting
is a valuable management tool, and the introduction of current purchasing power
accounting in a supplementary financial statement in no way precludes the use of
replacement cost for internal management control purposes, price-setting, or,
where appropriate, the revaluation of fixed assets in the ordinary accounts in
accordance with established practice.

3 Because current purchasing power accounting is concerned primarily with the
effects of inflation on the measurement of the profits of, and the purchasing power
invested in, an undertaking (e.g. by the equity shareholders in the case of a company, or by the nation as a whole in the case of a public enterprise), it uses a
measure of the change in the power of money to purchase commodities of the type
that consumers in general buy.

4 For example, if an individual shareholder wishes to consider how inflation has affected his financial position as between two dates, he will be concerned with the effect on
his power to purchase the goods and services he usually buys. No index of changes
in the purchasing power of consumers in general is perfect, because people's tastes
and purchasing patterns differ. As in other human affairs, a workable approximation has to be used. Statisticians have given a great deal of thought to devising
indices that will provide a good indication of the effect of general price changes on
consumers. The retail price index has been selected for CPP adjustments because
it is regarded as the best available indicator of changes in the general purchasing
power of money to consumers.

Monetary effects in CPP accounting

5 The effects of inflation on the interests of equity shareholders created by net
holdings of monetary assets or of net monetary indebtedness are no less real for
being the result of financial, as distinct from physical, conversion processes. The

results of financial expertise on the part of boards are as important to their share-holders as those of other management qualities. Monetary effects are real, as many small savers know to their cost. It is true that in some cases distribution of a monetary gain could have an adverse effect on liquidity. Availability of liquidity is, however, a separate question from the measurement of profitability.

Excessive asset values in CPP accounting

It has been suggested that to adjust asset values on a CPP basis could raise them above their 'true' value to the company. However, the rules for calculating the CPP amounts make it clear that if the adjusted asset value is believed to be in excess of an amount currently justified by its future expected contribution to the business (e.g. the net realizable value of a current asset) the CPP adjusted figure should be written down accordingly, just as should be done with the unadjusted figure in the absence of general inflation. In the case of fixed assets the existence of such a situation implies in effect that the depreciation provision on the earlier, non-adjusted, basis has been inadequate.

6

The nature of replacement cost accounting

'Replacement cost accounting' is not a single well-defined technique, but rather a family of techniques. Replacement cost accounting does not isolate and record the effects of changes in the general purchasing power of money, but selects and gives effect to those specific price changes, arising for whatever reason, which have an impact on the costs and revenues of the business concerned. In replacement cost accounting the underlying concept of profit on a transaction is based on the difference between the selling price of an article and the cost of its replacement at the date of sale, and is thus different from that inherent in the historical cost basis which measures profit, either in historic pounds or in pounds of current purchasing power, as the difference between selling price and original cost. Replacement cost accounting therefore aims to show the maintenance or otherwise of the physical assets of a business rather than the maintenance of the amount of purchasing power (historic or current) originally invested in the assets. It may therefore be regarded as management orientated rather than shareholder orientated because the shareholder is likely to be concerned with the general purchasing power of his investment.

7

The term 'replacement cost accounting' has been used to describe methods of accounting which include among others:

8

(a) showing freehold and leasehold property at current market values;

(b) showing all fixed assets and depreciation at current replacement values;

(c) showing fixed assets and stock, with depreciation and cost of sales, at current replacement values;

(d) as in (c), with the equity interest adjusted for the general price level change, and with monetary assets and liabilities at their original money values, with consequential adjustments to profit.

In all these and similar cases, replacement costs might be arrived at by estimating current market values or by applying specific price indices, each of which was believed to be a reasonable indicator of the replacement cost of the asset or class of assets concerned. In using a replacement cost method, therefore, a wide degree

9

Appendix 1   STATEMENTS OF STANDARD ACCOUNTING PRACTICE

Accounting for changes in the
purchasing power of money

of discretion and subjective judgement enters in each separate case into the choice of the adjustment factor, and a general index for adjustment of asset values cannot be prescribed.

10   The replacement cost of an asset can rise or fall when there is no change at all in the general price level (i.e. when there is no inflation). Relative price changes may be due to technological, economic, social or legal factors.

11   The fact that the question of replacement cost is separate from that of CPP correction does not prevent the reporting of information on replacement cost to shareholders where this is considered to be relevant. This can be done, if desired, in a supplementary accounting statement, additional to and separate from the CPP supplementary statement, or where appropriate by adjustment of the ordinary accounts.

12   It should be noted, however, that the attempt to make replacement cost adjustments can give rise to very considerable difficulties of calculation and in some cases, e.g. where there is technological change, the result may be virtually meaningless unless the replacement cost is calculated for the whole of a particular industrial complex.

STATEMENTS OF STANDARD ACCOUNTING PRACTICE

Accounting for changes in the purchasing power of money

Appendix 2

This appendix is for general guidance and does not form part of the Provisional Statement of Standard Accounting Practice.

EXAMPLE OF THE PRESENTATION OF A SUPPLEMENTARY CURRENT PURCHASING POWER STATEMENT

The example has been prepared in order to illustrate how the figures of a company might be presented in the supplementary current purchasing power statement. It should be emphasized that the following example is only one method of presenting the information required by the Standard and is not obligatory. Indeed it is desirable that companies should experiment with different methods of presentation during the early years of the use of this Standard.

SUMMARY OF RESULTS AND FINANCIAL POSITION ADJUSTED FOR THE EFFECTS OF INFLATION (NOTE 1)

	Historical basis		Current purchasing power basis	
	£000 Last year (1)	£000 This year (2)	£000 This year (3)	£000 Last year (4)
RESULTS FOR THE YEAR				
Sales	1,920	2,110	2,190	2,134
Profit before taxation (see note 2)	205	215	175	195
Taxation	82	86	86	89
Profit after taxation	123	129	89	106
Dividends	60	60	61	65
Retained profit for the year	63	69	28	41
FINANCIAL POSITION AT END OF YEAR				
Net current assets	490	556	561	533
Fixed assets less depreciation	558	566	700	714
	1,048	1,122	1,261	1,247
Less: Loan capital (see note 3)	200	200 200	200 216	
Deferred taxation	39	44	44 42	
	239	244	244	258
Total equity interest	809	878	1,017	989
RATIOS				
Earnings per share (p) (based on 500,000 shares in issue)	24·6	25·8	17·8	21·2
Dividend cover (times)	2·1	2·2	1·5	1·6
Return on total equity interest (%)	15·2	14·7	8·8	10·7
Net assets per share (£)	1·6	1·8	2·0	2·0

Notes

(1) The figures in the current purchasing power basis columns were arrived at by converting the corresponding figures in the historical basis columns by reference to the changes in a general price index between the dates of the original transactions and the end of 'this year'. The current purchasing power basis figures for both this and last year are measured in pounds of purchasing power at the end of 'this year'. The general price index used was that specified in Provisional Statement of Standard Accounting Practice No. 7. The Retail Price Index at the end of this year was 139·3 and at the end of last year was 129·0. Both figures are based on January 1974=100.

As the Inland Revenue do not at present accept CPP basis accounting, taxation liabilities are calculated by reference to profits on the historical basis and no adjustment therefore is made to the tax charge in the CPP basis column.

Appendix 2   STATEMENTS OF STANDARD ACCOUNTING PRACTICE

Accounting for changes in the
purchasing power of money

(2) Profit before taxation
How the difference between profit on a historical basis and on a current purchasing power basis is made up.

	This Year £000		Last Year £000
PROFIT BEFORE TAXATION (historical basis) . .	215		205
Adjustment to convert to current purchasing power basis:			
STOCK			
Additional charge based on restating the cost of stock at the beginning and end of the year in pounds of current purchasing power, thus taking the inflationary element out of the profit on the sale of stocks	(37)		(25)
DEPRECIATION			
Additional depreciation based on cost, measured in pounds of current purchasing power, of fixed assets . .	(25)		(17)
MONETARY ITEMS			
Net gain in purchasing power resulting from the effects of inflation on the company's net monetary liabilities .	12		10
SALES, PURCHASES AND ALL OTHER COSTS			
These are increased by the change in the index between the average date at which they occurred and the end of the year. This adjustment increases profit as sales exceed the costs included in this heading	10		7
		(40)	(25)
PROFIT BEFORE TAXATION			
(Current purchasing power basis at end of year under review) .		175	180
Adjustment required to update last year's profit from last year's pounds to this year's pounds			15
PROFIT BEFORE TAXATION			
(Current purchasing power basis at end of this year) .		175	195

(3) The loan capital at the beginning of 'this year' amounted to £200,000. £200,000 at the beginning of this year is equivalent in purchasing power to £216,000 at the end of this year (because inflation has been 8 per cent during the year). As the company's liability to the providers of loan capital is fixed in money terms this liability has declined during the year in real terms from £216,000 to £200,000. This reduction of £16,000 in the company's obligation in terms of current purchasing power is included in the net gain on monetary items of £12,000 shown in note 2

Appendix 3

This appendix is for general guidance and does not form part of the Provisional Statement of Standard Accounting Practice.

OUTLINE OF A METHOD* OF CONVERSION FROM BASIC ACCOUNTS TO SUPPLEMENTARY CURRENT PURCHASING POWER STATEMENTS

The method of conversion may be divided into four basic stages:

(1) Figures for items in the balance sheet at the beginning of the year are converted into pounds of purchasing power at the beginning of the year as follows:

   (a) non-monetary items are adjusted for changes in the purchasing power of the pound since they were acquired or revalued;

   (b) monetary items are, by definition, already expressed in terms of pounds of purchasing power at the beginning of the year, and therefore require no conversion.

*There are other methods of conversion. Full details will be found in *Accounting for Inflation: A working guide to the accounting procedures,* published by The Trustees of Chartered Accountants' Trust for Education and Research of The Institute of Chartered Accountants in England and Wales.

Accounting for changes in the
purchasing power of money

(2) Figures for items in the balance sheet at the beginning of the year are then updated (see definition, paragraph 31), from pounds of purchasing power at the beginning of the year to pounds of purchasing power at the end of the year.

(3) Figures for items in the balance sheet at the end of the year are converted into pounds of purchasing power at the end of the year as follows:

    (*a*) non-monetary items are adjusted for changes in the purchasing power of the pound since they were acquired or revalued;

    (*b*) monetary items are, by definition, already expressed in terms of pounds of purchasing power at the end of the year, and therefore require no conversion.

(4) The difference between the total equity interest in the converted balance sheets at the beginning and end of the year (after allowing for dividends and the introduction of new capital), is the profit or loss for the year measured in pounds of purchasing power at the end of the year. This profit or loss can be analysed by producing a profit and loss account including figures expressed in pounds of purchasing power at the end of the year in the same detail as in the company's basic profit and loss account or in a more summarized form if desired. In addition to these items the converted profit and loss account should contain a figure for the net loss or gain in purchasing power resulting from the effects of inflation on the company's net monetary assets or liabilities.

Note

In stages 1 and 3 the figures for non-monetary items after conversion need to be reviewed, in the case of stocks, in the light of the test of lower of cost (in pounds of purchasing power at the respective balance sheet dates) and net realizable value, and in the case of fixed assets in the light of their estimated value to the business. It may then be necessary to make appropriate provisions against the converted figures. Consideration will also need to be given to the adequacy of the charge for depreciation on freehold and long leasehold property and whether it may be necessary to include in the deferred tax account in the supplementary statement an amount for the corporation tax on any chargeable gain which would arise on a sale of the assets at the date of the balance sheet at the amount shown in the supplementary statement (see paragraph 21).

Appendix 4   STATEMENTS OF STANDARD ACCOUNTING PRACTICE

Accounting for changes in the
purchasing power of money

Appendix 4

This appendix is for general guidance and does not form part of the Provisional
Statement of Standard Accounting Practice.

AN INDEX OF PRICES OF CONSUMER GOODS AND SERVICES (JANUARY 1974=100)

Year	Index	Percentage increase/ (decrease) over the previous year	Factor*
1914	11·1		8·84
1915	13·7	23	7·16
1916	16·2	18	6·06
1917	19·6	21	5·01
1918	22·6	15	4·34
1919	23·9	6	4·10
1920	27·7	16	3·54
1921	25·1	(9)	3·91
1922	20·4	(19)	4·81
1923	19·4	(5)	5·06
1924	19·5	1	5·03
1925	19·6	1	5·01
1926	19·1	(2)	5·14
1927	18·7	(2)	5·25
1928	18·5	(1)	5·30
1929	18·2	(1)	5·39
1930	17·6	(4)	5·57
1931	16·4	(7)	5·98
1932	16·0	(3)	6·13
1933	15·6	(3)	6·29
1934	15·7	1	6·25
1935	15·9	1	6·17
1936	16·4	3	5·98
1937	17·2	5	5·70
1938	17·4	1	5·64
1946	29·4		3·34
1947	31·4	6·8	3·12
1948	33·8	7·6	2·90
1949	34·6	2·4	2·84
1950	35·6	2·9	2·76
1951	38·8	9·0	2·53
1952	41·2	6·2	2·38
1953	41·9	1·7	2·34
1954	42·6	1·7	2·30
1955	44·1	3·5	2·22
1956	46·0	4·3	2·13
1957	47·5	3·3	2·07
1958	48·8	2·7	2·01
1959	49·1	0·6	2·00
1960	49·6	1·0	1·98
1961	51·0	2·8	1·92
1962	53·0	3·9	1·85
1963	54·0	1·9	1·82
1964	55·8	3·3	1·76
1965	58·4	4·7	1·68
1966	60·7	3·9	1·62
1967	62·3	2·6	1·57
1968	65·2	4·7	1·50
1969	68·7	5·4	1·43
1970	73·1	6·4	1·34
1971	80·0	9·4	1·23
1972	85·7	7·1	1·14
1973	93·5	9·1	1·05
1973 (Dec. 31)	98·1		1·00

*The factor by which expenditure would have to be multiplied to convert it into pounds of current purchasing power at 31st December 1973.

Accounting for changes in the
purchasing power of money

Notes

(1) Although the retail price index for a month relates to a point in time within the month, for all practical purposes it can also be taken as being the index at the end of the month.

(2) It is not suggested that companies will need to analyse their expenditure on fixed assets as far back as 1914, but the index has been provided to assist those companies who may in exceptional circumstances require an index that far back.

(3) If an index number is required for any month from January 1974 to date then use the relevant general index of retail prices (see paragraph 25 for sources of this index). For example the general index of retail prices for February 1974 is 101·7.

(4) To ascertain the index number for any month prior to January 1974 divide the annual index for the relevant year given in this appendix by the average retail price index for the same year and multiply the result by the retail price index for the desired month. For example, to ascertain index for March 1960:

Annual index for 1960 (from this appendix) (January 1974 = 100) . . 49·6

Average retail price index for 1960 (from Method of Construction and Calculation of the index of retail prices) (17th January 1956 = 100) . . . 110·6

Index of retail prices for March 1960 110

Therefore index for March 1960 (January 1974 = 100) . . . .
   (49·6 ÷ 110·6) × 110 . . . . 49·3

Index

215